LEARN TO PLAY CHAMPIONSHIP

SCRABBLE®

Jump-start your game with:

☐ Frequent rack rearrangement: Learn the surefire system of word-finding from the pros

☐ Your two best friends: the blank and the S—four rules to finding seven-letter bonus plays and maximizing your score

☐ Rack management and tile exchanges—secrets of winning plays

☐ The right attitude—how to avoid the traps

☐ Questions and answers to improve your play

EVERYTHING SCRABBLE® can put you in the winner's circle of the game all America loves!

JOHN D. WILLIAMS, JR., is the Executive Director of the National **SCRABBLE®** Association and **SCRABBLE®**'s national spokesman. JOE EDLEY is the editor of the *SCRABBLE® News* and the only two-time winner of the National SCRABBLE® Championship.

EVERYTHING SCRABBLE®

JOE EDLEY

AND

JOHN D. WILLIAMS, JR.

POCKET BOOKS

New York   London   Toronto   Sydney   Tokyo   Singapore

SCRABBLE® is a registered trademark of Hasbro, Inc., manufacturer of the SCRABBLE® Brand Crossword game. The game board, tiles, tile holders, and all other components of the game referred to and/or depicted in this publication are © Milton Bradley Company, all rights reserved.

Words and definitions from *The Official SCRABBLE® Players Dictionary*, 2nd edition, used with the permission of Merriam-Webster.

An *Original* Publication of POCKET BOOKS

POCKET BOOKS, a division of Simon & Schuster Inc.
1230 Avenue of the Americas, New York, NY 10020

Copyright © 1994 by John D. Williams, Jr., and Joe Edley
Front cover photo by Jeremiah Dine

Library of Congress Cataloging-in-Publication Data

Edley, Joe.
    Everything SCRABBLE® / Joe Edley and John D. Williams, Jr.
        p.   cm.
    ISBN 0-671-86686-9
    1. SCRABBLE® (Game)   I. Williams, John D., Jr.   II. Title.
GV1507.S3E35   1994
793.73S—dc20   94-32849
                                                         CIP

First Pocket Books trade paperback printing January 1995

10 9 8 7 6 5 4 3 2 1

POCKET and colophon are registered trademarks of
Simon & Schuster Inc.

Puzzle design by Sally Ricketts

Printed in the U.S.A.

I dedicate this book to my parents, Marian and Morris Edley, and my wife, Laura Marlene Klein, alias "Keen Animal Allurer," for their continuing support. Also to John D. Williams, Jr., for giving me the opportunity, joyfully, to promote the game and for his efforts to make this book a comprehensive and entertaining read. Finally, to all the ardent fans, who share the joy and camaraderie of this wonderful word game.

—Joe Edley

I would like to thank my father, who gave me a love of words; Jane Ratsey Williams, who gave me encouragement and more; Kristen and Alexandra, who grew up in "SCRABBLE® Central"; and to Joe Edley, who made me a serious player. Also thanks to Alfred Mosher Butts, who started it all.

—John D. Williams, Jr.

The authors would like to acknowledge Jerry Lerman and Rita Norr for their excellent advice; Sally Ricketts for her patience and fine work; our editors Paul McCarthy and Eric Tobias; Regula Noetzli, who kept the faith; and Cathy Meredith, who saw the wisdom in all of this.

CONTENTS

P A R T ▪ O N E

GETTING BETTER QUICKLY: ONE GOOD TURN FOLLOWS ANOTHER

P A R T ■ F I V E

APPENDICES: FACTS, TRIVIA, AND WORD LISTS   251

130 - J, x, z
24 - 2 letters
271 - 3 letter
62 - Q
192 - words no vowels

ABOUT THIS BOOK:
What It Is and How to Use It

This is the most comprehensive book ever published about the SCRABBLE®
game. Authored by the only two-time winner of the National SCRABBLE®
Championship and the Executive Director of the National SCRABBLE® Association, it was written to increase your knowledge of virtually every aspect
of the game, from the SCRABBLE game's history and culture to learning
how to increase your vocabulary; from learning how to manage your rack
to understanding what it takes to become national champion. And to make
this educational book fun, we have included a total of over a thousand puzzles. This book was written for anyone who has ever played a SCRABBLE
game, from novice to expert.

We expect that some people will read the book straight through and others
will simply want to browse and use it as a reference. With all these readers
in mind, we have broken the book up into parts.

Sprinkled throughout the book are puzzles of varying difficulty designed
to help you retain what you'll learn from reading the text. If you spend time
trying to solve them, you will learn more. If you can't solve a puzzle within
a reasonable amount of time, you might want to look up the answer. We've
suggested a time limit in most cases. At some future time you might try the
puzzles again to see if you can solve them faster or without looking up the
answers. Doing so will develop your abilities even further.

As you will see throughout the text, there will be talk of "bingos"—that
is, scoring a 50-point bonus for using all seven letters on your rack. For
expert and championship players, bingos are an essential, constant part of
the game. For less experienced players, this fact may seem a little intimidating, as many of them have never seen, let alone scored, a bingo.

The examination of bingos is not intended to intimidate, but to encourage
you to reach beyond your current skills. You may surprise yourself!

Part One (Chapters 1 through 8) is devoted to teaching you the basic SCRABBLE® Brand Crossword Game skills. For the novice, a thorough understanding of the principles of this section will raise your scores considerably with very little effort. Please remember to use the Glossary at the end of the book, if necessary. We introduce many commonly used SCRABBLE terms that may be unfamiliar.

Part Two (Chapters 9 through 15) delves deeper into more advanced concepts of play. While we recommend that both novices and experts read these chapters, you will get more out of them after you've practiced the exercises in Part I.

Part Three (Chapters 16 through 18) is loaded with puzzles that will tease, test, and develop your skills. Try them! The puzzles are graded—the more stars, the harder the puzzle.

Part Four (Chapters 19 through 23) will take you beyond your living room for a glimpse of the game's inventor, Alfred Butts, the SCRABBLE culture, and competitive SCRABBLE® game Club and Tournament play. We also include fifteen examples of outstanding SCRABBLE game play, and a special chapter on how to introduce the game to children. The game can help teach a variety of skills and combines learning with fun!

For those of you who haven't yet seen an *Official SCRABBLE® Players Dictionary (OSPD)* or its 2nd Edition *(OSPD2)*, we recommend you read **Chapter One** to familiarize yourself with the ins and outs of using the OSPD2.

Chapter Two is devoted to teaching novices how to form words on the board and the notations used throughout this book. Make sure you understand this chapter before reading further.

We recommend **Chapter Three** for everyone who hasn't yet learned the ninety-four two-letter words. They are the foundation for virtually all SCRABBLE game skills. In fact, we suggest that you play the SCRABBLE game with the two-letter word list in front of you until you learn them by heart.

We'll bet that **Chapter Four** is more important than most of our readers will immediately think. If you don't frequently rearrange the tiles on your rack, you will miss many easy high-scoring plays. Check out this chapter, whether you're a novice or an expert.

Chapter Five is, broadly speaking, at the heart of excellence in the SCRABBLE game. If you are able to see and utilize the open bonus squares, also known as "hot spots," you will consistently score more points. We present several puzzles here that will help to develop your skills. Novices and experts alike can learn from this chapter.

Chapter Six is all about the dreaded Q. Sure it's worth 10 points, but if you don't have a U you'll probably be in a quandary about what to do.

Believe it or not, you don't need a U to play the Q! Play your next game armed with this chapter and the Q won't seem so daunting.

Chapter Seven will show you how to earn big scores! Most people we've talked with don't know how to find seven- and eight-letter bonus plays, known as bingos, which earn an extra 50 points. It's not difficult, but it does require that you learn and remember a few common combinations of letters. If you solve the puzzles in this chapter, we predict you'll dramatically increase your bingo output.

Chapter Eight will show you that each play has two parts: the score and the "leave." The "leave" is the set of letters remaining on your rack after you've played, but before you've drawn new tiles. Your skill at the game will develop quickly as you learn how to combine scoring big and saving good combinations of letters.

In **Chapter Nine** we explore in more depth how to think like a topnotch player. We recommend reading this chapter carefully. Look at each example rack and think about what you would do before reading the analysis. Then incorporate our suggestions into your thinking.

Chapter Ten goes into depth about when you should exchange tiles. Most novices we've encountered are hesitant to do so, thinking that it's always better to score *some* points rather than *no* points. Wrong!

Chapter Eleven explores how you can make the most of both of the super tiles: the S and the blank.

Chapter Twelve will give you insights on how the champions learned the words, and how you can too, painlessly, and even have fun doing so.

Chapter Thirteen will show you how to take advantage of the J, X, and Z. You can learn all the unusual three- and four-letter J, X, and Z words by solving the puzzles while referring to this brief list.

Chapter Fourteen will show you how to take advantage of the developing spatial patterns on the board as the game progresses. Knowing how to "open" or "close" the board can give you a decided advantage, even if you're behind.

Chapter Fifteen is all about phoney words. In SCRABBLE Club and Tournament play, if a phoney word is played, it remains in play unless challenged off the board. We present several examples of when you might want to play a phoney or challenge your opponent. For tournament players, whether you're a novice or expert, this chapter is a must.

Chapter Sixteen will show you that it's not enough just to know the words; you'll want to be able to find them on your rack. This chapter has four different kinds of puzzles designed to improve your overall word-finding ability.

Chapter Seventeen will give you extensive practice finding words and the best places to play them.

Chapter Eighteen is for the word buff who likes real challenges. This chapter has some stumpers that will keep you busy for many hours.

In **Chapter Nineteen,** we'll introduce you to Alfred Butts, the inventor of the SCRABBLE® game.

You'll learn all about clubs and tournaments in **Chapter Twenty.** Those of you who are thinking about entering organized competitive SCRABBLE play will have the most to gain here.

Chapter Twenty-one is for budding experts only. We lay our cards on the table in this chapter. If you want to be one of the best, this chapter will tell you how! Most people have the capacity to become SCRABBLE experts. It simply takes time, practice, and learning the proper skills. It's all here.

Chapter Twenty-two will show you exactly the kinds of skills the top players have. Here are fifteen wonderful plays that we hope will convey why we think the SCRABBLE game is so exciting.

Chapter Twenty-three will show you how to introduce the SCRABBLE game to children. Whether you want to start your five-year-old with SCRABBLE® for Juniors, or your eight-year-old with the regular SCRABBLE® Brand Crossword Game, this chapter will give you many of the dos and don'ts.

Appendix One clarifies many often-asked questions about the rules. **Appendix Two** has a variety of facts and figures that will delight trivia buffs. **Appendix Three** is all about the National SCRABBLE Association. What do we do? How can you join? If you have any questions about the SCRABBLE game, we're your complete resource. **Appendix Four** has some extremely useful word lists drawn directly from *The Official SCRABBLE® Players Dictionary*. You will probably want to refer to these lists frequently.

The **Glossary** has all the definitions for the SCRABBLE game lingo we've used throughout the book.

Enjoy!

INTRODUCTION

"Spellbound"

It was the middle of the night and I was certain my wife was asleep. So I was startled when she abruptly sat up in bed and squinted at me through the dim haze of my night-light. As she stared at me, her look became a blend of bewilderment and disdain. "Has it come to this?" she finally said.

She did not even wait for a reply as she rolled back over to sleep. With luck, she'd spend a few more hours in a dreamworld where husbands don't wake up in the middle of the night to study secret word lists.

There was no denying it: After years of being on the fringes of the national SCRABBLE® scene, I had become a bona fide "word nerd." And, like people all across the U.S. and Canada, I was preparing for my first official SCRABBLE tournament. This meant committing to memory words that most people never heard of, would never use, and lived very happily without knowing. But to the SCRABBLE enthusiast, they are critical. Among the basics were the eight Q words without a U and the 94 two-letter words. And these were only the beginning.

Actually, my wife was getting off easy. She could have married the retired military officer who spent his days calculating the probability of seven-letter plays on the first draw. Almost every day he'd spend a couple of hours drawing seven SCRABBLE tiles out of a bag and writing down the letters. Then he'd see if there was indeed a seven-letter play in the combination. Next, he'd put the tiles back in, shake the bag, and start the process all over again. By his own calculation, he had done this several thousand times, recording each "play."

With reams of crumpled legal yellow pads as proof, he determined there is a 10 percent probability that SCRABBLE experts should expect a seven-letter play—a bingo—to start their game. It should come as no surprise that this man once described his apartment in the following way: SCRABBLE draperies, a SCRABBLE wastebasket, SCRABBLE bedspread. He slept in SCRABBLE pajamas.

While this gentleman's love of the game tended toward the obsessive, his dedication was by no means rare. We are a country of special-interest groups, and the SCRABBLE world is like any other, whether it be Elvis fans, sky divers, baseball card collectors, Trekkies, or golfers. We have our own superstars, prodigies, groupies, and leaders. We have a body of knowledge— word lists, strategies, training techniques—that dazzles everyone from the humble inventor of the game himself to the casual living room player.

Like most subcultures, our membership cuts across a wide cross-section of the continent. It includes celebrities, prison inmates, doctors, teachers, truck drivers, teenagers, the old and the young, the competitive and the amateur, and just about everyone else. Some of us got here because we love words, others because we love games. Still others play because they love people. Some play occasionally, some play every single day of their lives. When a human being is not available to compete, a computer opponent will more than test one's skill.

Before you get too overwhelmed by all of this, here is the most important thing of all to know about the SCRABBLE game. The game is a classic, which means two things. The first is that it's completely different every single time you play it. The second is that you can enjoy it at every level, whether you play once a year on a rainy summer day, once a month on a visit to your aunt, or every day of your life. This book is meant to celebrate all of those levels and the people at them.

I turned back to my wife, who was still sleeping peacefully. Looking at things objectively, I guess I could understand her amusement at my growing fascination with competitive SCRABBLE. It was getting late and I really needed sleep. Turning off the light, I decided I'd had enough of word lists for the night. Maybe just a few anagrams before drifting off. . . .

JOHN D. WILLIAMS, JR.

I have always been a game-player. In fact, the first memory I have of playing a game was at five years old. Our extended family of ten people—including aunts, uncles, and cousins—all played a game of Monopoly®. Working as a team, my father and I won by being the first to build on the purples— Mediterranean and Baltic.

From there, I graduated to chess, pocket pool, table tennis, and a variety of other board games such as backgammon, Othello®, and Mastermind®. One of my diversions, as a rather unusual teenager, was solving puzzles, including finding the smaller words that could be formed from the letters in larger words. Though I eventually studied mathematics in college, my heart wasn't in it.

During my twenties, while studying psychology and philosophy and trying to "find myself," I learned the correct approach to a winning competitive attitude. When I heard about the first National SCRABBLE® Championship in 1978, I believed in my heart that I could become a SCRABBLE game expert and that this might ultimately lead to a profession. My head told me that was ridiculous, for although I had played many different games, I'd never focused on one game long enough to consider making it my profession.

To realize my goal, late in 1978 I took a job as a night watchman and studied SCRABBLE on the job. In 1980, I won the National SCRABBLE Championship. That's a long story in itself. I hope to put it into print someday. I was the runner-up in 1985 and finished third in 1983. In 1988, John Williams needed an expert to be part of the administration at the National SCRABBLE® Association. For more than six years, John and I have devoted our time to promoting and improving the organized SCRABBLE scene.

After directing the past several national tournaments, I came back to play in 1992 and won my second National SCRABBLE® Championship. It's been my goal for years to be able to share the joys of the SCRABBLE game with others. This book represents a significant part of my continuing efforts toward that goal. Whether you want to be a champion or just want to beat your uncle Jim, we're sure you'll find some useful information and improve your abilities by reading this book.

Joe Edley

EVERYTHING
SCRABBLE®

The History of SCRABBLE®

Ironically, the entire world has heard of SCRABBLE® Brand Crossword Game, but hardly anyone knows how it got here. Many people assume it has been here for centuries—most certainly invented by the Romans or at the very least, the English. Actually, the story is an American classic.

The year was 1931, the depths of the Great Depression. Alfred Mosher Butts was a young out-of-work architect living in his hometown of Pough-keepsie, New York. In an attempt to earn some extra money, he set out to invent a game. Butts had always liked anagrams and crosswords, so he used that as his inspiration.

Analyzing existing games, Butts determined they fell into three basic cate-gories. There were "numbers" games, such as bingo and dice. There were "move" games, such as chess and checkers. And then there were "word" games, such as anagrams and crossword puzzles. Between his interest in words and his architect's love of structure and order, Butts decided to work on a word game that utilized a grid concept. In addition, he wanted to create a game that combined both luck and skill, with stronger emphasis on skill. He also liked the idea of a hundred tiles. As he began his first set of sketches, Butts called his boardless anagram game idea Lexiko, which later evolved into the board game Criss Cross Words.

Alfred M. Butts next began an exhaustive analysis of the English language, particularly examining word structure. The most obvious dynamic, he knew, was that while there were twenty-six letters in the language, some appeared far more frequently than others. For example, he quickly determined that vowels are used far more frequently than consonants, with the vowel E being the most common. To verify his theories, Butts painstakingly studied the front page of *The New York Times*, doing letter-by-letter counts. He kept detailed charts of how many times each letter appeared—or didn't appear!

It was this research that enabled Butts to assign values to each letter in a SCRABBLE game, while also determining how many of each should be available as game pieces. Hence there are twelve Es, worth only 1 point each, and only one Z, worth 10 points. Butts's basic cryptographic analysis of our language and his original scheme for tile distribution have stood the test of time for three generations of SCRABBLE game players and over billions of games played.

The game boards for the prototype of Criss Cross Words were hand-drawn with architectural equipment, reproduced by blueprinting, and pasted on folding cardboard checkerboards. The tiles were blueprinted and then glued to quarter-inch plywood and cut into squares to match the size of the board.

Throughout the years, the physical aspect of the game went through some subtle changes. For example, one version of the game had 109 letters and 1 blank. Another prototype began play in the upper left-hand corner of the board—similar to the way one traditionally starts a crossword puzzle. However, the basics have remained the same.

From about 1932 through 1938, Alfred Butts continued to make the Lexiko sets by hand and to give them to friends, many of whom became instant devotees of the new game. To his disappointment, however, almost every single established game manufacturer in the United States turned down the new idea. Most found it interesting, but felt it did not have the elements for mass appeal. In 1938 he stopped producing Lexiko, and then sold to individuals its offspring, Criss Cross Words, until 1942. That's when he met a bookseller named Charles Ives, who began manufacturing Criss Cross Words until the war forced him to stop in 1943. It was at this time that Butts was introduced to an entrepreneur named James Brunot, an owner of one of the few original Criss Cross Game sets. In time, Brunot was to add his marketing genius to the project.

Sidelined by World War II and an infusion of new work, both Butts and Brunot were forced to keep the project as a low priority until 1947. Then things began to move. First, some refinements were made in the basic play of the new game. For example, they agreed to rearrange the premium squares—triple letter, double word, etc.—for more exciting and varied scoring opportunities. They also simplified the rules, which had been lengthy and complicated. They were fine for someone as brilliant as Alfred Butts and his friends, but not for a mass market.

Next Brunot and Butts agreed on a new name—SCRABBLE® Brand Crossword Game. It was then that Brunot and his family became convinced that the game was ready for the mass market. Alfred Butts, who had very little time to develop the game, quickly authorized Brunot and his wife to produce and sell it. With this in mind, the ambitious young couple formed the Production and Marketing Company and set up shop in their Newtown, Connecticut, home.

Before long, game production became too complicated for the Brunots' home. They rented a small abandoned schoolhouse in Dodgingtown, Connecticut, where they and a friend turned out about twelve games per hour, stamping letters on the wooden tiles one at a time. Later, boards, boxes, and tiles were made elsewhere and sent to the fledgling factory for assembly and shipping.

The first four years were a struggle, so Brunot kept his other job to support the family. In 1949, for example, the Brunots made 2,400 sets but lost $450. But year by year, the numbers of orders increased as news of this wondrous new game began to spread, chiefly by word of mouth.

By 1952, the Brunots acknowledged they could no longer keep pace with the growing demand. They reached an agreement with Selchow & Righter, a Bay Shore, New York, game manufacturer, to market and distribute the game in the U.S. and Canada. Founded in 1867, Selchow & Righter was a family business, best known for manufacturing the game classic "Parcheesi, A Royal Game of India." The Brunots would retain the SCRABBLE® name.

Selchow & Righter had another classic on its hands. By the midfifties, in fact, SCRABBLE had become a legitimate national craze, as stories appeared in newspapers and magazines and on television. The demand was so great that for three years game orders were very carefully allocated in order that all areas of the continent could receive their fair share. By 1954, over four million sets had been sold.

Over the next two decades, it seemed as if everyone in America owned a SCRABBLE game. Sales remained steady, and the game eventually expanded into versions in Spanish, Italian, Russian, Hebrew, French, Braille, and large type. In 1972, Selchow & Righter purchased the trademark "SCRABBLE" from James Brunot's Production and Marketing Company, giving it exclusive rights to all SCRABBLE® Brand products and entertainment services in the U.S. and Canada. Two other companies were to divide the rights for the rest of the world.

In 1986, Selchow & Righter was sold to Coleco Industries, manufacturers of Cabbage Patch dolls. Three years later, Coleco declared bankruptcy, and its primary assets—most notably SCRABBLE and Parcheesi—were purchased by the nation's leading game manufacturer, the Milton Bradley Company. Based in East Longmeadow, Mass., Milton Bradley, in an effort to expand the line, added a new Deluxe Travel SCRABBLE®, a Super SCRABBLE® Gameboy for Nintendo owners and Sesame Street SCRABBLE®.

Milton Bradley also realized the value of competitive SCRABBLE game play for keeping alive the "SCRABBLE game culture" in the U.S. and Canada.

The company helps underwrite the National SCRABBLE® Association, based in Greenport, New York; and hosts the biennial National SCRABBLE® Championship. The company also created the respected national School SCRABBLE® Program, a classroom-tested curriculum which utilizes the word game as a learning tool in the nation's schools. While Milton Bradley prefers not to discuss sales figures, it's safe to say SCRABBLE is not only very much alive, but still growing.

GETTING BETTER QUICKLY:
One Good Turn Follows Another

These first eight chapters are especially written both for the novice player and for those more experienced players who've never used *The Official SCRABBLE® Players Dictionary*, 2nd Edition.

We've simplified and included in these chapters all the basic skills you'll need in order to enjoy playing an exciting and skillful SCRABBLE game.

❏ Learn how the *OSPD2* differs from other dictionaries
❏ Learn the ninety-four two-letter words
❏ Learn how to rearrange your tiles on your rack so that words will appear effortlessly
❏ Learn how to use the bonus squares to maximize your score
❏ Learn the Q words that don't use a U, as well as all the three-, four-, and five-letter Q words
❏ Learn how to find seven- and eight-letter words on your rack
❏ Learn how to save good combinations of letters to increase your odds of drawing better tiles

1

LOOK IT UP: *The Official SCRABBLE® Players Dictionary,* 2nd Edition

If you want to get serious about the SCRABBLE® game, sooner or later you are going to need *The Official SCRABBLE® Players Dictionary.* It's the "bible" of SCRABBLE word game enthusiasts and, like any important book, has a story.

Back in the dark ages, if two people were playing the SCRABBLE game, chances are they occasionally had an argument about which words were acceptable. To help decide these arguments, there have always been a variety of excellent dictionaries on the market. But while Aunt Ethel from Wyoming always used one dictionary, Uncle Dave from Nebraska used another. Invariably you could watch them battle the merits of their favorite words or non-words late into the evening.

To clear this potential word-game roadblock, Selchow & Righter, the game's manufacturer, decided in 1975 to publish an official SCRABBLE dictionary. One of the challenges facing the company was how to get the word experts to agree upon the words. Should it be an unabridged dictionary? Or should it simply contain the words used in everyday English?

The end result—*The Official SCRABBLE® Players Dictionary*—fell somewhere in between the two extremes. Based on listings from five popular dictionaries, it lists only two- to eight-letter words. Longer words are included as inflections of shorter words (UNLIKELIEST is the superlative of UNLIKELY). To be included in the *OSPD*, a word had to be found in two of the five most popular American dictionaries. At the time, that meant the *Webster's Seventh Collegiate Dictionary, Webster's New World Dictionary,* the *Random House Collegiate Dictionary,* the *American Heritage Dictionary,* and the *Funk & Wagnalls College Dictionary.*

When it was finally published in 1978, the *OSPD* included over a hundred thousand words. This was a SCRABBLE game player's dream!

As one might imagine, there are arguments over why certain words are included or excluded. With the number of unusual words, some people are unconvinced that the words come solely from popular dictionaries. Yet, for all its faults, the *OSPD* is the breakthrough that SCRABBLE needed to surge in popularity. Now any two North Americans could play using the same word source.

There are still the occasional gripes over the brief or unusual definitions (KANE is defined as KAIN, which you then have to look up and discover is "a tax paid in produce or livestock"), and few people are certain how to pronounce many of the words, since there are no pronunciation marks in the *OSPD*. However, the original *OSPD* edition in 1978 was generally praised as an excellent reference for settling any SCRABBLE game word disagreement.

In 1991, the Milton Bradley Company, the game's new manufacturer, and Merriam Webster published *The Official SCRABBLE® Players Dictionary, 2nd Edition.*

Here are some hints on using *The Official SCRABBLE® Players Dictionary, 2nd Edition:*

A) Only one definition is given for each word. Often the common meaning will be bypassed to illustrate an unusual usage. For example, IMP is listed as a verb, and is defined: "to graft feathers onto a bird's wing." The verb usage is necessary to show that IMPED and IMPING are acceptable. For the purposes of the game there was no need to mention other definitions.

B) There are special RE- and UN- lists, which include hundreds of words not defined in the text. Make sure you look at both the text and the list when verifying RE- or UN- words. The lists are printed right after the text entries for RE and UN.

C) Unless an -ING word is defined as a noun, it doesn't take an S. For example, PLAY is defined as a verb. As such, PLAYING is the present participle and is acceptable. Instead of listing PLAYING separately, it is simply shown as: "PLAY -S, -ED, -ING, to engage in amusement or sport." Since there is no separate listing for PLAYING as a noun, PLAYINGS is not acceptable. However, FLYING is acceptable, as it is listed as a noun— "N: pl. -S the operation of an aircraft"—and so its plural FLYINGS is acceptable.

D) If a word is listed in boldface, or as an inflection of a boldfaced word, then it is acceptable. Example: FOCUS is listed and so it is acceptable. Also listed and acceptable are: FOCUSED, FOCUSING, FOCUSES, FOCUSSED, FOCUSSING, and FOCUSSES.

E) There are many verbs that take an ER at the end. After all, if you can PLAY, then there can be a PLAYER. One can BAKE, and s/he is a BAKER. However, not all verbs can be so altered. One may PART, but there is no PARTER listed in the *OSPD2*. All cases where verbs may be made into nouns by adding ER are listed in the *OSPD2*.

F) Although foreign words are not generally considered acceptable, there are many words in the *OSPD2* which seem foreign. That's because if a word has no adequate substitute in English, then the original foreign word is considered acceptable. For example, almost all foreign coins are acceptable. You will find words like PESETA (a monetary unit of Spain) and XU (a Vietnamese coin) acceptable, as well as QAID (a Muslem leader) and SAHIB (sir; master—used as a term of respect in colonial India).

G) Some words are listed in boldface more than once. For instance, BRIT-TLE is listed as an adjective, and shows the inflections BRITTLER and BRITTLEST. If someone challenges BRITTLED, an inexperienced word judge might assume, after seeing this entry, that BRITTLED is unacceptable. Wrong! BRITTLE is *also* listed separately as a verb, and can be inflected as BRITTLED, BRITTLING, and BRITTLES. So when you can't find an entry, be sure you check above and below the expected alphabetic positioning of a word for an alternate listing.

H   Occasionally someone will play an uninflected, acceptable word of more than eight letters, such as PETROLEUM. The National SCRABBLE® Association uses, both at tournament and club play, *Merriam-Webster's Collegiate Dictionary*, 10th Edition, to verify words of nine letters or more.

While there may always be discussions about which words should or should not be acceptable, we must always defer to the *OSPD2*, so that we are all playing by the same rules. We should not forget that the *OSPD2* allows equal chances to all players.

Now that you've been introduced to the *OSPD2*, let's look at a few basic SCRABBLE game rules that you'll need to know.

THE ABCs: HOW TO MAKE PLAYS AND SCORE BONUS POINTS
A Word About Notations, Diagrams, and Puzzles

Below is a representation of a SCRABBLE® Brand Crossword Game board. Following it are explanations for some of the symbols used in this book.

	A	B	C	D	E	F	G	H	I	J	K	L	M	N	O	
	TWS			DLS			TWS				DLS			TWS		**1**
		DWS				TLS			TLS				DWS			**2**
			DWS			DLS		DLS				DWS				**3**
	DLS			DWS			DLS				DWS			DLS		**4**
					DWS					DWS						**5**
		TLS	**Z₁₀**			TLS			TLS				TLS			**6**
		E₁	DLS		**H₄**		DLS	**A₁**	**X₈**	**E₁**			DLS			**7**
	TWS	**E₁**	DLS	**W₄**	**A₁**	**T₁**	**C₃**	**H₄**			DLS			TWS		**8**
	O₁		DLS		**L₁**		DLS		DLS			DLS				**9**
	C₃	**L₁**	**O₁**	**U₁**	**T₁**		TLS			TLS			TLS			**10**
	K₅			DWS	**E₁**					DWS						**11**
	DLS			DWS	**R₁**		DLS				DWS			DLS		**12**
			DWS			DLS		DLS				DWS				**13**
		DWS				TLS			TLS				DWS			**14**
	TWS			DLS			TWS				DLS			TWS		**15**

DIAGRAM 2-1

TWS = TRIPLE WORD SCORE

When a TWS square is covered, the player covering it scores triple the value of the sum of the individual letters of the word covering the TWS. Example: Adding the letters R, O, and K in Diagram 2-1, forming ROCK, scored R (1) + O (1) + C (3) + K (5) = 10 x 3 = 30 points. Notice that ROCK was played after CLOUT but before ZEE.

DWS = DOUBLE WORD SCORE

When a DWS square is covered, the player covering it scores double the value of the sum of the individual letters of the word covering the DWS. Example: The play of HALTER in Diagram 2-1 scored 4 (H) + 1 (A) + 1 (L) + 1 (T) + 1 (E) + 1 (R) = 9 x 2 = 18 points.

TLS = TRIPLE LETTER SCORE

When a TLS square is covered, the value of the letter covering the TLS is tripled. Example: For the play of ZEE in Diagram 2-1, the Z alone was worth 3 x 10 = 30 points.

DLS = DOUBLE LETTER SCORE

When a DLS square is covered, the value of the letter covering the DLS is doubled. Example: For playing AXE in Diagram 2-1, the X alone was worth $8 \times 2 = 16$ points.

It's also wise to keep in mind another way to score points quickly. As mentioned earlier, there is an additional 50-point bonus if you use all seven tiles on your rack, commonly known as playing a bingo.

? = BLANK

The blank tile is worth zero points and is represented in the text as a question mark—"?"

Recording Plays

Notice the numbers 1 through 15 printed down the right side of the board on Diagram 2-1, as well as the letters printed across the bottom. With their help we can describe any square of the board with only a letter and number. Thus, the center square is represented as either 8H or H8.

When the *number* is listed first, the play is *horizontal*. That shows that the word is played across a row. When the *letter* is listed first, the play is *vertical*. That shows that the word is played down a column.

Example

In Diagram 2-1 the opening play of WATCH is recorded as: WATCH 8D. The 8D represents the square which is in the eighth row and intersects the D column, and is the location of the *first letter* of the word. The second play, HALTER, is recorded as HALTER E7. The E7 represents the square which is in the E column and intersects the seventh row, and is the square on which the word begins.

Who Plays First?

Here's how you determine who plays first at the start of the game: The players each randomly choose one tile from the pool. The player who draws the letter closest to the beginning of the alphabet plays first. Drawing a blank tile automatically earns first play. If the drawn tiles are identical, the players draw again. After it is determined who goes first, all drawn tiles are returned to the pool and the first player draws seven new tiles to start the game.

Whoever is first to play begins the game by forming a word with two or more letters, playing it horizontally or vertically so that one of the letters covers the pink center Double Word Square.

Note that in most diagrams in this book we make the first play horizontally. We've found that most people play the first word that way, though there is absolutely nothing wrong with starting vertically. Also note that we often print the score of a play next to the beginning square. Example: PARTY 8D (26 points). This signifies that the word "party" was played beginning on the 8D square, moving across the board horizontally, and earned 26 points.

Basic Play-Making 101

After the first play, there are *four ways* to add words to the board. The official rules included with the game mention only three. We haven't changed the rules; we're just redefining those three ways to make it even easier to understand.

1. Play *through* an existing word.

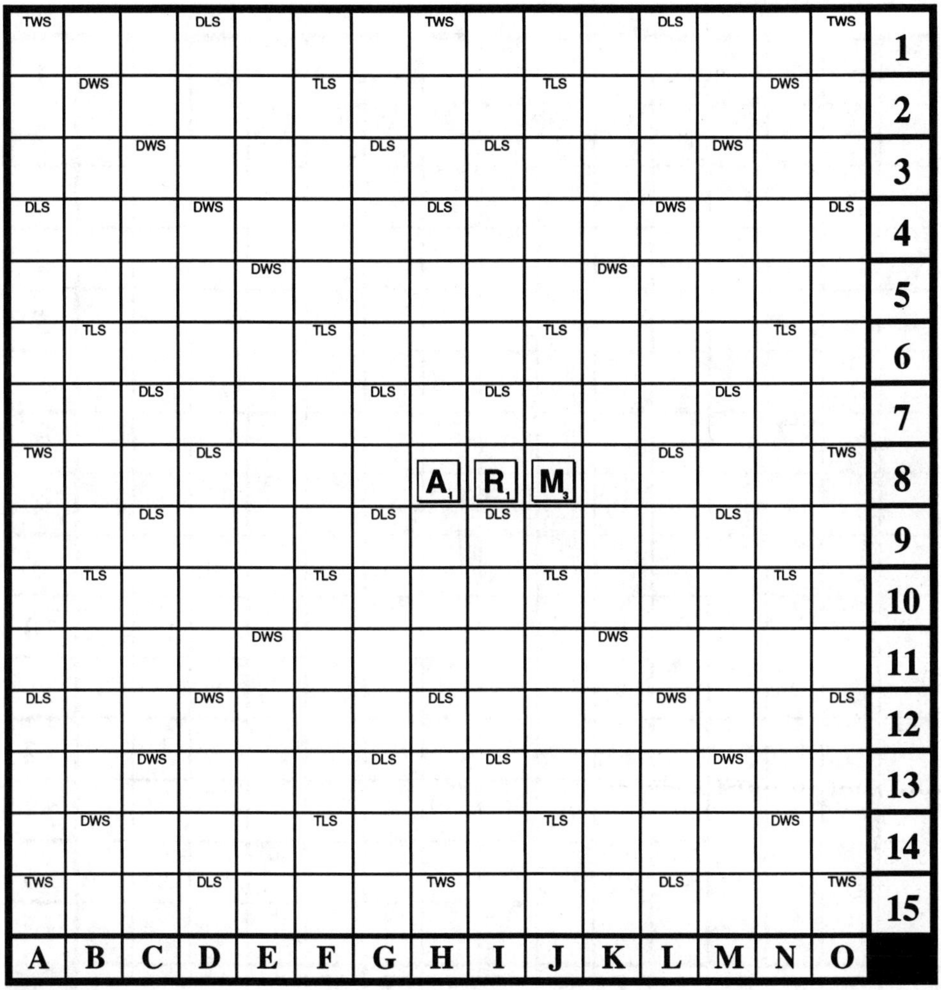

TWS			DLS				TWS				DLS			TWS	**1**
	DWS				TLS				TLS				DWS		**2**
		DWS				DLS		DLS				DWS			**3**
DLS			DWS				DLS				DWS			DLS	**4**
				DWS					DWS						**5**
	TLS				TLS				TLS				TLS		**6**
		DLS				DLS		DLS				DLS			**7**
TWS			DLS				**A**	**R**	**M**			DLS		TWS	**8**
		DLS				DLS		DLS				DLS			**9**
	TLS				TLS				TLS				TLS		**10**
			DWS						DWS						**11**
DLS			DWS				DLS				DWS			DLS	**12**
		DWS				DLS		DLS				DWS			**13**
	DWS				TLS				TLS				DWS		**14**
TWS			DLS				TWS				DLS			TWS	**15**
A	**B**	**C**	**D**	**E**	**F**	**G**	**H**	**I**	**J**	**K**	**L**	**M**	**N**	**O**	

DIAGRAM 2-2

Example

Imagine that Diagram 2-2 is your game position. Your rack is: C G H I L N Y

What would you play?

You may play *through* one of the letters of the word ARM to form your play. Some choices are: CLANG H6 (8 points), HIM J6 (16), RICH I8 (10), CHAIN H6 (10) and LAYING H7 (12).

2. *Add* a letter to the front or back of an existing word and play perpendicular to that word. This is commonly known as playing a "hook" word, or "hooking."

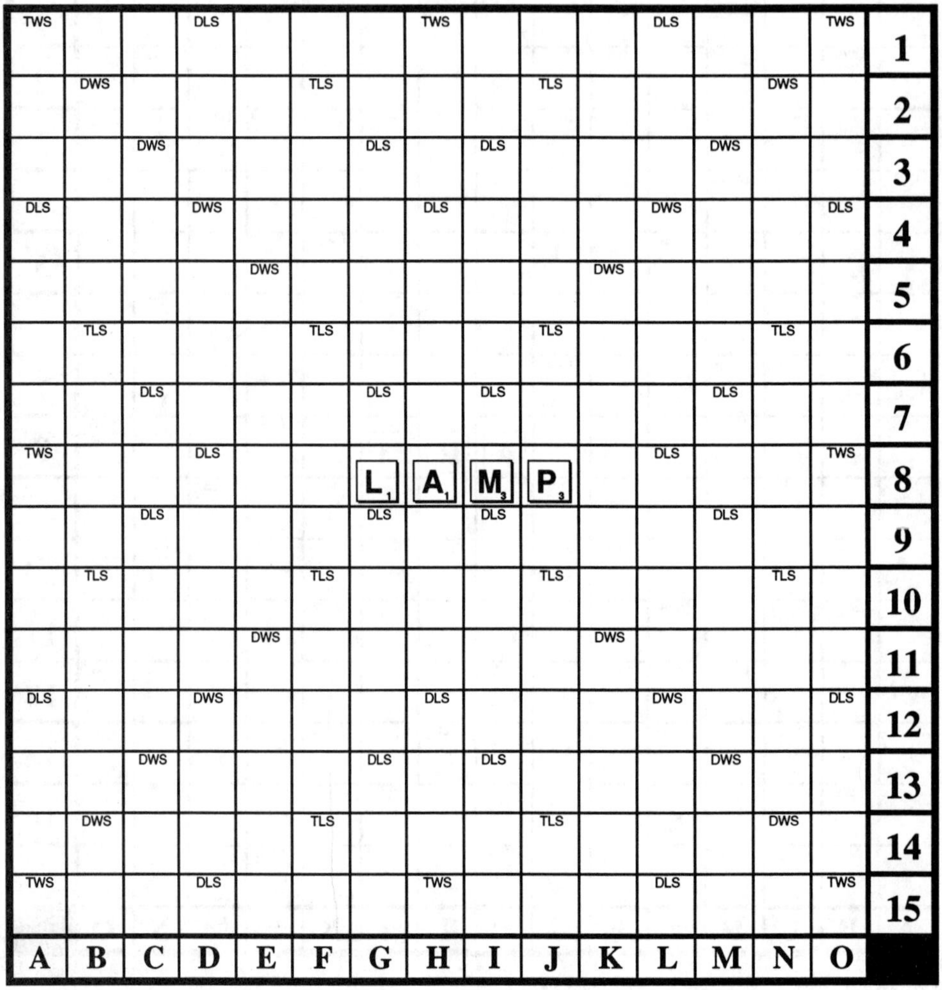

TWS			DLS				TWS				DLS			TWS	**1**
	DWS				TLS				TLS				DWS		**2**
		DWS				DLS		DLS				DWS			**3**
DLS			DWS				DLS				DWS			DLS	**4**
				DWS					DWS						**5**
	TLS				TLS				TLS				TLS		**6**
		DLS				DLS		DLS				DLS			**7**
TWS			DLS			**L₁**	**A₁**	**M₃**	**P₃**		DLS			TWS	**8**
		DLS				DLS		DLS				DLS			**9**
	TLS				TLS				TLS				TLS		**10**
				DWS					DWS						**11**
DLS			DWS				DLS				DWS			DLS	**12**
		DWS				DLS		DLS				DWS			**13**
	DWS				TLS				TLS				DWS		**14**
TWS			DLS				TWS				DLS			TWS	**15**
A	**B**	**C**	**D**	**E**	**F**	**G**	**H**	**I**	**J**	**K**	**L**	**M**	**N**	**O**	

DIAGRAM 2-3

Example

Imagine Diagram 2-3 is your game position. Your rack is: A B C L N O Y

What would you play?

You may add the C to LAMP to form CLAMP and form another word played vertically on the board. Some choices are: CLAY F8 (22 points), BACON F6 (28) COB F8 (24) COY F8 (27) LACY F6 (22)

3. *Extend* a word by adding letters either to the front or back or to both the front or back.

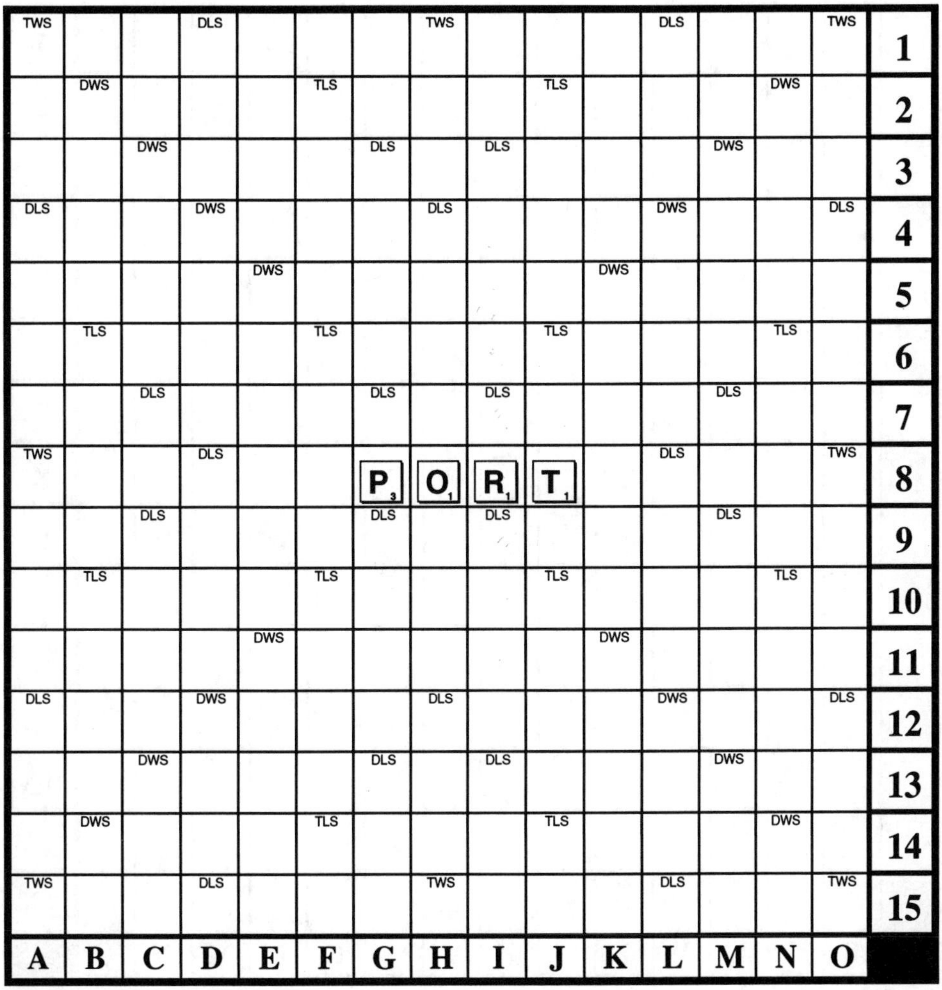

TWS			DLS				TWS				DLS			TWS	**1**
	DWS				TLS				TLS				DWS		**2**
		DWS				DLS		DLS				DWS			**3**
DLS			DWS				DLS				DWS			DLS	**4**
				DWS						DWS					**5**
	TLS				TLS				TLS				TLS		**6**
		DLS				DLS		DLS				DLS			**7**
TWS			DLS			**P₃**	**O₁**	**R₁**	**T₁**		DLS			TWS	**8**
		DLS				DLS		DLS				DLS			**9**
	TLS				TLS				TLS				TLS		**10**
			DWS						DWS						**11**
DLS			DWS				DLS				DWS			DLS	**12**
		DWS				DLS		DLS				DWS			**13**
	DWS				TLS				TLS				DWS		**14**
TWS			DLS				TWS				DLS			TWS	**15**
A	**B**	**C**	**D**	**E**	**F**	**G**	**H**	**I**	**J**	**K**	**L**	**M**	**N**	**O**	

DIAGRAM 2-4

Example

Imagine Diagram 2-4 is your game position. Your rack is: A D E E I M R

What would you play?

You may extend PORT in a variety of ways: REPORT 8E (8 points), DE-PORT 8E (9), PORTER 8G (9), REPORTED 8E (13), IMPORT 8E (10), IM-PORTED 8E (15), and REIMPORTED 8C (18).

4. Play *parallel* to an existing word, forming two or more words on the same play.

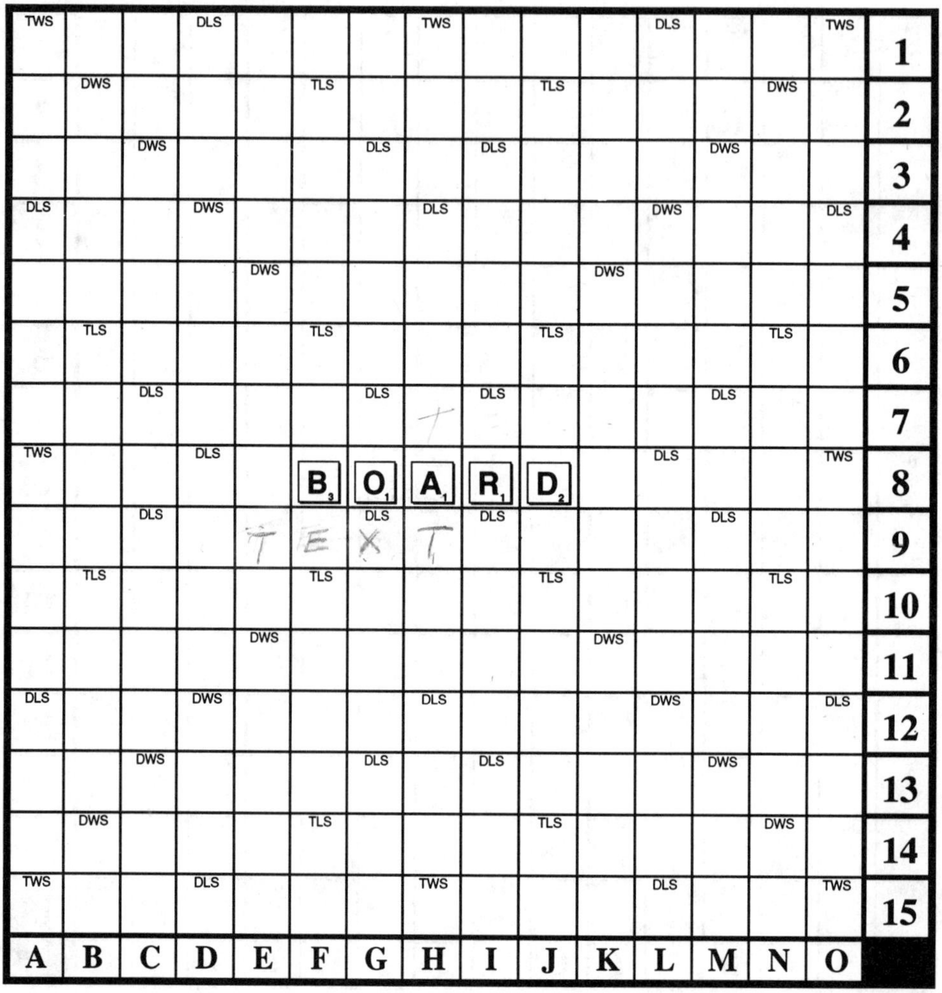

TWS			DLS				TWS				DLS			TWS	**1**
	DWS				TLS				TLS				DWS		**2**
		DWS				DLS		DLS				DWS			**3**
DLS			DWS				DLS				DWS			DLS	**4**
				DWS						DWS					**5**
	TLS				TLS				TLS				TLS		**6**
		DLS				DLS		DLS				DLS			**7**
TWS			DLS			**B₃**	**O₁**	**A₁**	**R₁**	**D₂**		DLS		TWS	**8**
		DLS				DLS		DLS				DLS			**9**
	TLS				TLS				TLS				TLS		**10**
			DWS							DWS					**11**
DLS			DWS				DLS				DWS			DLS	**12**
		DWS				DLS		DLS				DWS			**13**
	DWS				TLS				TLS				DWS		**14**
TWS			DLS				TWS				DLS			TWS	**15**
A	**B**	**C**	**D**	**E**	**F**	**G**	**H**	**I**	**J**	**K**	**L**	**M**	**N**	**O**	

DIAGRAM 2-5

Example ———————————————————

Imagine Diagram 2-5 is your game position. Your rack is: A C E R T T X

What would you play?

You may play parallel to BOARD, with several choices: CRATE 9B (12 points), which also forms BE; CATER 9C (18), which also forms BE and OR; and TEXT 9E (42), which also forms BE, OX, and AT.

Once you learn that BA is acceptable (it means "the eternal soul in Egyptian mythology"), then TAX 9E (39 points) is possible, which forms OX as well.

With both plays, TEXT 9E and TAX 9E, the X is played on a Double Letter Score and helps form two words simultaneously. This means that the X is scored as a double letter (16 points) for *each* word it helps form. This is important to remember, since once you learn this principle, you'll be able to score 32 points for just the X when it forms two words at once. And on a Triple Letter Score, the X can score you 48 points when it spells two words at once!

But remember, once a letter is played, later words that use that letter don't earn the bonus square it covers. That bonus is only good the first time it's used.

Knowing the rules in this chapter is your starting point for SCRABBLE excellence. Your first step forward is learning the ninety-four two-letter words in Chapter Three.

3 IT TAKES "TWOS" TO TANGLE

The two-letter words are without question the most critical building blocks to improving your game. In fact, the National SCRABBLE® Association routinely advises new members that learning "the twos" will almost automatically increase their scoring average by 30 to 40 points a game.

These two-letter gems are priceless, for a couple of reasons. First, they will increase your scoring opportunities by allowing more parallel plays. Second, knowing the twos opens up many more spots for scoring, often allowing you to play a bingo where there would otherwise be no place on the board. Few things in the game are more frustrating than having a bingo with nowhere to play it!

It's also encouraging to realize that you already know many of the two-letter words, and that the rest are relatively easy to learn. For example, there are several common sources of two-letter words.

One is the musical scale: DO, RE, MI, FA, SO, LA, TI. Another is the Greek alphabet, a terrific source for both twos and unusual threes, such as XI, MU, NU, RHO, CHI, and more. Then there is the alphabet itself, where most letters have their own spellings. For example, all of the following are real words: EF (F), EM (M), EN (N), AR (R), ES (S), and EX (X). Some threes include CEE, DEE, GEE, VEE, and ZEE. Here is an example of how a two-letter word can make a +50-point play all by itself:

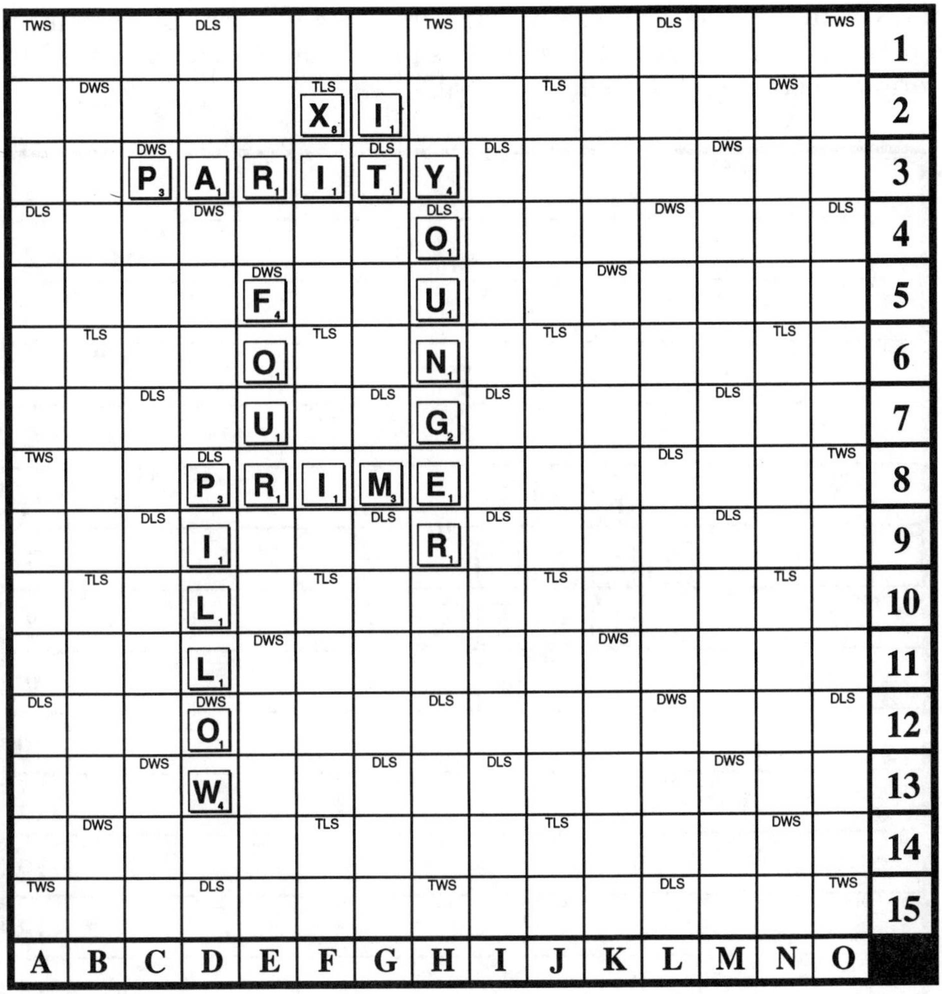

	A	B	C	D	E	F	G	H	I	J	K	L	M	N	O
1	TWS			DLS				TWS				DLS			TWS
2		DWS				X(8)	I(1)			TLS				DWS	
3			P(3)	A(1)	R(1)	I(1)	T(1)	Y(4)	DLS				DWS		
4	DLS			DWS				O(1)				DWS			DLS
5					F(4)			U(1)			DWS				
6		TLS			O(1)	TLS		N(1)		TLS				TLS	
7			DLS		U(1)		DLS	G(2)	DLS				DLS		
8	TWS			P(3)	R(1)	I(1)	M(3)	E(1)				DLS			TWS
9			DLS		I(1)		DLS	R(1)	DLS				DLS		
10		TLS			L(1)	TLS				TLS				TLS	
11					L(1)						DWS				
12	DLS			DWS	O(1)			DLS				DWS			DLS
13			DWS		W(4)		DLS		DLS				DWS		
14		DWS				TLS				TLS				DWS	
15	TWS			DLS				TWS				DLS			TWS

DIAGRAM 3-1

As you can see in Diagram 3-1, playing the word XI above and parallel to the word PARITY allows you to score with the X in both directions, making for a 52-point play. You could have also played XU in the same spot, assuming you had also learned the two-letter word UT. This would have not only scored big, but also enabled you to get rid of the X and U, both tough letters to carry on your rack if you are trying to build a seven-letter word and earn the 50-point bonus for using all your tiles. (See Chapter Seven.)

Diagram 3-2 shows an example using the word KA, a favorite of many SCRABBLE® players. That's because it can take a third letter to form several three-letter words. They include: KAB, KAE, KAF, KAS, KAT, KAY, OKA, and **SKA**. In fact, you can easily learn these eight words by remembering the phrase "Betsy's Foot." All the letters in that phrase can be added to KA to form an acceptable three-letter word!

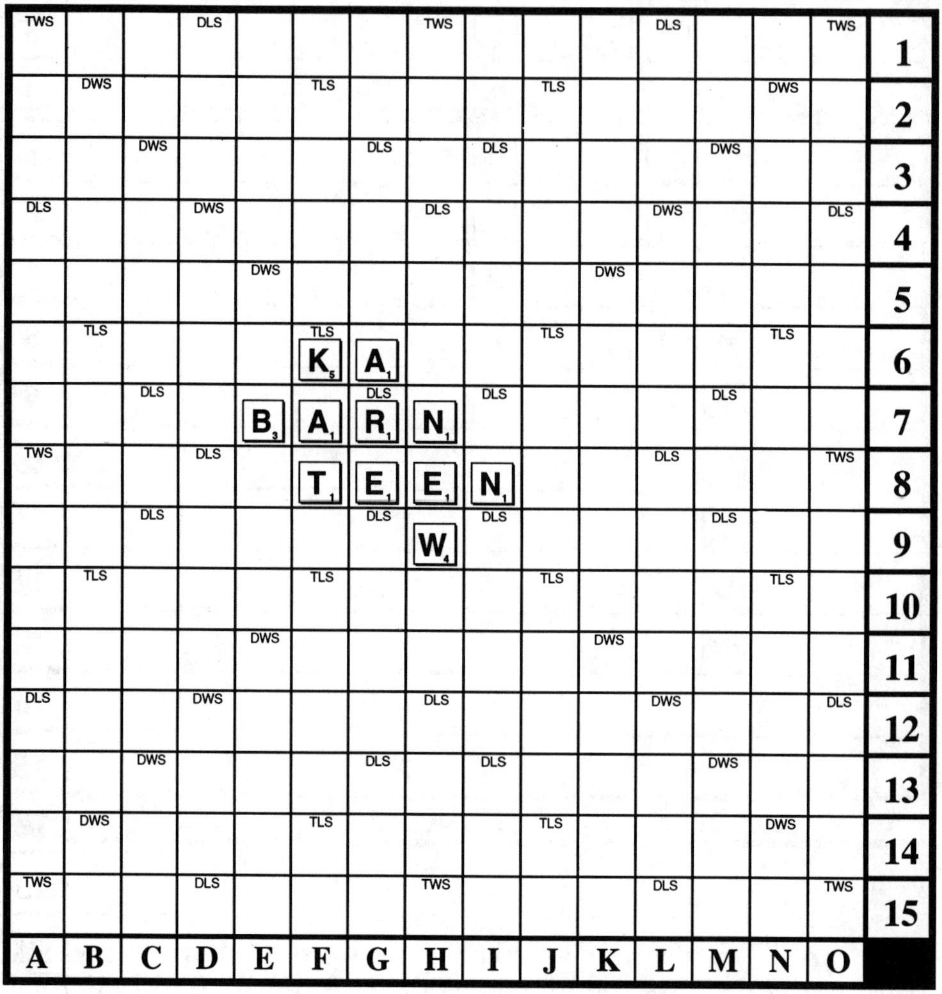

	A	B	C	D	E	F	G	H	I	J	K	L	M	N	O	
	TWS			DLS				TWS				DLS			TWS	**1**
		DWS				TLS				TLS				DWS		**2**
			DWS				DLS		DLS				DWS			**3**
	DLS			DWS				DLS				DWS			DLS	**4**
					DWS						DWS					**5**
		TLS				**K**	**A**			TLS				TLS		**6**
			DLS		**B**	**A**	**R**	**N**	DLS				DLS			**7**
	TWS			DLS	**T**	**E**	**E**	**N**				DLS			TWS	**8**
			DLS				**W**		DLS				DLS			**9**
		TLS				TLS				TLS				TLS		**10**
				DWS								DWS				**11**
	DLS			DWS				DLS				DWS			DLS	**12**
			DWS				DLS		DLS				DWS			**13**
		DWS				TLS				TLS				DWS		**14**
	TWS			DLS				TWS				DLS			TWS	**15**
	A	**B**	**C**	**D**	**E**	**F**	**G**	**H**	**I**	**J**	**K**	**L**	**M**	**N**	**O**	

DIAGRAM 3-2

Just played: KA 6F 36 points

In Diagram 3-2, knowledge of the two-letter words pays off with the 36-point play of KA. It also points out another good function of the twos: allowing you to score well without opening up much scoring opportunity for your opponent. And while you don't want to play your entire game in such a "closed" fashion, there are definitely situations when it makes good sense strategically. (See Chapter Fourteen on open and closed boards.)

As we said earlier, the two-letter words are also valuable because they open up opportunities. Diagram 3-3 shows an example of how knowledge of the twos resulted in a high-scoring play on a somewhat closed board.

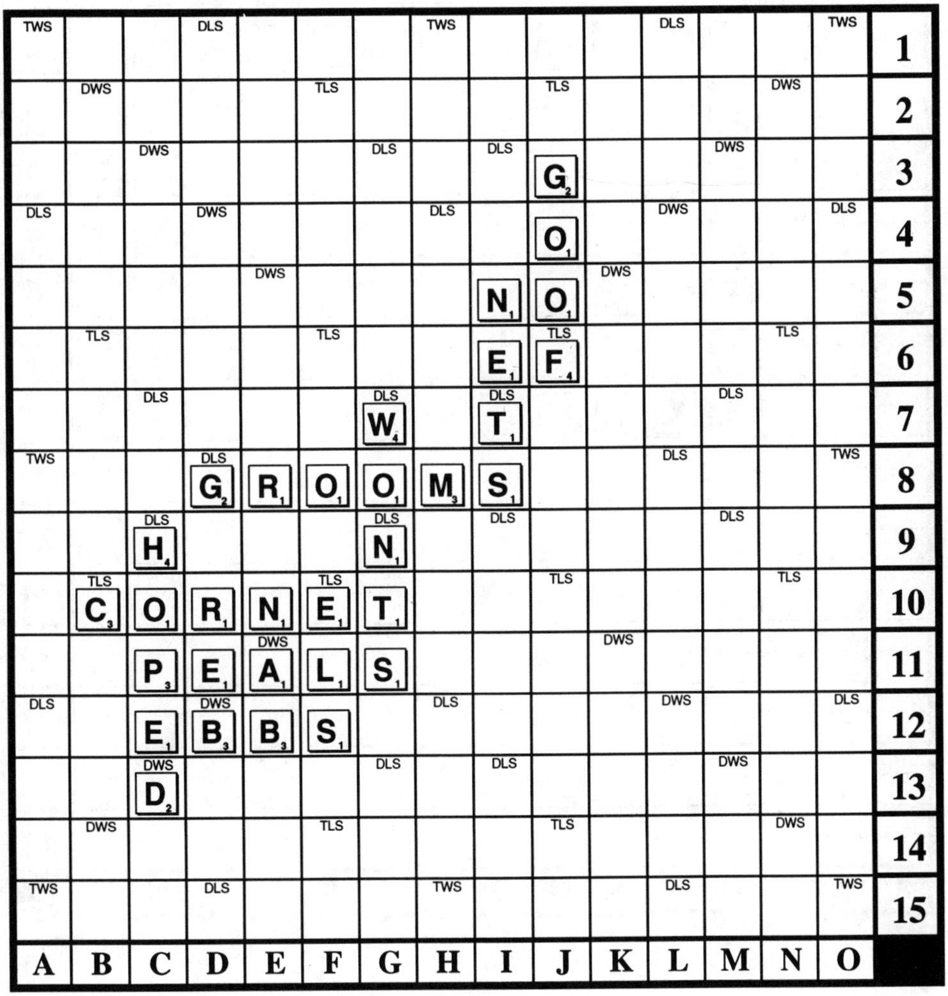

A	B	C	D	E	F	G	H	I	J	K	L	M	N	O	#
TWS			DLS				TWS				DLS			TWS	1
	DWS				TLS				TLS				DWS		2
		DWS				DLS		DLS	G_2			DWS			3
DLS			DWS				DLS		O_1		DWS			DLS	4
				DWS				N_1	O_1	DWS					5
	TLS				TLS			E_1	F_4				TLS		6
		DLS				W_4		T_1				DLS			7
TWS			G_2	R_1	O_1	O_1	M_3	S_1			DLS			TWS	8
		H_4				N_1		DLS				DLS			9
	C_3	O_1	R_1	N_1	E_1	T_1			TLS				TLS		10
		P_3	E_1	A_1	L_1	S_1				DWS					11
DLS		E_1	B_3	B_3	S_1		DLS				DWS			DLS	12
		D_2				DLS		DLS				DWS			13
	DWS				TLS				TLS				DWS		14
TWS			DLS				TWS				DLS			TWS	15

DIAGRAM 3-3

Rack: A F G L O O V   Play: GOOF J3 31 points

In Diagram 3-4 is an example of how knowledge of the twos allowed a player to not only score a bingo for an extra 50 points, but to earn a Triple Word Score as well. Note that DIALING could also be played at 9H, but for far fewer points.

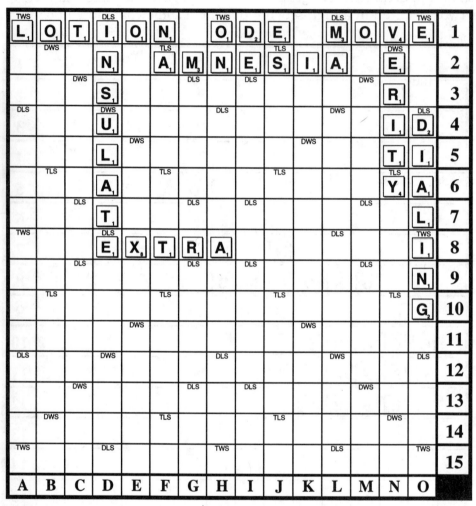

DIAGRAM 3-4

Rack: A D G L I I N   Play: DIALING O4 (95 points)

You can see why when someone asks the National SCRABBLE® Association how s/he can become an expert, the first thing we say is: Learn the twos.

Below is a list of all ninety-four two-letter words in *The Official SCRABBLE Players Dictionary*. Next, you will want to be able to find those high-scoring plays that will take advantage of your knowledge of the twos. To do that means learning how to rearrange the tiles on your rack. Next stop: Chapter Four.

The 94 Acceptable Two-Letter Words

AA: *n* pl. -S rough, cindery lava

AD: *n* pl. -S an advertisement

AE: *adj* one

AG: *adj* pertaining to agriculture

AH: *interj*—used to express delight, relief, or contempt

AI: *n* pl. -S a three-toed sloth

AL: *n* pl. -S an East Indian tree

AM: present 1st person sing. of be

AN: *indefinite article*—used before words beginning with a vowel

AR: *n* pl. -S the letter R

AS: *adv* to the same degree

AT: *prep* in the position of

AW: *interj*—used to express protest, disgust, or disbelief

AX: *v* -ED, -ING, -ES to work on with an ax (a type of cutting tool)

AY: *n* pl. -S aye

BA: *n* pl. -S the eternal soul in Egyptian mythology

BE: *v* AM, ARE, ART, WAS, WERE, WAST, WERT, BEEN, BEING to have actuality

BI: *n* pl. -S a bisexual

BO: *n* pl. -S a pal

BY: *n* pl. -S a pass in certain card games

DA: *prep* of; from—used in names

DE: *prep* of: from—used in names

DO: *n* pl. -S the first tone of the diatonic scale

EF: *n* pl. -S the letter F

EH: *interj*—used to express doubt

EL: *n* pl. -S an elevated railroad or train

EM: *n* pl. -S the letter M

EN: *n* pl. -S the letter N

ER: *interj*—used to express hesitation

ES: *n* pl. ESES the letter S (also spelled ESS)

ET: a past tense of EAT

EX: *n* pl. EXES the letter X

FA: *n* pl. -S the fourth tone of the diatonic musical scale

GO: *v* WENT, GONE, GOING, GOES to move along

HA: *n* pl. -S a sound of surprise

HE: *n* pl. -S a male person

HI: *interj*—used as a greeting

HM: *interj*—used to express thoughtful consideration

HO: *interj*—used to express surprise

ID: *n* pl. -S a part of the psyche

IF: *n* pl. -S a possibility

IN: *v* INNED, INNING, INS to harvest

IS: present 3rd person sing. of BE

IT: *pron* the 3rd person sing. neuter pronoun

JO: *n* pl. JOES a sweetheart

KA: *n* pl. -S the spiritual self of a human being in Egyptian religion

LA: *n* pl. -S the sixth tone of the diatonic musical scale

LI: *n* pl. -S a Chinese unit of distance

LO: *interj*—used to attract attention or to express surprise

MA: *n* pl. -S mother

ME: *pron* the objective case of the pronoun I

MI: *n* pl. -S the third tone of the diatonic musical scale

MM: *interj*—used to express assent or satisfaction

MO: *n* pl. -S a moment

MU: *n* pl. -S a Greek letter

MY: *pron* the possessive form of the pronoun I

NA: *adv* no; not

NE: *adj* born with the name of (also NEE)

NO: *n* pl. NOS or NOES a negative reply

NU: *n* pl. -S a Greek letter

OD: *n* pl. -S a hypothetical force of natural power

OE: *n* pl. -S a whirlwind off the Faeroe Islands

OF: *prep* coming from

OH: *v* -ED, -ING, -S to exclaim in surprise, pain, or desire

OM: *n* pl. -S a mantra used in contemplation of ultimate reality

ON: *n* pl. -S the side of the wicket where a batsman stands in cricket

OP: *n* pl. -S a style of abstract art

OR: *n* pl. -S the heraldic color gold

OS: *n* pl. OSA, OSSA, or OSAR either an orifice, a bone, or an esker

OW: *interj*—used to express sudden pain

OX: *n* pl. OXEN or OXES a hoofed mammal or clumsy person

OY: *interj*—used to express dismay or pain

PA: *n* pl. -S a father

PE: *n* pl. -S a Hebrew letter

PI: *v* PIED, PIEING, PIING, or PIES to jumble or disorder

RE: *n* pl. -S the second tone of the diatonic musical scale

SH: *interj*—used to urge silence

SI: *n* pl. -S ti

SO: *n* pl. -S the fifth tone of the diatonic musical scale

TA: *n* pl. -S an expression of gratitude

TI: *n* pl. -S the seventh tone of the diatonic musical scale

TO: *prep* in the direction of

UH: *interj*—used to express hesitation

UM: *interj*—used to indicate hesitation

UN: *pron* pl. -S one

UP: *v* UPPED, UPPING, UPS to raise

US: *pron* the objective case of the pronoun we

UT: *n* pl. -S the musical tone C in the French solmization system, now replaced by do

WE: *pron* the 1st person pl. pronoun in the nominative case

WO: *n* pl. -S woe

XI: *n* pl. -S a Greek letter

XU: *n* pl. XU a monetary unit of Vietnam

YA: *pron* you

YE: *pron* you

4 REARRANGING YOUR TILES MAKES WORDS APPEAR!

We have observed many new SCRABBLE® game players struggling unnecessarily to find words with their seven tiles. Why do they struggle? That's easy! They think that a word will simply occur to them if they sit and *stare* at their rack of seven letters. That's definitely *not* the best way to go about finding good plays.

We advise that you get into the habit of moving the tiles around on your rack frequently, often randomly. Words will appear before your eyes, often like magic! As you become more experienced, you will learn which combinations of letters will produce more words than others.

Let's show you what we mean. This might be a good time to pull out your own SCRABBLE set and use an actual rack and letters. Try to spell a common seven-letter word with these letters:

A E G N O S T

Below are some sample arrangements. Examine each one only briefly before going on to the next one. After you become experienced moving tiles on your rack, finding such words may become commonplace. The answer is at the end of this chapter. Note: TANGOES is not acceptable.

A E G N O S T	T O N A G E S	T E A G O N S	E T A G O N S
N O G A T E S	S T O N A G E	G A N T O E S	S E N T A G O
G E T A N O S	O G E N T A S	A N T O G E S	E N G O A T S
N O S T A G E			

Here's a surefire system for moving tiles on your rack in order to be thorough in your search for words:

Imagine you have just four tiles on your rack: A, B, D, and E. These can be arranged into twenty-four different possible arrangements. How fast can you form all twenty-four arrangements? Experts can do it in their heads in just a few seconds. If you can manipulate the tiles quickly enough, checking for words as you go, you can probably learn to do it in less than a minute. Start by putting them in alphabetical order. Note any letters that form a word. Here's the list: ABDE, ABED, ADBE, ADEB, AEBD, AEDB, BADE, BAED, BDAE, BDEA, BEAD, BEDA, DABE, DAEB, DBAE, DBEA, DEAB, DEBA, EABD, EADB, EBAD, EBDA, EDAB, EDBA.

Of course, in one turn you'll never be able to form all the arrangements of a typical rack of seven different letters (there are 5,040 of them). But as you learn how to combine letters, you usually won't need to use this systematic approach for more than four letters at a time.

To really burn this system into your memory, try the following exercise just once: Take the lettered tiles A, E, P, R, and S and form all 120 arrangements: Start with AEPRS, AEPSR, APERS, etc. This exercise will give you the experience and practice you need to know how to move your tiles on your rack. While you're doing it, try to recognize the twelve acceptable five-letters words spellable with these exact letters. Only eight of them are common words. You'd need an unusually good vocabulary to recognize the rest. You'll find all twelve words at the end of the chapter.

To help develop your word-finding ability, we suggest practicing with the chart below. Find several words that use each pair or triplet of consonants. By knowing how consonants go together, you'll become more efficient at rearranging combinations of letters to form words. For example: using the B, you might find BLACK, BLIMP, BLUE, CLIMB, LAMB, SYMBOL, BROWN, BRICK, HERB, CURB, and MARBLE.

Once you're able to find the words on your rack, you will want to be able to use the bonus squares on the board to boost the scores of your words. Chapter Five will show you exactly how to do that.

Common Combinations of Consonants

TWO-LETTER COMBOS

B: BL, MB, BR, RB
C: CH, CK, CL, CR, NC, RC, SC, CT
D: DL, DG, DR, LD, ND, RD

F: FL, LF, FR, RF
G: GH, DG, GL, LG, GN, NG, GR, RG
H: CH, GH, PH, SH, TH, WH
K: CK, LK, KL, NK, KN, RK, SK
L: BL, CL, DL, LD, FL, LF, GL, LG, KL, LK, LM, PL, LP, RL, LS, SL, LT, TL, LV, WL
M: MB, MP, LM, RM, SM
N: NC, ND, NG, GN, NK, KN, RN, NS, SN, NT, WN
P: PH, PL, LP, MP, RP, PR, SP, PT
R: BR, RB, CR, RC, DR, RD, FR, RF, GR, RG, RK, RL, RM, RN, PR, RP, RS, RT, TR, RV, WR
S: SC, SH, SK, SL, LS, NS, SM, SN, SP, PS, RS, ST, SW
T: CT, FT, TH, LT, TL, NT, PT, TR, RT, ST, TW
V: LV, RV
W: WH, WL, WN, WR, SW, TW

THREE-LETTER COMBOS

CHR, CKL, GHT, LCH, NCH, NDL, NGL, NKL, RCH, RDL, RGL, RST, RTH, SCH, SCR, SHR, SPL, SPR, STR, TCH, THR

ANSWERS: CHAPTER 4

AEGNOST = ONSTAGE

AEPRS = APERS, APRES, ASPER, PARES, PARSE, PEARS, PRASE, PRESA, RAPES, REAPS, SPARE, SPEAR.

5 MAXIMIZE YOUR SCORING: Head for the "Hot Spots"

In theory, there are often several hundred different possible plays you can make on any one turn. How should you choose which ones are the best? Naturally, your first priority is the score. The higher the score, the better the play, usually. This chapter is devoted to helping you find those high-scoring plays. In Chapters Eight and Nine we'll explore how to determine which of those choices is best strategically. We suggest you use a board and have a set of tiles in front of you when you try some of the puzzles in this chapter. You're more likely to have an easier time solving them, as well as better success simulating actual game situations.

Very simply: **Use the bonus squares!** We also call them "hot spots," because they can lead you to earn an explosive number of points. They are where the action is! And while one bonus square is good, we advise, if you can: **Cover Two Bonus Squares at Once!**

1. Bonus Squares and Parallel Play:

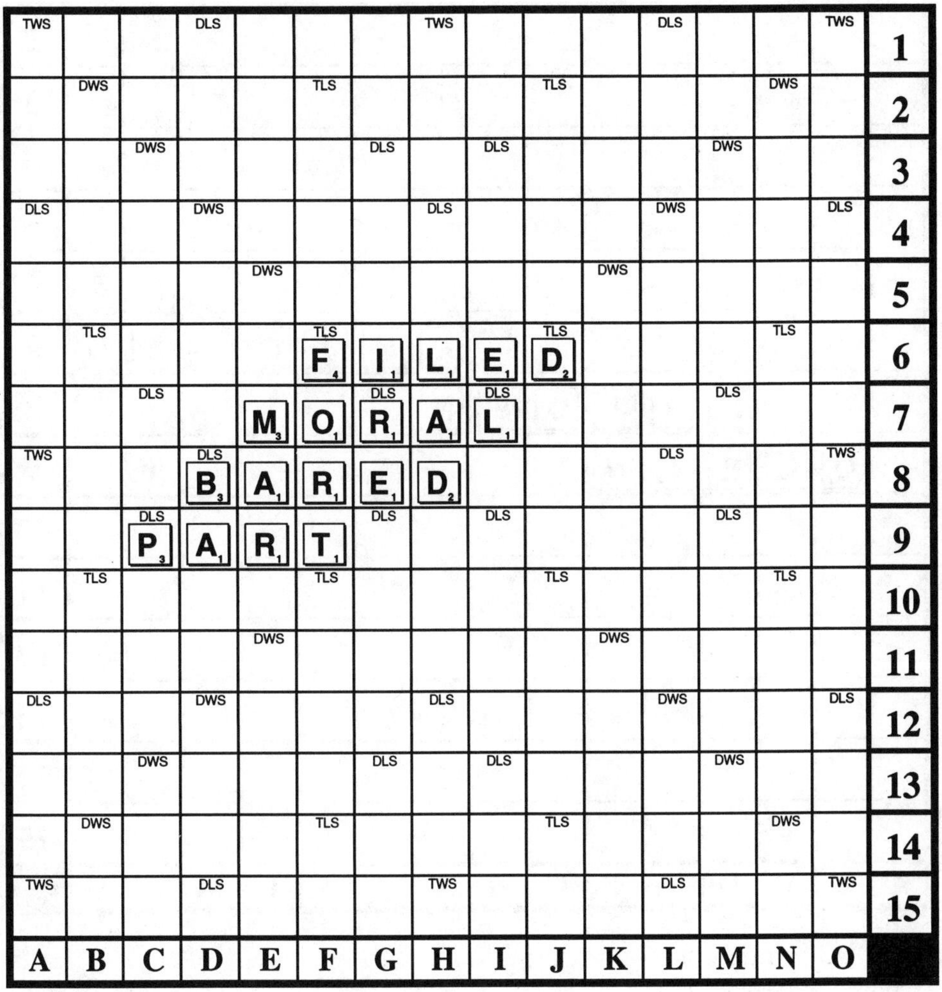

	A	B	C	D	E	F	G	H	I	J	K	L	M	N	O	
	TWS			DLS				TWS				DLS			TWS	**1**
		DWS				TLS				TLS				DWS		**2**
			DWS				DLS		DLS				DWS			**3**
	DLS			DWS				DLS				DWS			DLS	**4**
					DWS						DWS					**5**
		TLS				TLS	F₄ I₁ L₁ E₁ D₂		TLS				TLS			**6**
			DLS				M₃ O₁ R₁ A₁ L₁	DLS				DLS				**7**
	TWS			DLS			B₃ A₁ R₁ E₁ D₂				DLS			TWS	**8**
			DLS				P₃ A₁ R₁ T₁	DLS				DLS				**9**
		TLS				TLS			TLS				TLS			**10**
				DWS				DWS								**11**
	DLS			DWS			DLS				DWS			DLS		**12**
			DWS			DLS		DLS				DWS				**13**
		DWS			TLS			TLS				DWS				**14**
	TWS			DLS			TWS				DLS			TWS		**15**

DIAGRAM 5-1

Always look for plays parallel and adjacent to words already on the board. Often such plays will score many more points than most others. Example: In Diagram 5-1, the play of PART also formed BA, MAR, and FORT, scoring a total of 25 points, whereas PART itself only scored 9. That's a bonus of 16 extra points for playing parallel to another word.

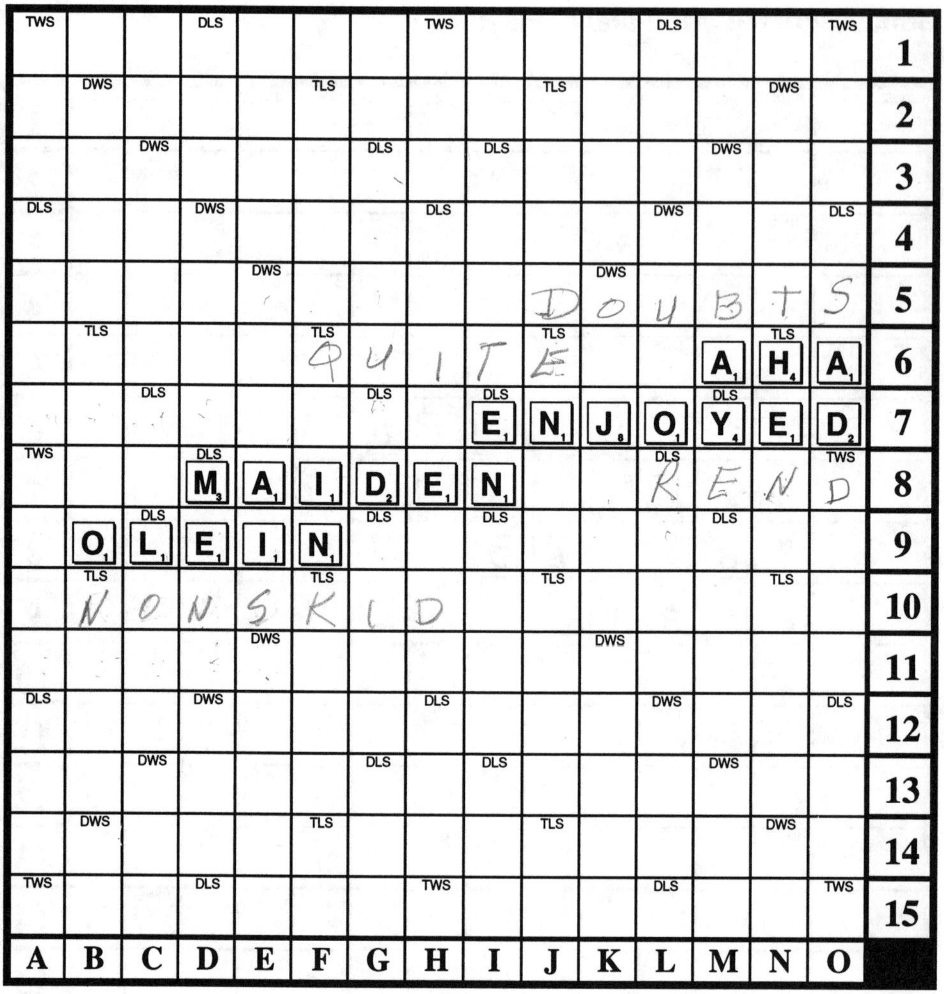

DIAGRAM 5-2

Find an outstanding way to play each of the following words onto Diagram 5-2. As you find a place for each word, remove the word from the position and go on to the next word. Answers on page 59.

Time limit: 20 minutes

1. REND
2. DOUBTS
3. NONSKID
4. QUITE

2. Triple Letter -Triple Letter:

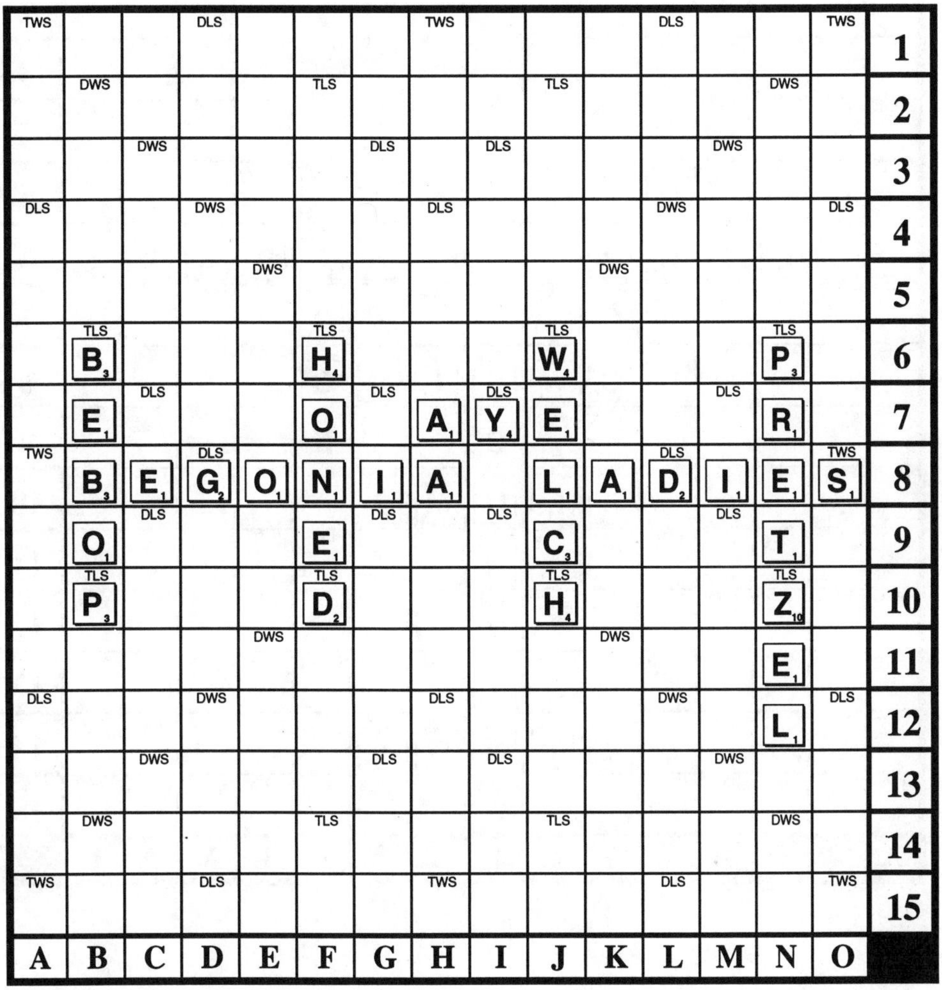

	A	B	C	D	E	F	G	H	I	J	K	L	M	N	O
1	TWS			DLS				TWS				DLS			TWS
2		DWS				TLS				TLS				DWS	
3			DWS				DLS		DLS				DWS		
4	DLS			DWS				DLS				DWS			DLS
5					DWS						DWS				
6		**B**				**H**				**W**				**P**	
7		**E**	DLS			**O**	**A**	**Y**	**E**				DLS	**R**	
8	TWS	**B**	**E**	**G**	**O**	**N**	**I**	**A**		**L**	**A**	**D**	**I**	**E**	**S**
9		**O**	DLS			**E**	DLS		DLS	**C**			DLS	**T**	
10		**P**				**D**				**H**				**Z**	
11					DWS						DWS			**E**	
12	DLS			DWS				DLS				DWS		**L**	DLS
13			DWS				DLS		DLS				DWS		
14		DWS				TLS				TLS				DWS	
15	TWS			DLS				TWS				DLS			TWS

DIAGRAM 5-3

Because the twelve Triple Letter Score squares are aligned in the same four rows and columns, look for opportunities to use two of them when you have several high-point tiles. These combinations can be formed on the B, F, J, and N columns as well as on rows 2, 6, 10, and 14.

#	A	B	C	D	E	F	G	H	I	J	K	L	M	N	O
1	TWS			DLS				TWS				DLS			TWS
2		DWS				TLS				TLS				DWS	
3			DWS				DLS		DLS				DWS		
4	DLS			DWS				DLS				DWS			DLS
5					Q_{10}						B_3				
6		C_3	U_1	T_1	U_1	P_3				H_4	A_1	R_1	D_2	Y_4	
7			DLS		A_1		DLS		DLS		R_1		DLS		
8	TWS			DLS	D_2	O_1	W_4	S_1	I_1	N_1	G_2	DLS			TWS
9			DLS				DLS	O_1	DLS		E_1		DLS		
10		TLS				P_3	L_1	U_1	M_3	B_3				TLS	
11					DWS			N_1			DWS				
12	DLS			DWS				D_2				DWS			DLS
13			DWS				DLS	I_1	DLS				DWS		
14		DWS				Z_{10}	I_1	N_1	C_3	Y_4				DWS	
15	TWS			DLS				G_2				DLS			TWS

DIAGRAM 5-4

Example

In Diagram 5-3, BEBOP, HONED, WELCH, and PRETZEL are worth 23, 21, 29, and 44 points, respectively. In Diagram 5-4, CUTUP, PLUMB, HARDY, and ZINCY are worth 21, 23, 28, and 47 points.

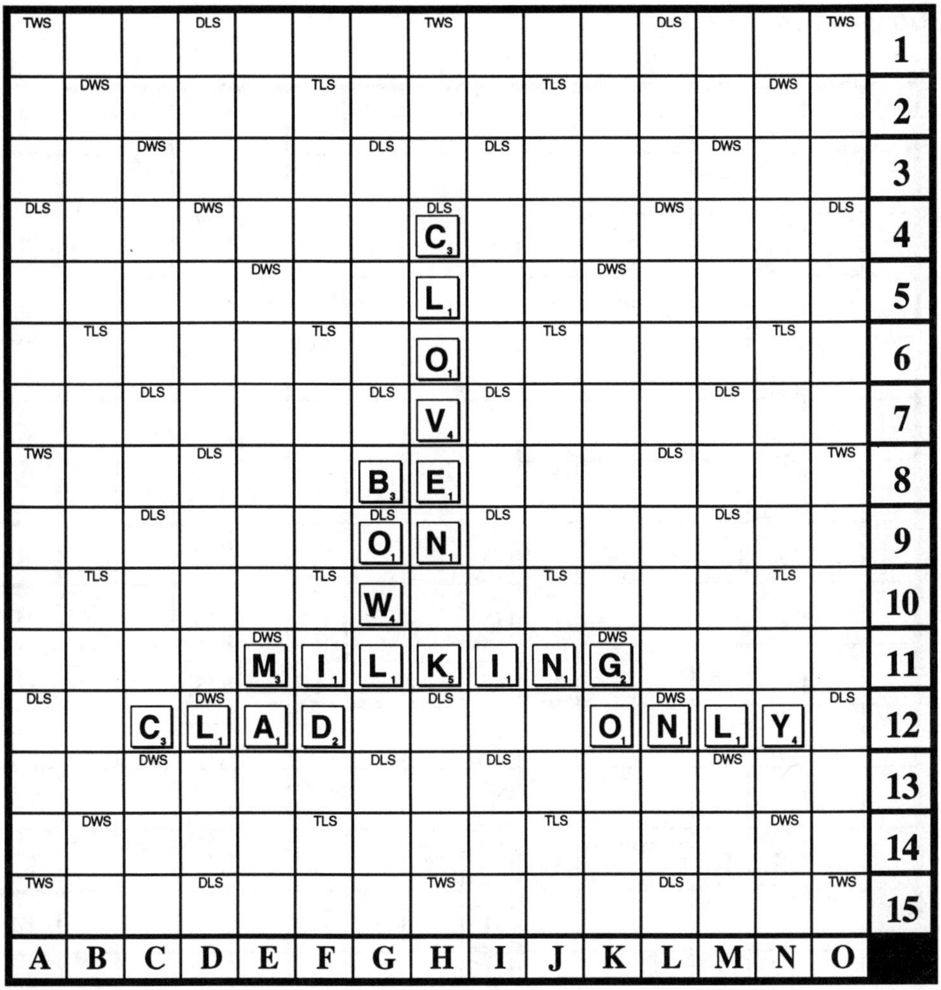

DIAGRAM 5-5

	A	B	C	D	E	F	G	H	I	J	K	L	M	N	O	
1	TWS			DLS				TWS				DLS			TWS	**1**
2		DWS				TLS				TLS				DWS		**2**
3			DWS				DLS		DLS				DWS			**3**
4	DLS			DWS				C				DWS			DLS	**4**
5					DWS			L			DWS					**5**
6		TLS				TLS		O		TLS				TLS		**6**
7			DLS				DLS	V	DLS				DLS			**7**
8	TWS			DLS			B	E				DLS			TWS	**8**
9			DLS				O	N	DLS				DLS			**9**
10		TLS				TLS	W			TLS				TLS		**10**
11					DWS	M	I	L	K	I	N	G				**11**
12	DLS		C	L	A	D		DLS				O	N	L	Y	**12**
13			DWS				DLS		DLS				DWS			**13**
14		DWS				TLS				TLS				DWS		**14**
15	TWS			DLS				TWS				DLS			TWS	**15**

Your rack: I M N P P R T

Use Diagram 5-5 and the letters IMNPPRT to find a play covering two TLSs. The highest-scoring, common-word answer is on page 59. Time limit: 10 minutes.

3. Double Letter-Double Word:

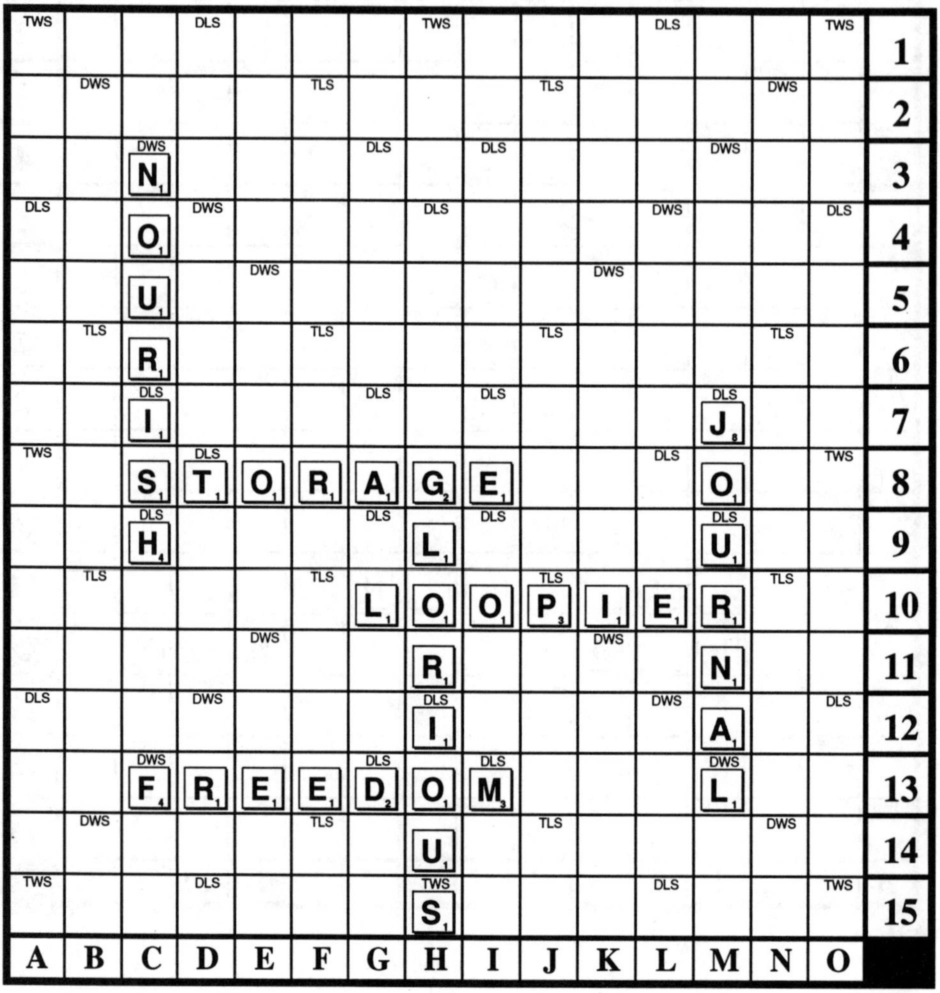

A	B	C	D	E	F	G	H	I	J	K	L	M	N	O	
TWS			DLS				TWS				DLS			TWS	**1**
	DWS			TLS				TLS				DWS			**2**
		N				DLS		DLS				DWS			**3**
DLS		O	DWS				DLS				DWS			DLS	**4**
		U		DWS						DWS					**5**
	DWS	R			TLS				TLS				TLS		**6**
		I				DLS		DLS				J			**7**
TWS		S	T	O	R	A	G	E			DLS	O		TWS	**8**
		H				L		DLS				U			**9**
	TLS				TLS	L	O	O	P	I	E	R	TLS		**10**
				DWS		R				DWS		N			**11**
DLS			DWS			I	DLS				DWS	A		DLS	**12**
		F	R	E	E	D	O	M				L			**13**
	DWS				TLS		U		TLS			DWS			**14**
TWS			DLS				S				DLS			TWS	**15**

DIAGRAM 5-6

When you have opportunities to use a Double Word Score square, don't overlook using the Double Letter Score squares as well. You may even have an opportunity to use *two* DLSs with one DWS. These can be commonly formed on rows 3 and 13 or columns C and M. Less frequently, you may be able to use two DLSs in one play on rows 4 and 12 or on columns D and L.

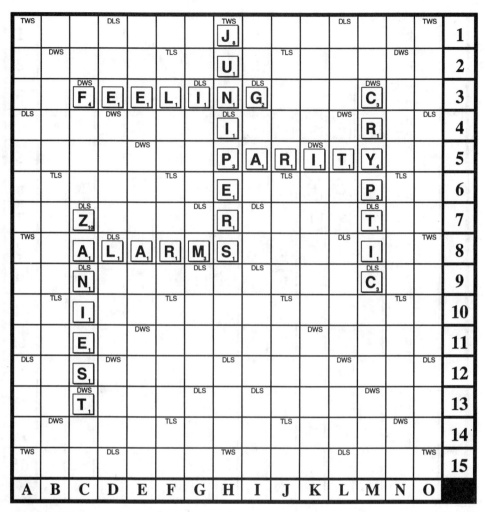

DIAGRAM 5-7

Example

In Diagram 5-6, NOURISH, FREEDOM, and JOURNAL are worth 30, 36, and 46 points respectively. In Diagram 5-7, FEELING, CRYPTIC, and ZANIEST are worth 28, 40, and 54.

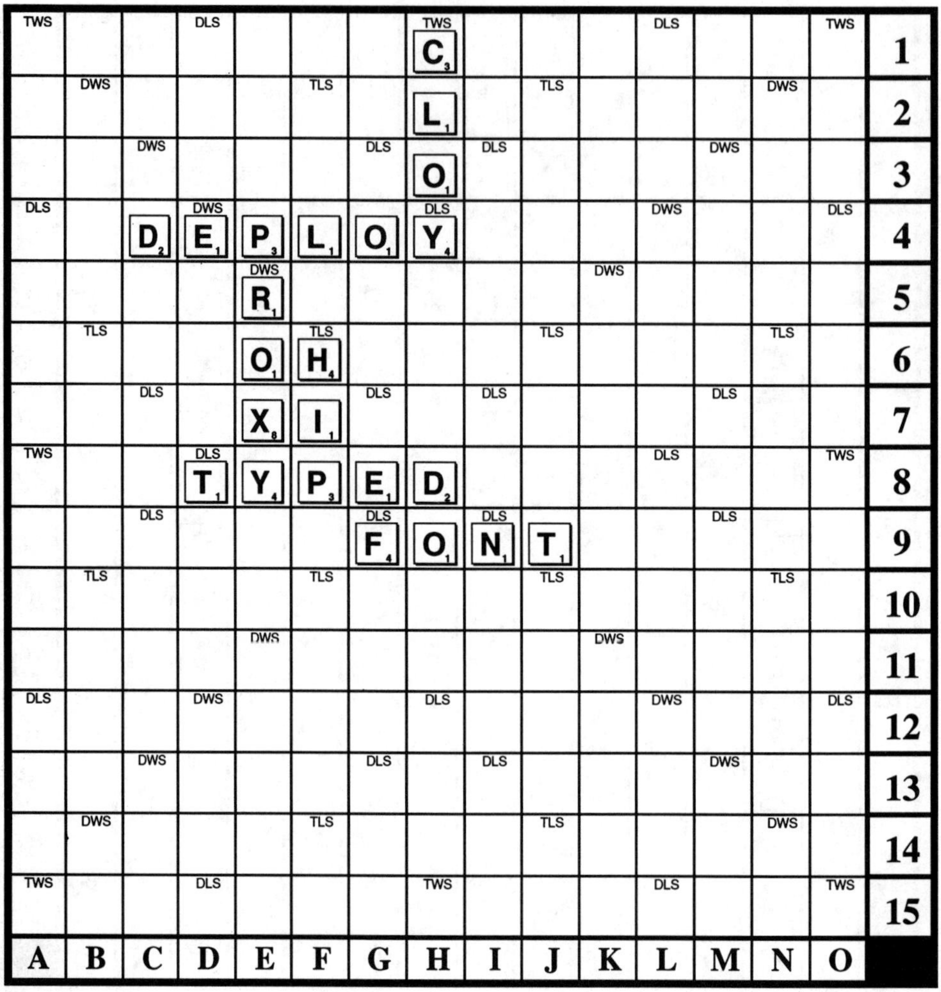

DIAGRAM 5-8

Your rack: B E G N R S V

Use Diagram 5-8 and the letters BEGNRSV to find a play that earns at least one DLS and one DWS. Answer on page 59.

Time limit: 10 minutes

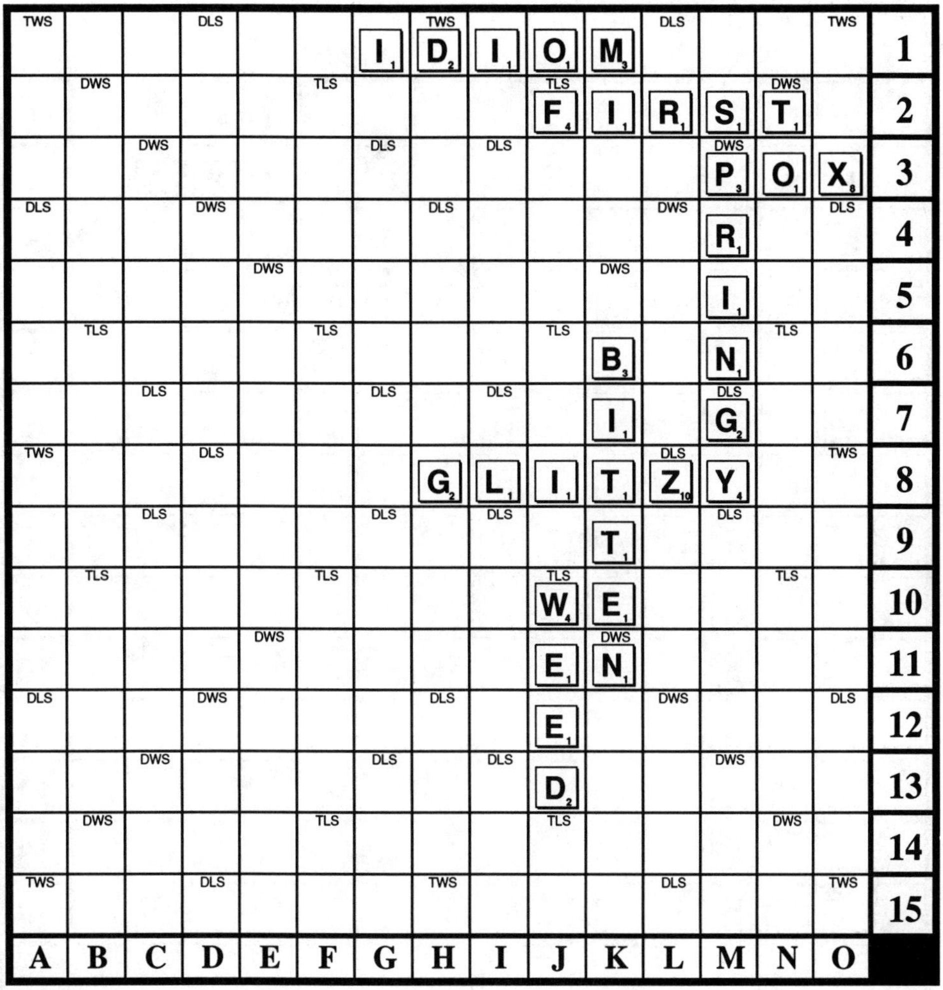

DIAGRAM 5-9

Your rack: A E F I O P R

Use Diagram 5-9 and the letters AEFIOPR to find a play that earns at least one DLS and one DWS. The highest-scoring common-word answer is listed on page 59.

Time limit: 10 minutes

4. Triple Letter-Double Word

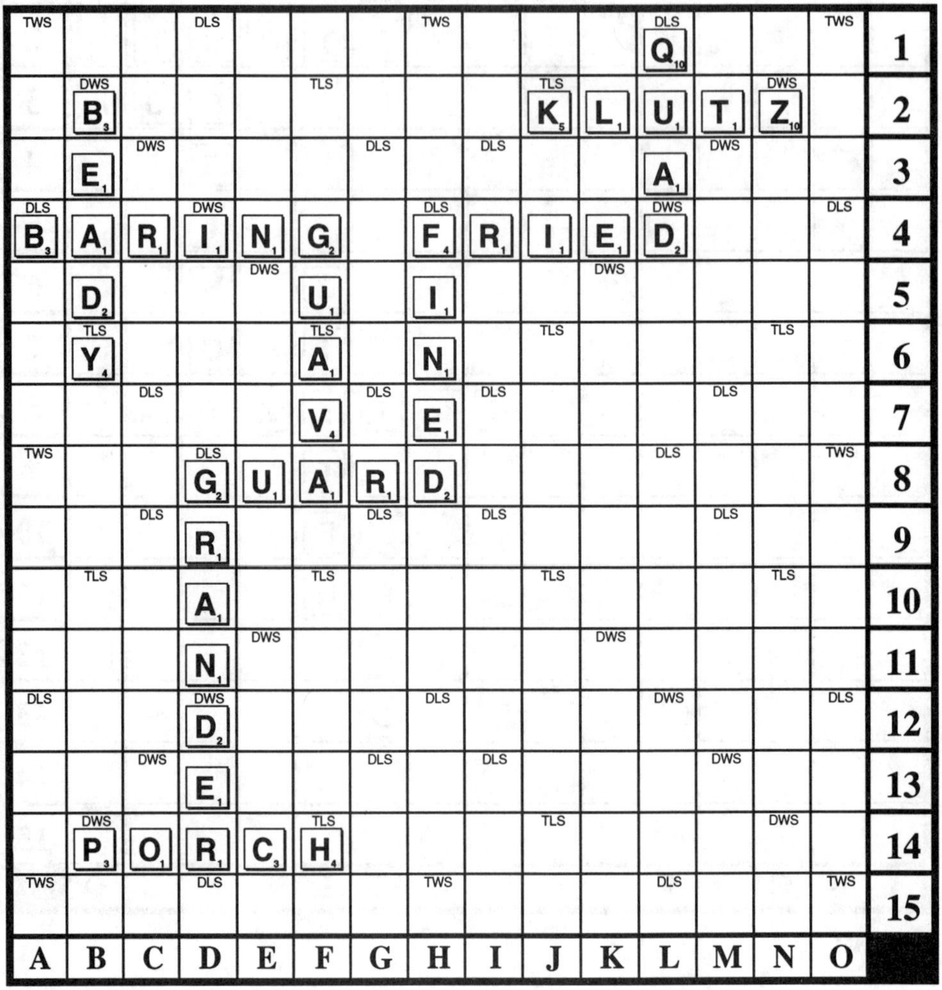

	A	B	C	D	E	F	G	H	I	J	K	L	M	N	O	
1												Q				1
2		B								K	L	U	T	Z		2
3		E										A				3
4	B	A	R	I	N	G		F	R	I	E	D				4
5		D				U		I								5
6		Y				A		N								6
7						V		E								7
8				G	U	A	R	D								8
9				R												9
10				A												10
11				N												11
12				D												12
13				E												13
14		P	O	R	C	H										14
15																15

DIAGRAM 5-10

Four of the DWSs have Triple Letter Score squares four spaces away. By combining these two squares, you can score as much as 70 points or more with a Q or Z. With the 4-point tiles (F, H, V, W, and Y) you can often score more than 30 points. These combinations can be formed on rows 2 and 14 and columns B and N.

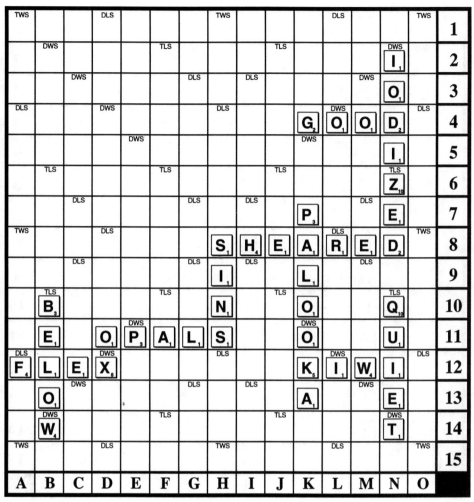

DIAGRAM 5-11

Example

In Diagram 5-10, BEADY, PORCH, and KLUTZ are worth 38, 40, and 56 points, respectively. In Diagram 5-11, BELOW, QUIET, and IODIZED are worth 32, 68, and 76 points.

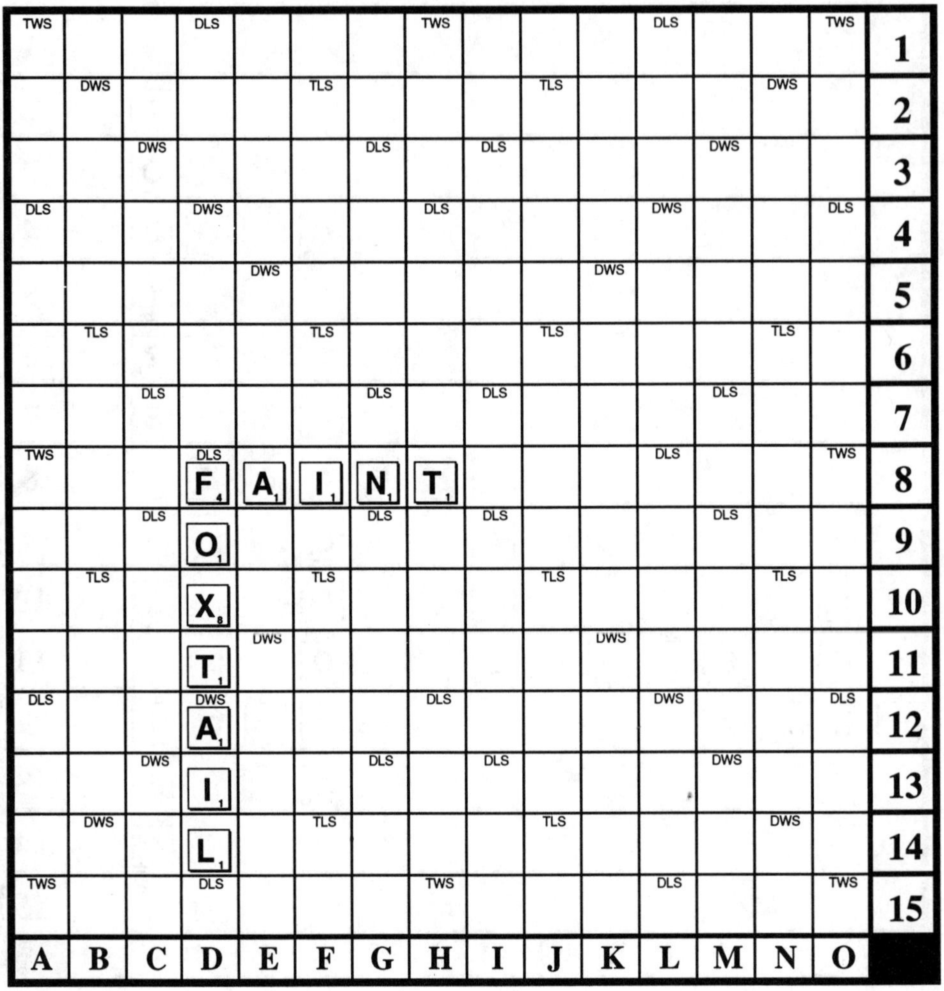

DIAGRAM 5-12

Your rack: A E E I O R Z

Use Diagram 5-12 and the letters AEEIORZ to find a play that covers both a DWS and TLS. The highest-scoring answer is on page 59.
Time limit: 10 minutes

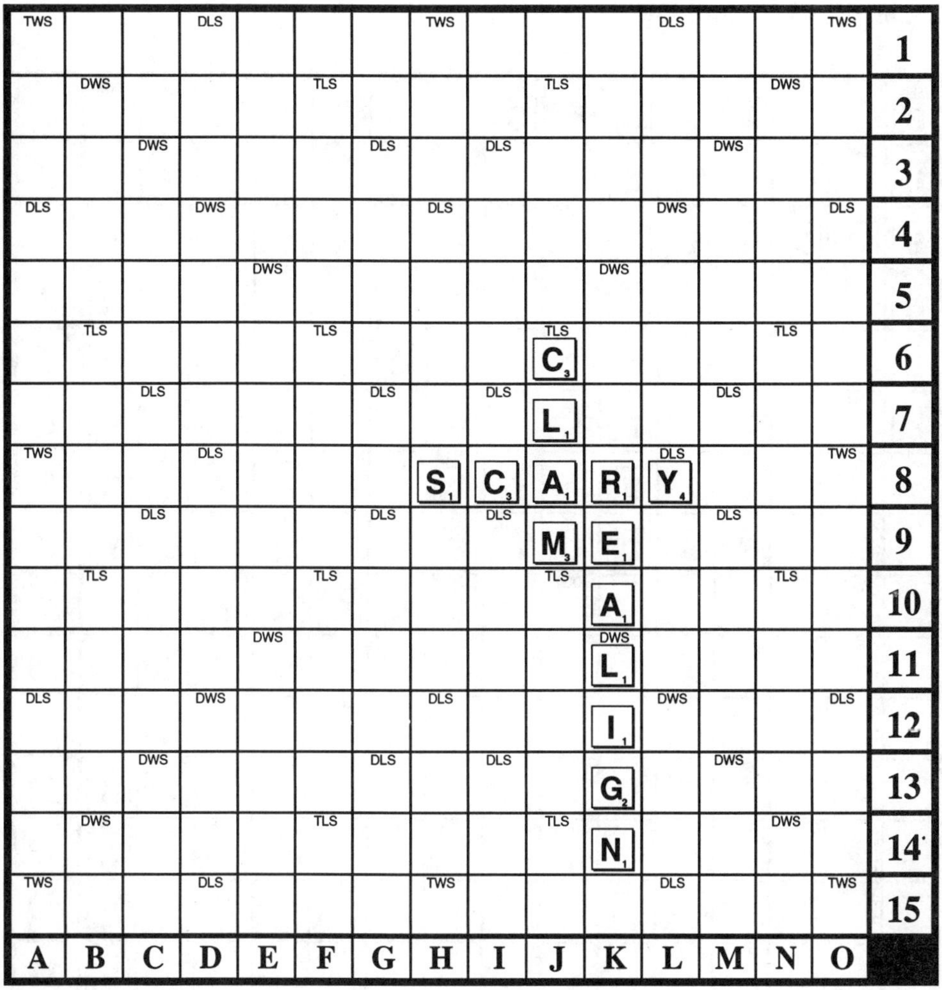

A	B	C	D	E	F	G	H	I	J	K	L	M	N	O	
TWS			DLS				TWS				DLS			TWS	1
	DWS				TLS				TLS				DWS		2
		DWS				DLS		DLS				DWS			3
DLS			DWS				DLS				DWS			DLS	4
				DWS						DWS					5
	TLS				TLS			C_3	TLS				TLS		6
		DLS				DLS		L_1				DLS			7
TWS			DLS			S_1	C_3	A_1	R_1	Y_4	DLS			TWS	8
		DLS				DLS		M_3	E_1			DLS			9
	TLS				TLS				A_1				TLS		10
				DWS					L_1	DWS					11
DLS			DWS				DLS		I_1		DWS			DLS	12
		DWS				DLS		DLS	G_2			DWS			13
	DWS				TLS				N_1				DWS		14
TWS			DLS				TWS				DLS			TWS	15

DIAGRAM 5-13

Your rack: A E K N O P W

Use Diagram 5-13 and the letters AEKNOPW to find a play that covers both a TLS and DWS. The highest-scoring common-word answer is on page 59.

Time limit: 10 minutes

5. Triple Word-Double Letter

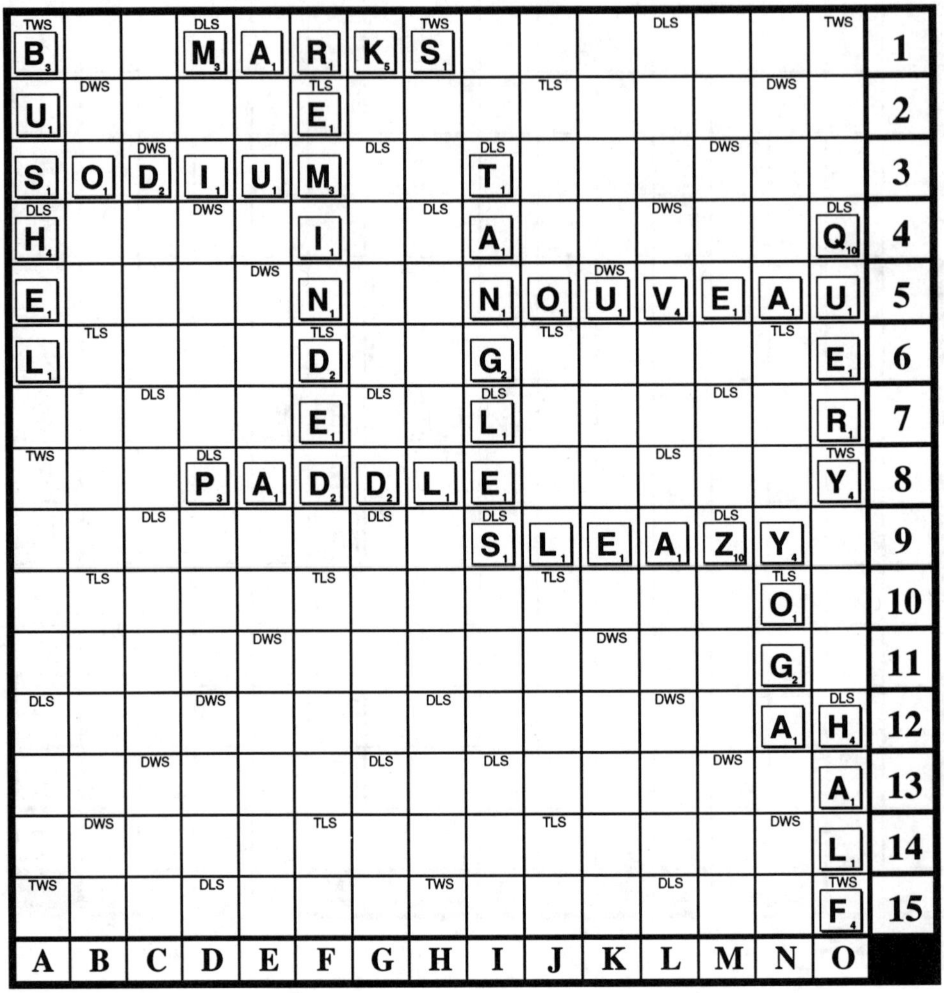

	A	B	C	D	E	F	G	H	I	J	K	L	M	N	O	
1	B			M	A	R	K	S								1
2	U				E											2
3	S	O	D	I	U	M			T							3
4	H				I				A						Q	4
5	E				N				N	O	U	V	E	A	U	5
6	L				D				G						E	6
7					E				L						R	7
8				P	A	D	D	L	E						Y	8
9									S	L	E	A	Z	Y		9
10														O		10
11														G		11
12													A	H		12
13														A		13
14														L		14
15														F		15
	A	B	C	D	E	F	G	H	I	J	K	L	M	N	O	

DIAGRAM 5-14

The TWS can be a potent weapon for earning high scores. Try to use it with the Double Letter Score square a few spaces away. You can form such combinations in two different ways. One way is along the edges of the board on rows 1 and 15 and columns A and O. The other way is to cover one of the middle TWS squares at either 1H, A8, H15, or O8 while playing toward or away from the center of the board.

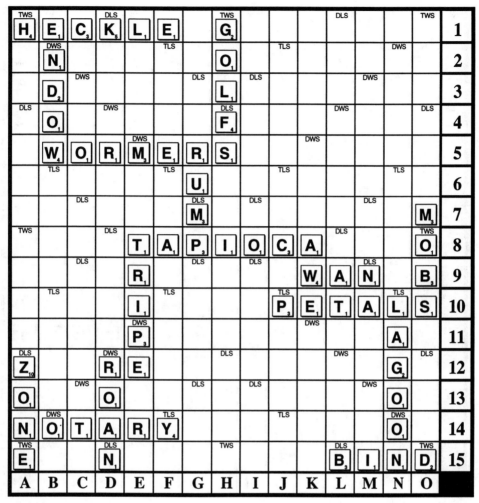

DIAGRAM 5-15

Example

In Diagram 5-14, MARKS, BUSHEL, HALF/AH, and QUERY score 42, 45, 51, and 81 points, respectively. In Diagram 5-15, BIND, HECKLE, and ZONE score 30, 60, and 69 points, while GOLFS/WORMERS is worth 51 points.

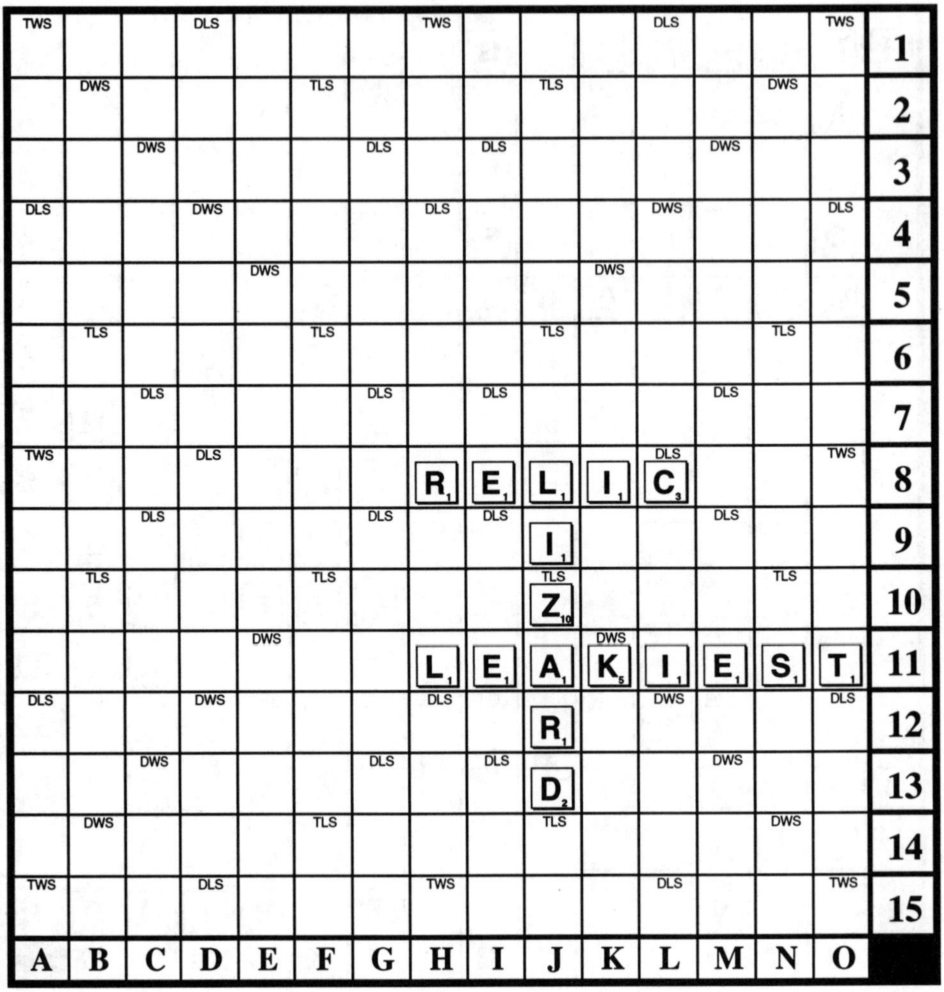

A	B	C	D	E	F	G	H	I	J	K	L	M	N	O	
TWS			DLS			TWS					DLS			TWS	1
	DWS			TLS			TLS					DWS			2
		DWS			DLS		DLS				DWS				3
DLS		DWS				DLS					DWS			DLS	4
			DWS				DWS								5
	TLS			TLS			TLS				TLS				6
		DLS			DLS		DLS				DLS				7
TWS			DLS			R	E	L	I	C	DLS			TWS	8
	DLS				DLS		DLS	I			DLS				9
	TLS			TLS			TLS	Z			TLS				10
			DWS			L	E	A	K	I	E	S	T		11
DLS		DWS				DLS		R		DWS	DWS			DLS	12
		DWS			DLS		DLS	D			DWS				13
	DWS			TLS			TLS					DWS			14
TWS			DLS			TWS					DLS			TWS	15

DIAGRAM 5-16

Your rack: A B E G H N R

Use Diagram 5-16 and the letters ABEGHNR to find a play that covers both a TWS and a DLS. The highest-scoring common word answer is listed on page 59.

Time limit: 10 minutes

6. Double-Doubles

	A	B	C	D	E	F	G	H	I	J	K	L	M	N	O	
	TWS			DLS				TWS			DLS			TWS		**1**
		DWS				TLS				TLS				DWS		**2**
			DWS				DLS		DLS				DWS			**3**
	DLS			DWS				DLS **P₃**				DWS			DLS	**4**
					DWS **H₄**	**O₁**	**W₄**	**L₁**	**I₁**	**N₁**	DWS **G₂**					**5**
		TLS				TLS		**A₁**			TLS				TLS	**6**
			DLS				DLS	**T₁**	DLS				DLS			**7**
	TWS			DLS			**C₃**	**O₁**	**W₄**			DLS			TWS	**8**
			DLS				DLS	**O₁**	DLS				DLS			**9**
		TLS				TLS		**N₁**			TLS				TLS	**10**
					DWS **P₃**	**E₁**	**A₁**	**S₁**	**A₁**	**N₁**	DWS **T₁**					**11**
	DLS			DWS				DLS				DWS			DLS	**12**
			DWS				DLS		DLS				DWS			**13**
		DWS				TLS				TLS				DWS		**14**
	TWS			DLS				TWS			DLS			TWS		**15**

DIAGRAM 5-17

Covering two Double Word Score squares at the same time is called playing a "Double-Double," and written DWS-DWS.

There are four places that account for almost all double-doubles. (see Diagrams 5-17 and 5-18).

The DWS-DWS is worth **four** times the value of the sum of the tiles. If all seven tiles are 1-pointers, that's 28 points. However, play a DWS-DWS with a Q or Z and you can score 64 points without even using all your tiles!

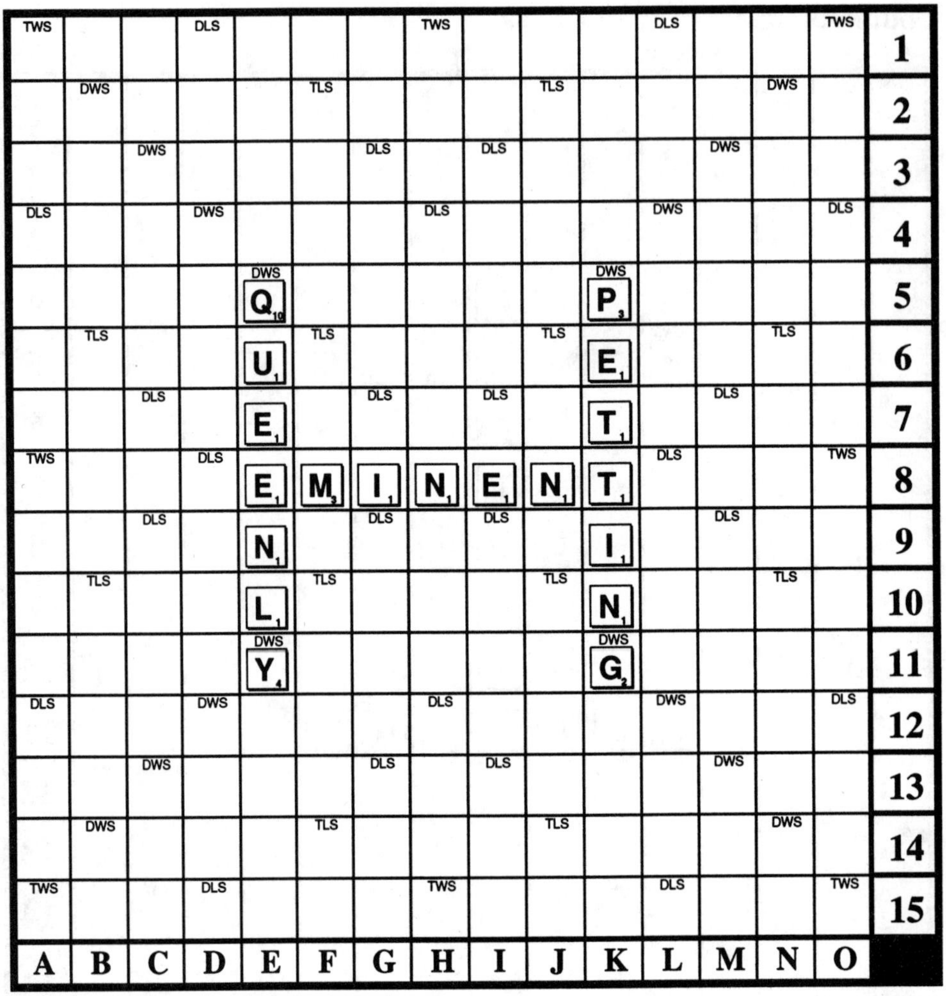

DIAGRAM 5-18

Example

In Diagram 5-17, PEASANT and HOWLING score 36 and 56 points, respectively. In Diagram 5-18, PETTING and QUEENLY score 40 and 76.

Double-Doubles can happen as early as the second play of a game. If the first player covers any Double Letter Score square along the eighth row (8D or 8L) or the H column (H4 or H12), the second player will have a chance for a DWS-DWS.

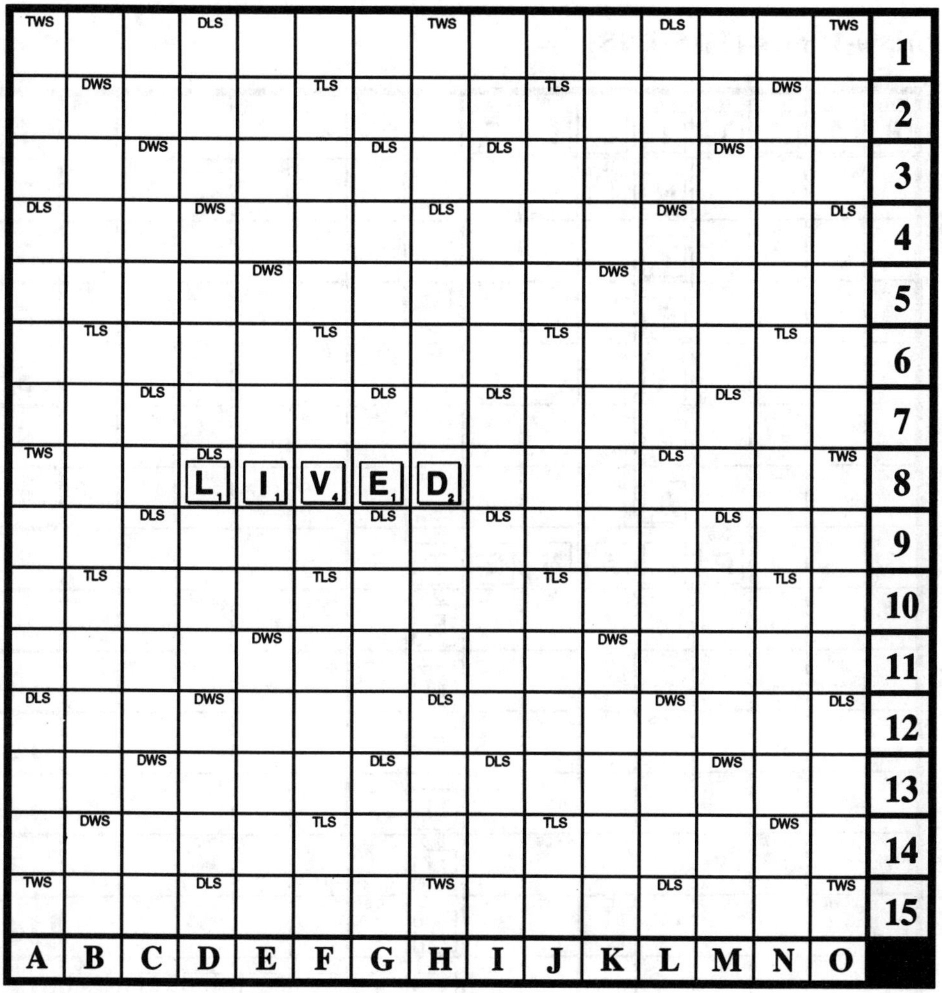

DIAGRAM 5-19

Your rack: A D E E H T V

Use Diagram 5-19 and the letters ADEEHTV to find a play that covers both DWSs along the E column. Answer on page 59.
Time limit: 10 minutes

7. Triple-Triples (TWS-TWS)

TWS **P₃**	A₁	R₁	T₁	DLS I₁	C₃	L₁	TWS E₁			DLS		TWS			**1**
	DWS			**N₁**	TLS			TLS			DWS				**2**
		DWS		**T₁**		DLS		DLS			DWS				**3**
DLS			DWS	**E₁**			DLS			DWS			DLS		**4**
			DWS	**R₁**				DWS							**5**
	TLS			**V₄**	TLS			TLS				TLS			**6**
		DLS		**A₁**		DLS		DLS			DLS				**7**
TWS			DLS **P₃**	L₁	A₁	N₁	E₁	**T₁**			DLS		TWS		**8**
		DLS				DLS		DLS **E₁**			DLS				**9**
	TLS				TLS			**M₃** TLS				TLS			**10**
			DWS					**P₃**	DWS						**11**
DLS			DWS			DLS		**O₁**			DWS		DLS		**12**
		DWS			DLS			DLS **R₁**			DWS				**13**
	DWS				TLS			**A₁** TLS				DWS			**14**
TWS			DLS			TWS	**F₄**	L₁	A₁	N₁	DLS K₅	I₁	N₁	TWS G₂	**15**
A	B	C	D	E	F	G	H	I	J	K	L	M	N	O	

DIAGRAM 5-20

A Triple-Triple is the pinnacle of the SCRABBLE scoring experience. That's when you play across two red Triple Word Score squares on the same play, giving you **nine** times the value of the sum of your letters. At a minimum, when you don't use all your letters and two blanks are employed, your score will be 54 points. Commonly, TWS-TWSs will earn about 122 to 140 points (this includes the 50-point bonus for using all your tiles). Because it's worth so much, you should always take some time to look for one if it seems you have a chance.

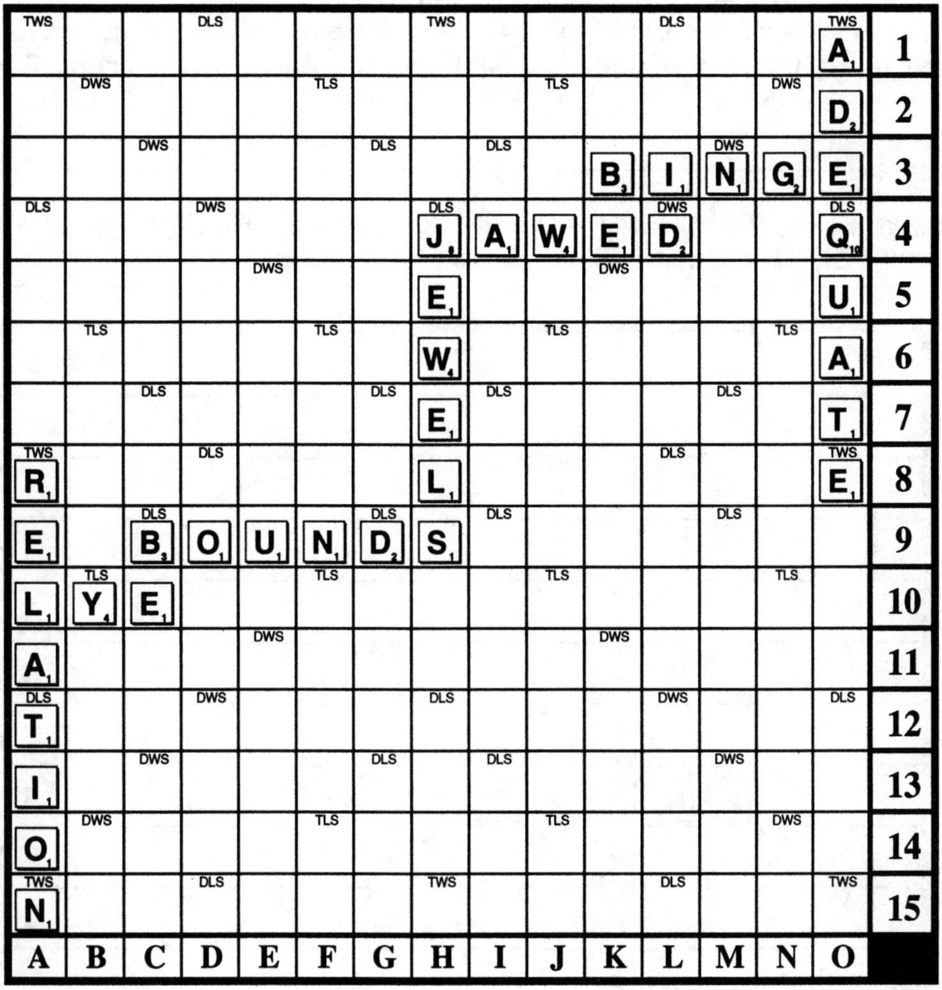

DIAGRAM 5-21

It may take hundreds of games before you ever have the luck to play one, because most players avoid giving their opponents such opportunities. And when they do, you're not likely to have just the right tiles you'll need. But when it does happen, watch the points pile up!

Lest you think that you won't ever play a Triple-Triple, we're happy to tell you that at virtually every SCRABBLE game tournament there are a few Triple-Triples played. At most tournaments, the highest single play is often worth more than 130 points.

You'll play Triple-Triples only on rows 1 and 15 or columns A and O. We've never seen or heard of it happening, but if you should miraculously cover three TWSs with one play, forming a 15-letter word, that's worth 3x3x3 = 27 times the value of the sum of the individual letters. We've seen an imaginary game made up that scored over 3800 points, playing two Triple-Triple-Triples!

Example

In Diagram 5-20, PARTICLE and FLANKING score 167 and 239 points, respectively. In Diagram 5-21, RELATION and ADEQUATE score 131 and 302.

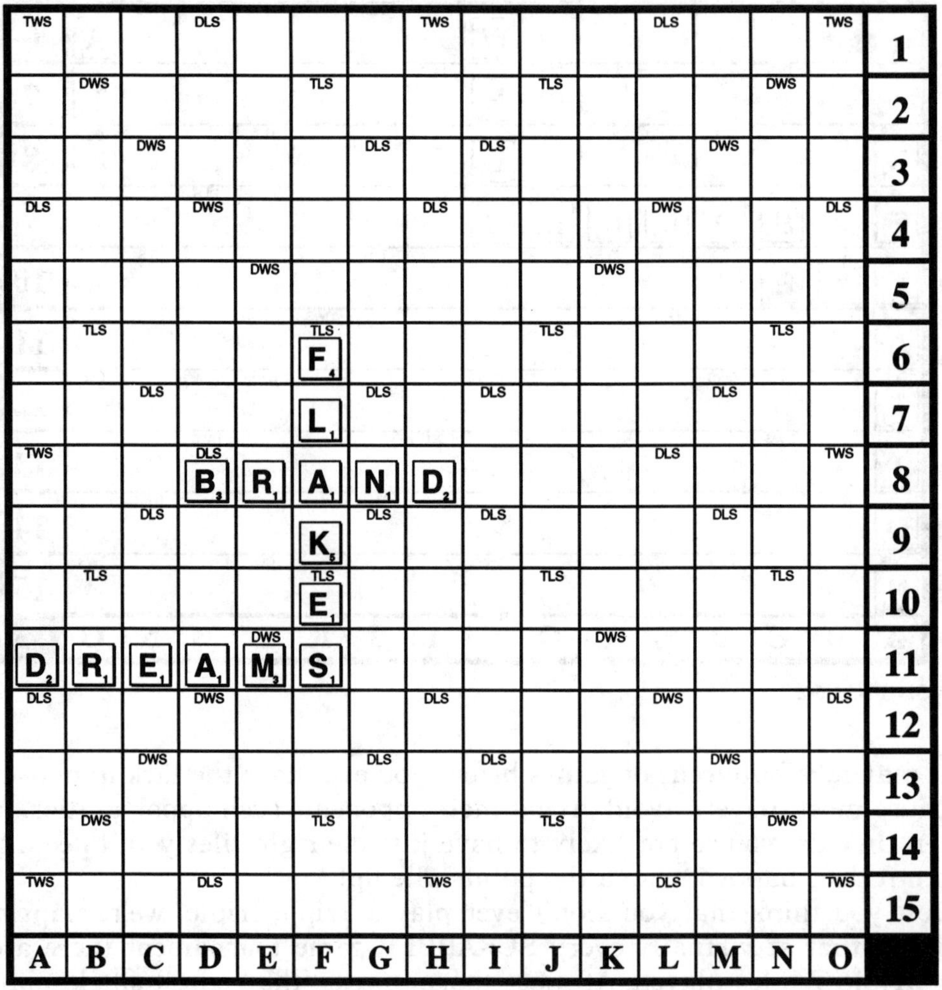

	A	B	C	D	E	F	G	H	I	J	K	L	M	N	O	
	TWS			DLS				TWS				DLS			TWS	**1**
		DWS				TLS				TLS				DWS		**2**
			DWS				DLS		DLS				DWS			**3**
	DLS			DWS				DLS				DWS			DLS	**4**
					DWS					DWS						**5**
		TLS				TLS / F				TLS				TLS		**6**
			DLS			L	DLS		DLS				DLS			**7**
	TWS			DLS / B	R	A	N	D				DLS			TWS	**8**
			DLS		K		DLS		DLS				DLS			**9**
		TLS				TLS / E				TLS				TLS		**10**
	D	R	E	A	DWS / M	S					DWS					**11**
	DLS			DWS				DLS				DWS			DLS	**12**
			DWS				DLS		DLS				DWS			**13**
		DWS				TLS				TLS				DWS		**14**
	TWS			DLS				TWS				DLS			TWS	**15**

DIAGRAM 5-22

Your rack: G I I M N O S

Use Diagram 5-22 and the letters GIIMNOS to find a TWS-TWS play. Answer on page 59.

Time limit: 10 minutes

Bonus Square Bonanza

In each of the following diagrams, use the given rack to find a play that covers the two bonus squares listed. Answers on page 59.

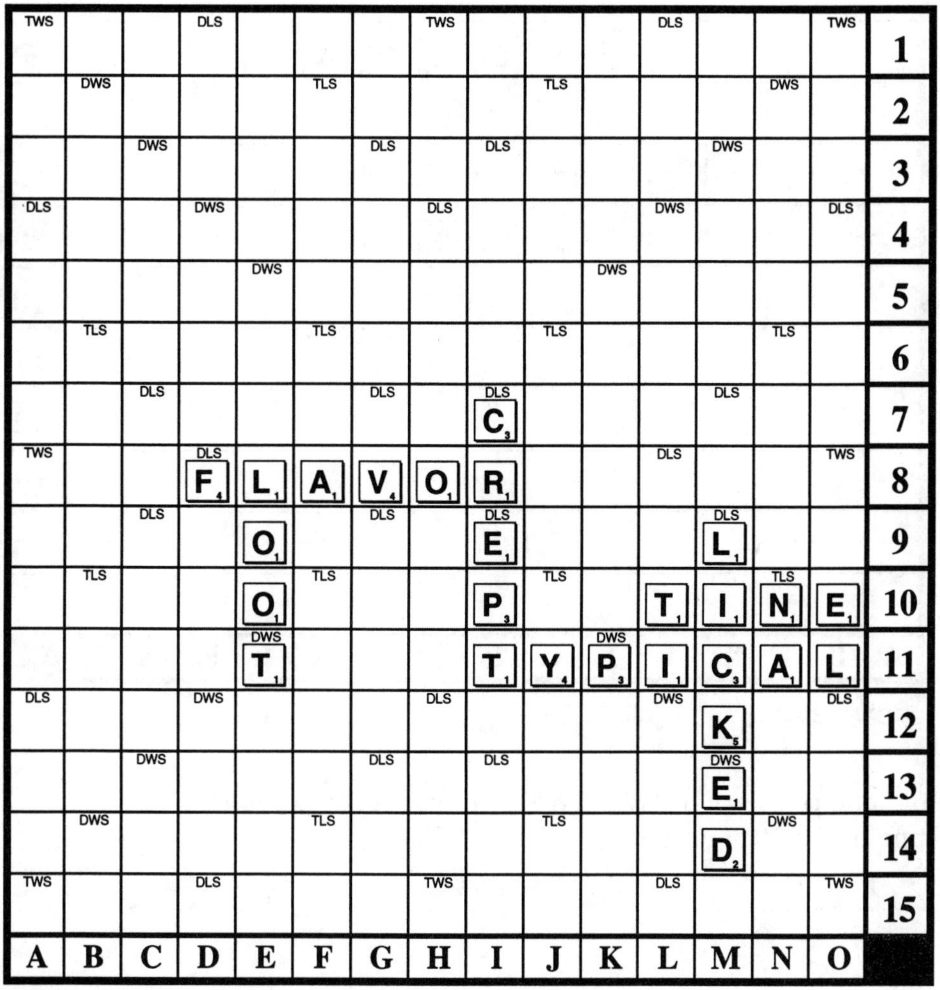

A	B	C	D	E	F	G	H	I	J	K	L	M	N	O	
TWS			DLS				TWS				DLS			TWS	**1**
	DWS				TLS				TLS				DWS		**2**
		DWS				DLS		DLS				DWS			**3**
DLS			DWS				DLS				DWS			DLS	**4**
				DWS						DWS					**5**
	TLS				TLS				TLS				TLS		**6**
		DLS				DLS		**C**				DLS			**7**
TWS			**F**	**L**	**A**	**V**	**O**	**R**			DLS			TWS	**8**
		DLS		**O**		DLS		**E**				**L**			**9**
	TLS			**O**	TLS			**P**	TLS	**T**	**I**	**N**	**E**		**10**
				T			**T**	**Y**	**P**	**I**	**C**	**A**	**L**		**11**
DLS			DWS				DLS				DWS	**K**		DLS	**12**
		DWS				DLS		DLS				**E**			**13**
	DWS				TLS				TLS			**D**	DWS		**14**
TWS			DLS				TWS				DLS			TWS	**15**

DIAGRAM 5-23

Find the TWS-TWS. Your rack: E H N R S S T

Time limit: 10 minutes

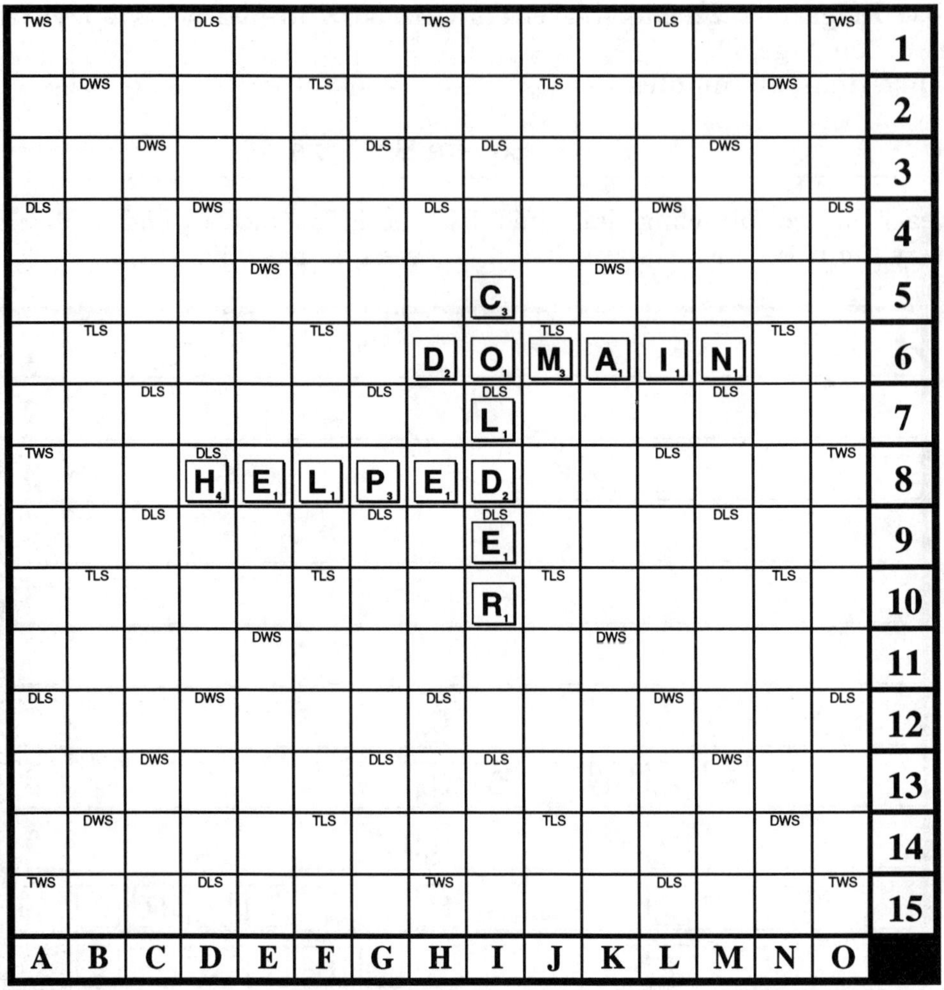

DIAGRAM 5-24

Board tiles:
- C₃ at I5
- D₂ O₁ M₃ A₁ I₁ N₁ (DOMAIN) across row 6 (H6–M6)
- L₁ at I7
- H₄ E₁ L₁ P₃ E₁ D₂ (HELPED) across row 8 (D8–I8)
- E₁ at I9
- R₁ at I10

Find one of the two DWS-DWSs. Your rack: B D I N O S T
Time limit: 10 minutes

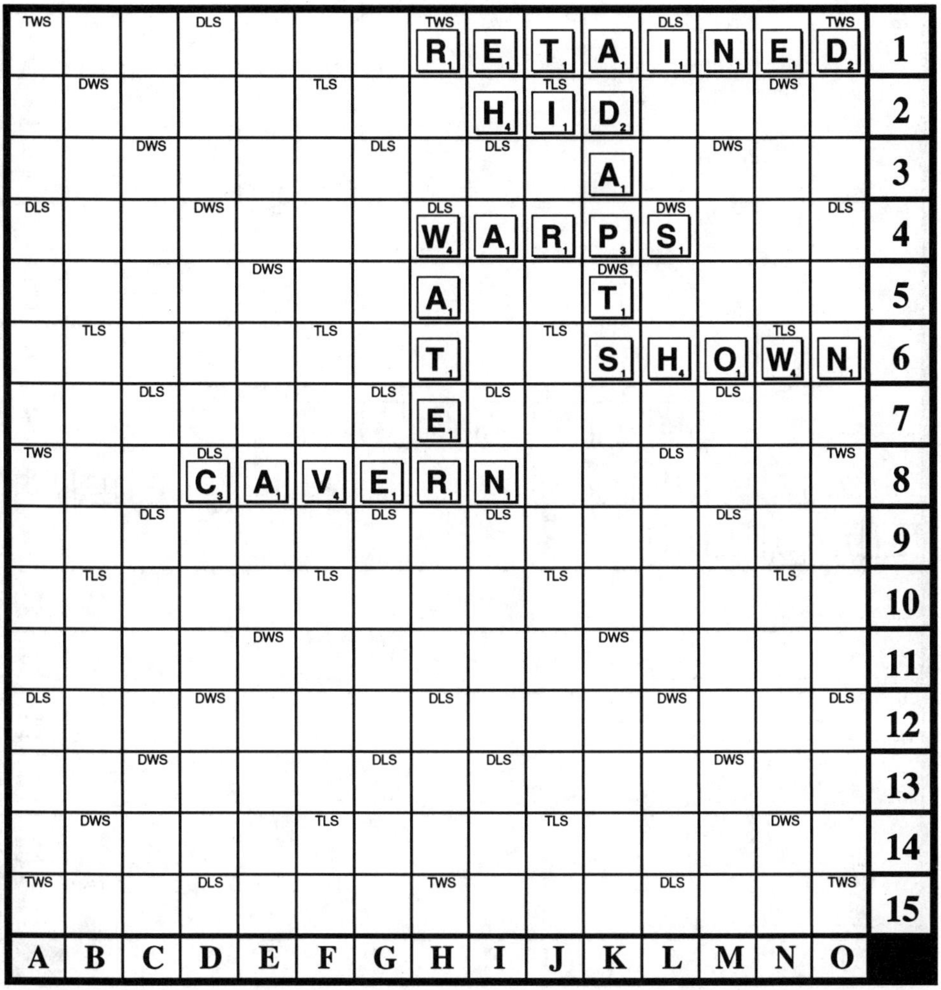

	A	B	C	D	E	F	G	H	I	J	K	L	M	N	O	
	TWS			DLS			TWS **R**	**E**	**T**	**A**	DLS **I**	**N**	**E**	TWS **D**		1
		DWS			TLS		**H**	**I**	TLS **D**				DWS			2
			DWS			DLS		DLS	**A**			DWS				3
	DLS			DWS			DLS **W**	**A**	**R**	**P**	DWS **S**			DLS		4
					DWS		**A**			DWS **T**					5
		TLS			TLS		**T**		TLS	**S**	**H**	**O**	TLS **W**	**N**		6
			DLS			DLS	**E**	DLS			DLS				7
	TWS		DLS **C**	**A**	**V**	**E**	**R**	**N**			DLS		TWS		8
			DLS			DLS		DLS			DLS				9
		TLS			TLS			TLS			TLS				10
				DWS				DWS							11
	DLS			DWS			DLS			DWS			DLS		12
			DWS			DLS		DLS			DWS				13
		DWS			TLS			TLS			DWS				14
	TWS			DLS			TWS			DLS			TWS		15

DIAGRAM 5-25

Find the highest-scoring TWS-DLS. Your rack: A G H M T U Y
Time limit: 10 minutes

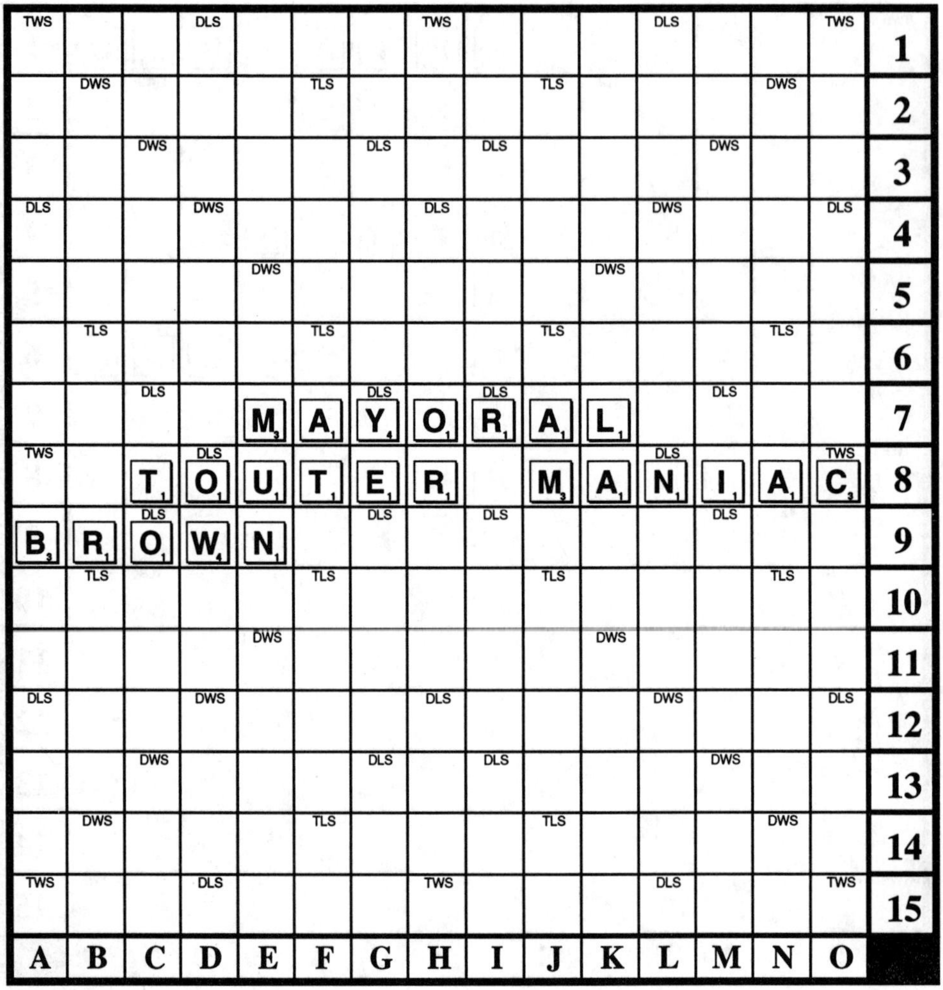

DIAGRAM 5-26

Find the highest-scoring DWS-TLS. Your rack: C I O Q S T U
Time limit: 10 minutes

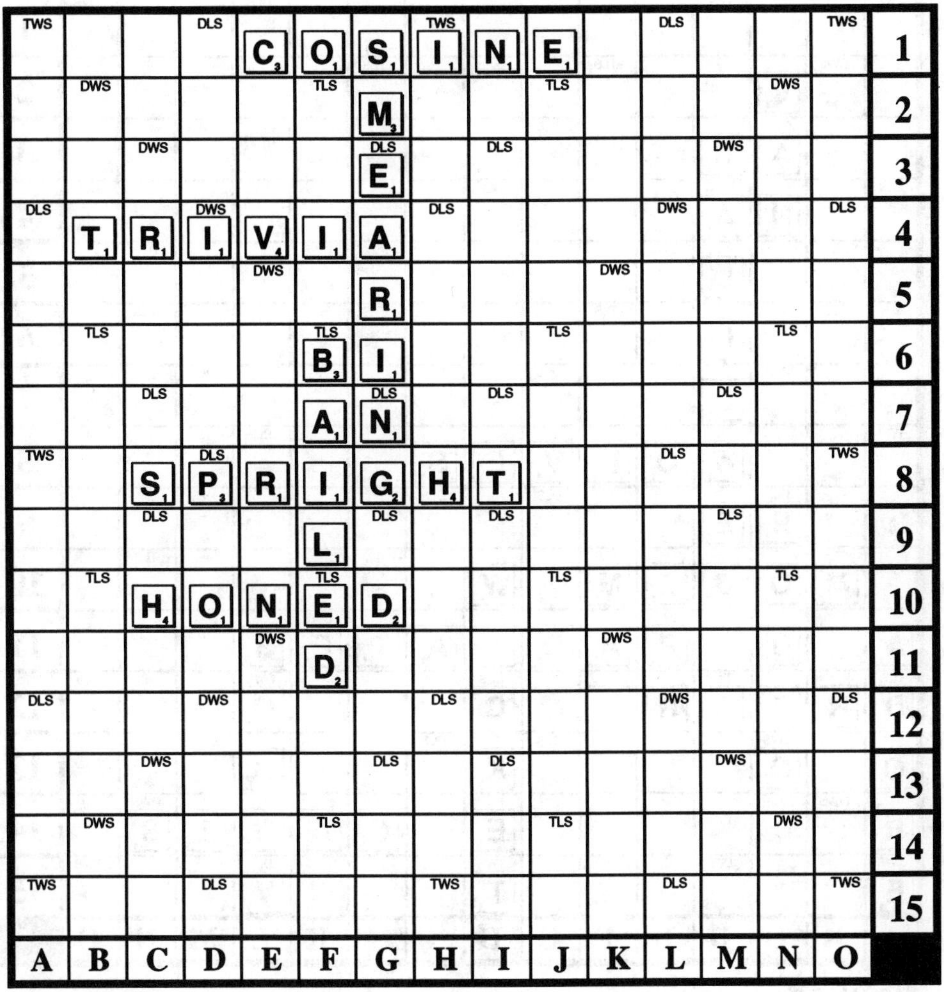

DIAGRAM 5-27

Find the highest-scoring DWS-DLS. Your rack: B C E I K L U
Time limit: 10 minutes

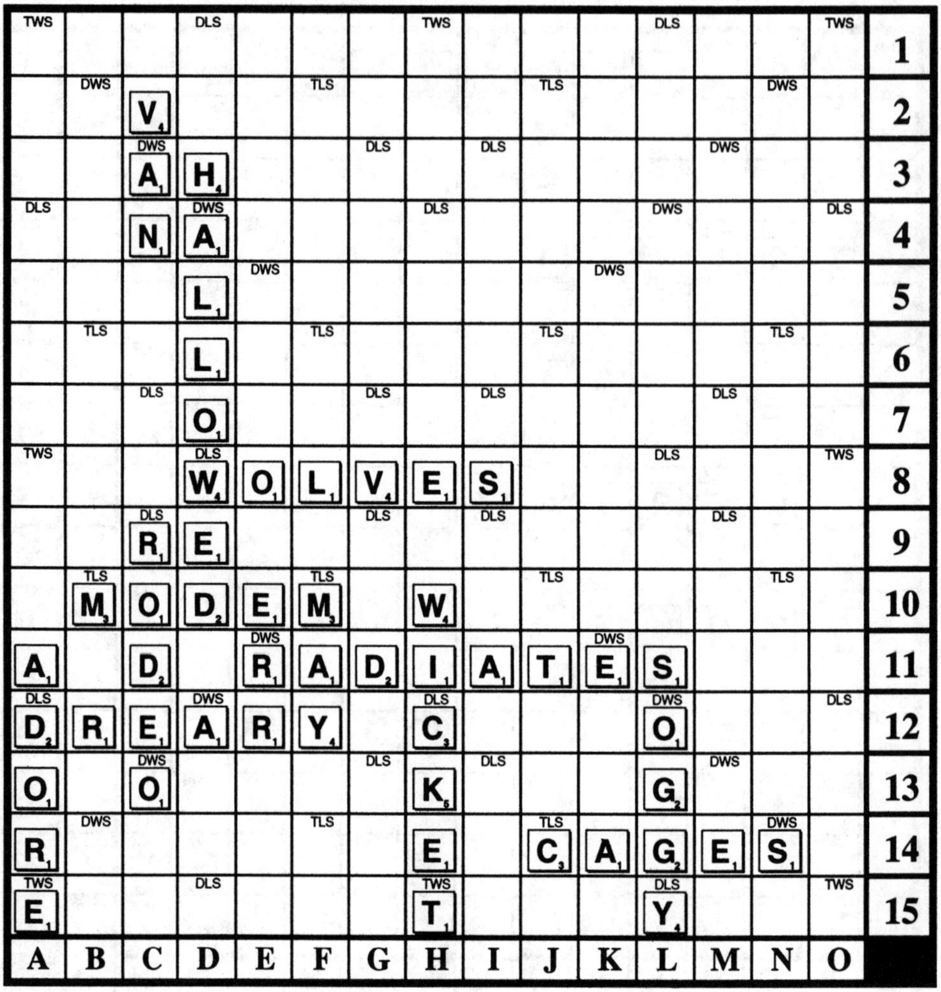

DIAGRAM 5-28

Find the highest-scoring TLS-TLS. Your rack: A E F I L O P
Time limit: 10 minutes

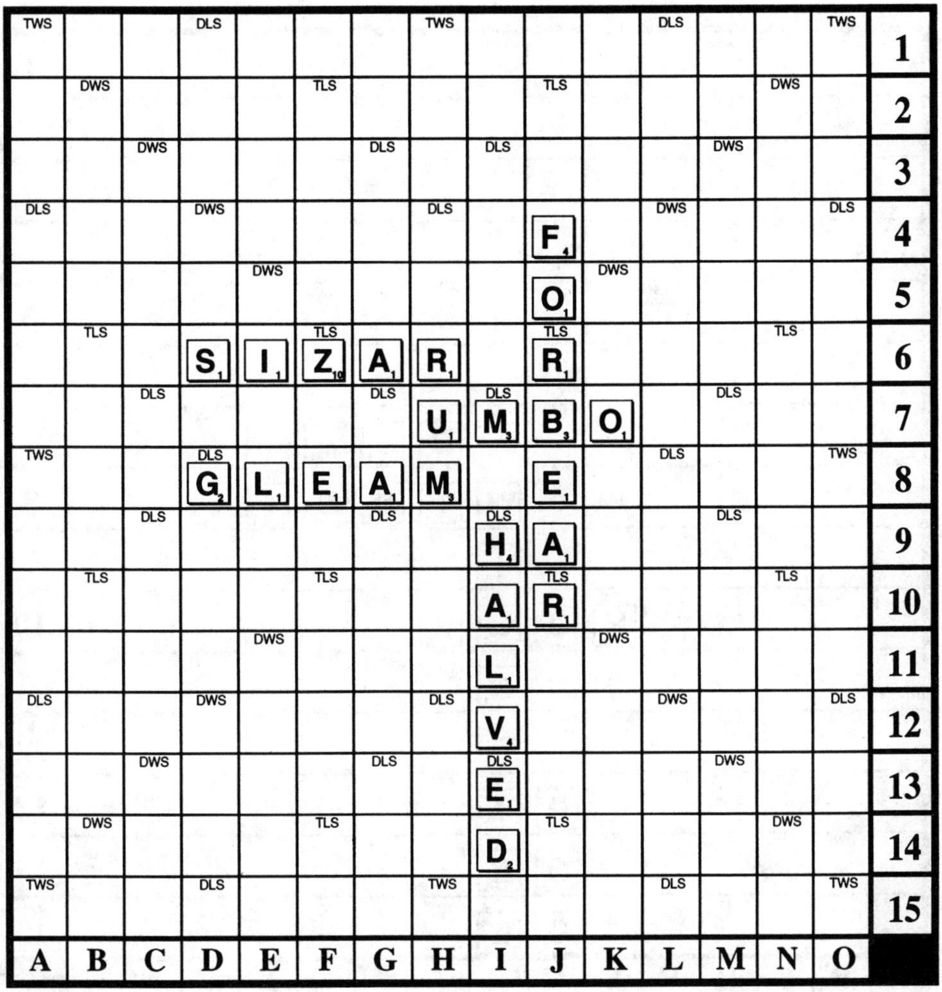

DIAGRAM 5-29

Find the outstanding parallel play. Your rack: A D E E R R R
Time limit: 15 minutes. This is a toughie!

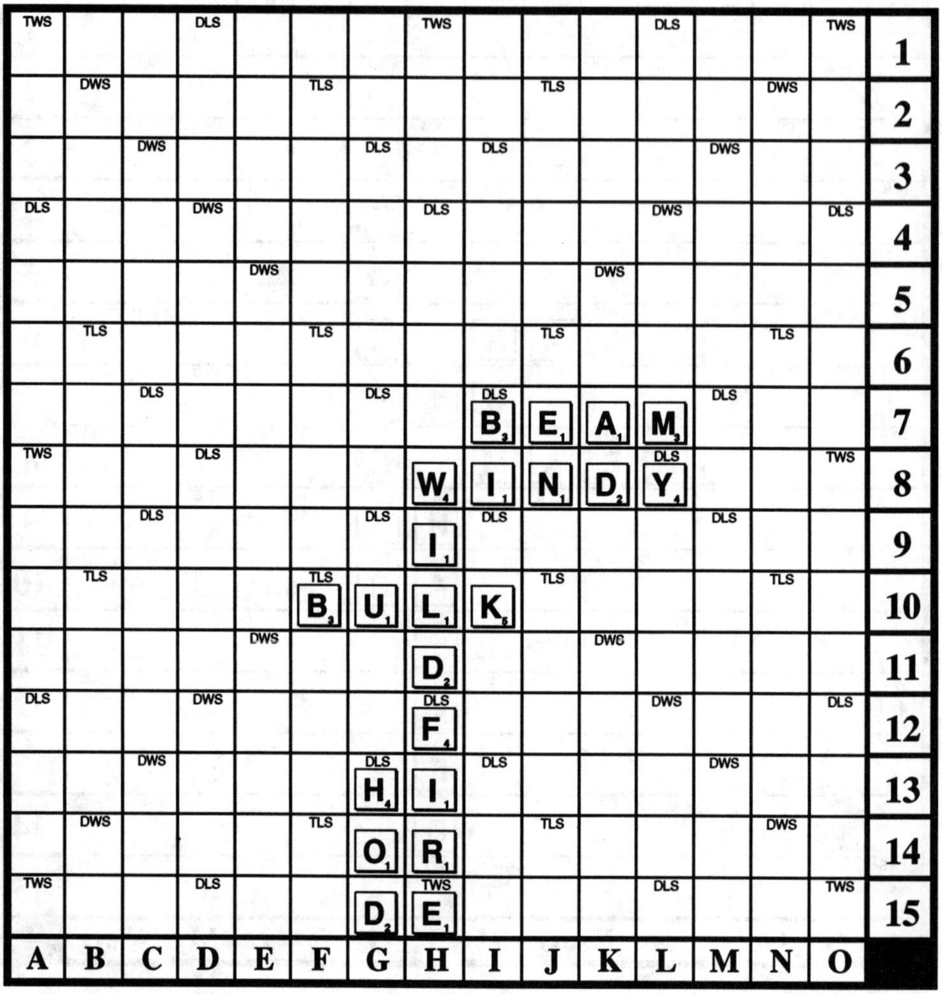

DIAGRAM 5-30

Find the outstanding parallel play. Your rack: A A D L M P R
Time limit: 10 minutes

One of the major stumbling blocks to scoring well is drawing the Q without a U. Chapter Six shows you some important words that will help clear your rack of the Q quickly.

DIAGRAM 5-2: 1. REND 8L 48 points; 2. DOUBTS 5J 36; 3. NONSKID 10B 105; 4. QUITE 6F 43.

DIAGRAM 5-5: PROMPT 6F 24.

DIAGRAM 5-8: GOVERNS 3G 39.

DIAGRAM 5-9: FAIRER 4H 26.

DIAGRAM 5-12: REALIZE 14A 72.

DIAGRAM 5-13: KNOWN 14J 44.

DIAGRAM 5-16: BREATH O7 45.

DIAGRAM 5-19: DEVIATE E5 44.

DIAGRAM 5-22: MISDOING A8 167.

DIAGRAM 5-23: SHELTERS O8 108.

DIAGRAM 5-24: BANDITS K5 40; BASTION K5 36.

DIAGRAM 5-25: NAUGHTY O6 54.

DIAGRAM 5-26: ACQUITS N8 76.

DIAGRAM 5-27: BRICKS C3 38.

DIAGRAM 5-28: PILAF 6B 24.

DIAGRAM 5-29: REORDER K5 50.

DIAGRAM 5-30: MILD 9G 33.

6

YOUR FOURTH-GRADE TEACHER, MRS. KLEINFELDER, LIED TO YOU
You *Can* Have Words with a Q and No U

Veteran SCRABBLE® game competitors will tell you that the Q can be your best friend in a game—or your worst nightmare. As long as you have a U or a blank, it can be a guaranteed pointmaker. Should you find yourself with a Q and no U or blank, consider your options carefully.

As soon as you draw a Q, you should be aware of how many Us have been played and how many remain in the bag. Remember, there are only four of them. Also, carefully assess the merit of using a blank as a U. Depending upon your tiles, the blank may simply be worth more as a building block for a future bingo. With two blanks, you should certainly use one of them to rid yourself of the Q. Your second option is to play off your other tiles, scoring as well as possible while waiting to draw a U. This may work for a turn or two, but the odds are against this strategy being successful beyond that.

Your chief concern near the end of the game is to make sure you don't get caught with an unplayed Q, as this may add 20 points to your opponent's score and can very easily cost you the match. In fact, if all the Us have been played, you should give strong consideration to exchanging the Q— and perhaps some other unwanted tiles. It may be as good as making a 20-point play, as your opponent could now get stuck with it! Just remember: as soon as there are fewer than seven tiles in the bag, you may no longer exchange tiles.

Of course, there is a third option, long practiced by SCRABBLE game enthusiasts at all levels—the Q-without-U words. These extraordinarily valuable words, which will help you to both score points and clear your rack of "unworkable" tiles at the same time, are listed below. Learn them!

QAID: *n* pl. -S. A variation of caid, a Muslim leader.

QANAT: *n* pl. -S. A system of underground tunnels and wells in the Middle East.

QAT: *n* pl. -S. Variation of kat, an evergreen shrub.

QINDAR: *n* pl. -DARS or -DARKA. Variation of QINTAR, a monetary unit of Albania.

QINTAR: *n* pl. -S. See above.

TRANQ: *n* pl. -S. Variation of trank (i.e., tranquilizer).

QOPH: *n* pl. -S. KOPH, a letter of the Hebrew alphabet.

FAQIR: *n* pl. -S. Variation of FAKIR, a Hindu ascetic.

Also of note: UMIAQ, BUQSHA, and QIVIUT.

Here's one more hint to keep in mind: Be mindful of the words AID and AT. These two words can be used by either you or your opponent to dump the Q. So whenever you are about to play either of them, ask yourself if it will help or hinder your efforts to win.

In general, whenever you get the Q, try to get it off your rack by whatever means possible, as soon as possible. That's how to use the Q to your advantage.

Playing the Q

With each of the following four-letter combinations, a Q may be added to form a word after rearranging the five letters. Review the list of Q words on page 62 before trying this exercise. You may want to redo these puzzles occasionally in the future until you can determine all the words without reviewing the list. Answers on page 62.

1. EIRU
2. AIMU (2 words)
3. ANTU
4. EEUU
5. ASTU
6. EOTU (2 words)
7. ESUU
8. IPUU
9. AANT
10. ETUU
11. HOTU
12. HRSU
13. INOU
14. AISU (2 words)
15. EFIU
16. ANRT
17. EORU
18. AKUY
19. AENU
20. EIPU (2 words)

QAT	MAQUI	QUAYS	QUITE
QUA	PIQUE	QUEAN	QUITS
AQUA	QAIDS	QUEEN	QUODS
QAID	QANAT	QUEER	QUOIN
QATS	QOPHS	QUELL	QUOIT
QOPH	QUACK	QUERN	QUOTA
QUAD	QUADS	QUERY	QUOTE
QUAG	QUAFF	QUEST	QUOTH
QUAI	QUAGS	QUEUE	QURSH
QUAY	QUAIL	QUEYS	ROQUE
QUEY	QUAIS	QUICK	SQUAB
QUID	QUAKE	QUIDS	SQUAD
QUIN	QUAKY	QUIET	SQUAT
QUIP	QUALE	QUIFF	SQUAW
QUIT	QUALM	QUILL	SQUEG
QUIZ	QUANT	QUILT	SQUIB
QUOD	QUARE	QUINS	SQUID
AQUAE	QUARK	QUINT	TOQUE
AQUAS	QUART	QUIPS	TRANQ
EQUAL	QUASH	QUIPU	TUQUE
EQUIP	QUASI	QUIRE	UMIAQ
FAQIR	QUASS	QUIRK	USQUE
FIQUE	QUATE	QUIRT	

DIQUAT

While you may now be able to make good 25-to-35-point plays, your next jump will take you further than you imagine. Anybody can learn how to find seven- and eight-letter words! You only need to practice looking for them with the right tools. Up ahead—Chapter Seven!

ANSWERS: CHAPTER 6

1. QUIRE	6. QUOTE, TOQUE	11. QUOTH	16. TRANQ
2. MAQUI, UMIAQ	7. USQUE	12. QURSH	17. ROQUE
3. QUANT	8. QUIPU	13. QUOIN	18. QUAKY
4. QUEUE	9. QANAT	14. QUAIS, QUASI	19. QUEAN
5. SQUAT	10. TUQUE	15. FIQUE	20. EQUIP, PIQUE

7 BINGOS: HOW TO MAKE SEVEN- AND EIGHT-LETTER PLAYS

A bingo is a play that uses all seven letters of a player's rack. This scores 50 extra bonus points, and is at the heart of consistent winning. Experts usually play two or three bingos in an average game, and they are constantly thinking about how to develop a bingo rack.

We've known many casual players who've never laid down a bingo. What's the secret to finding these plays? It's actually not all that mysterious. First, know which letters commonly combine together to form easy-to-see word beginnings and endings. Then look for them on your rack.

Example

The three letters G, I, and N can be combined as ING to form the ending of many words. ENDING, HAVING, FLOWING, and COMING are just four of the thousands of words ending in ING. Once you see ING on your rack, all you need to do is rearrange the other four letters (remember from Chapter Four that there are only twenty-four possible arrangements), which shouldn't take more than a minute to explore once you're experienced at it.

Some of the other most common endings are: ED, ER, IER, IEST, and IES. Of word beginnings, UN and RE are two of the most frequently played. An extensive list of such word beginnings and endings is printed at the end of this chapter. The more familiar you are with them, the quicker you'll achieve those 50-point bonuses. By moving the tiles around on your rack, you will learn to see the useful letter combinations without much effort.

BINGO PRACTICE #1:

Find the common word that can be spelled with each set of letters below. In each case the word will either begin or end with one of the following sets of letters:

Beginnings: **EM, EN, EX, FORE, HEAD, HAND, IM, IN, ISO, MID**
Endings: **ED, EE, ENCE, ENT, ER, EST, FORM, FUL, GHT, ISH**

We recommend that you play with actual tiles on a rack as you would while playing a game, instead of trying to find the words in your head. Answers on page 75.

Example

In Set A, # 1 is ABELMMS. If you compare these seven letters with the possible beginnings and endings above, you may notice that the answer word can only begin with EM, since there is no other matching beginning or ending.
  Time limit per set: 30 minutes
  Average Score: 5 correct   Good Score: 7 correct   Expert Score: 9 correct

SET A	SET B	SET C	SET D
1. ABELMMS	1. BEIILMMO	1. AEFOPRW	1. AEILOSST
2. EIOOPST	2. ADEEHST	2. AEELMNS	2. ADDEHOR
3. ADEINPRS	3. ACDEEINU	3. EGLNPRU	3. EEINNPTT
4. FIMNORU	4. AEGSTUV	4. EEIORRTX	4. EEELMOPY
5. CEEEILNN	5. BEIKLNR	5. IIMNOPRS	5. AGHIRSY
6. EFHLLPU	6. AGHIRSTT	6. DEFLLOU	6. ACEFORST
7. GHIILRS	7. ACEHNNT	7. ACEEINRS	7. AABDHLLN
8. AGHILRT	8. BDEMSTU	8. ACDEHKLO	8. DGHIIMNT

BINGO PRACTICE #2:

Beginnings: **MIS, NON, OUT, OVER, POST, PRE, RE, SEA, SUB, UN**
Endings: **ATE, GRAM, IA(L), IBLE, IC, ICAL, IER, IES, IEST, IFY**

Answers on page 75.

SET A	SET B	SET C	SET D
1. BEEIORTV	1. ABEGINO	1. ADINNORY	1. EIIPRSTU
2. AEHIOPRU	2. EINNSSTU	2. EEEIMPRR	2. ABDEILU
3. ACIILNOR	3. DEENNOPU	3. DFIILOSY	3. ACELNNU
4. ABEELSSU	4. EGHIOSTU	4. ADEEMORT	4. EEGIPRST
5. DEEEINRR	5. ABDEILMN	5. AEEGLMRT	5. CDEEIIMP
6. EENNNOSS	6. ADELNORV	6. AEEHORSS	6. AEFNORST
7. EEIILLRV	7. ACDOPRST	7. ACCILMO	7. BEEGMRSU
8. AAEGILTT	8. AMORSTTU	8. CDEIMOST	8. ACEILMPS

FINDING BINGOS OVER THE BOARD

Use the following diagrams as your board positions. Try to find the playable eight-letter bingos with each of the three given racks. This will teach you to use an existing letter on the board plus your seven-letter rack. We list the choice of beginnings or endings to use in the answers. Answers on page 75.

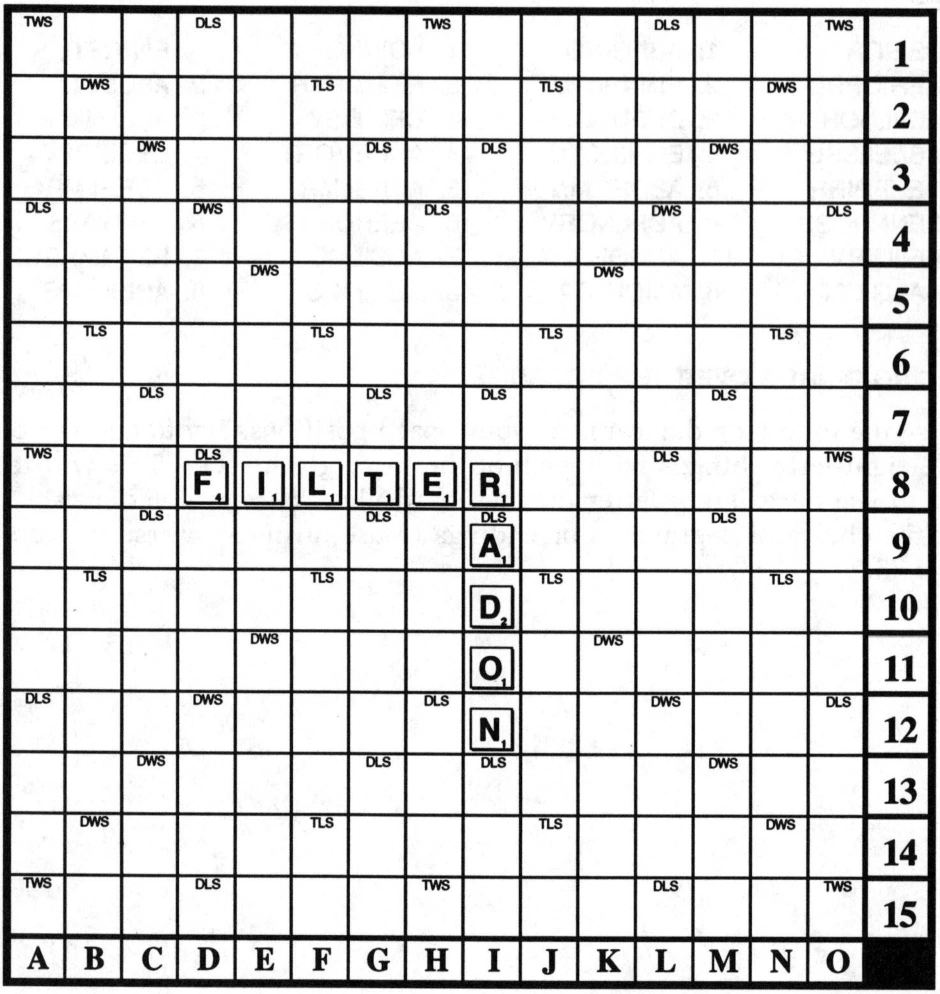

DIAGRAM 7-1

Beginnings: **CON, IN, OUT, RE, UN**

Endings: **ABLE, ED, ENT, IES, TION**

Rack #1: **D D E E F I R**

Rack #2: **A E I N R T V**

Rack #3: **A A C N O T V**

Time limit: 20 minutes

Average Score: 1 correct

Good Score: 2 correct *Expert Score:* 3 correct

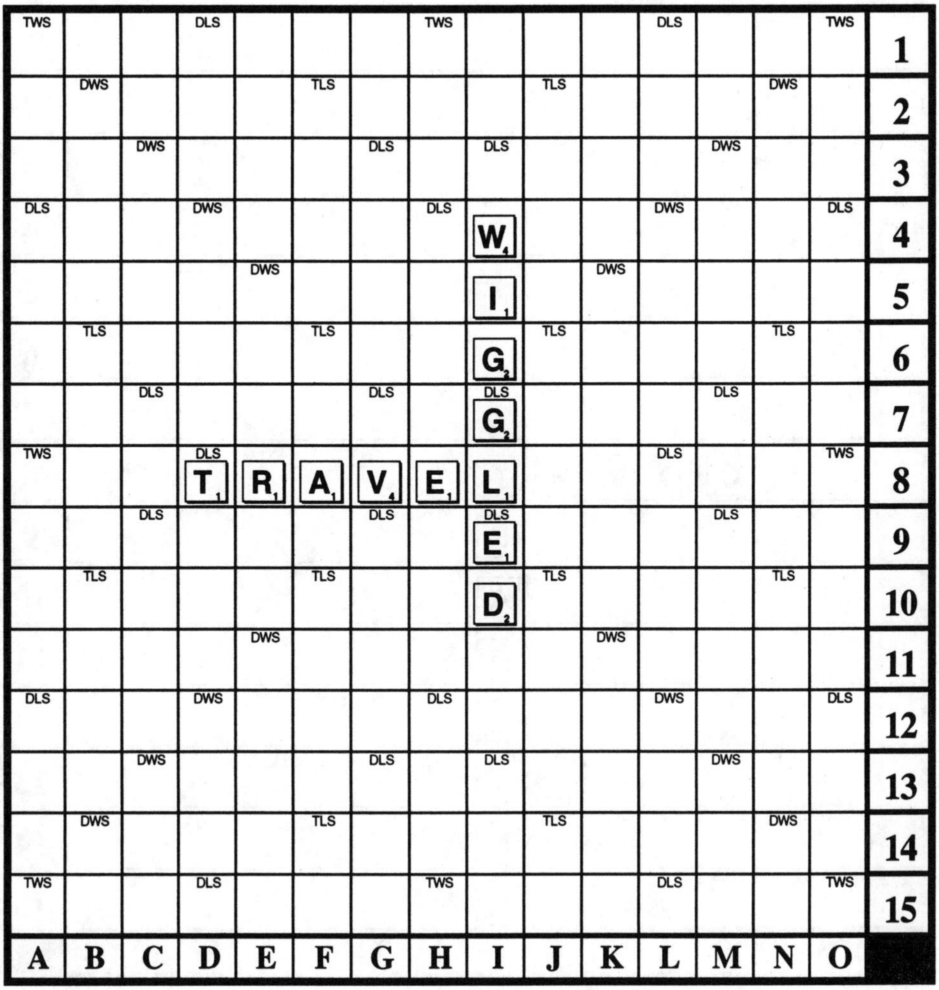

DIAGRAM 7-2

Beginnings: **CON, IN, OUT, RE, UN**

Endings: **ABLE, ED, ENT, IES, TION**

      Rack #1: **D E N R U W Y**

      Rack #2: **I L N O O S U**

      Rack #3: **B D E E L L O**

Time limit: 20 minutes

Average Score: 1 correct

Good Score: 2 correct   *Expert Score:* 3 correct

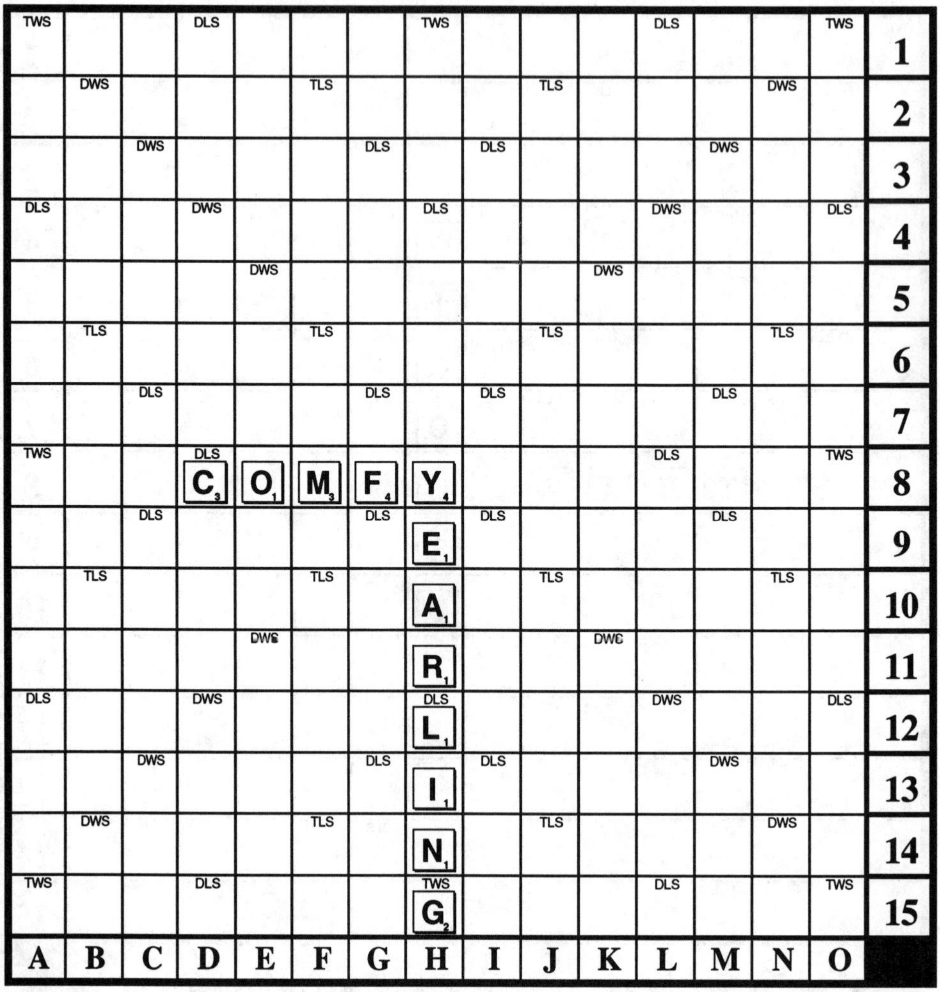
COMFY
YEARLING

DIAGRAM 7-3

Beginnings: **CON, IN, OUT, RE, UN**

Endings: **ABLE, ED, ENT, IES, TION**

Rack #1: **C E N O O R T**

Rack #2: **E E I N P T T**

Rack #3: **D E N O S U V**

Time limit: 20 minutes

Average Score: 1 correct

Good Score: 2 correct *Expert Score:* 3 correct

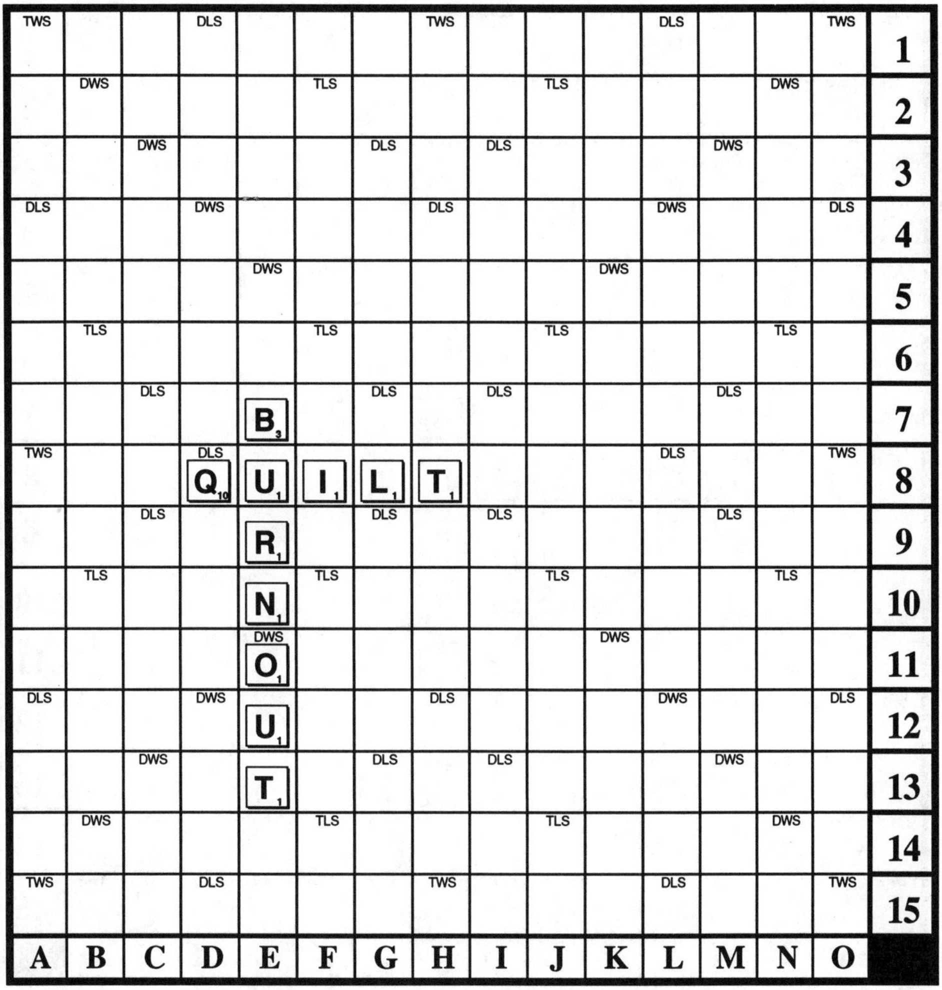

DIAGRAM 7-4

Beginnings: **CON, IN, OUT, RE, UN**
Endings: **ABLE, ED, ENT, IES, TION**
Rack #1: **G I L N O T Y**
Rack #2: **A B D E F I N**
Rack #3: **A B C E I N T**

Time limit: 20 minutes
Average Score: 1 correct

Good Score: 2 correct   *Expert Score:* 3 correct

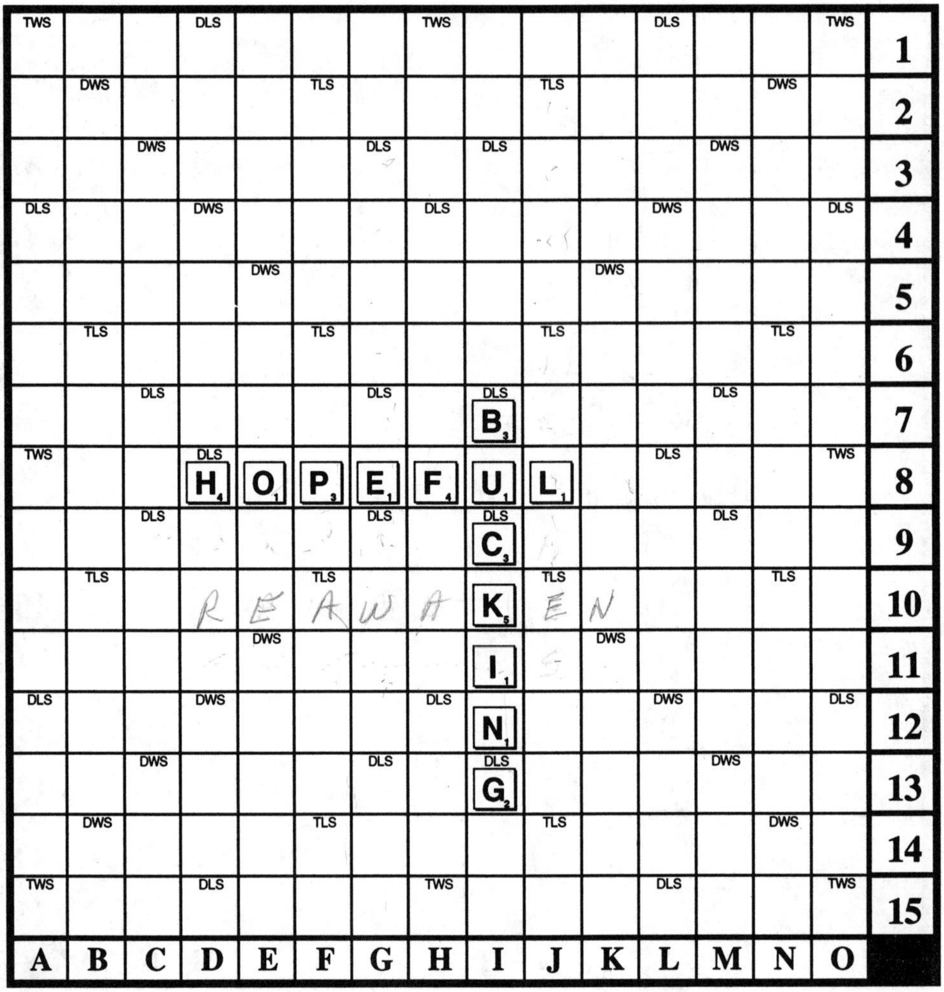

DIAGRAM 7-5

Beginnings: **CON, IN, OUT, RE, UN**
Endings: **ABLE, ED, ENT, IES, TION**

Rack #1: **A A E E N R W**
Rack #2: **A A D I L M S**
Rack #3: **A C F I I P S**

Time limit: 20 minutes
Average Score: 1 correct

Good Score: 2 correct   *Expert Score:* 3 correct

Finding a Place for Your Seven-Letter Bingo

It's one thing to find a seven-letter word on your rack; it's another to find a place for that bingo on a board crowded with letters. The secret is to look for hook words and parallel plays. Look at the following diagrams and follow the directions. In each case you will be asked about finding a place for your bingo. Answers on page 75.

TWS			DLS			TWS			DLS			TWS			**1**
	DWS			TLS			TLS			DWS					**2**
		DWS			DLS		DLS			DWS					**3**
DLS			DWS			DLS			DWS			DLS			**4**
			DWS				DWS								**5**
	TLS			TLS			TLS			TLS					**6**
		DLS			DLS		DLS	E A R D R U M			DLS				**7**
TWS		DLS P	A	N	T	R	Y			DLS	A	TWS A	L		**8**
		DLS R			DLS	E	DLS E	L	I	E	DLS S	T		**9**
	TLS	O		TLS			TLS				TLS H			**10**
		M	DWS					DWS			W			**11**
DLS		DWS P			DLS			DWS		A	DLS			**12**
	DWS	T		DLS		DLS			DWS	R				**13**
	DWS			TLS			TLS			DWS T				**14**
TWS		DLS			TWS			DLS			TWS				**15**

A	B	C	D	E	F	G	H	I	J	K	L	M	N	O

DIAGRAM 7-6

Your rack: E A R D R U M

Find an allowable place to play the bingo EARDRUM in Diagram 7-6. Time limit: 10 minutes

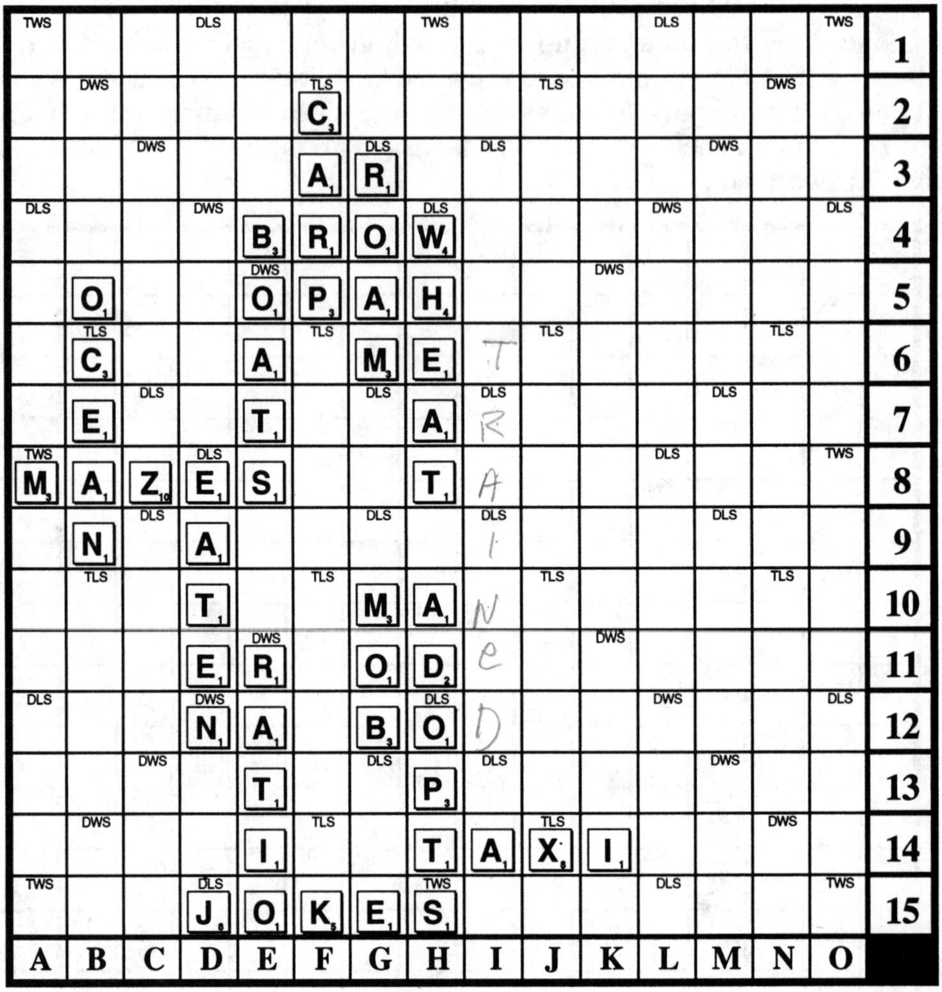

DIAGRAM 7-7

Your rack: T R A I N E D

At what place in Diagram 7-7 can you play TRAINED, using all seven tiles in the rack and forming only acceptable words? Time limit: 10 minutes

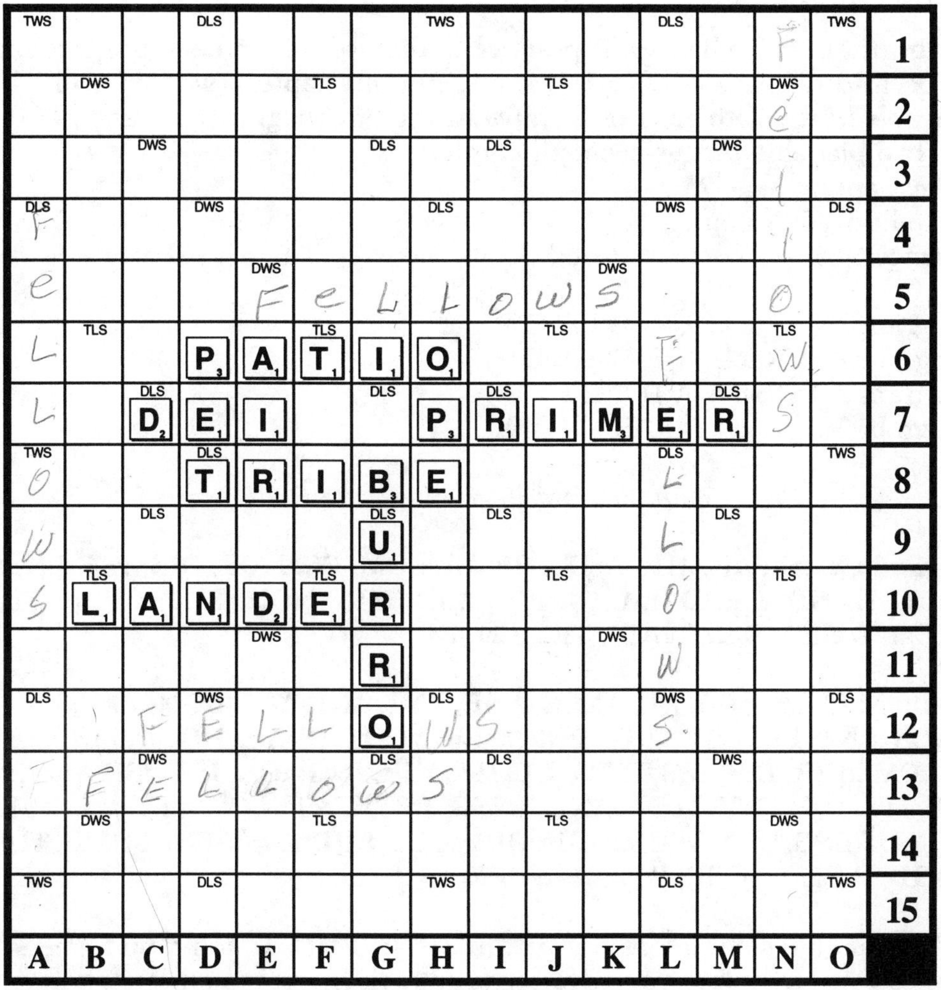

DIAGRAM 7-8

Your rack: F E L L O W S

There are five common ways to position your bingo in Diagram 7-8. Where are they and which one gives you the most points? Time limit: 15 minutes

BINGO PRACTICE #3:

Now that you've had some practice finding seven- and eight-letter words, go back to diagrams 2-2, 2-3, 2-4, and 2-5 in Chapter Two. Try to find the playable bingo with each of the given racks. In Diagrams 2-2 and 2-4 there are two playable bingos each, all common words.

Answers on page 75.

Time limit: 30 minutes.

Average Score: 2 correct   Good Score: 3 correct   Expert Score: 4 correct

Diagram 2-2: Rack: C G H I L N Y
Diagram 2-3: Rack: A B C L N O Y
Diagram 2-4: Rack: A D E E I M R
Diagram 2-5: Rack: A C E R T T X

Common Word Beginnings and Endings

Beginnings: AB, AD, AIR, ANTI, BE, BI, COM, CON, DE, DIS, EM, EN, EX, FORE, HAND, HEAD, IM, IN, ISO, MID, MIS, NON, OUT, OVER, POST, PRE, RE, SEA, SEMI, SUB, TRI, UN, UP.

Endings: ABLE, AGE, AL, ANCE, ANE, ANT, ARY, ATE, DOM, EAU, ED, EE, ENCE, ENT, ER, EST, FISH, FORM, FUL, GHT, GRAM, HOOD, IA(L), IBLE, IC, ICAL, IER, IES, IEST, IFY, ILE, ILY, INE, ING, ION, ISE, ISH, ISM, IST, ITE, ITY, IUM, IVE, IZE, LAND, LESS, LET, LIKE, LOGY, LY, MAN, MEN, MENT, NESS, OID, OSE, OUGH, OUS, OUT, SHIP, SIS(SES), SOME, TURE, WARD, WEED, WISE, WOOD, WORM.

There is only one more jump to make in PART I. You won't often find bingos to play unless you save on your rack the common letters that frequently form them. Chapter Eight tells you how to do it.

Bingo Practice # 1:

A.	B.	C.	D.
1. EMBALMS	1. IMMOBILE	1. FOREPAW	1. ISOLATES
2. ISOTOPE	2. HEADSET	2. ENAMELS	2. HOARDED
3. SPRAINED	3. AUDIENCE	3. PLUNGER	3. PENITENT
4. UNIFORM	4. VAGUEST	4. EXTERIOR	4. EMPLOYEE
5. LENIENCE	5. BLINKER	5. IMPRISON	5. GRAYISH
6. HELPFUL	6. STRAIGHT	6. DOLEFUL	6. FORECAST
7. GIRLISH	7. ENCHANT	7. INCREASE	7. HANDBALL
8. ALRIGHT	8. DUMBEST	8. HEADLOCK	8. MIDNIGHT

Bingo Practice # 2:

A.	B.	C.	D.
1. OVERBITE	1. BEGONIA	1. NONDAIRY	1. PURITIES
2. EUPHORIA	2. SUNNIEST	2. PREMIERE	2. AUDIBLE
3. IRONICAL	3. UNOPENED	3. SOLIDIFY	3. UNCLEAN
4. SUBLEASE	4. TOUGHIES	4. MODERATE	4. PRESTIGE
5. REINDEER	5. MANDIBLE	5. TELEGRAM	5. EPIDEMIC
6. NONSENSE	6. OVERLAND	6. SEASHORE	6. SEAFRONT
7. LIVELIER	7. POSTCARD	7. COMICAL	7. SUBMERGE
8. TAILGATE	8. OUTSMART	8. DOMESTIC	8. MISPLACE

DIAGRAM 7-1: 1. DIFFERED D5 or D6 82 points. Give yourself extra credit for also finding REDEFIED H2 68; and/or FRIENDED 12E 78 2. INTERVAL F1 71 3. VACATION E3 76.

DIAGRAM 7-2: 1. UNDERWAY F2 69; 2. SOLUTION D4 66; 3. BELLOWED 4D 80. or BOWELLED 4G 80

DIAGRAM 7-3: 1. CONCERTO D8 76 or D5 74 points; 2. PENITENT, 14B 74; 3. UNSOLVED 12D 74.

DIAGRAM 7-4: 1. OUTLYING 12D 82; 2. FINDABLE G2 69; 3. INCUBATE 12B 76.

DIAGRAM 7-5: 1. REAWAKEN 10D 69. Notice that AWAKENER 10G 69 points is also possible. 2. MALADIES G2 64; 3. PACIFIES G2 68.

DIAGRAM 7-6: EARDRUM 7G 86.

DIAGRAM 7-7: TRAINED I6 85.

DIAGRAM 7-8: The five starting squares are: A4, 13A, 13B, N1, and 5E. FELLOWS 5E scores the most, 126. Give yourself extra credit for finding FELLOWS N3. PRIMERO is a type of card game.

DIAGRAM 2-2: CHARMINGLY, 8F: 116. ACHINGLY H8 104.

DIAGRAM 2-3: BALCONY 9C 88.

DIAGRAM 2-4: DIAMETER J3 69, or DREAMIER I1 63, or I7 65.

DIAGRAM 2-5: EXTRACT E4: 91.

8 MINDING YOUR Ps, Qs, AND EVERYTHING ELSE
Introduction to Rack Management

No matter how skilled you are at word games, as a SCRABBLE® Brand crossword game player you will be at the mercy of the tiles you draw. You might be an expert, but if you draw TUUVVWW (a well-known expert once drew this opening rack) and your novice opponent draws AEINRST, you probably won't be leading after the first play. Of course, during a series of games the luck factor is less important, since generally each player will get his or her fair share of blanks and Ss. The expert, however, knows how to consistently manage his or her rack well. We often hear about experts at tournaments from their opponents: "S/he drew all the good tiles! I couldn't do a thing!" While this can and does happen, there are ways to enhance your chances of drawing a balanced, high-scoring rack.

To balance your rack means to save the better combinations of letters. The ideas in this chapter are so important for improving your SCRABBLE game skills that we've created a handy anagram to help you remember:

UNBALANCED RACK = CAN EARN BAD LUCK

We'll use a question-and-answer approach to express some of the ideas in this chapter.

Novice: I have trouble with Cs on my rack. Someone once said that a C is a good letter and better than a P, but I like Ps much better. What's really true?

Expert: Each person's vocabulary will to a certain extent determine how valuable each letter is to them. Hence the best play for one person may not be the best play for someone else. Computer tests based upon the results of thousands of SCRABBLE games show this order of most-to-least valuable letters: Blank, S, E, X, Z, R, A, H, N, C, D, M, T, I, J, K, L, P, O, Y, F, B, G, W, U, V, Q. However, you should be warned that this list was generated by a computer knowing *all* the words in the OSPD.

Novice: Why should that matter?

Expert: Suppose you want to become a good SCRABBLE game player and so you start, for some odd reason, by learning all the words spelled with a V. After you have learned them all, you may find that the V is a very valuable letter, much more valuable than the C. That's because whenever you draw the V, you can almost always use it for a good score, since you know so many words using it. When you draw a C, on the other hand, you don't know many words using it, so you have more difficulty with the C than the V.

Novice: How do I determine which letters are best for me?

Expert: Though you may usually rely on the list above, instead of focusing too much energy on individual letters, we advise you to spend some time each turn determining which *combination of letters* you'd like to have left on your rack *after* your play.

For example, you have AABIILN. You see the play BANAL for 25 points. That's not a bad score! However, you notice that ALIBI will score 20. Which do you choose? Look at the difference between the "leaves" for both plays. (A leave is the group of letters left on your rack *after* you have made a play and *before* you have replenished your rack.) After BANAL you will be left with II. After ALIBI you have AN. Which do you think will reap better results next turn?

If you don't know, try this experiment: Choose five random tiles from the tile bag and add the II combination to form a new seven-letter rack. Find your best play using a position from any SCRABBLE game in progress. Now take away the II and add the AN to form a slightly different rack. Find your best play again on the same game-in-progress. Repeat this experiment twenty times with twenty random racks and keep track of how many points you scored with both the II rack and the AN rack. It should be apparent that the AN is much more likely to help you score well than the II. Is the AN leave worth the 5 points you will lose by playing ALIBI? Most times it will be worth it! Think of a good play as having two parts—what you score, and what tiles are left on your rack. This example shows off, in part, a worthwhile principle to remember: ***You don't want to duplicate any letter on your rack unless it's an E.*** Duplicate letters take away your flexibility to form more words. So, if you have two of any letter but the E, make sure you look for plays that use at least one of these letters.

Novice: What if I have two Ss? I know that Ss are valuable tiles. Should I save two of them at the cost of a few points?

Expert: It's true that Ss are very valuable. However, two Ss don't necessarily make for a better rack. If you can get an extra 3 or 4 points for the second S, we suggest you use it. See Chapter Eleven for more discussion on how to use Ss.

Another principle we can learn from the above example is to **keep approximately the same number of vowels and consonants in your leave.** This means that if you play five tiles, keep one vowel and one consonant. If you play three tiles, keep two vowels and two consonants. If you play only one tile, you should probably be close to a bingo, and your chances will be enhanced if you save three vowels and three consonants.

When you must leave an odd number of tiles on your rack, it's usually a good idea to leave one extra consonant. That's true largely because there are more three-, five-, and seven-letter words with one extra consonant than an extra vowel. Another reason is that if you draw too many vowels, which are worth only 1 point, you won't often have a high-scoring play; whereas, if you have too many consonants, you're more likely to make a good play, since you may have one or more high-point consonants to use on a bonus square.

One last principle to remember is: If possible, **hold as few high-point tiles as possible in your leave.** The high-point tiles and their values are: B (3), C (3), D (2), F (4), G (2), H (4), J (8), K (5), M (3), P (3), Q (10), V (4), W (4), X (8), Y (4), and Z (10). The high-point tiles are worth more because they are generally less frequently used to spell words. So, the more high-point tiles you have in your rack, the fewer choices you'll have for plays.

Those of you who hesitate to believe this principle may point to all the times you've had several letters like the X, Z, M, and P and one or two vowels that enable you to make a play of 30 or more points. It's true: Having three or four high-point tiles *in addition to* a few vowels may give you points galore. However, if you don't draw vowels with those consonants, you may be wishing you had used those high-pointers earlier. Plus, you will find that bingos are *much* harder to draw with three or more high-point tiles. Therefore, we advise you to try to keep a good balance of 1-point tiles.

One last reason to use those high-point tiles is that you'll rarely be able to play five or six tiles with three or more high-pointers in your rack. Keep in mind that your best bet to draw the Ss, blanks, a steady flow of Es, and the X and Z is by playing more rather than fewer tiles each turn.

Novice: Okay, I understand that I should save the good combinations. But which are they?

Expert: That's a good question. Before we tackle it, here is one important point to remember: Any accurate assessment of how you should manage your rack in any *specific* position must include the configuration of the words on the game board. That's because you may want to make certain plays for reasons other than rack balance. Having said that, we'll assume for this discussion that none of the board positions have distinguishing features that will influence the rack leave, unless we say otherwise.

LEAVE: 1 letter

If you're using six tiles and leaving one, you can look at the list on page 76 to see which letters are more valuable. The blank, S, E, and X are the four best tiles to keep. Imagine your rack is AEGLNPT and you're trying to decide between playing TANGLE or PLANET, and they're about the same number of points. The list shows that the P is generally more useful than the G, so play TANGLE.

The blank and S are the two most valuable tiles. If you are able to make a good play with six tiles and still keep the blank or S, you are accomplishing the typical rack-balancing goal. Nonetheless, check the board carefully to see if you may have overlooked a really outstanding play using the S or blank.

It's a good idea to think "two words" whenever you have an S, because adding an S to a word on the board and playing perpendicular to it is one of the best ways to score more points.

With the blank on your rack, if you don't see a bingo, you should ask yourself if you can score at least 20 to 30 more points using the blank. If so, play it. If not, save it for a later play.

Chapter Eleven discusses how to use Ss and blanks to find bingos.

LEAVE: 2 letters

We've already said that it's better to save one vowel and one consonant. Which ones are best? Use the valuable-letter list to determine which vowels and consonants are best to keep. If you're trying to decide between leaving AL and ER, you can see that the E is better than the A and the R is better than the L, so ER is a better leave than AL. Similarly, HI is a better leave than GO.

For someone just beginning to learn how to play, this method of evaluation is an excellent guide. But keep in mind that it's not perfect. For instance, though the chart shows otherwise, most experts would keep DE instead of CE, and AL instead of AK. In both cases, the expert is thinking about playing bingos. We'll discuss more about rack balance and bingos in Chapter Nine.

LEAVE: 3 or 4 letters

In general, the best leaves have combinations of one or two vowels (preferably the E and A or two Es) and two of the following consonants, in decreasing order of preference: S, R, N, T, and L. Why is this a good formula for a three- or four-tile leave? Mostly because you'll draw bingo racks more often if you save these letters. Furthermore, if you draw one or two high-point tiles and no bingo, then these three or four 1-pointers will usually combine well with them to form good-scoring five- or six-letter words.

There is one exception to this three-tile leave rule. The E is such a useful letter that keeping it with another vowel and a consonant for a three-tile leave is not often discouraged, although other factors may affect your decision.

LEAVE: 5 letters

Not counting the variety of special-scoring and board considerations that can occur, there are a limited number of reasons for playing only two tiles and leaving five.

1. You are "fishing" for a bingo by keeping five dynamic tiles, such as AERST, that will lead you to bingos on your next turn a significant percentage of the time. In that case you need only learn: Which five-tile combinations are worthy of fishing with?

There aren't many we would waste a turn to fish with, but here are most of them: AERST, AENST, AELST, ADEST, ADERS, AELRS, EIRST, EINST, EORST, ENOST, EENST, EERST, AENRT, and EINRT. Keep in mind that the first six are the best and the last two are the least desirable. There are exceptional situations where certain letters already on the board may inspire you to fish with less spectacular leaves. However, as a general rule we don't suggest developing this habit.

2. You earn a good score with a two-letter word. Example: You play AH for 28 points, EX for 36, WE for 24, or JO for 52. When you play any of these or similar choices, chances are you're not keeping AERST. In the majority of cases you simply want to keep a balance of two or three vowels and three or two consonants. Example: AABEHIR. You play AH for 28 points, keeping ABEIR. However, if you have AAEHIOR, playing AH leaves you with AEIOR, which is very unbalanced and may lead to a horrible next rack. You might instead want to sacrifice as many as 5 or 10 points to keep a much better leave. For instance, playing ARIA for 20 points, and thus keeping EHO, gives you much better chances for a higher score next turn.

LEAVE: 6 letters

As with the five-tile leave, you should avoid using only one tile unless you score really well or are fishing for a bingo. Here are ten six-letter leaves that you can comfortably fish with: AEINST, AEIRST, AEINRT, AEINRS, EINORS, EINOST, AENRST, EINRST, ENORST, and AEERST. Appendix Four lists all the bingos that can be formed with these leaves. Such a six-letter leave is often called a "six-letter stem," since each is the foundation for many bingos.

To those of you who've never played a bingo: We suggest that if you follow these rack-balancing guidelines and review, even occasionally, Appendix Four, you will soon surprise yourself with your increased scores.

This completes Part I—your first course.

P A R T · T W O

ADVANCED PLAY:
Graduating to the Next Level

What distinguishes a good home SCRABBLE® game player from an experienced club player? The following chapters will answer that question and show you how to improve your play even further. Expect, however, greater complexity in our discussions. These chapters are not intended for beginners. Our intention in Part II is to take an experienced player one or more steps ahead toward becoming an expert. However, we do encourage novices to read these chapters, since there are many insights here that can be grasped by anyone.

Chapter Nine discusses rack balancing in more depth. Chapter Ten presents ideas that may change your thinking about exchanging tiles. Chapter Eleven is a must for anyone who wants to score more points with the S and blank tiles. In Chapter Twelve, we'll show you which words you should learn to help you the most, while four top players give you their secrets for word power. Chapter Thirteen adds yet more words to your arsenal—the three- and four-letter J, X, and Z words. Chapter Fourteen will explain "open" and "closed" boards and how you can take advantage of them to win more games. Chapter Fifteen will give you the information you need about those phoneys that every topnotch player knows and will use against you.

9 ADVANCED RACK MANAGEMENT: POINTS VS. LEAVE

In this chapter we want to further explore rack balancing by giving you several racks and several choices for plays. Then we'll tell you how the expert thinks about each rack. Advanced players strive to build bingo racks as quickly as possible. In general, the major concerns are: How many points is each play worth, and how good is the leave? Whether it's better to score more points or keep a better leave is not always easy to answer, even by the best players.

Here are a few other things to keep in mind as you read this chapter:

Our analysis assumes that the reader is at least familiar with the ideas in Chapters Seven and Eight. If you haven't read those pages, you definitely won't benefit as much from this chapter.

For the purposes of learning these specific ideas, the reader should consider only the choices provided and disregard other plays s/he might find. Unless we otherwise specify, assume that when a play is suggested, all the letters come from the given rack.

For any specific board position and rack, there will be a variety of other considerations besides rack balance that can affect your decisions. In these pages, we delve into these ideas enough to get you started thinking along winning ways. Ultimately, you will have to learn by experience how to choose the best plays. And since SCRABBLE® game strategy is by no means complete, we leave it to the aspiring player to discover new ideas that expand the boundaries of current theory.

Finally, we advise you to read our analysis while simultaneously assessing your ability to follow our advice. For example: If you haven't yet tried any of the bingo exercises in Chapter Seven, and if you haven't yet become familiar with how to find bingos, some of the analysis found in this chapter may not exactly apply to you. Once you are able to find bingos with the more common letters, the one- and two-point tiles (ADEGILNORSTU?), you may find this chapter more useful. To help your bingo skills grow, we've designed an exercise at the end of Chapter Eleven that can show you just how powerful having three vowels, three consonants, and a blank can be. It will be well worth trying. Note that in this chapter the leave after each play is given in parentheses.

Rack #1: A B C E I N V

Novice: I see VICE (BAN), VIBE (ACN), CAB (EINV), CAVE (BIN), and CABIN (EV), all for 16 to 20 points. Which should I play?

Expert: You might choose any of the words but CAVE or CABIN. After CABIN, the EV leave makes your rack particularly vulnerable to bad luck, since you'll have five chances to draw high-point tiles. The V does not usually combine well with other high-point tiles, unless you draw the OR for the prefix OVER-. After CAVE, the BIN leave is much inferior to the other leaves.

Otherwise, consider: You have three high-point tiles (B, C, and V) that don't combine well together. Your goal should be to use at least two of them for your next play. That's because, in general, you should never leave two high-point tiles on your rack. It reduces your bingo chances enormously. (The CH combination is a notable exception.)

Each of the first three words gives you a reasonable leave. Let's compare VICE and VIBE: Which is the better leave, ABN or ACN? In general, we would choose to play VIBE, since the C is much superior to the B. That's particularly true when you're looking for bingos; many more seven- and eight-letter words have a C than a B.

Now compare VIBE with CAB: Some experts might instead play CAB in order to keep the balanced EINV leave, which is bingo-prone if you don't draw another high-point tile. But your best decision will depend on an honest evaluation of your own vocabulary. So if you know many seven- and eight-letter words spelled with the V, the EINV will lead you to a bingo often enough to make this leave worthwhile.

As you might guess from our lack of a definitive answer, not all experts will agree on how to play this rack. We wanted to show you from the start that there is often a wide range of opinions on what to play. We believe that what's most important is for us to show you the thought process behind the decision, rather than that there is always one right answer.

Rack #2: A A M O O T T

Novice: I see ATOM (AOT) 20 points, MOTTO (AA) 18, and TOMATO (O) 16. I'm not sure which is best.

Expert: Though only 16 points, TOMATO is the best choice. The most important reasons are that it allows you to draw six new tiles and it minimizes the duplication of letters. In general, it's better to play six tiles instead of four in order to have a better chance to draw the blanks and Ss and the valuable J, X, and Z. The only common exceptions are when you play four tiles and save three terrific letters, such as ERS, ENS, EST, ERT, ENR, or ENT, to name a few. When you save these tiles you give yourself a good chance either to draw a bingo or to make a five- or six-letter follow-up play.

Rack #3: E H I I O U V

Novice: I see HIVE (IOU) 20 points, HOVE (IIU) 20, and VIE (HIOU) 12. What should I do?

Expert: Sometimes you have to trust that your letters will improve. In this case that means playing HIVE (not HOVE because of the II leave) for 20 points even though you keep the horrible IOU leave. You can expect that you may have to exchange letters next turn if you don't draw well, but taking 20 points now and hoping to draw well next turn is better than taking zero now and risking who-knows-what-you-will-draw next time.

Even as we say this, there are probably a few experts who would exchange five tiles, keeping the EH. That's a decision often made based on other considerations, such as who's ahead, by how much, and what tiles have been played.

Rack #4: A E L O S T T

Novice: Should I play TO (AELST) 6 points or TOTAL (ES) 15?

Expert: Even if you can't find an eight-letter bingo using a tile on the board, you should realize that you are very close to a seven-letter bingo. Assuming there are at least two places on the board to play bingos, you should rid yourself of just two tiles, saving AELST, and hope for a bingo next turn. As we discussed in Chapter Eight, this is called fishing, and all the best players do it occasionally. AELST is a powerful five-letter leave. There are 238 different seven-letter words that include these letters. See page 80 for other strong five-letter leaves.

Rack #5: A B E L R R V

Novice: I have three different ways to play the word VERBAL. One way uses only the BLRV, saving AER and scoring 25 points. Another way is to play VERBAL using all six tiles from my rack, saving an R and scoring 25. The last way is to play through an E on the board, keeping ER and scoring 24. Both blanks and one A have already been played, but no Ss or Rs are on the board yet, and this is only my fourth play of the game. I can also play BRAVER and keep the L, scoring 28. All my choices seem nearly equal, since they all keep the board open for seven-letter words. Is one of my plays better than the others?

Expert: You can eliminate BRAVER, since the L leave is much inferior to any of the others. The extra point or two is not worth keeping the L. Using six tiles and keeping the R isn't bad, but it doesn't compare to either other leave, ER or AER. The ER combination is so dynamic that you should try to keep these letters even at the cost of a few points. The only question now is whether you should keep the A or not. The AER combination is quite good, as long as you don't draw too many vowels. Since there are plenty of As left in the bag, I advise you to play yours, keeping only ER. If you were to perform a thousand trials that compared drawing to ER or AER at this stage of the game, you'd find that you would generally have more balanced racks after keeping ER than AER.

Rack #6: L N O R V W ?

Novice: I see VOWER or VOWEL, both through an existing E on the board. Both plays score 22 points. I also see VOW for 26 points and VON for 28 points, both using three of my tiles. With all these choices it's not at all clear to me what to do.

Expert: What's most important here? With a blank on your rack your priority is to build a bingo in the next few turns! To that end you must make the play that gives you the best leave without sacrificing too many points. Of the choices listed, VOWEL gives you the best leave (NR?). Why? Because after VOW and VON, the three consonants left (LNR or LRW) make it harder to draw a bingo rack next turn. While after VOWER, the LN? leave is some-what less powerful than the NR? leave after VOWEL. You can assume that because the R is much closer to the beginning of the most-to-least valuable letter-list.

Rack #7: A I L O S S Y

Novice: My choices are SOYA (ILS) 22 points, SILO (ASY) 20 points, NOISY (ALS) 20 points (N on the board), SLAYS (IO) 35 points, and LOYAL (ISS) 23 points with an L on the board. I'd like to play an S, but I don't think I should use both of them. Is that true?

Expert: This is a typical choice for many double-S racks: There are a variety of plays using one S for about the same number of points; there is one play not using either S and a play using both Ss for many more points. The decision you reach will depend on factors other than simply rack balance. However, if rack balance is your only concern, then our opinion is to choose the SAL leave over all others and play NOISY. That's because you have a better chance to bingo after this leave than with any other.

Keep in mind that if you think you won't need a bingo to win or that you won't be able to play one later in this game, you will probably want to take the points with SLAYS. That's because you don't need to save the Ss for a bingo. Some novices get caught up with the idea of saving Ss and forget that the *S is for Scoring!*

Rack #8: A A A D E R W

Novice: This is my first rack of a game, and I am first. I see AWARD (AE) (8H) 22 points, and WARED or WADER (AA) (8D) 26. I like getting rid of two As with AWARD. It's probably worth it to lose 4 points and have a better leave.

Expert: You're right! AWARD is better than either WARED or WADER. However, there's an even better play! If you have looked at the two-to-make-three letter list, you may have noticed the word AWA. It's an adverb meaning "away." As an opening play, it scores only 12 points. Most players discount AWA immediately, since it scores so many fewer points than the other plays. But oddly, this play has been shown by computer analysis to be best. However, before we explain why, we will repeat what we said earlier: The computer analysis is based upon the player's knowing all the bingos. If you haven't developed your bingo skills, you may not actually benefit as much as some other players from AWA.

Here's the reason AWA is so good: After playing AWA 8F 12 points, you have the very powerful ADER leave. If you played this exact position a thousand different times, each time drawing three tiles to ADER, you would find that your rack created a second-turn bingo a significant fraction of times. Your overall two-turn total after turns one and two would, in general, be more than after any other first play.

The other significant difference between AWA and the other five-tile plays is that AWA gives away fewer scoring opportunities to your opponent. That means your opponent will generally score fewer points after you play AWA than s/he will after WARED, WADER, or AWARD.

Rack #9: E I N O R S Y

Novice: I see OY (EINRS) 10 points, IRONY (ES) 30, and NOISY (ERS) 20, which uses an S already on the board. Which do you prefer?

Expert: All three plays leave dynamic tiles. The ERS leave is the best three-letter leave you can have without a blank. However, with most positions and scores, you should simply play IRONY for 30 points. That's because the ES leave after playing IRONY is also excellent. And in most cases, the extra 10 points are worth taking. But if IRONY were only 22 to 25 points, you might seriously consider playing NOISY and keeping the ERS instead.

If you're behind in the score so much that you must play a bingo to win, play OY. The EINRS leave is better than just ERS. But in most other cases, when the score is closer, you sacrifice too many points by playing OY for only 10 points.

Rack #10: E F I L N O P

Novice: I see several plays: FLOP (EIN) 28 points, FELON (IP) 34, FILE (NOP) 24, FOP (EILN) 28, and FLOE (INP) 30. There are sixty-five tiles on the board already, and neither blank has been played. I'm ahead by 30 points before my play.

Expert: Since you're going to be nearly a bingo ahead after your turn, your main concern is how to stay ahead. By playing five tiles (FELON 34) and keeping IP, you maximize your chances of drawing a blank, which is vital if you want to keep your opponent from playing a bingo. The IP leave, though not as bingo-prone as EIN or EILN, will generally allow you a decent play next turn. Plus, FELON is your biggest scoring play. That's important!

Rack #11: B D I O P T X

Novice: The board is fairly open, with several bonus squares available. The only choices I see are BIPOD (TX) 30 points and two different places for POX (BDIT) worth either 36 points or 35 points. I think I should take the extra 6 points, but the leave, BDIT isn't that great. The score is about even. Neither blank and only one S has been played.

Expert: You should sacrifice the points to play BIPOD. That's because on the open board you're likely to play the X next turn for at least 36 points. And the TX leave is much superior to BDIT, while you have two extra chances to draw an S or blank.

Rack #12: C E I L O W Y

Novice: The game is three-quarters over with the blanks and Ss on the board. I don't see any places to put a bingo even if I had one, though there are two TLSs open next to As. I'm ahead by 5 points. I have several choices: COWY (EIL) 30 points; YOWIE (CL) 28; YOWL (CEI) 32; WILCO (EY) 28; YOW (CEIL) 28.

Expert: Without the prospect of a bingo, you want to make as good a play next turn as you will this turn. With that in mind, play WILCO. The EY leave will allow you to play parallel to a TLS for at least 28 points since YA and YE are both acceptable twos.

Rack #13: A D E I R V Y

Novice: We've each taken only five turns, playing two bingos apiece. The score is very close, but the board is wide open. There is an open D, N, and T in separate parts of the board that can be used to spell eight-letter bingos. I see IVY (ADER) for 20 points, DAVY (EIR) for 30, and VARIED (Y) for 35.

Expert: The ADER leave after IVY is the best of your three leaves. However, because the score is close, you need every point you can get, while still giving yourself bingo chances. That's why you should choose DAVY. With three useful consonants open, the EIR leave acts effectively like a leave of DEIR, EINR, or EIRT, any one of which could earn you a bingo next turn.

Finally, even though VARIED is 5 points more, the Y leave has much less potential for scoring a bingo, even if it does earn 28 points next turn.

Rack #14: A A E N O T Z

Novice: I'm behind by 80 points with only twenty-five tiles left to play, though the board is fairly open for playing bingos. Both blanks and three Ss are on the board already. My choices are AZOTE (AN) 40 points, ZOA (AENT) 32, or ZONATE (A) 36.

Expert: You're far enough behind so that you need a bingo to win. In order to build a bingo, you must sacrifice the extra points by playing ZOA. The AENT leave is too good to pass up. By comparison, playing ZONATE effectively gives up the game. That's because you're using up all your good tiles, and are unlikely to draw a bingo with just the A leave. And while AZOTE is 10 extra points with a decent leave, you're still far less likely to bingo than after playing ZOA.

Others may argue that by playing more tiles you give yourself a better chance to draw the last S. That's true. But drawing the S doesn't guarantee a bingo, and we simply wouldn't pass up the powerful AENT leave.

Rack #15: A H I J M O W

Novice: I'm behind by about 50 points with a very open board. There are lots of good bonus squares to play on. I have three plays that score from 30–35 points: HAJ (IMOW) 32, HAJI (MOW) 33, and MHO (AIJW) 34. Plus, three words—MOW (AHIJ) 34 points, HOW (AJIM) 35, or JOW (AHIM) 39—can be played vertically down the board starting on the same square, K9, which places the O alone on row 10 just to the right of a Triple Letter Square. Playing HAJ sets up the I hook for HAJI, but my opponent might have an I and take it.

Expert: You won't be any closer to a bingo after any of your choices, so that shouldn't be your major concern. Instead, ask yourself how each of your plays will set up a play for your other high-point tiles next turn. You're right to be afraid of the HAJ/I setup. In another position, with different scores, you might consider it. Instead, by playing HOW and leaving AJIM, you may be able to play JO across while coming down with JAM parallel to HOW and score more than 55 points. There is no reason to assume your opponent will block your setup with so many other bonus squares to choose from. And even if your opponent takes your setup, you'll likely score at least 30 points on this open board, which is all you'd expect after making any other play now.

No matter how well you balance your rack, you're bound to draw poor tiles occasionally—everyone does. Is it advisable to exchange tiles, or is it more important to play a word, any word? Chapter Ten shows you how to determine when to exchange tiles.

10 BAG IT!
When to Exchange Your Tiles

Chances are that at one time or another during most SCRABBLE® games you will say to yourself: "I can't find a decent play. Maybe I should exchange tiles." (Actually, we've known some players whose language in these situations is a lot more colorful.) We're going to show why it's to your advantage to exchange tiles more often than you'd probably expect. Then we'll explain when to do it.

Here are the main factors to consider:

1) What are your options for plays, and how many points are they worth?

Whenever your rack of letters looks really hopeless (say you have 3 Is and 2 Os) you should still take time to find whatever plays are possible. One of the characteristics that distinguishes the better players from the novices is the ability to take seemingly terrible combinations of letters and find plays that score well. You won't be able to make a good, sound decision about whether to exchange or not until you know all your choices.

Let's look at an example:

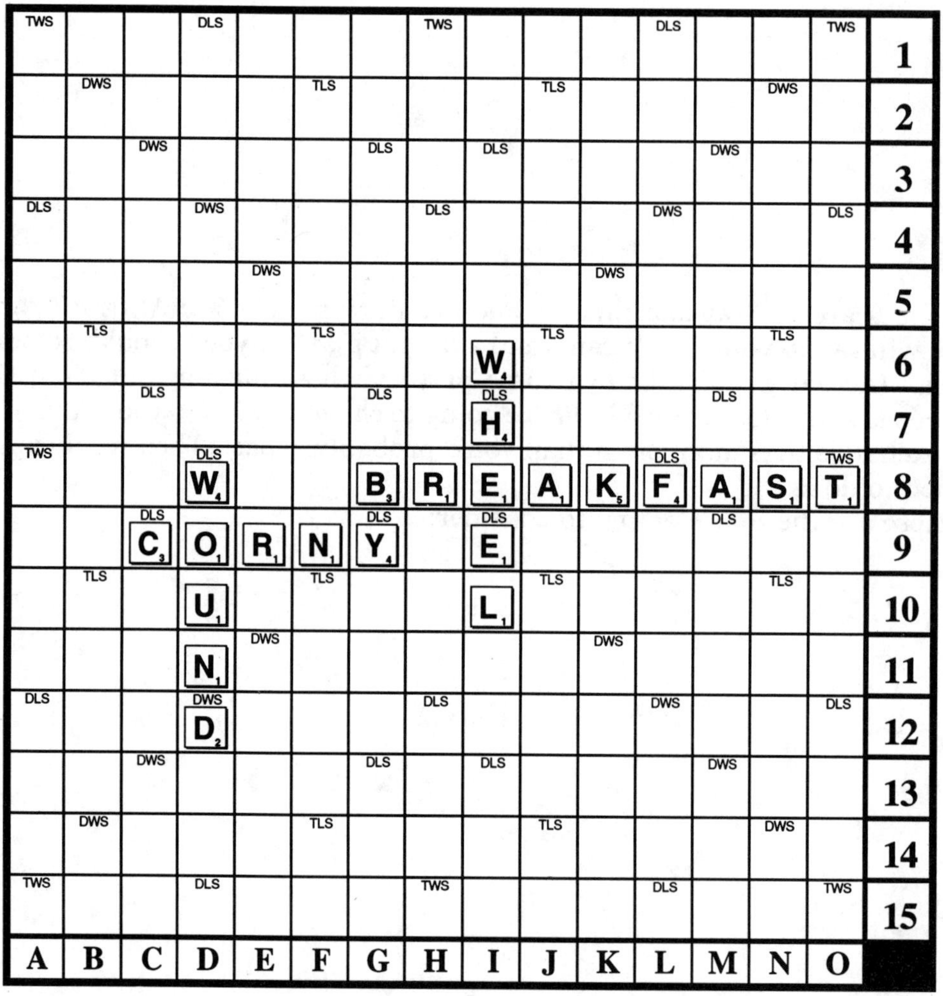

DIAGRAM 10-1

Your score: 40   Opponent's score: 113
Rack #1: AFIIIOO   Rack #2: ADIIIOO

What would you do with each rack, faced with the position shown in Diagram 10-1?

Rack #1: First look at your choices. Three choices are FA, OF, or IF. These can be played parallel to BREAKFAST, with the F falling on the 7M square. Considering the score of these plays—between 20 and 23 points—one might think they're not so bad. However, as we've seen from Chapter Nine, the five-vowel leave is so bad that on the next turn you're not likely to improve your rack. Being as far behind as you are, you can't expect to win this game unless you play a bingo. Keeping five vowels is not the way to do that!

What are the other common word choices? OAF at C11 or E11, WOO 6I, SOFA N8, ALOOF 10H, WAIF 6I, and INFO 11C. You would be left with: IIIO, AFIII, IIIO, III, IIOO, or AIIO. Each of these is so weak that, given the few points you'd be scoring, you are much better off trying to draw Ss and blanks by exchanging tiles. A good rule of thumb is: Unless you score 20 points or more, don't ever leave yourself with three vowels and no consonants, especially if you need a bingo to win. Also, avoid leaving one consonant and three vowels, unless the score is relatively close and you see no better choice.

Now imagine that you have Rack #2: ADIIIOO.

If you know the word OIDIA (n.pl. a type of fungus), that is an excellent play and much better than exchanging tiles. OIDIA plays best at either J10 or H2. Though we don't recommend keeping two vowels, you have good bingo chances if you draw three consonants. However, there is an even better play available, a four-voweled six-letter word many of our readers are familiar with. Can you find it? See page 104 for answer.

	A	B	C	D	E	F	G	H	I	J	K	L	M	N	O	
	TWS			DLS				TWS				DLS			TWS	**1**
		DWS				TLS				TLS				DWS		**2**
			DWS				DLS		DLS				DWS			**3**
	DLS			DWS				DLS				DWS			DLS	**4**
					DWS						DWS					**5**
		TLS				TLS				TLS				TLS		**6**
			DLS				DLS	**F**	DLS				DLS			**7**
	TWS			**F**	**O**	**R**	**M**	**A**	**L**			DLS			TWS	**8**
			DLS				DLS		**A**				DLS			**9**
		TLS				TLS			**K**	TLS				TLS		**10**
				P	**O**	**L**	**I**	**T**	**E**		DWS					**11**
	DLS			DWS				**D**	**E**	**T**	**A**	**I**	**L**	**S**	DLS	**12**
			DWS				DLS		DLS				DWS			**13**
		DWS				TLS				TLS				DWS		**14**
	TWS			DLS				TWS				DLS			TWS	**15**

DIAGRAM 10-2

Rack: A L N U U U U   Using Diagram 10-2, what would you do?

It's worth noting another example of a mistake that novices often make. Big-Ego Bob has just drawn all four Us! His rack reads ALNUUUU. He's silently bemoaning his fate and waiting for his opponent to play so that he can exchange tiles. When his opponent finally does play, it is a bingo, DE-TAILS, for 66 points, which opens up the S in the middle of a triple-triple column. Of course, he congratulates his opponent and says, sarcastically: "That was tough to find!" and then he exchanges seven tiles rather quickly. But what did he miss? Had he taken some time to look, he probably would have seen a good common-word play, for a reasonable 21 points, that would have dumped six of his tiles! Can you find it? Answer on page 104.

The point of this example is to make you aware that your opponent's play may turn your poor rack into a diamond in the rough! Always look to see how your opponent's last play has changed the board for you.

2) If you exchange now, what will your chances be next turn to make a significantly better play?

On each turn, try to estimate the chances of your playing a bingo in the next several turns, both after exchanging and after playing a word on the board. Ask yourself one or both of the following questions:

A) "Suppose I make a play now. If I draw average tiles, will I be able to play a bingo next turn? How about the following turn?" If the answer is yes, then you may want to play a word.

B) "After making this play, will my leave be so awkward that even after a reasonably good draw, will I still take more than two turns to bingo?" If so, then you may want to exchange now.

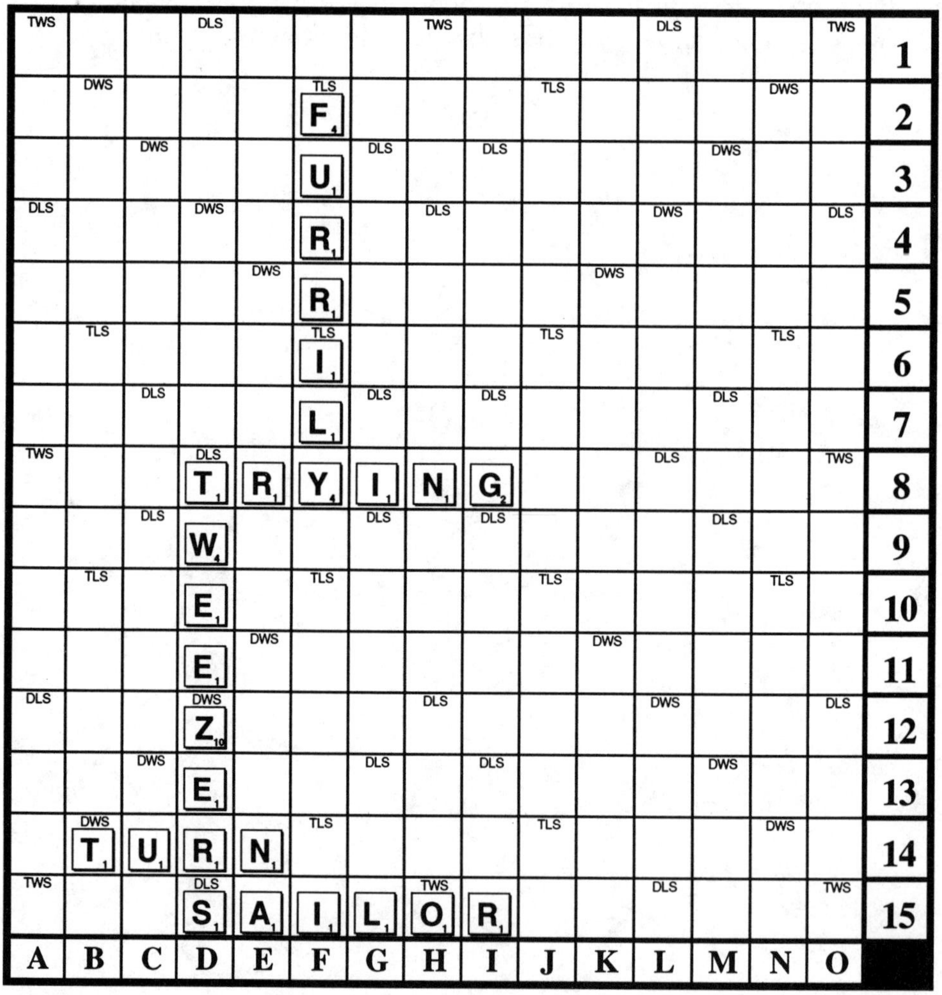

DIAGRAM 10-3

Your Score: 37   Opponent's Score: 149
Rack: A B F K M V W   What do you do?

Using Diagram 10-3, if you make the nice-looking play of FAME 13A 28 points, your rack leave will be BKVW. These are extremely awkward tiles. Even with the best of draws you won't bingo for at least two turns, and more probably three or four. Since you won't win without a bingo, being so far behind, you can't afford to play FAME. You must either exchange all seven tiles or keep the AM combination for use on row 13 next turn. However, our preference is to exchange all seven, especially with the blanks missing. Who knows? Maybe you'll draw the X and use row 13 anyway for 40-plus points! Note: If you were only 40 to 60 points behind, then FAME would be a terrific play. It's only because you need a bingo so desperately that you must exchange.

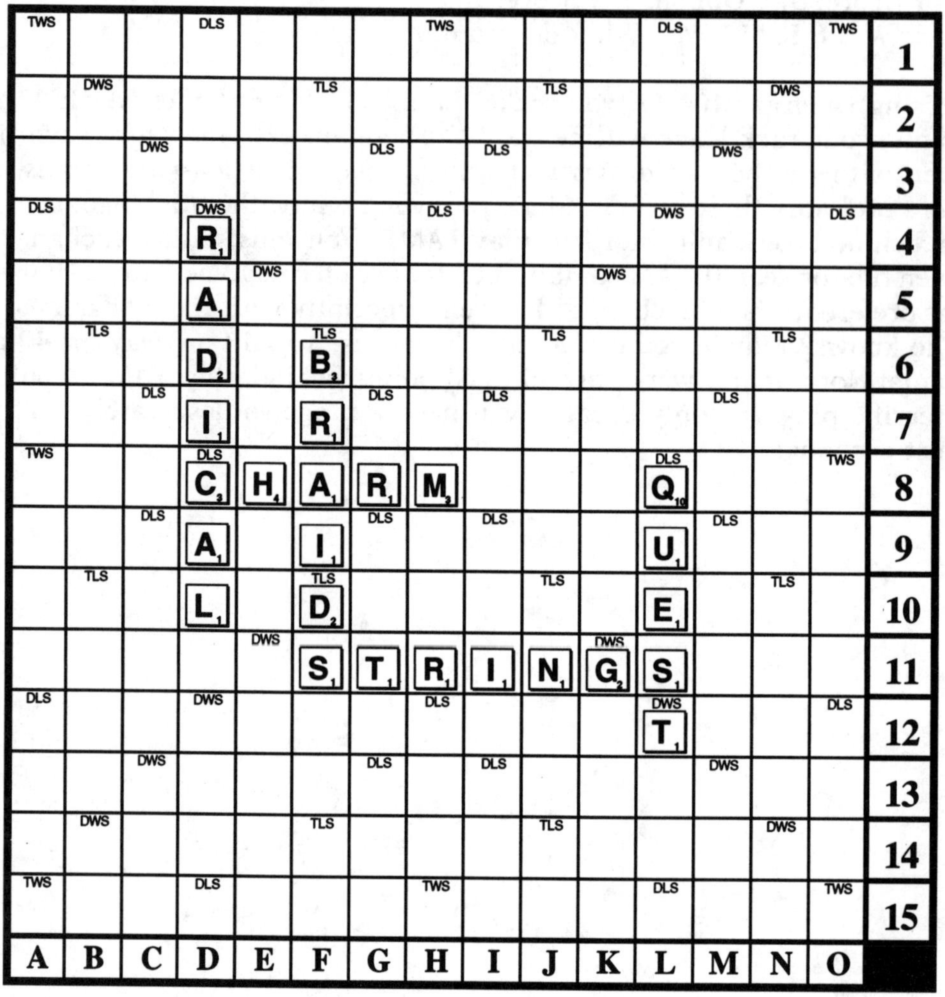

DIAGRAM 10-4

Rack: L M R R T T U   The score is even. What would you do?
Bonus question: What high-scoring word can you play with an O added to your rack?

Refer to Diagram 10-4. Should you exchange? If so, what? The most apparent play seems to be TRAM 5B 12 points. Other plays just don't score as well or use enough tiles to balance the rack adequately. MURAL 5A 14 points is not as tempting, because you open the TWSs for a paltry 14 points. While you shouldn't avoid playing to the board edge when scoring well, there is no reason to give your opponent such a juicy opening without compensation. Two extra points are not enough!

But what will happen the next turn after TRAM? By scoring 12 points now you keep LRTU. Let's look at the hot spots. You will have only three chances to draw an I to make QUIT 8L 39 points, and only three chances to draw an A or an E plus a high-point consonant to make a five-letter word starting at C9 and playing down to the DWS at C13.

There's one other nice hot spot for which you only need one tile. Add an O to your rack and you can score 45 points. Can you guess what the play is? Even if you don't know the word, which is somewhat obscure, creative players will often look for the chance to add prefixes or suffixes to words already played, even if they're not certain of their validity. Answer on page 104.

Now let's imagine that you do exchange five tiles and then play one of these high-scoring possibilities next turn. We suggest that your score for your next turn alone will probably total more than both turns together if you play TRAM now. The odds of drawing an I or O after an exchange of five tiles at this point in the game is roughly 62 to 64 percent.

Because of that, we don't suggest playing. Instead we suggest you exchange five tiles, saving the TU. That's because LRTU is not a good leave—you won't often draw a bingo to these tiles and even if you do, unless you draw an S, there are few places to play a bingo on this board. Secondly, having five chances to draw either an O or I or other good combinations outweighs the 12 points gained now. Keep in mind that if the O-play or QUIT or the C column hot spots weren't available, then TRAM might very well have been a better play.

3) How many points will you score for both this turn and next turn, in total, if you don't exchange now?

Say that you don't exchange but instead play for 10 points. Next turn your rack doesn't improve that much, and you are forced to play for 10 points again, for a total of 20 points in two turns. Now suppose that you exchange this turn, scoring zero points. Your rack improves significantly, so that you score 30 points next turn. That's a total of 30 points for the two turns. We can say that exchanging was worth 10 extra points to you.

Of course, you may be wondering: If I think about exchanging now, how am I going to determine how many points I'll score next turn when I don't know what my letters will be?

The luck of the draw keeps you from knowing exactly what you'll have. But with time and experience, you will probably develop a good idea about your scoring chances in most positions if you do the following:

Imagine that you play this exact position and rack a thousand times. Imagine the varieties of racks you'd draw. If you exchange five hundred times, you will naturally draw a blank and/or an S a certain number of times. You'll also draw a well-balanced rack a certain number of times. And you'll draw the good 3- and 4-point tiles a certain number of times in order to make good four-, five-, or six-letter plays that justify your exchange. Of course, you'll also draw poor combinations of letters some number of times, but fewer times than most people imagine! Likewise, imagine making a play five hundred times drawing to the weak leave. What kinds of plays will you usually have next turn?

It would also help you to understand this principle of "imagining" by actually taking one position and rack and replaying it fifty to a hundred times just to gain experience about what can happen. This process will give you invaluable insight that you'll be able to use in your real games! After you have enough SCRABBLE game experience, it's likely you'll develop a strong sense of the probabilities for drawing tiles. It's very much like the experienced gin rummy or poker player who knows his chances of getting a good card. Of course, it also helps to have an awareness of what tiles have already been played. You can read more about that in Chapter Twenty-one.

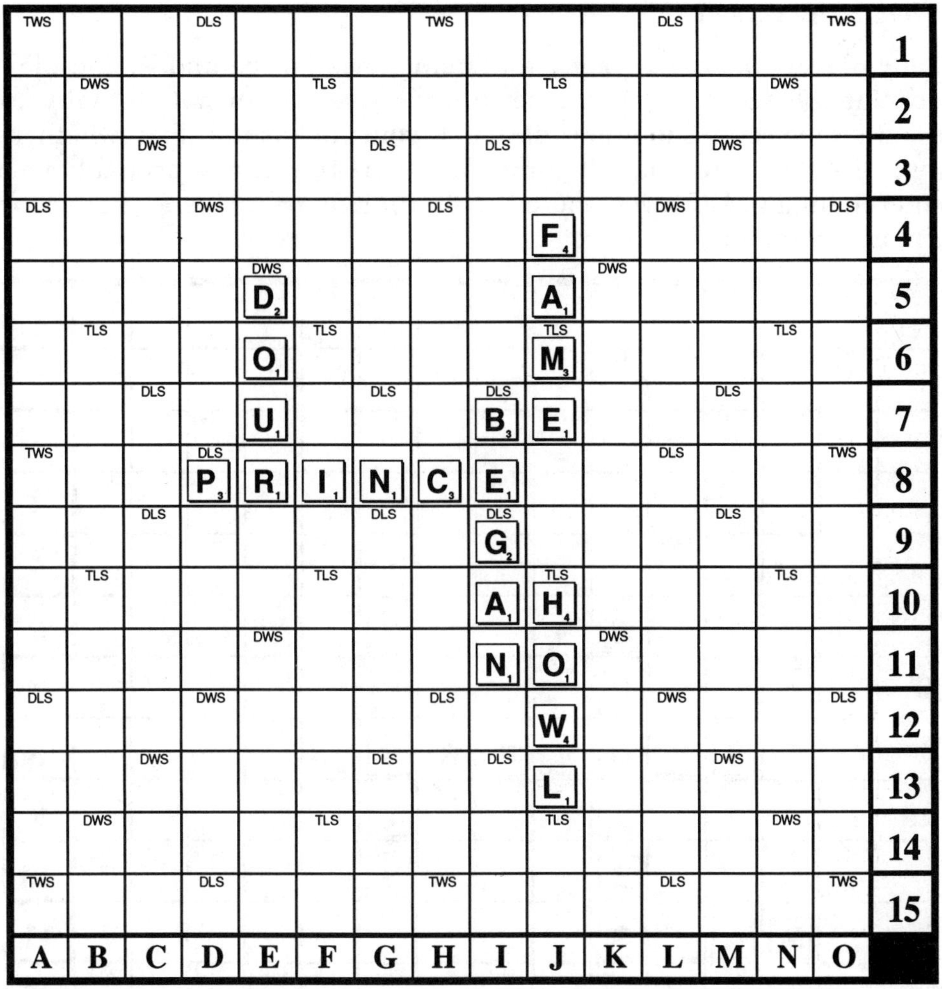

DIAGRAM 10-5

Rack: A A A L L O O   The score is even. What would you do?

Some potential plays are ALOOF 4F 9 points, FOAL 4J 14, MOOLA 6J 9, WOOL 12J 14, or ALA K4 19. Most experts would tell you that regardless of the score, they would rather exchange five or six tiles (keeping an A or AL for use along the K column) than take points now and keep three vowels or even AAL (after ALOOF or MOOLA). There are blanks and Ss and Es to be drawn. If you play a word now, you have little chance of playing a bingo soon.

4) What's the score?

Many players believe wrongly that being ahead or behind should play an important role in deciding whether to exchange tiles or not. Actually, most of the time the score shouldn't matter! If your rack is that bad, whether the score is even, or you're up 70 points or down 70, you will probably benefit from exchanging. However, there are exceptions to this rule. Let's look at one more example:

A	B	C	D	E	F	G	H	I	J	K	L	M	N	O	
TWS			DLS			TWS				DLS			TWS		1
	DWS			TLS			TLS				DWS				2
		DWS			DLS		DLS				DWS				3
DLS			DWS			DLS				DWS			DLS		4
				DWS				DWS							5
	TLS			TLS	W			TLS	Z			TLS			6
		DLS			H	DLS		DLS	E		DLS				7
TWS			C	L	O	V	E	R	S		DLS		TWS		8
		DLS			L	DLS		DLS	T		DLS				9
	TLS				E			TLS	Y			TLS			10
		M	A	T	S					DWS					11
DLS		P	A	D		DLS				DWS			DLS		12
		D	O	G		DLS		DLS			DWS				13
	DWS			TLS				TLS				DWS			14
TWS			DLS			TWS				DLS			TWS		15

DIAGRAM 10-6

Rack: C D M O R T V Consider Diagram 10-6 when:
a) You're 70 points ahead. What would you do?
b) You're 70 points behind. What would you do?

Analysis: a) The board is not conducive for playing bingos. Because of that, and because you're ahead, you want to close the board down as much as possible, even if you don't score many points. Your opponent can play a bingo down the H column. If you can block this, it's going to be very difficult for him or her to place a bingo on the board, and your chances of winning increase dramatically. Which play blocks the best and results in the best leave? Some choices are: DROVE (CMT), COVER (DMT), CORVET (DM), VECTOR (DM), MOVER (CDT), and COVERT (DM). Of these choices, we like COVERT because it uses five tiles and keeps two consonants instead of three. It also leaves no new openings. The weaker VECTOR allows for an S-hook, since VECTORS is also a word, while CORVET opens up the letter C for bingos.

b) If you are 70 points down, the last thing you want to do is close up the board. You'll need an open board to play your bingo when and if you develop one. We suggest exchanging five or six tiles (keep R or RT, since by counting letters we know that the vowel-consonant ratio of the tiles in the bag is about 1-1).

SUMMARY FOR WHEN TO EXCHANGE:

1. **What are your options?** It's important to be systematic and examine all the rows and columns for scoring potential.

2. **How quickly will you bingo?** Consider playing a word. If you estimate that it will take at least three or four turns to develop a bingo rack, and you can't find a play that satisfies you, then seriously consider exchanging now.

If you are like most casual players, who don't average at least one bingo a game, please be patient. As you practice the exercises in Chapter Seven, your bingo skills will grow.

3. **Compare your total score for this and your next turn:**
a) After you've exchanged.
b) When you form words both turns.
Compare (a) and (b). If you think there is a very good chance that you'll score enough points in the future by exchanging now, then seriously consider doing so.

Since you can't know for certain what possibilities your opponent will open up for you, assume that what's available now is all there will be next turn. You might even consider that one of the hot spots available now won't be there next turn. In the end, it all boils down to experience and paying attention to the probabilities.

There will be times when instead of wanting to exchange, you'll have the opposite challenge: too many choices for good plays. That may be particularly true when you draw a blank or S. It's not always easy to find a bingo with a blank. And with an S on your rack, you may be torn between playing it and saving it. Chapter Eleven will show you what to do.

ANSWERS: CHAPTER 10

Diagram 10-1: AIKIDO K6 22.

Diagram 10-2: UNUSUAL O9 21.

Diagram 10-4: OUTCHARM 8A 45.

---

11 YOUR TWO BEST FRIENDS: THE BLANK AND THE S

When you draw the blank, it will be the most valuable tile on your rack. Why? Because you will be able to form more bingos with a blank on your rack than with any other letter!

Now that you have practiced finding bingos in Chapter Seven, let's see how the blank can help even more (note that "?" will represent the blank):

Suppose you have the rack BDNORW?. You only have one vowel, so the chances are that if there is a bingo, the blank will have to be used as a vowel. Notice the D on the rack. From the list of common endings, you know that ED is a great combination. Try it; you just have to rearrange BNORW. Answer on page 118.

Of course, this was a relatively easy example; there weren't too many choices for what to make the blank. Unfortunately, it won't always be this easy.

The key to finding bingos with the blank is to be systematic and thorough. Follow these guidelines and you will improve your blank-bingo skills over time.

Guidelines for Finding Bingos with Blanks

1. Check your vowel-consonant ratio.

Here are some general rules to follow:

If you have **six vowels,** you most probably won't have a bingo; there are only a handful of eight-letter words with six vowels. (See Appendix Four.) With **five vowels** you may have one of the few five-vowel seven-letter words, such as SEQUOIA or MIAOUED. Or perhaps you may have one of the three hundred or more five-vowel eight-letter words, like AQUANAUT or PEEKA-BOO. But otherwise, you aren't likely to have a bingo. If you have **four vowels,** the blank will probably need to be a consonant. If you have **three vowels,** the blank may be either a vowel or consonant. If you have only **two vowels,** the blank will probably be a vowel. However, there are many seven-letter words with only two vowels. Here you should see how your consonants fit together. Do you have the TCH or GHT combination? These can lead you to words such as WATCHES or SIGHTED. If you have only **one vowel,** the blank will almost always have to be a vowel. Of course, there are exceptions. There are some six-letter words with only one vowel that take an S to form a bingo. Examples: FRIGHT, SPRAWL, STRING, and SCRIMP.

2. Which of the bingo-prone tiles do you already have?

The letters that work best to form seven- and eight-letter words, beginning with the best in each category, are the vowels E, A, and I and the consonants S, R, N, T, and L. The D also works really well, but mostly if you have an E for the ED ending. Finally, the G is excellent, although usually only when you have ING or the less useful ending AGE.

What we mean is that if you are looking for the "right" vowel, imagine the blank is first an E, then an A, and then an I. If you need a consonant, imagine the blank is first an S, then an R, N, T, and finally L.

If you already have some of these letters, then go on to the next letter. That's because *you're much more likely to find a bingo with seven different letters than with one letter that's repeated.* The only exception to this is with the letter E. If you have one, you can easily have a bingo with a second E. That's because the E is extremely versatile. For example, hundreds of words either begin with RE or end in ER or ED—or, for that matter, with the E alone.

Example 1

You have A E I N S V ?. What should you imagine the blank to be, a vowel or a consonant? First notice that you have three vowels and three consonants, so the blank might easily be either. In this case, we advise looking at the consonants first. Why? Remember Guideline #1: You already have the three common vowels. Plus, it is very common for bingos to have at least two of the four letters LNRT. As we look at the most bingo-prone letters— E, A, I, S, R, N, T, and L—notice that you are missing the R, T, and L. Since the R is the first consonant listed that we don't already have, let's try it first. Can you find a seven-letter word with the letters A E I N S V adding an R?

Again, we advise that you take the actual tiles and move them around on your rack. The answer is on page 118. Now try the blank as a T. There are three common words using the letters A E I N S V and a T.

Can you find them? The answer is on page 118.

Example 2

Your rack is B E M N O R ?. Can you find a seven-letter word with these tiles?

Since you have only two vowels, your last letter will probably be a vowel. But which? First try BEMNOR + E, then BEMNOR + A, and finally BE-MNOR + I. Give yourself at least a minute with each combination before moving on to the next, moving the tiles around at least every few seconds. The answer is on page 118.

3. Use your high-point tiles to help lead you to a bingo.

One of the reasons that some tiles are worth more points than others is that they aren't as frequently found in the English language and are harder to use. However, each of the sixteen high-point tiles (B, C, D, F, G, H, J, K, M, P, Q, V, W, X, Y, and Z) has its own particular style of showing up in seven- and eight-letter words. Each is commonly found in certain arrangements with other letters. For example, the B will often be paired with the R or L to form BR or BL combinations such as BROWN, BRICK, BLUE, or NIMBLE. The F will often be combined with a T or a Y, or even the UL duo, to form FT, FY, or FUL combinations such as LOFT, RIFT, NOTIFY, EDIFY, CAREFUL, or HARMFUL. See pages 26 and 74 for a list of useful combinations.

Example 3

You have the rack H I N R S U ?. As soon as we notice that we don't absolutely need to have an extra vowel, we should automatically look to use our one high-point tile, the H, in one of its familiar "settings." On page 74 we see that the H can often be placed after IS at the end of a word. Let's see how that affects our search. We have NRU? left. Try playing with these tiles! If you look at NISH first, you may find more than one bingo. See page 118 for the complete list.

Other bingos with a blank will likewise be easier to find if you use your high-point tile to guide you.

4. Remember the common beginnings and endings, and then use them to find your blank bingos.

To summarize what we've said:

How to Find Bingos Using a Blank

1. Consider the vowel-consonant ratio.
2. Look for the best bingo tiles: vowels E, A, and I and consonants S, R, N, T, and L. Avoid duplicating a letter already on your rack unless it's an E.
3. Use your high-point tiles to guide your search.
4. Remember the common beginnings and endings and use the blank to form them. Example: IE? can be imagined as IED, IER, or IES.

Quiz: Test yourself again and find the bingos using the following sets of six letters and a blank tile. In each case there is only one common word to be found. We suggest using actual tiles to help simulate playing the game. We also suggest that after three to five minutes of searching, you look at the hint on page 118. We list the letter the blank must be to spell each word.

This quick search-and-look-up method can both train your mind to find the common letter arrangements and help you to avoid becoming too frustrated with *not* finding the words. It's better to look it up and move on!

BLANK BINGO QUIZ

1. CIRRTU?	6. ADEHMT?	11. EEFLMS?	16. EGPSTU?
2. CFILNY?	7. AGMSTU?	12. EEFFIT?	17. EGNOTV?
3. ANOOTV?	8. ALLRTY?	13. EEISTZ?	18. ENNOTV?
4. AEGSVY?	9. DEELNV?	14. EEKOTY?	19. IIOTTU?
5. ADFHLN?	10. DLLNOW?	15. EENNTU?	20. IMNORT?

Answers will be found on page 118.

A Blank Without a Bingo

What happens when you have a blank, but you can't find or play a bingo? The answer depends on two conditions:

1. Do you have a play using the blank that scores at least 20 to 30 points more than if you don't use your blank? Look at Diagram 11-1.

	A	B	C	D	E	F	G	H	I	J	K	L	M	N	O	
	TWS			DLS				TWS				DLS			TWS	1
		DWS				TLS				TLS				DWS		2
			DWS				DLS		DLS				DWS			3
	DLS			DWS			DLS					DWS			DLS	4
					DWS							DWS				5
		TLS				TLS				TLS				TLS		6
			DLS				**M**	**A**	**J**	**O**	**R**	**E**	**D**			7
	TWS			**G**	**L**	**U**	**E**	**D**				**T**	**A**	**L**	**K**	8
			DLS	**L**				**O**	**V**	**A**		DLS				9
		TLS		**A**		TLS				TLS				TLS		10
				Z	DWS						DWS					11
	DLS			**Y**			DLS					DWS			DLS	12
			DWS				DLS		DLS				DWS			13
		DWS				TLS				TLS				DWS		14
	TWS			DLS				TWS				DLS			TWS	15

DIAGRAM 11-1

Rack: L N O O R X ?

What should you do? You can play *XU* 10J and score a huge 49 points. Or you can simply play *LOX* K9 and score only 27, but hope to bingo next turn. The best answer to this question may differ for each player. If you are able to find bingos with ease, and think you will have no trouble finding one next turn, then you should probably sacrifice the points this turn. However, if you haven't yet mastered the skills involved in finding bingos, you might want to take the extra points now. In each case, you will be making the best decision based upon your clearest assessment of your personal skills.

A	B	C	D	E	F	G	H	I	J	K	L	M	N	O	#
TWS			DLS				TWS				DLS			TWS	1
	DWS				TLS				TLS				DWS		2
		DWS				DLS	C	DLS				DWS			3
DLS			P	E	B	B	L	E	S		DWS			DLS	4
F	A	M	I	L	Y		A		E	DWS					5
	TLS				TLS		R		X				TLS		6
		DLS				DLS	I	DLS	Y			DLS			7
TWS			DLS			H	O				DLS			TWS	8
		DLS				A	N	DLS				DLS			9
	TLS	V	A	L	U	E	D		TLS				TLS		10
				DWS						DWS					11
DLS			DWS				DLS				DWS			DLS	12
		DWS				DLS		DLS				DWS			13
	DWS				TLS				TLS				DWS		14
TWS			DLS				TWS				DLS			TWS	15

DIAGRAM 11-2

Your rack: L M O O P Z ?

Using Diagram 11-2, you can play *TOPAZ* B2 70 points. That's like playing a bingo! There is no other play available that scores 40 points without using the blank. You should jump at the chance to make this play!

2. What are your winning chances with or without a bingo?

If you can assess that you don't need a bingo to win, you might simply want to make your highest scoring play. However, if you realize that you need a 70- to 90-point play to win the game, then you must sacrifice the points now in order to have a good chance later on to get that bingo.

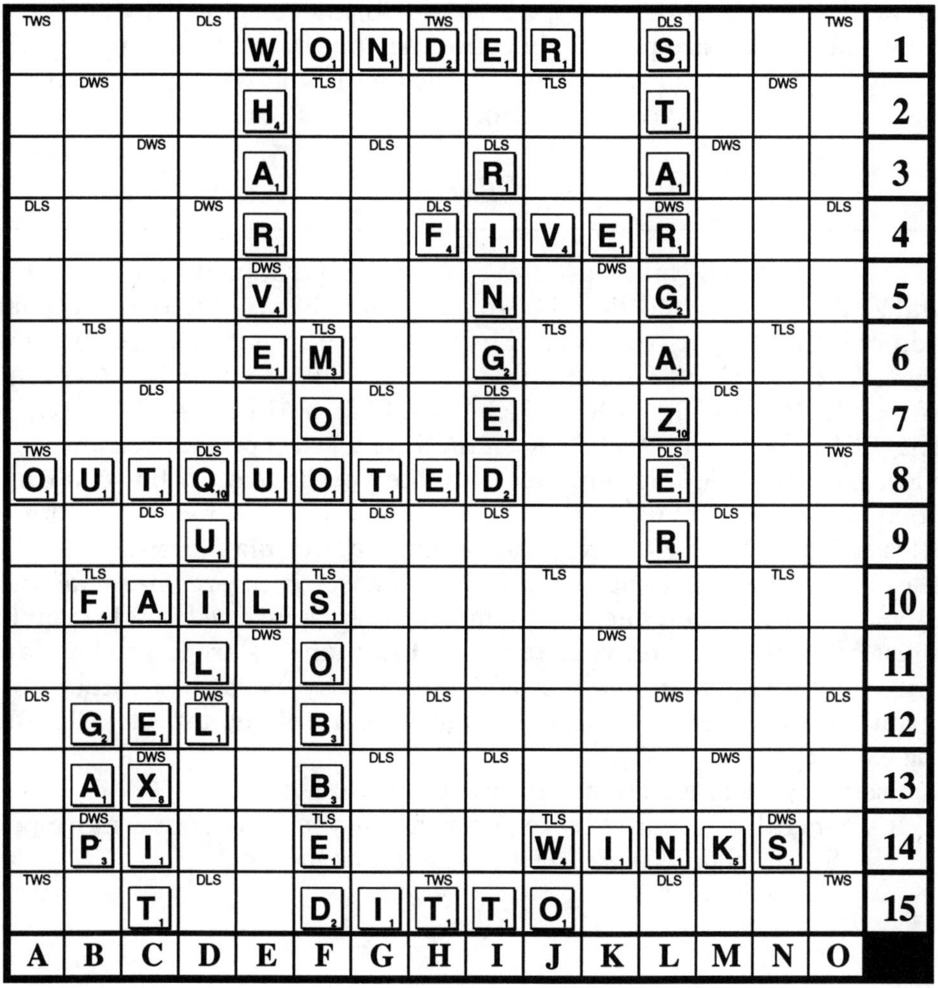

	A	B	C	D	E	F	G	H	I	J	K	L	M	N	O	
					W	O	N	D	E	R		S				1
					H							T				2
					A			R				A				3
					R		F	I	V	E		R				4
					V			N				G				5
					E	M		G				A				6
						O		E				Z				7
	O	U	T	Q	U	O	T	E	D			E				8
				U								R				9
	F	A	I	L	S											10
				L	O											11
	G	E	L		B											12
	A	X			B											13
	P	I			E					W	I	N	K	S		14
		T				D	I	T	T	O						15

DIAGRAM 11-3

Your rack: C E I J P R ?

You're behind 80 points and playing on Diagram 11-3. You see three excellent plays: PROJECT C2 40, JAPER 4A 42, and JEEPS 8K 39. But you need to use your blank for each of them. If you play any of these, you'll be 60 to 70 points down after your opponent's next play and have little chance to play a bingo without the blank. And you will definitely need the bingo to win. So these options don't leave much hope of your winning. What are your other choices? You can play JIN L12 20 points, JEU B6 26, or JERK M11 30. By not using your blank, you now have a reasonable chance to build a bingo within two or three plays, which may bring you close to victory. None of these three plays are perfect, because they all block some bingo lines and leave two high-point tiles. However, occasionally you will be forced to make these kinds of plays if you want to have *any* realistic chance to win.

"S" as in SCORE!

Like the blank, the S can be used to score a bundle of points. It can not only pluralize most nouns and singularize most verbs but is invaluable as a letter to add in front of other words. For instance, there are many words beginning with A, C, H, L, M, N, P, and T that take an S in front: AIL, AND, CAMP, COW, CREAM, HALE, HARP, LUSH, LEAVE, MALL, MART, NOW, NIP, PARE, PELT, TONE, and TILT, to name just a few. For that reason we call the S a good hook letter. However, suppose you have an S but can't find a particularly good play using it. What should you do? Do you use it for 2 or 3 extra points? Or do you save it for a much better play later on?

The answer to that is not so simple, because there are many factors at play, such as: a) are you ahead or behind, and by how much? b) Do you have not just one but two Ss on your rack? c) How many Ss are left to be played? and d) exactly how many points will you score by using the S? Your ability to evaluate these conditions adequately is part of the art of SCRABBLE game excellence.

To use the S most effectively, follow these guidelines:

1. It's generally accepted by experts that if you can score 8 more points using the S, you should use it. Here's a good example:

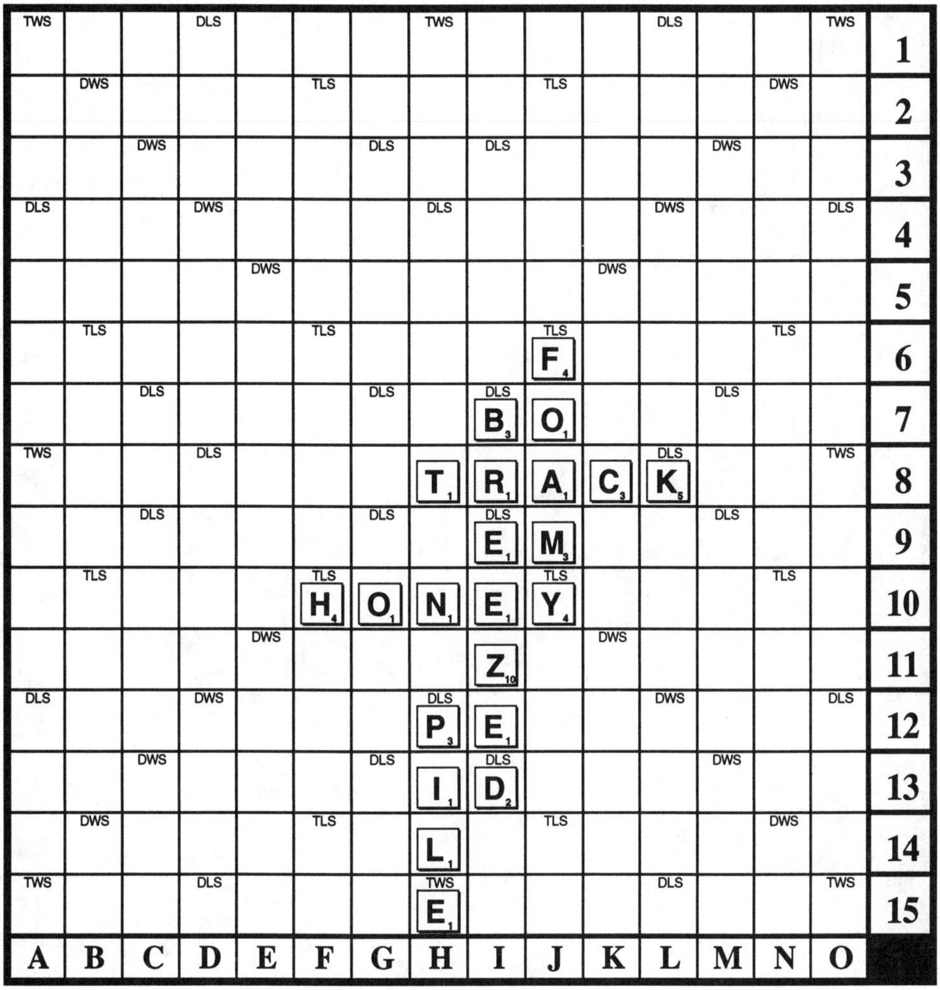

DIAGRAM 11-4

Your rack: A I L O S U V

Playing on Diagram 11-4, if the choices you find are VIOLA K2 or 11B for 21 points or VIOLAS M3 32, you can be comfortable playing away the S for 11 extra points. Of course, if you see the word SOUVLAKI L2 you'll earn a whopping 80 points.

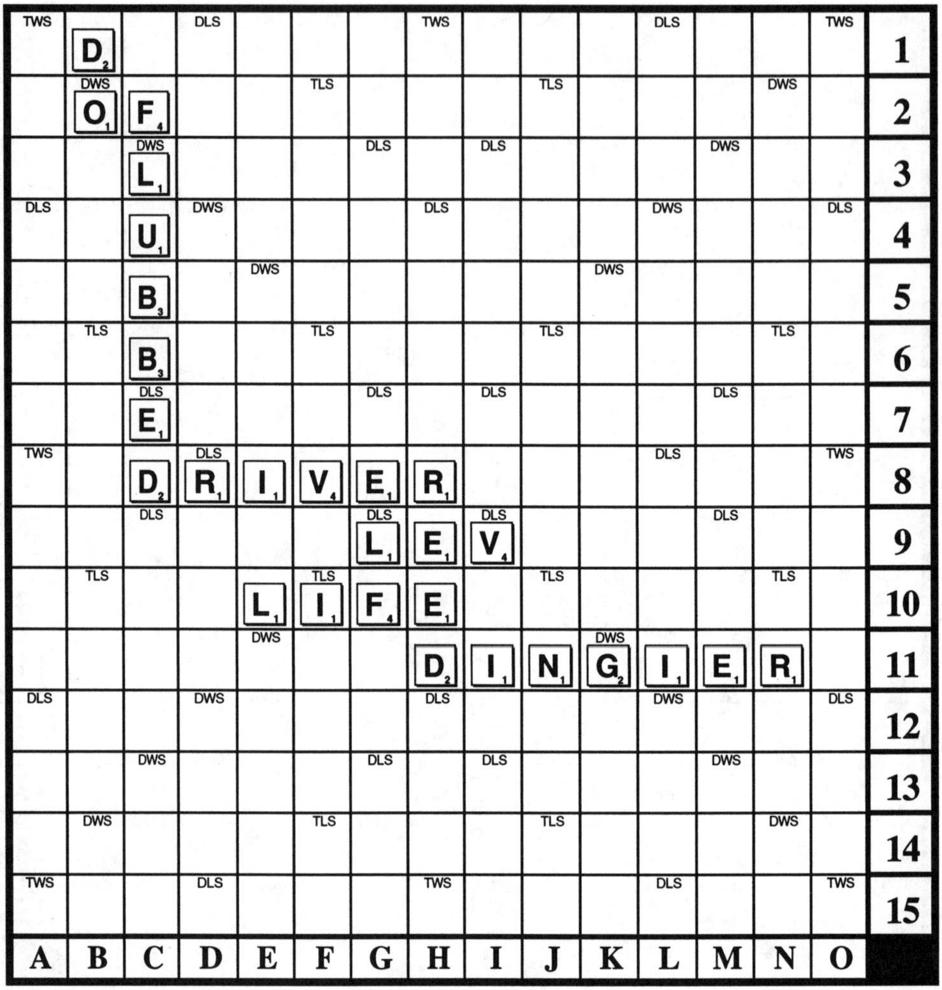

DIAGRAM 11-5

Your Rack: A E I N N O S

In Diagram 11-5, the score is nearly even. You see either ANIONS 12C 21 points or ION 11D 12. Though the S gives you 9 extra points, the letters AENS remaining on your rack after playing ION are so bingo-prone that many experts would choose the lesser-scoring move.

2. If you have two Ss, you may part with one of them for fewer than 8 extra points. Because the second S usually doesn't help you much to build a bingo, you're better off getting rid of it for a few extra points. The exception to this rule is if you have one of the endings LESS or NESS. In that case you should examine your rack thoroughly for a bingo. Let's look at an example.

TWS			DLS				TWS				DLS			TWS	**1**
	DWS				TLS				TLS				DWS		**2**
		DWS				DLS		DLS				DWS			**3**
DLS			DWS				DLS				DWS			DLS	**4**
				DWS		K₅				DWS					**5**
	TLS				TLS	E₁			TLS				TLS		**6**
		DLS				E₁ DLS		DLS				DLS			**7**
TWS			DLS D₂	R₁	I₁	P₃	T₁				DLS			TWS	**8**
		DLS				I₁ DLS		DLS				DLS			**9**
	TLS				TLS	N₁			TLS				TLS V₄		**10**
			DWS	S₁	I₁	G₂	N₁	A₁	L₁	DWS			E₁		**11**
DLS			DWS			H₄	O₁	E₁	D₂		DWS	R₁		DLS	**12**
		DWS				R₁ DLS	A₁	P₃	T₁	O₁	DWS R₁	S₁			**13**
	DWS				TLS				TLS			DWS	E₁		**14**
TWS			DLS			TWS				DLS	B₃	O₁	D₂	TWS Y₄	**15**
A	B	C	D	E	F	G	H	I	J	K	L	M	N	O	

DIAGRAM 11-6

Your Rack: A D G M O S S

Playing on Diagram 11-6, you find DOGMA H1 42 points. But you can score 5 more points with DOGMAS in the same place. Should you? Yes! Saving the extra S here isn't worth sacrificing 5 points.

3. If you don't have a bingo, but you do have *nearly* a bingo, then you may want to play off one or two tiles, saving the S and other bingo-prone letters in order to try and bingo next turn. This is called "fishing" and was discussed in Chapter Eight.

A	B	C	D	E	F	G	H	I	J	K	L	M	N	O	
TWS			DLS				T				DLS			TWS	1
	DWS			TLS			I	TLS				DWS			2
		DWS			DLS		M	DLS			DWS				3
DLS			DWS				E	F	F			DWS		DLS	4
				DWS			L	A	B	E	L				5
	TLS				TLS		O	R	TLS				TLS		6
		DLS				DLS	O	M			DLS				7
TWS			P	A	R	K	E	D			DLS			TWS	8
		H	E	X		DLS		DLS			DLS				9
	TLS		T		TLS				TLS				TLS		10
		B	A	I	T						DWS				11
DLS			L				DLS				DWS			DLS	12
		DWS			DLS			DLS				DWS			13
	DWS			TLS				TLS				DWS			14
TWS			DLS			TWS					DLS			TWS	15

DIAGRAM 11-7

Your Rack: E E I N Q R S

You are playing on Diagram 11-7. Because you can't play the Q, and because the EEINRS leave is so strong, you would be wise to sacrifice a turn to exchange the Q. The odds are very high that you will have a bingo next turn. Note that some experts prefer exchanging EQ, saving EINRS.

Imagine you have an E and a blank on your rack. Now combine any one of the two-letter vowel combinations below on the left with any one of the three-letter 1-point-consonant combinations on the right. With *every* such seven-letter rack, there will *always* be a bingo. And in almost every case, there will always be a *common-word bingo* available. The exceptions are: E? + EULST = ELUATES, TELEDUS, EUSTELE, UNSTEEL, or ELUENTS; + IULNR = URNLIKE or PURLINE; + EOLNT = TOLUENE; + EULNT = TEENFUL, TOLUENE, ELUENTS, or UNSTEEL. In some cases there are more than fifty bingos available! (See Appendix Four.) See page 118 for one example of each of the one hundred combinations. How many can you find? We suggest you spend about ten to fifteen minutes with each combination trying to find at least one bingo.

E ? +

A E	L	N	R
A I	L	N	S
A O	L	N	T
A U	L	R	S
E I	L	R	T
E O	L	S	T
E U	N	R	S
I O	N	R	T
I U	N	S	T
O U	R	S	T

As we've seen in this chapter, you don't have to memorize the dictionary to hone your SCRABBLE game skills. However, there are a few types of unusual words that you will enjoy knowing. Learning new words will give you more choices for each turn, which will increase your opportunity for developing your decision-making abilities. Chapter Twelve will show you what words to focus on.

BDNORW?: BROWNED or RUBDOWN

AEINSV?: EVANISH, NAVVIES, VAHINES, INVADES, ALEVINS, EVASION, NAIVEST, NATIVES, RAVINES, SAVINES, VAINEST, VALINES, and VINASSE.

BEMNOR?: EMBROWN, EMBRYON, and BROMINE.

HINRSU?: UNHAIRS, BURNISH, URCHINS, FURNISH, RUNTISH, RUSHING, NOURISH.

BLANK BINGO QUIZ: HINTS (blank given): 1. E; 2. A; 3. I; 4. O; 5. U; 6. C; 7. N; 8. E; 9. I; 10. A; 11. A; 12. N; 13. R; 14. N; 15. A; 16. A; 17. I; 18. C; 19. N; 20. O.

BLANK BINGO QUIZ: ANSWERS
1. RECRUIT; 2. FANCILY; 3. OVATION; 4. VOYAGES; 5. HANDFUL; 6. MATCHED; 7. MUSTANG; 8. ALERTLY; 9. LIVENED; 10. LOWLAND; 11. FEMALES; 12. FIFTEEN; 13. ZESTIER; 14. KEYNOTE; 15. UNEATEN; 16. UPSTAGE; 17. VETOING; 18. CONVENT; 19. TUITION; 20. MONITOR.

Answers to One-Point Tile Bingo Practice:
E? + **AELNR** = RELEARN; + **AELNS** = ENABLES; + **AELNT** = LEANEST; + **AELRS** = LEADERS; + **AELRT** = LEATHER; + **AELST** = RELATES; + **AENRS** = ENDEARS; + **AENRT** = GREATEN; + **AENST** = NEGATES; + **AERST** = CREATES; + **AILNR** = LANKIER; + **AILNS** = SALIENT; + **AILNT** = INFLATE; + **AILRS** = DERAILS; + **AILRT** = RETAILS; + **AILST** = DETAILS; + **AINRS** = ARSENIC; + **AINRT** = FAINTER; + **AINST** = SEATING; + **AIRST** = WARIEST; + **AOLNR** = LOANERS; + **AOLNS** = RELOANS; + **AOLNT** = TOENAIL; + **AOLRS** = ORACLES; + **AOLRT** = GLOATER; + **AOLST** = LOCATES; + **AONRS** = REASONS; + **AONRT** = SENATOR; + **AONST** = DONATES; + **AORST** = COASTER; + **AULNR** = UNCLEAR; + **AULNS** = UNSEALS; + **AULNT** = ANNULET; + **AULRS** = SURREAL; + **AULRT** = TEARFUL; + **AULST** = SULFATE; + **AUNRS** = SAUNTER; + **AUNRT** = URINATE; + **AUNST** = PEANUTS; + **AURST** = STATURE; + **EILNR** = RELINED; + **EILNS** = LICENSE; + **EILNT** = TENSILE; + **EILRS** = REPLIES; + **EILRT** = REPTILE; + **EILST** = LEFTIES; + **EINRS** = EROSION; + **EINRT** = TRAINEE; + **EINST** = INTENSE; + **EIRST** = RECITES; + **EOLNR** = ERELONG; + **EOLNS** = ENCLOSE; + **EOLNT** = TOLUENE; + **EOLRS** = RESOLVE; + **EOLRT** = ELECTOR; + **EOLST** = OMELETS; + **EONRS** = ENDORSE; + **EONRT** = OFTENER; + **EONST** = DENOTES; + **EORST** = STEREOS; + **EULNR** = UNREELS; + **EULNS** = UNREELS; + **EULNT** = TOLUENE; + **EULRS** = REPULSE; + **EURLT** = LECTURE; + **EULST** = UNSTEEL; + **EUNRS** = ENSURED; + **EUNRT** = TENURES; + **EUNST** = ENTHUSE; + **EURST** = REQUEST; + **IOLNR** = LOONIER; + **IOLNS** = LESIONS; + **IOLNT** = ELATION; + **IOLRS** = BOILERS; + **IOLRT** = POLITER; + **IOLST** = VIOLETS; + **IONRS** = SENIORS; + **IONRT** = ORIENTS; + **IONST** = NOTICES; + **IORST** = LOITERS; + **IULNR** = URNLIKE; + **IULNS** = LINEUPS; + **IULNT** = UTENSIL; + **IULRS** = LEISURE; + **IULRT** = REBUILT; + **IULST** = LUSTIER; + **IUNRS** = INJURES; + **IUNRT** = TRIBUNE; + **IUNST** = MINUTES; + **IURST** = GUTSIER; + **OULNR** = LOUNGER; + **OULNS** = COUNSEL; + **OULNT** = OUTLINE; + **OULRS** = OURSELF; + **OULRT** = TROUBLE; + **OULST** = LOUDEST; + **OUNRS** = SURGEON; + **OUNRT** = FORTUNE; + **OUNST** = TONGUES; + **OURST** = DETOURS.

12 IT'S YOUR WORD AGAINST MINE: BUILDING A BETTER VOCABULARY

You are playing your next-door neighbor in your weekly best-two-out-of-three SCRABBLE® games match. You are both reasonably competitive, intelligent, and have equal understanding of the fundamental game strategies. Who's usually going to win?

Given these conditions, the two most important factors that will determine the victor in these games are tile selection and vocabulary. Short of using X-ray vision, there is very little you can do about assuring yourself great tiles every time you play. So the single best thing you can do is learn as many words as possible.

This means quality as well as quantity. For example, it is far better that you know the seventeen Q words without a U (see Chapter Six) than a few hundred nine-letter words. And you'll be far better served knowing words with a high proportion of vowels (Appendix Four) than you will knowing a handful of impressive, but obscure, medical terms.

The first place to start in building a SCRABBLE vocabulary is the two-letter words, which we discussed in Chapter Three. The next step is to learn the 955 three-letter words in *The Official SCRABBLE® Players Dictionary*. These are the centerpiece of the National SCRABBLE® Association's beginner's word sheet, and they are listed in Appendix Four.

Also in the National SCRABBLE® Association New Member Kit is a sampling of what the experts call "vowel dumps." Anyone who has played even a few games knows the frustration of having a rack that is reminiscent of "Old MacDonald Had a Farm"—EIEIO—or for that matter the letters AU-AUA. This vowel-heavy situation is inevitable for SCRABBLE players at all levels, and the best way to be prepared is to know these invaluable words.

The National SCRABBLE® Association's list of important words to memorize also includes the most common and/or short usages of the heavy artillery—the J, Q, X, and Z. These are about 340 words that you will use again and again as you try to match the high-scoring tiles on your rack with open "hot spots" on the board. Many of these are discussed in Chapters Six and Thirteen.

Before you get too intimidated by all these lists and how long they seem, it's important to put everything in perspective. For example, all the specialized words we've just talked about come to a total of 1,200 or so. Even better, there is a very good chance you already know at least half of them. Don't believe it? As you use Appendix Four, go ahead and cross out in pencil all the words you already know. You'll be surprised.

Now you are faced with learning only 500-750 new words, a very achievable task. Given the natural interest in words that helped draw you to the SCRABBLE game in the first place, this should not be too difficult. And consider the rewards. We estimate that you'll increase your SCRABBLE scoring average a full 100 points a game if you learn these starter lists and use the words effectively.

Learning new words can be approached in any number of ways. Here are some ideas that have worked over the years for champions and casual players alike.

GENERAL CURIOSITY

People remember unusual words for a variety of reasons. Many know them from years of doing crossword puzzles. Some have areas of expertise—medicine, gardening, zoology—which expose them to hundreds of uncommon words and terms. Still others seem to indiscriminately know or discover strings of related words.

For example, John Williams has always been fascinated by the "genie family," as he calls it. Everyone knows that word, of course, as the creature who rose from Aladdin's lamp, in addition to other appearances throughout folklore and mythology. However, the term provides word magic as well; using both singular and plural forms, it has all the following alternative spellings:

GENIE: genies, jin, jins, jinn, jinns, jinnee, jinni, djin, djins, djinn, djinns, djinni, and djinny.

That's fourteen different forms of the same word! More important, it gives you many different options when you have the J, a high-scoring tile.

A favorite example of Joe Edley's is a G word—ganef. It means a "thief," and its variations include:

GANEF: ganefs, ganev, ganevs, ganof, ganofs, gonef, gonefs, gonif, gonifs, goniff, goniffs, gonof, gonofs, gonoph, and gonophs.

There are countless other examples of these types of words throughout *The Official SCRABBLE® Players Dictionary*. They are particularly easy to learn, because they are inherently interesting and one form of the word is usually an extension or twist on another. While this is an admittedly arbitrary and random form of learning new words, it is certainly effortless. You should be propelled by your curiosity alone!

Another random method of learning new words is to simply read the dictionary. Many players buy an extra copy of *The Official SCRABBLE® Players Dictionary* and black out all the words they already know. Then, over time, in fifteen-minute or half-hour doses, they browse through the book. It offers brief definitions—as opposed to pure word lists—and many people find that helpful as well.

Remember, of the hundred thousand or more words in the *OSPD*, chances are you know as many as one-third of them already. In fact, everybody knows more words than they think; they just don't use many of them on a regular basis—until they start playing the SCRABBLE game. To prove this, sit down with a friend and open up *The Official SCRABBLE® Players Dictionary*. Choose six random pages and test how many of the words you know between the two of you. You'll be very surprised.

It's also important to know that when learning new words for the purpose of playing the SCRABBLE game, one doesn't necessarily have to take time to learn meanings. You only have to know if it takes an S, ING, or other inflection. (Understandably, word purists take offense at this idea.)

HINTS FROM THE EXPERTS

If you have your sights set on becoming a legitimate, top-ranked SCRABBLE expert, you are going to have to employ some of the more systematic methods of learning new words. It is like training for competition. Some people can swim laps for hours, while others would rather run ten miles than swim a hundred feet. So find a regimen to learn words that is best suited to your personality.

We have interviewed four of the most renowned word experts in the history of competitive SCRABBLE play and asked each to give us his secret for adding to one's vocabulary. Here are some of their recommendations:

Peter Morris, a teacher and graduate student in English literature at Michigan State, has been a SCRABBLE expert since he was a teenager. He is the only person to have won both the American National SCRABBLE®

Championship (1989) and the World SCRABBLE® Championship (1991). An avid sports fan and a player of many games, Peter is the first to admit he does not like to study or learn new words as much as most other experts seem to. As a result, he has developed ways he feels are time-efficient for learning new words.

The first thing Peter recommends is to simply go to the nearest SCRABBLE game club in your area. (A North American club roster listing every club is available with NSA membership.) "After each game, wander around and look at all the boards," he advises. "You will see the same words appear over and over again, simply because these words have letters that players save, and so, inevitably, they are played repeatedly."

He especially emphasizes that you should always keep an eye out for words that get rid of bad tiles. A perfect example would be the words JUBA or VUG. The latter is especially good because its reverse—GUV—is good as well. In fact, reversible words or words that use the same letters as each other are some of the easiest to learn and remember. Other examples are:

KOA, OAK, OKA
AVER, RAVE, VERA
CHI, HIC, ICH
ELMY, YLEM

It's Peter's feeling that some people spend too much time learning obscure seven- and eight-letter words that will hardly ever be used. It's better that you learn the ones that will most likely appear again and again. For instance, AEEINRT will occur on your rack repeatedly as you learn to save these excellent letters. So you would do well to learn the following three words: RETINAE, TRAINEE, and ARENITE. His advice to beginners: Play a lot, learn from those better than you, and study board positions.

We have one word of caution for you, however, when learning new words from other players' boards: Make sure you look up the unfamiliar words, since some players get away with phoneys!

Joel Wapnick, a music professor at McGill University in Montreal, is renowned in the SCRABBLE world for his enormous vocabulary. He was the 1983 national SCRABBLE® champion, and runner-up at both the 1992 National SCRABBLE® Championship and the 1993 World SCRABBLE® Championship. He is said to have learned up to fifteen thousand new words in the six months previous to winning the national championship.

Joel says one of the first things he did was to go through the entire *Official SCRABBLE® Players Dictionary* and identify all the two- to five-letter words that he did not know. He then took these words and put them into a list to study. As he recorded a word, he would also note any good anagrams of the word beside it. It's Joel's theory that you might as well learn both the word and its anagrams at the same time. A couple of examples would be:

ALIEN: ALINE, ELAIN, ANILE, LIANE
COSINE: CONIES, ICONES, OSCINE

Joel says time management is the key to learning new words. He often carries word lists with him and uses stolen moments to hone his vocabulary. A long wait in a doctor's office, a traffic jam, or a late-starting meeting are all small opportunities to learn a couple of new words. "Find your own area of weakness and create your own list and exercise," Wapnick suggests. He also mentions learning niche categories, like the Q-without-U list and words that don't take an S. These are especially helpful for defensive play.

Mike Baron, a clinical psychologist in Albuquerque, New Mexico, is one of America's best-known SCRABBLE players and foremost word experts. Mike has also run one of the oldest and most successful SCRABBLE game clubs in America, introducing scores of "living room" players to the world of competitive SCRABBLE.

A veteran of eight National SCRABBLE® Championships, Mike has written more about words and word lists than anyone else. Like Peter Morris, Mike believes the goal is "to get the best payoff with the least amount of studying." As a result, his specialty is breaking down words into logical groupings and analyzing their letter patterns for easy learning.

Consistent with the NSA's dictum, Baron says to learn the two- and three-letter words first. He feels the best way to do this is to write out the two- and three-letter word lists twice from memory, studying the omissions after each effort. Along with the threes and the J, Q, X, and Z lists, Baron feels four-letter words are more important than many players realize. Why? He maintains that in any given SCRABBLE game, 75 percent of the words will consist of two, three, or four letters. After you master these, Baron advises you should learn the top hundred "bingo stems," which will be discussed in the advanced strategy chapters.

Joe Edley, the coauthor of this book, is the 1980 and 1992 national SCRAB-BLE® champion, the only person in history to ever win the event twice. He was also the third-place finisher in the 1983 Nationals and came in second in 1985, as well as taking fourth place in the 1991 World SCRABBLE® Championship. Trained as a mathematician, Joe takes a very systematic but fun approach to learning new words.

"Basically, I just play a variation of the word game many of us played as children. It's played by choosing a large word and then seeing how many smaller words you can make from it." Joe says it's fast and easy and captures the essence of SCRABBLE—making new words from a jumble of letters. "Do this fifteen to twenty minutes a day several times a week," Joe says, "and within a year you'll not only know hundreds of new words, but you'll be able to find them on your rack!" At first, it will help you learn all the two- and three-letter words, then with practice the fours and fives.

When Joe practices this exercise, he invariably uses a nine- or ten-letter word. However, here is an example of a very common word—HANDLE—and all the words that can be made from it. In all, there are fifty-eight words contained in its letters!

ad	ae	ah	al	ale	an	and	ane
da	dah	dahl	dal	dale	de	deal	dean
del	den	dhal	edh	eh	el	elan	eland
eld	en	end	ha	had	hade	hae	haed
haen	hale	haled	hand	handle	he	head	heal
held	hen	la	lad	lade	laden	land	lane
lea	lead	lean	led	lend	na	nae	nah
naled	ne						

Of course, you are going to need a method to check and see how many of the possible words you have found. There are several options for this. One is the *Webster's Word Game Word Finder,* by Bruce Wetterau, another is a good anagramming computer program, and a third is the Franklin Electronic *The Official SCRABBLE® Players Dictionary.* All will help you gauge your progress. Whatever your method for learning new words, do it! Because if you want to get better, and beat your opponents, it all comes down to your word against theirs.

Of the new words we advise you to learn, the short J, X, and Z words will be among the most useful. With the help of some puzzles, Chapter Thirteen will teach these words to you.

13 THE HEAVY ARTILLERY— J, X, AND Z

While the 10-point Q is often a difficult tile to play, the other high-point tiles—the J, X, and Z—are generally much easier to place for large scores. Using those tiles on bonus squares can earn 40 to 80 points in one play! Learn the unusual, but acceptable, three- and four-letter J, X, and Z words listed on page 130. Opportunities to play these words will occur repeatedly.

New players frequently ask which one of these high-point tiles is the best. The X is by far the best, due to its versatility. Because AX, EX, XI, OX, and XU are all acceptable, you will often be able to form plays worth 36 to 52 points by using the X on one of the bonus squares and making parallel plays with letters already on the board. The Z is second to the X, followed by the J.

To help you learn the unusual four-letter words containing J, X, and Z, first review the four-letter word list on page 130. Keep referring back to the list when you have trouble remembering the words.

Each of the following three-letter combinations takes either the J, X, or Z to form a four-letter word. Most of the time you'll have to mix up the letters to properly spell the word. We've marked either a 2 or 3 next to a letter combination if two or three of the letters J, X, or Z can be added to form a word. A star (*) next to a number means that one of the answer words has an anagram. Example: In 45, EST will form words with any of the letters J, X, or Z, and one of the words has an anagram.

Most of the answer words are obscure, so please review the word list on page 130 before trying this exercise.

JXZ QUIZ

1. CEH	*11. AOT	21. ELO	31. ADH	41. OOR
2. EMY	12. DOY -2	22. ACR	32. IOR	42. EIN -2
3. BEU -2	13. GIN	23. AIR	33. AOS	43. AIO
4. IIT	14. OOU	24. EFU	34. AAL	44. EPR -2
5. EEF	15. ALR	25. STY	35. INY	*45. EST -3
6. ETU	16. IPY	*26. AEL -2	36. ORY	46. EOY -2
7. ACL	17. ART	27. ANO -2	37. DIN	47. BEI -3
8. AAT	18. EOP	28. ISY	38. AEE	*48. AEN
9. DIO	19. OKU	29. ABU	*39. APU	*49. ENO -3
10. IRT	20. AII	30. EHU	40. ILL -2	*50. ADE -3

As you repeat the exercise in the future, your word knowledge will improve, until such time that you'll probably find you won't need the list at all!

Here are three more puzzle diagrams to practice using the J, X, and Z. In each case, the answers will list a variety of plays not asked for specifically, in order to give you an idea of the numerous choices available in each position.

	A	B	C	D	E	F	G	H	I	J	K	L	M	N	O	
	TWS			DLS				TWS				DLS			TWS	**1**
		DWS			TLS									DWS		**2**
			DWS			DLS		DLS **R**					DWS			**3**
	DLS			DWS			DLS	**O**			DWS	**O**	**M**	**E**	DLS **N**	**4**
					DWS		**B**	**U**	**N**	**N**	DWS **Y**					**5**
		TLS				TLS		**N**	TLS	**O**				TLS		**6**
			DLS			DLS		DLS **D**		**N**		DLS				**7**
	TWS			DLS **B**	**A**	**R**	**O**	**N**	**S**		**D**	DLS			TWS	**8**
		DLS				DLS		DLS			**A**	DLS				**9**
		TLS				TLS			TLS		**I**			TLS		**10**
				DWS							DWS **R**					**11**
	DLS			DWS			DLS				**Y**	DWS			DLS	**12**
			DWS			DLS		DLS					DWS			**13**
		DWS			TLS					TLS				DWS		**14**
	TWS			DLS				TWS				DLS			TWS	**15**

DIAGRAM 13-1

Your rack: A D E G G I J

There are many excellent plays available on Diagram 13-1 using the given rack. In fact, there are three different places on the board where you can make plays worth 40 points or more. Can you find some of the 26-point-or-better spots? Answers on page 131.

Time limit: 20 minutes   Average Score: 1 correct   Good Score: 2 correct   Expert Score: 3 correct

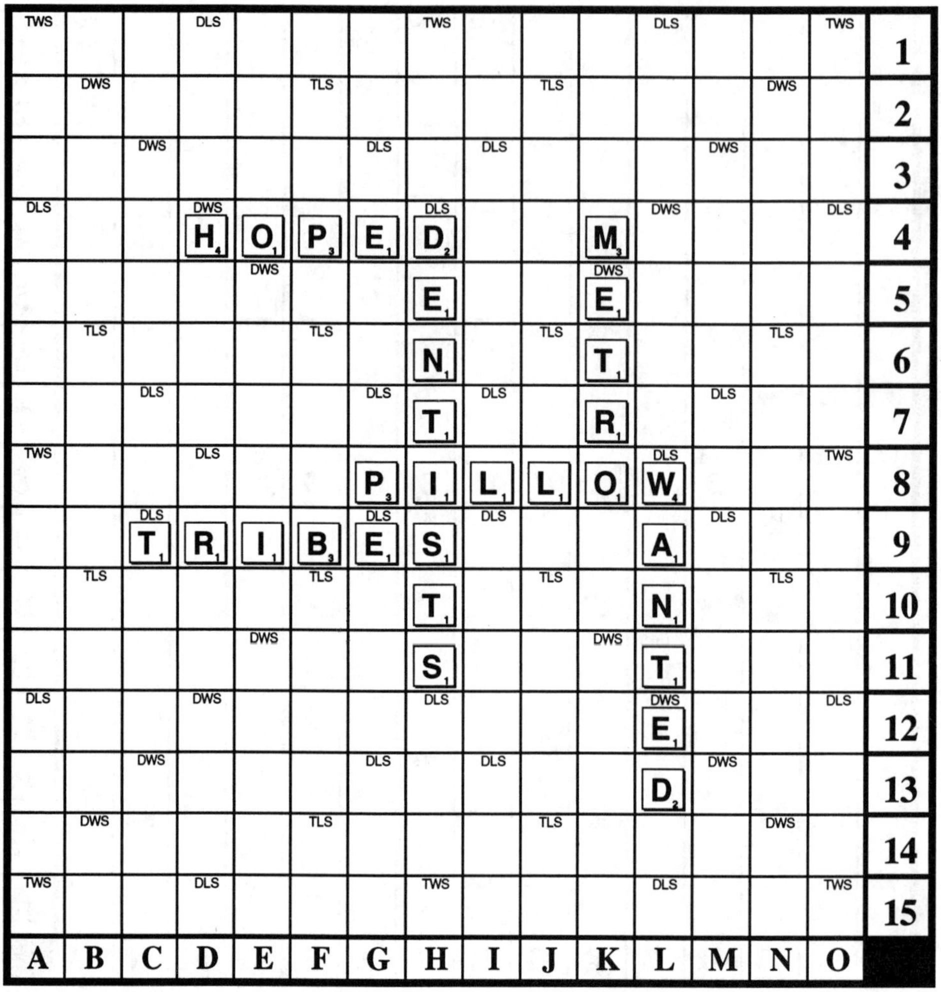

DIAGRAM 13-2

Your rack: A G I M O U X

Diagram 13-2 is open for many high-scoring X plays. As you explore, try to find several 50-plus point plays.

Time limit: 20 minutes   Average Score: 1 correct   Good Score: 2 correct   Expert Score: 3 correct

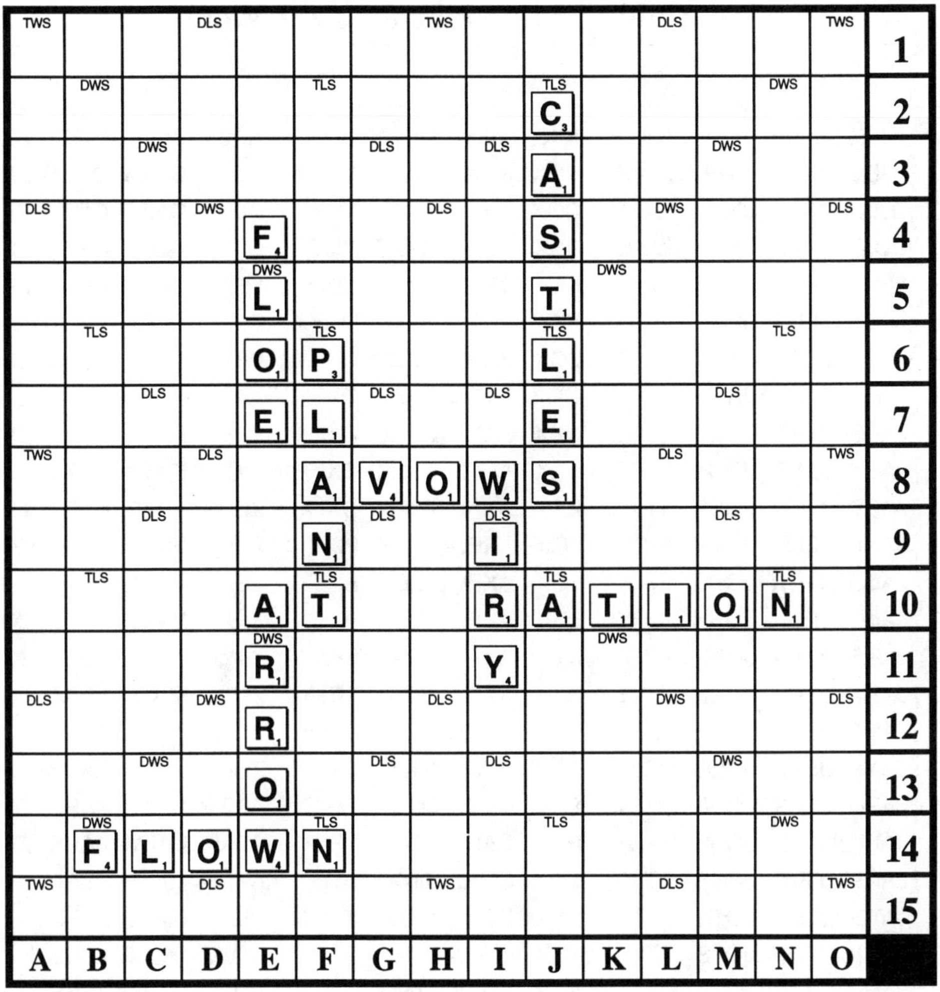

DIAGRAM 13-3

Your rack: E N O O T Y Z

Use Diagram 13-3 to find the four different hot spots that each allows you to make at least one play of 50-plus points.

Time limit: 20 minutes

Average Score: 1 correct   Good Score: 2 correct   Expert Score: 3 correct

It takes more than word knowledge to win SCRABBLE® games. After the first thirty or so tiles are on the board, it's often an advantage for either player to know how and where to play to prepare the board's open spaces for the latter stages of the game. In Chapter Fourteen we show you how to "open" or "close" the board and when to do it.

The Three- and Four-Letter J-X-Z Words

	J					X					Z		
HAJ	AJAR	JAWS	JILL	JOWS	AXE	SIX	DOXY	MIXT	ADZ	COZY	OOZY	ZEKS
JAB	AJEE	JAYS	JIMP	JOYS	BOX	SOX	EAUX	MOXA	AZO	CZAR	ORZO	ZERO
JAG	DJIN	JAZZ	JINK	JUBA	COX	TAX	EXAM	NEXT	BIZ	DAZE	OUZO	ZEST
JAM	DOJO	JEAN	JINN	JUBE	DEX	TUX	EXEC	NIXE	COZ	DOZE	OYEZ	ZETA
JAR	FUJI	JEED	JINS	JUDO	FAX	VEX	EXES	NIXY	FEZ	DOZY	PHIZ	ZIGS
JAW	HADJ	JEEP	JINX	JUGA	FIX	VOX	EXIT	ONYX	FIZ	FAZE	PREZ	ZILL
JAY	HAJI	JEER	JISM	JUGS	FOX	WAX	EXON	ORYX	WIZ	FIZZ	PUTZ	ZINC
JEE	HAJJ	JEES	JIVE	JUJU	GOX	XIS	EXPO	OXEN	ZAG	FOZY	QUIZ	ZING
JET	JABS	JEEZ	JOBS	JUKE	HEX	ZAX	FALX	OXES	ZAP	FRIZ	RAZE	ZIPS
JEU	JACK	JEFE	JOCK	JUMP	KEX	APEX	FAUX	OXID	ZAX	FUTZ	RAZZ	ZITI
JIB	JADE	JEHU	JOES	JUNK	LAX	AXAL	FIXT	OXIM	ZED	FUZE	RITZ	ZITS
JIG	JAGG	JELL	JOEY	JUPE	LEX	AXED	FLAX	PIXY	ZEE	FUZZ	SIZE	ZOEA
JIN	JAGS	JEON	JOGS	JURA	LOX	AXEL	FLEX	PREX	ZEK	GAZE	SIZY	ZOIC
JOB	JAIL	JERK	JOHN	JURY	LUX	AXES	FLUX	ROUX	ZIG	HAZE	SPAZ	ZONE
JOE	JAKE	JESS	JOIN	JUST	MIX	AXIL	FOXY	SEXT	ZIP	HAZY	TZAR	ZONK
JOG	JAMB	JEST	JOKE	JUTE	NIX	AXIS	HOAX	SEXY	ZIT	IZAR	WHIZ	ZOOM
JOT	JAMS	JETE	JOKY	JUTS	OXO	AXLE	IBEX	TAXA	ZOA	JAZZ	ZAGS	ZOON
JOW	JANE	JETS	JOLE	MOJO	OXY	AXON	ILEX	TAXI	ZOO	JEEZ	ZANY	ZOOS
JOY	JAPE	JEUX	JOLT	PUJA	PAX	BOXY	IXIA	TEXT	ADZE	LAZE	ZAPS	ZORI
JUG	JARL	JIAO	JOSH	RAJA	PIX	CALX	JEUX	VEXT	AZAN	LAZY	ZARF	ZYME
JUN	JARS	JIBB	JOSS	SOJA	POX	COAX	JINX	WAXY	AZON	MAZE	ZEAL	
JUS	JATO	JIBE	JOTA		PYX	COXA	LUXE	XYST	BIZE	MAZY	ZEBU	
JUT	JAUK	JIBS	JOTS		RAX	CRUX	LYNX		BOZO	MOZO	ZEDS	
RAJ	JAUP	JIFF	JOUK		REX	DEXY	MAXI		BUZZ	NAZI	ZEES	
TAJ	JAVA	JIGS	JOWL		SEX	DOUX	MINX		CHEZ	OOZE	ZEIN	

Answers to JXZ four-letter word quiz:
1. CHEZ; 2. ZYME; 3. JUBE, ZEBU; 4. ZITI; 5. JEFE; 6. JUTE; 7. CALX; 8. TAXA; 9. OXID; 10. RITZ; 11. JOTA, JATO; 12. DOXY, DOZY; 13. ZING; 14. OUZO; 15. JARL; 16. PIXY; 17. TZAR; 18. EXPO; 19. JOUK; 20. IXIA; 21. JOLE; 22. CZAR; 23. IZAR; 24. FUZE; 25. XYST; 26. AXEL, AXLE, LAZE; 27. AXON, AZON; 28. SIZY; 29. JUBA; 30. JEHU; 31. HADJ; 32. ZORI; 33. SOJA; 34. AXAL; 35. NIXY; 36. ORYX; 37. DJIN; 38. AJEE; 39. JAUP, PUJA; 40. JILL, ZILL; 41. ORZO; 42. NIXE, ZEIN; 43. JIAO; 44. PREX, PREZ; 45. JEST, JETS, SEXT, ZEST; 46. JOEY, OYEZ; 47. JIBE, IBEX, BIZE; 48. JANE, JEAN; 49. JEON, EXON, OXEN, ZONE; 50. JADE, AXED, ADZE, DAZE.

Answers to JXZ, Diagram 13-1: The four plays worth 36 points or better are: DJIN O1 36; JADING 7G 42; JAGGED (or JIGGED) 2F 43; and JADE 3L 50. Other high-scoring plays are: JAGGED E7 32; JAGGIER 3C 34, or F2 34; JIG 10J 27; JEAN O1 33; JAGG 2F 38; JAG 9C 26.

Diagram 13-2: The three 50-plus X-plays are MOXA or MAXI at 5C 53 points and AXIOM 8A 54. Other high-scoring plays are: MOXA L1 40, or L3 45, or M12 36; XU M9 36; AXIOM 5A 41, or L1 42, and GOX (or MIX) 5C 45 (47) or L3 39 (41). Advanced players may discover OXIME 5D 59.

Diagram 13-3: The four highest-scoring hot spots are: across row 15 beginning at 15F; down from D1–4; down from H11–15; across row 4H–L. The plays are: OOZY or OYEZ 15F 50 points; ZONE D1 56; ZESTY 4H 54; and OZONE H11 77. Other high-scoring plays include: COZEY 2J 38; OOZE 15F 41; OOZY H10 38; TROOZ 12D 48; SNOOZY 4J 44; ZONER 12A 48; ZONATE 10B 35; ZOO D2 34.

14

SPACE EXPLORATION: WHEN THE BOARD IS CLOSED OR OPEN

Look at the following two board positions:

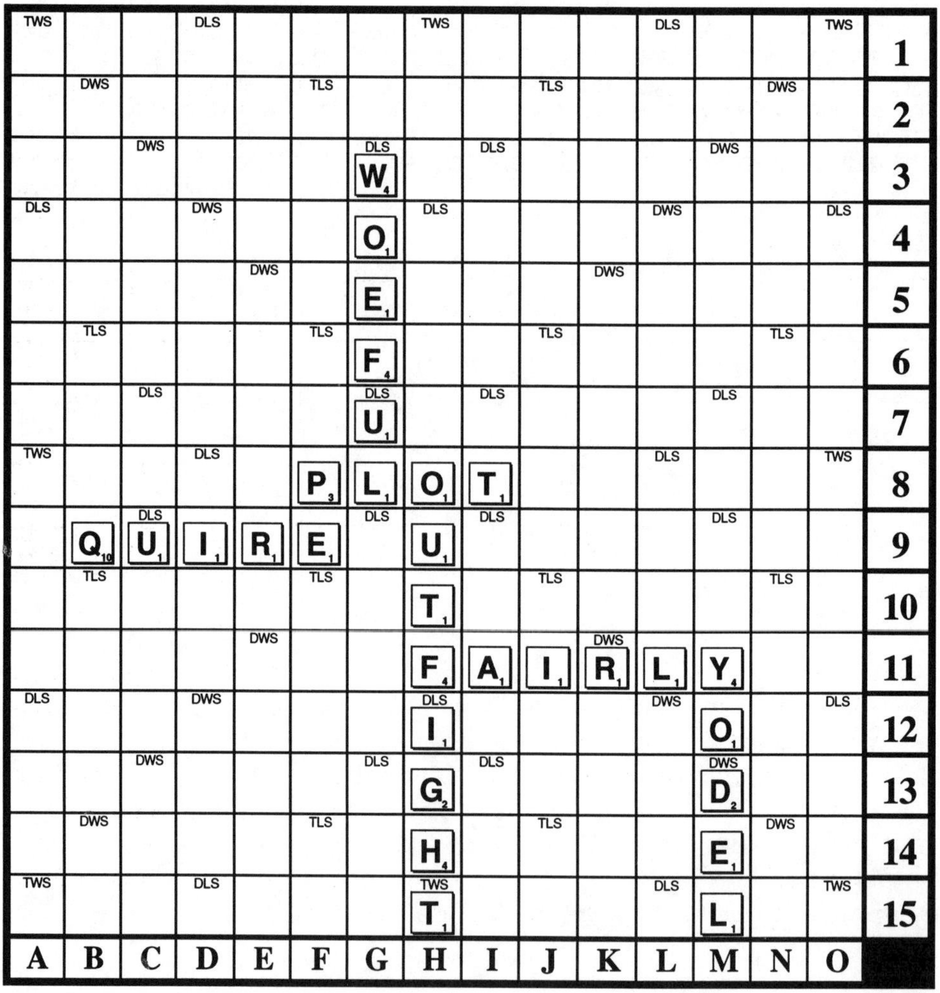

	A	B	C	D	E	F	G	H	I	J	K	L	M	N	O	
	TWS			DLS				TWS				DLS			TWS	**1**
		DWS				TLS				TLS				DWS		**2**
			DWS			DLS **W**		DLS				DWS				**3**
	DLS			DWS		**O**		DLS			DWS				DLS	**4**
					DWS	**E**				DWS						**5**
	TLS				TLS	**F**			TLS				TLS			**6**
			DLS			DLS **U**		DLS				DLS				**7**
	TWS			DLS		**P**	**L**	**O**	**T**			DLS			TWS	**8**
	Q	**U**	**I**	**R**	**E**	DLS **U**		DLS				DLS				**9**
	TLS				TLS	**T**			TLS				TLS			**10**
				DWS		**F**	**A**	**I**	**R**	DWS **L**	**Y**				**11**
	DLS			DWS		DLS **I**				DWS	**O**			DLS	**12**
			DWS			**G**		DLS			DWS **D**				**13**
		DWS				TLS **H**			TLS		DWS **E**				**14**
	TWS			DLS		TWS **T**				DLS	**L**			TWS	**15**

DIAGRAM 14-1

DIAGRAM 14-2

	A	B	C	D	E	F	G	H	I	J	K	L	M	N	O	
	TWS			DLS				TWS				DLS			TWS	1
		DWS				TLS				TLS				DWS		2
			DWS				DLS		DLS				DWS			3
	DLS			DWS				DLS				DWS			DLS	4
					DWS					DWS						5
		TLS				TLS				TLS				TLS		6
			DLS				T	O		DLS				DLS		7
	TWS			DLS	B	R	I	N	G				DLS		TWS	8
			DLS	R			Y		DLS			V	DLS			9
		TLS		U			X			V		E		TLS		10
				N				P		I	F	S				11
	DLS			T			A	W	E			T			DLS	12
			I	S	O	L	A	T	E	D			DWS			13
		DWS		C	A	C	H	E			TLS			DWS		14
	TWS			F	A	D	E	S				DLS			TWS	15

If the score is even, which board would you rather have to play on, Diagram 14-1 or Diagram 14-2? In this case there is no right or wrong answer. That's because without knowing your rack, your winning chances are the same with either position. But how you answer, or where your inclination lies, may give you an insight into your "SCRABBLE® game personality."

What are the significant differences between these two positions? The main difference is that Diagram 14-1 is very open. An "open" position has many opportunities for scoring points. For example:

1) With an S you can play SQUIRE and spell another word vertically on column A, earning a Triple Word Score—for example, DOGS A6 33 points.

2) You can play at H1–4—for example, PLOW H1 53.

3) If you have an IN combination, the G on 13H might help you form an ING bingo at 13A–H.

4) A high-point tile can play on 14J–N—for example, JIBED 14J 62.

5) You might find a double-double playing through the E at 5G.

6) You can play at 15L–O; for example, FLEX 15L 54.

With all these possibilities, both players may score many points as the game progresses.

Now consider Diagram 14-2. It is a very closed board on which there are very few scoring possibilities. Can you find any rows or columns open for earning large scores? If either player has an S, then column I allows for bingos ending in S, by forming BRINGS. There is one other possible bingo line: H1–8. An ING bingo would fit very nicely from H1–8 and open up rows 1–5. Otherwise, a word like TIME or TIMED starting at F7 might give someone as much as 26 or 28 points.

As we have said, your chances on either of these boards are about equal. Regardless of how "lucky" your tiles are, opening up the board or closing down existing hot spots will often determine the outcome of your games. While it's not in the scope of this book to fully explain every conceivable nuance of strategy, there are a few basic ideas that you should know.

One general principle is this: **When you are ahead you want to limit your opponent's chances to catch up,** so you want to **keep the board closed.** This usually forces your opponent to open the board. When s/he does, you hope to take advantage of those openings to increase your lead.

When you are behind you need to keep the board open to allow you to score enough to overtake your opponent. That means you will sometimes want or need to risk opening the board for your opponent.

When the score is close, with neither player ahead by more than 30 points, it's not always clear what to do. Many times you will simply disregard the concept of "openness" or "closedness" and just make your best play, taking into consideration only how much you score and how good your leave is.

How can you create the kind of board position that's advantageous for you? Let's look at two examples.

	A	B	C	D	E	F	G	H	I	J	K	L	M	N	O	
	TWS			DLS				TWS				DLS			TWS	**1**
		DWS				TLS				TLS				DWS		**2**
			DWS				DLS		**V**				DWS			**3**
	DLS			DWS			**F**	**E**	**R**	**R**	**Y**	DWS			DLS	**4**
					DWS	**Q**		**E**			DWS					**5**
		TLS				**U**		**R**		TLS				TLS		**6**
			DLS		**M**	**I**	DLS	**E**	DLS				DLS			**7**
	V			**B**	**L**	**A**	**Z**	**E**	**D**			DLS			TWS	**8**
	I		DLS		**R**		DLS		DLS				DLS			**9**
	A	**D**			**B**	TLS				**J**			**H**	TLS		**10**
		A		**C**	**L**	**I**	**P**	**P**	**E**	**D**	DWS		**U**			**11**
	E	**M**		DWS	**E**			**H**		**T**	**O**	**E**	**S**		DLS	**12**
	A		**W**				DLS	**O**	DLS				**K**			**13**
	S	**W**	**A**	**D**	**D**	**L**	**I**	**N**	**G**	TLS			DWS			**14**
	Y		**X**	DLS				**E**				DLS			TWS	**15**

DIAGRAM 14-3

Your Score: 220   Opponent's Score: 300
Your Rack: A E F I N S T

Using Diagram 14-3, what would you play with the above rack?

ANALYSIS: You're too far behind to win without playing a bingo. You have very good tiles. In fact, you have the bingo FAINEST, meaning "gladdest," but it doesn't play. Here are the bingo hot spots: 1) Through the R or Y on the K or L columns; 2) Down to or through B on the D column; 3) Across row 3 ending in IVE through the V at 3I (forming EF and ER as well); and

4) Down column N to the H and/or U in HUSK. Despite having four bingo spots, if your opponent plays through the R at 4K, two of those spots will be gone. And you're unlikely to be able to use the B at D8 unless you draw an L for an -ABLE or -IBLE word.

So, realistically, your best chance to bingo is on column N. Now suppose your opponent decides to play down the L column, ending his word in an E or A on L10 and forming EH or AH, neither of which takes an S. You'll only have the V or B to bingo through. That's not promising either!

Therefore, what you must do is create a new opening for yourself, while keeping most of your bingo-prone tiles. First off, which tiles should you consider playing? Ideally, you would play off just the F. By keeping SATINE you give yourself the best chance to bingo next turn. See Appendix Two for all the possible bingos using the six SATINE letters.

However, the problem is that you won't open any new bingo lines for yourself if you just play off the F (look at EF, 7I, or H8). The next best thing to do is play off the FI. There are several ways to do this. Do you see how one of them opens a dynamic bingo line? Look for the answer labeled Diagram 14-3 on page 141.

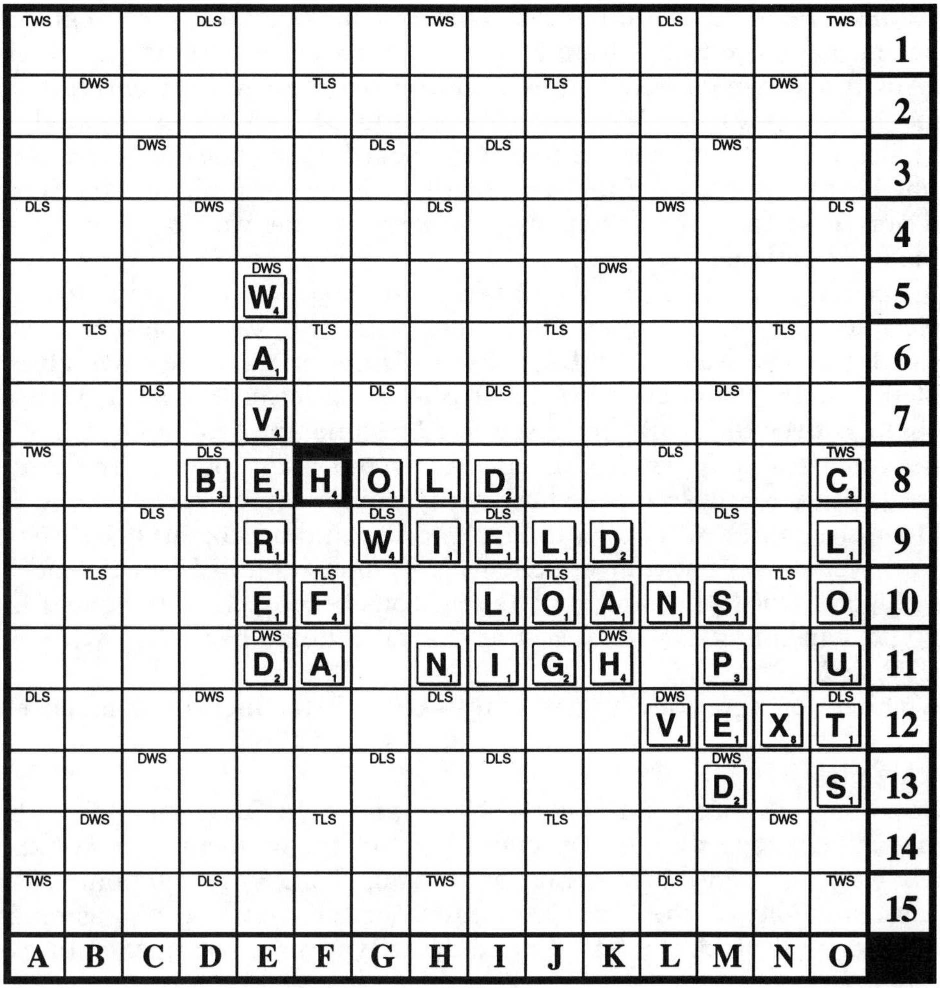

DIAGRAM 14-4

Your Rack: A B E G H I L
You are 70 points ahead playing on Diagram 14-4. What would you do?

ANALYSIS: This board is nearly closed down. There are two places for opening up the game. You can take a 100-point lead by playing NEIGH H11 30 points, and keeping ABL. Or you can take the TLS at 6F using BAGEL F2 25 or EH F5 31, or play on the DWS at D4 with BLAH D3 28, BAH D4 26, or even BELGA D1 27. Other plays don't score nearly enough to justify themselves.

Which of the choices do you like?

ANSWERS: Because you are ahead by so much, you don't want to give your opponent a chance to catch up by giving him a potentially large comeback play or bingo, which could happen if you open up several letters to play through. So, plays like NEIGH, BAGEL, and BELGA are eliminated; they are much too dangerous. Note that if the board were wide open, any of these might be the best play. But because there is so little chance for scoring, and you're so far ahead, you want to keep it that way by limiting your opponent's options.

Of the other choices, BLAH leaves an unbalanced rack with too many vowels and no scoring prospects for next turn. So, we are left with either EH or BAH. The leave after BAH (EGIL) is better than the leave after EH (ABGIL), mainly because the E is such a useful letter. However, we would choose EH over BAH only because the F2-F6 line, the best hot spot for your opponent after your BAH, will give away too many points. Try drawing several random racks and see how many points you can score along the F column after BAH! After EH, though the D column is open, it will tend to score fewer points for your opponent. Note that both FEH, PEH, and YEH are all good words, but are not so dangerous because your opponent is unlikely to win this game because s/he played a bingo beginning with either an F, P, or Y.

Whether you agree or disagree with BAH or EH, either one is an excellent choice. Of course, if you knew and found GALABIEH 6B 74 points, you would quickly play it.

Now imagine that you're *behind* by 70 points in Diagram 14-4 with the same rack. Disregarding the obscure bingo for the moment, you would definitely want to open the board up by playing NEIGH H11 30 points. That's because any play on the D or F column will either not be worth as much as NEIGH or will block the board unnecessarily. Unless you open it up you'll surely lose.

	A	B	C	D	E	F	G	H	I	J	K	L	M	N	O	
	TWS			DLS			TWS				DLS			TWS		**1**
		DWS	T		TLS			TLS					DWS			**2**
			A			DLS		DLS				DWS				**3**
DLS			J	A	G	G		DLS			DWS			DLS		**4**
					L					DWS R						**5**
	TLS				A		TLS				E			TLS		**6**
		DLS			Z		DLS M	O	DLS B		C		DLS			**7**
TWS			DLS B	E	L	O	W				O		DLS		TWS	**8**
	DLS					DLS T	E	DLS N	P	I	N	DLS S			**9**
	TLS				TLS			TLS A	L	O	O	TLS F			**10**
				DWS				DWS E							**11**
DLS			DWS			DLS		DWS D			DWS		DLS			**12**
			DWS		DLS		DLS				DWS				**13**
	DWS			TLS			TLS				DWS				**14**
TWS		DLS			TWS				DLS			TWS			**15**

DIAGRAM 14-5

Your Rack: A A C G K L N

You and your opponent are within 30 points of each other playing on Diagram 14-5. What do you do?

Suppose you are trying to decide between two plays: BLACK D8 26 points and FLACK N10 28. Which one do you prefer?

ANALYSIS: Either of these plays allows you a reasonably good leave: AGN. Since FLACK is worth 2 more points, one might argue that it is the better play. But look closely at what FLACK does to the board. If your opponent has an S, s/he could then play along the bottom of the board, earning a TWS that might make the difference in who wins the game.

While BLACK allows the opponent an S-hook, row 13 is not nearly so dangerous. That's because the DWS and DLS at 13C and 13G are relatively hard to use to make large scores, whereas after FLACK, all your opponent has to do to score more than 34 points is play a four-letter word with S as the third letter and the first letter being any tile worth more than 1 point. Also, it is much easier to end bingos with an S than it is to have the S in the first, second, third, or fourth position. Your opponent will bingo much more often after FLACK than after BLACK. You could wind up losing the game on this one play.

One more point: If you have an S on your rack instead of the N (AACGKLS), you might want to consider playing FLACK, because you have an immediate opportunity to score on row 15. However, how will you feel if your opponent takes the spot with his or her own S? What this means is that while some of the time you'll benefit from setting up your S, other times you'll get burned. Only your own experience—and knowing how many Ss and blanks are still out—can help you to learn what to do in situations like this.

Summary for Space Exploration:

Deciding whether to leave the board more or less open after your play is one of the most difficult decisions a player will encounter. Even the top experts think there is still a great deal to learn in this area. However, if you use the following guidelines you won't go far wrong:

1. When you are far ahead (70 or more points) you should generally close down the board as best you can, even at the expense of a few points. Wouldn't you be happy costing yourself 5 or 10 points if you keep your opponent from playing a bingo?

2. When you are 70 or more points behind, keep the board fairly open to bingos or high-scoring J, Q, X, or Z plays.

3. When you and your opponent are about even or are within 30 points of each other, always weigh these two factors: the openings you leave your opponent vs. your rack leave. When you have bingo-prone tiles, you may often decide to keep the board more open so you can play your bingos; when you have poor letters, you may want to keep the board more closed.

4. Always remember to use the above guidelines in the context of how your opponent plays. Against some opponents you might fare better by not making the theoretically "best" play. Again, only your own experience will help you make that determination.

Even when you've played your very best and taken a huge lead, your opponent may try to trick you with phoney words. Or, even if you are so far behind that you want to give up and start another game, you may be able to catch up and win with a phoney word. Does that seem unethical to you? Who plays phoneys and why? We'll give you the inside scoop about playing phoneys in Chapter Fifteen.

ANSWERS: CHAPTER 14

Diagram 14-3: Play FIB D6 8 points. This opens up the excellent C column (C1–C7) for any bingos ending in ES (forming EF and SI). Now there are two excellent bingo columns available for you. Your opponent won't be able to block them both. So, you will have a decent chance to catch up next turn.

15 IS IT A SOUTH AMERICAN SHRUB OR A PHONEY WORD?

In North American SCRABBLE® game Clubs and Tournaments, it is within the official rules to play phoney words. However, if your opponent challenges, the phoney comes off the board and you lose a turn. On the other hand, if your play is found acceptable, the challenger loses his or her turn. So there is a definite risk for the challenger.

In this chapter we'd like to discuss three major issues concerning phoneys.

1) Is it ethical to play phoneys?

Many players who have yet to play at NSA SCRABBLE® game Clubs and/or Tournaments think it is unethical to purposely play a nonword. Many of these same people play the game in part, to learn new words, and often enjoy conversing with their opponents about words during a game. If a word is played and they are unfamiliar with it, they might ask the player what the word means, fully expecting an accurate answer.

If this sounds like you or your friends, please know that you aren't alone! There are thousands of people who enjoy playing this way. We applaud this style and urge you to continue enjoying yourselves.

In fact, when children or young adults play the game, we recommend the dictionary as a tool. This way they are regularly encouraged to look up words they don't know. (However, we want to make it clear that we're not recommending that they browse through the dictionary looking for words to make a better play.) Later on, when their vocabulary is extensive enough, they might prefer to play with more "challenging" dictionary rules.

Organized competitive SCRABBLE game play in the U.S. and Canada is very different from the typical "living room" play. Players must not only learn which words are acceptable, but also be able to recognize phoney words. Here word meanings are less important, since no one has to define the words they play. Players consider it a valued skill to be able to challenge a nonword off the board. Because of this, the attitude of most club and tournament players is that any kind of play is acceptable as long as your opponent doesn't challenge.

Admittedly, this can lead to some higher scores, especially when an expert plays against a novice. Because the novice quickly becomes wary of challenging the expert after the first incorrect challenge, the expert can make virtually any play s/he wants, knowing the opponent won't dare question it. Because of the enormous advantage the expert has, most don't consider it ethical to play phoneys against novices. In order to even the match, many experts handicap themselves by allowing the novice free challenges. Regardless of your attitude toward playing phoneys, club and tournament players are happy being "challenged" in this way!

2) There are several situations during a game when you may benefit from playing a phoney word.

When You Have Little to Lose

Sometimes your game will seem hopelessly lost. For instance, suppose you're 150 points behind. At that point you notice that you can play an "almost" real word for a bingo or high score that might give you an outside chance to win. Since you have little to lose, you might as well try it! What's an "almost" real word? It's a phoney that looks and sounds as if it might or should be an acceptable word, but isn't, or you are *almost* sure isn't. For example, one expert tried the phoney PARODIZE against another expert in a crucial tournament game. Although it was eventually challenged and removed from the board, it cost the opponent eight minutes of precious time on his game clock just to ponder the acceptability of a "word" that could easily have meant: "to make a parody of."

In general, plausible phoneys are frequently "words" that have common prefixes or suffixes, so they seem familiar. RE, ER, or UN words are particular favorites. Would you be willing to challenge PARTERS, RETILES, or UNCARED? None of these are currently acceptable! RETILES is one of the more notorious phoneys, since most everyone can think of a sensible meaning and may even have used the "word" occasionally. We have seen many games won with this tactic that wouldn't have had a chance otherwise. Incidentally, PRATERS, LEISTER, STERILE, and DURANCE are the acceptable anagrams of those phoneys that won't be challenged off the board.

We suggest that you also be aware that the reverse tactic has also been used. Suppose your opponent lays down ZIGWURST? Would you know that it was a phoney? To us it seems so outrageously phoney that even an experienced player might reason: "That's so weird that my opponent must surely know it's good and is simply laying a trap for me!" While the opponent *is* laying a trap, s/he *knows* that it is a phoney.

We recall a tournament game between two experts in Reno, Nevada, where the bingo FOGHATS was played. In fact, it was an important play that helped win that game for the victor. The losing player knew he had seen the word before, but forgot that he had seen it on a special list of outrageous phoneys, instead of in the dictionary.

Several years later, another top expert was the victim of FOGHATS at the very same hotel in Reno. And he, too, recalled seeing the word in print. Of course, the original story had been talked about and published in the *SCRABBLE® News*, the official newsletter of the National SCRABBLE® Association. Over time, the details of the true events had been forgotten, but the word was remembered as being acceptable.

When You Want to Test Your Opponent

Suppose you are playing someone you've never played before. Does this person typically challenge words s/he doesn't know? You may have no idea. If you have the first turn, you might open the game with a phoney just to see what s/he does. If s/he doesn't challenge, this gives you valuable information about him or her. If s/he does challenge, what have you lost? Often, losing the first move is inconsequential.

Incidentally, you might want to open a game with a phoney because you know that your opponent *will* challenge. Here's why. We know a player who, in the 1993 World SCRABBLE® Championship, opened a game with the word GARROT. His rack included another T. He knew that GARROTTE is a good word. He was hoping that his opponent would challenge, remove his word, and then play an E in his first word, allowing him to play his eight-letter bingo next. Since there are 12 Es, that's not so farfetched.

Unfortunately for this expert, in the world championship the British-based Chambers English Dictionary is also used as a word source, and GARROT is listed in it. When the challenge came back *acceptable*, he was, ironically, somewhat disappointed. We should also add that because most of the contestants were playing with thousands of words they weren't necessarily familiar with, the rules were adjusted so that there was no penalty for an incorrect challenge.

When Your Opponent Has Just Lost a Challenge

You've just played MACRONS. Your opponent challenges and it is found acceptable! Now you've drawn letters that don't quite work together well, but you see a phoney that looks like a plausible word. Should you try it?

One of the best times to play a phoney is right after your opponent has just lost a challenge. After feeling the sting of one lost turn, s/he may not want to test the waters again just yet. We've seen this ploy used successfully hundreds of times!

When You Have a Variety of Good Plays

You have a blank and have found several playable bingos. Yet you see a phoney bingo that scores 15 more points than any of the other real words. Do you play it? Answer: Only if you think that your opponent will see your legitimate bingos. In that case s/he might assume that you wouldn't try a phoney when you have all those perfectly good words to play.

We don't advise using this strategy unless you are familiar with how your opponent usually thinks.

When You Score Few Points

You have an average rack and see no spectacular plays. However, you do see a phoney that looks plausibly like a real word. It scores 10 to 20 points and leaves you with a much better leave than any other play.

Often an opponent won't challenge a low-scoring play because s/he'll assume that the player probably has several acceptable low-scoring plays and wouldn't take a chance on losing a turn unless the phoney was worth something substantial. Once again, it pays to know your opponent's thinking habits and level of word knowledge before you try this.

When You Want the Game Decided on One Play

Let's say you have a moderate lead of 50 points. If you play a phoney bingo and raise that lead to 130 points at the halfway mark of the game, this can demoralize a less-than-expert opponent and make it extremely difficult for him or her to win. You may be able to coast to a victory. If you lose the challenge, what have you lost? You'll probably still have a lead after your opponent plays, though it may be a narrower one. But if your phoney uses a blank, you may be confident you'll play a bingo later and win anyway.

Playing the phoney simply puts enormous pressure on your opponent *right now.*

One well-known expert is known for occasionally playing phoneys against other experts in championship play. In one national championship he knowingly used a blank to play the phoney SALTANTS to take a 100-point lead in the crucial final game. He was fairly certain that his opponent would know the word SALTANT (which means "dancing and singing"), but not know that it is an adjective and does not take an S. In that situation, even if he had lost the turn, he would retain the blank and the lead, and so maintain good winning chances.

When You Want a Higher Point Spread

Tournaments are often won on "point spread." Point spread is the amount of points by which a game is won or lost. If you win 400 to 300, then your point spread for that game is +100 and your opponent's is −100. After each game your "total point spread" goes up or down, depending on whether you win or lose. Someone who has eight wins and a point spread of 609 points places higher than someone who finishes with eight wins and a point spread of 467. Therefore, when some players are fairly certain they will win a game and can afford to lose a turn, they may take a chance in playing a phoney in order to win by a larger margin!

When the Game Is Nearly Over

At the end of a game, one player may be stuck with a tile and not be able to play out. This frequently happens with the Q. At this point the opponent may continue taking turns until s/he plays all of his or her tiles on the board. If you see a phoney or a word you're not sure of, that scores well, why not try it? Losing a turn in this situation won't hurt at all. But be careful! If six consecutive turns score zero points, the game is over. That means that if your opponent passes three times in a row, and you play three consecutive challenged phoneys, the game is over.

3) When should you challenge a word you think is a phoney?

If you are certain a play is unacceptable, then it's usually right to challenge it. The only exception is when the phoney allows *you* to make a great play that you wouldn't have otherwise. Even then you should calculate exactly what advantage you gain from allowing the phoney. Here's an example:

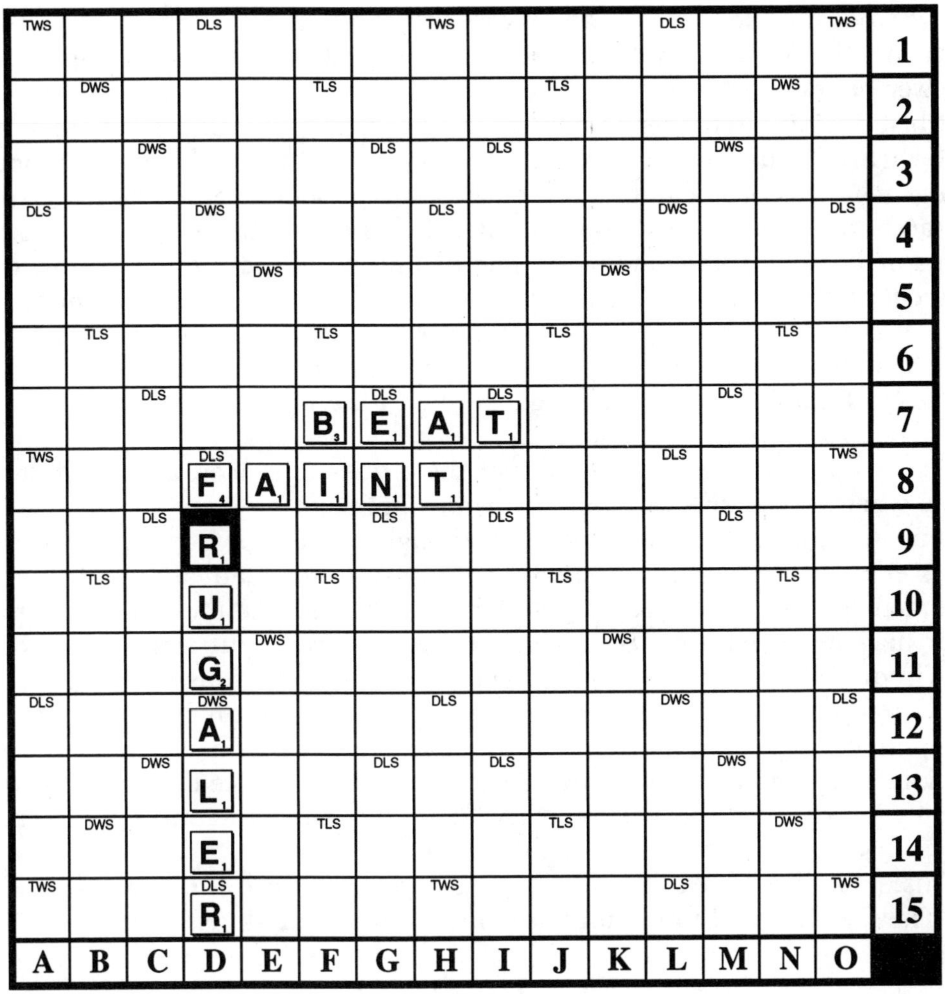

DIAGRAM 15-1

Your Score: 17   Opponent's Score: 24 (98??)
Your Rack: A A E E G S V   What do you do on Diagram 15-1?

Your opponent has just played FRUGALER. You immediately think, "No way!" but then you might ask, "If someone can be frugal, why can't they be frugaler?" Having looked at your ER list recently, you're fairly certain that it just didn't make it into the OSPD2. However, you notice that your opponent has other bingos, such as GRATEFUL or REGULAR, which would have been safer plays. Still undecided? Look at your rack and see what's possible for you after FRUGALER. Suddenly, you see a Triple-Triple through the R for 158 points! Clearly, you don't want to challenge your opponent's play, since it allows you to take a considerable lead. What is your big move? Answer below.

When deciding whether to challenge or not, keep in mind the following:

If you aren't sure that a word is a phoney, first consider who your opponent is and what his or her habits are concerning phoneys. Does s/he frequently or rarely play them? How sophisticated is his or her thinking? How strong is his or her word knowledge? Is s/he using any of the ploys mentioned in this chapter? If you don't challenge, do you have a reasonable chance to win? If not, then challenge. How often are your decisions correct when you have a strong desire to challenge? If your intuitions are sometimes wrong, be wary! Finally, *always* challenge the last play unless you are 100% sure it's good. You've nothing to lose.

The extent to which you can answer these questions accurately will determine whether you should challenge your opponent.

One final thought about phoneys: Although we've shown you many different scenarios about using phoneys purposely to your advantage, the most common reason people play a phoney *by far*, is because they think the play is or may be acceptable. So when you aren't sure about a word, consider how frequently your intuition has been accurate in previous situations. Take a few seconds to ask yourself if, deep in your heart, you believe the word is acceptable, or if you're indulging in wishful thinking. If you have a good track record, you might want to take the chance and make the play. If you're usually making up the words, then take extra time to consider alternate plays.

This ends Part II. We invite you to test yourself with the puzzles in Part III. They're designed to be fun while increasing your skills. Enjoy!

ANSWERS: CHAPTER 15

Diagram 15-1: AVERAGES 15A 158 points

PART THREE

PUZZLES:
Learning Can Be Fun!

In Part III we have assembled a wide variety of puzzles. Solving these puzzles will serve four functions:

1. It will be fun.
2. It will build vocabulary skills.
3. It will assess your word-finding abilities.
4. It will be more fun.

We've also suggested a time limit and an average, good, and expert score for most sets of ten puzzles so that you can gauge how well you're developing. We suggest you repeat any sets you find difficult. In this way you'll be able to measure your progress over time.

In Chapter Sixteen we have created four kinds of puzzles and assigned to each a level of difficulty based on a three-star scoring system. (The more stars, the greater the difficulty.) In Chapter Seventeen you will be challenged to find words over-the-board. These puzzles will better prepare you for your toughest opponent! Chapter Eighteen has some very tough puzzles. Check your schedule before beginning any of these.

16 HOOK WORDS, ANAGRAMS, FILL-INS, AND FRONT EXTENSIONS

In this chapter we're going to test your word-finding abilities in four different ways. We suggest that if you can't solve any given puzzle in a reasonable length of time, look up the answer. Then, at a much later time, try to solve it again. For most people it's surprisingly easy to forget the answers, so you'll be able to test how well you've improved over time. Our experience has shown that by practicing in this fashion you will be training yourself to find these same types of answers during actual game play. Time and again we've seen novices, who typically take five minutes or more to find a seven-letter word with their rack of letters, speed up their skills by a factor of ten in the course of a year or two.

HOOK WORDS

Find the one letter that can be added to the front of each of the following words to form a very common word. For each individual puzzle, a different letter may be needed. For instance, __ A G O N and __ A G M A take different first letters, a W and an M, and so on. We've deliberately presented many obscure, less common words so that, by association, you'll find it easier to remember both words. Our puzzle sections are designated with stars; the more stars, the harder the puzzles. The answers start on page 161.

Five-Letter Words*

Time limit per set: 20 minutes

Average Score: 6 correct   *Good Score:* 8 correct   *Expert Score:* 10 correct

SET A	SET B	SET C
1. __ HONG	1. __ PERM	1. __ NOME
2. __ AGON	2. __ HIDE	2. __ OMIT
3. __ IMID	3. __ PALS	3. __ HILI
4. __ ANTA	4. __ AGMA	4. __ HEIR
5. __ VIES	5. __ HOST	5. __ PICE
6. __ BACK	6. __ AGUE	6. __ LAID
7. __ VARY	7. __ IWIS	7. __ DEAL
8. __ FOUL	8. __ KING	8. __ RIAL
9. __ PRIG	9. __ PLAT	9. __ RIMY
10. __ EGER	10. __ LAKY	10. __ ROOD

SET D	SET E	SET F
1. __ EYED	1. __ LEFT	1. __ RUSK
2. __ FIRE	2. __ LIEN	2. __ MIRK
3. __ FOOT	3. __ GLOW	3. __ TROP
4. __ CONS	4. __ LOFT	4. __ VAIL
5. __ GAPE	5. __ LORY	5. __ BONY
6. __ LOBE	6. __ LUNT	6. __ VERY
7. __ GREE	7. __ HANT	7. __ APSE
8. __ MAGE	8. __ MELL	8. __ VOWS
9. __ HEAP	9. __ RUTH	9. __ WEAK
10. __ HEFT	10. __ NAVE	10. __ WELT

Six-Letter Words**

Time limit per set: 20 minutes

Average Score: 5 correct   *Good Score:* 7 correct   *Expert Score:* 9 correct

SET G

1. __ ACTOR
2. __ ADIOS
3. __ AGLET
4. __ AIVER
5. __ ALARY
6. __ ALDER
7. __ ALIGN
8. __ ALOES
9. __ AMBIT
10. __ AMENT

SET H

1. __ ANTIS
2. __ APTLY
3. __ ARBOR
4. __ ARGLE
5. __ ARGON
6. __ ARSON
7. __ ASCOT
8. __ ATMAN
9. __ AWFUL
10. __ BATED

SET I

1. __ BLEST
2. __ BORTS
3. __ CRAWL
4. __ CURVY
5. __ DRIFT
6. __ EAGER
7. __ EAGLE
8. __ EBBED
9. __ EDUCT
10. __ EGRET

SET J

1. __ ELECT
2. __ EMBER
3. __ ENURE
4. __ ERROR
5. __ EVERT
6. __ EXIST
7. __ GREED
8. __ HADED
9. __ HOOEY
10. __ HORAL

SET K

1. __ HOSEN
2. __ HUBBY
3. __ HYING
4. __ INDOW
5. __ IRADE
6. __ KETCH
7. __ LAPSE
8. __ LINGY
9. __ LIVES
10. __ LOGAN

SET L

1. __ LORAL
2. __ UNSET
3. __ RIGID
4. __ OSMIC
5. __ OVINE
6. __ SABLE
7. __ QUATE
8. __ RALLY
9. __ RAYON
10. __ RIFLE

Seven-Letter Words**

Time limit per set: 20 minutes

Average Score: 5 correct   *Good Score:* 7 correct   *Expert Score:* 9 correct

SET M	SET N	SET O	SET P
1. __ AGNATE	1. __ LEANLY	1. __ OXTAIL	1. __ RIDENT
2. __ ANTRUM	2. __ LIABLE	2. __ PENDED	2. __ ROUBLE
3. __ ARMFUL	3. __ LISTEN	3. __ RECKED	3. __ RUDELY
4. __ ARRANT	4. __ LOWERY	4. __ REPAID	4. __ RUMPLE
5. __ AUDING	5. __ LUMPEN	5. __ RACKET	5. __ SCENDS
6. __ ENFOLD	6. __ MARTEN	6. __ RATIFY	6. __ SPOUSE
7. __ ETHANE	7. __ MONGST	7. __ PRAISE	7. __ LAYOFF
8. __ GAINST	8. __ NEATEN	8. __ REASON	8. __ THEISM
9. __ STOUND	9. __ OFTEST	9. __ REFACE	9. __ OOLOGY
10. __ LATTEN	10. __ VENUES	10. __ PREACH	10. __ VERBID

Anagrams

Each of the following less common words has exactly one very common word as an anagram. For example, the anagram of CHAY is ACHY. Your task is to find the common words. After one or more trial runs through each set of puzzles, you may learn to go through this list fairly quickly. You then might want to test your recall of these obscure words by looking at the common words on the answer page and trying to find their anagrams on this page. Answers start on page 162.

Four-Letter Anagrams*

Time limit per set: 20 minutes
Average Score: 6 correct   *Good Score:* 8 correct   *Expert Score:* 10 correct

SET A	SET B	SET C	SET D	SET E
1. CHAY	1. ORAD	1. LATH	1. AWRY	1. OYER
2. POLY	2. EGAL	2. HILA	2. DOBY	2. NEIF
3. SIMP	3. KOTO	3. PIAL	3. BENE	3. FROE
4. BLAW	4. EPHA	4. IMAM	4. BREE	4. KEPI
5. BAHT	5. WONK	5. VINA	5. BONK	5. HYTE
6. ALEC	6. LAZE	6. MOLA	6. CEIL	6. METH
7. CAPH	7. FIAR	7. PALY	7. POCO	7. PLIE
8. CAKY	8. AGIN	8. MYNA	8. EDDY	8. LWEI
9. MARC	9. GAOL	9. PRAM	9. DELF	9. NEUK
10. YALD	10. HANT	10. NONA	10. OHED	10. FILO

Five-Letter Anagrams**

Time limit per set: 20 minutes

Average Score: 5 correct   *Good Score:* 7 correct   *Expert Score:* 9 correct

SET F	SET G	SET H	SET I
1. AAHED	1. MACLE	1. LAMED	1. NAEVI
2. DAMAR	2. ECLAT	2. DRAVE	2. ANOLE
3. MALAR	3. COMAE	3. HYDRA	3. UVEAL
4. BALDY	4. GAMIC	4. VIAND	4. YAMEN
5. RABID	5. MOCHA	5. AROID	5. TRAVE
6. TUBAE	6. NATCH	6. PAVID	6. TAWER
7. BIALI	7. ORACH	7. MONAD	7. IMAGO
8. CAGER	8. MALIC	8. EGRET	8. TONGA
9. CHELA	9. TAROC	9. ENATE	9. GOWAN
10. CHARE	10. MUSCA	10. FLEAM	10. THRAW

SET J	SET K	SET L
1. LARUM	1. LICHI	1. GREGO
2. BEDEL	2. ONTIC	2. GENOM
3. BERME	3. RUNIC	3. MOHUR
4. BOSUN	4. CUTIN	4. EPHOR
5. LUDIC	5. MONDE	5. THROE
6. SODIC	6. FONDU	6. VOILE
7. PUDIC	7. IMIDO	7. OWLET
8. TEUCH	8. REIFY	8. SLYPE
9. CIVET	9. GOFER	9. SULFO
10. VOCES	10. FLYTE	10. LOUGH

Seven-Letter Anagrams***

Time limit per set: 20 minutes

Average Score: 3 correct   *Good Score:* 5 correct   *Expert Score:* 8 correct

In sets M–O, the common-word anagrams all have either common beginnings or common endings (see page 74 for the list). We strongly recommend using letter tiles on a rack to solve these puzzles. Doing this will better simulate game play. An alternate method is to use pencil and paper and record different letter arrangements while trying to find the anagrams.

SET M	SET N	SET O	SET P
1. BISNAGA	1. AVODIRE	1. NILGHAI	1. USURPER
2. CATALOS	2. OVERSAD	2. NILGHAU	2. ANTISAG
3. VEDALIA	3. TEREFAH	3. SAINTLY	3. SPATHAL
4. DRAYAGE	4. HALTERE	4. SAVIOUR	4. CARIBES
5. ANAPEST	5. FINAGLE	5. BIOGENY	5. ABRIDGE
6. DOGBANE	6. REFUTAL	6. TUBULIN	6. BRAILLE
7. AMBONES	7. RIVAGES	7. RESTYLE	7. REBOANT
8. ECHIDNA	8. MUTAGEN	8. MITOGEN	8. HARICOT
9. CUMARIN	9. NEGATON	9. WETTISH	9. FAIENCE
10. OCTANOL	10. PREWRAP	10. NIVEOUS	10. GYRATED

SET Q	SET R	SET S	SET T
1. PAROLED	1. STYLATE	1. NOCTUID	1. DINKEYS
2. PANDITS	2. SURNAME	2. THICKEN	2. DUMMIES
3. DALTONS	3. FUNFAIR	3. POLEMIC	3. DENSITY
4. MADRONO	4. OOMPAHS	4. EXOTICS	4. VIROIDS
5. REAVING	5. OPUNTIA	5. COLONES	5. PERLITE
6. ALLONGE	6. ISSUANT	6. MONOECY	6. VESPINE
7. IMPASTE	7. BUNDIST	7. EMERSED	7. QUERIER
8. LATHERY	8. TURBINE	8. PREDIVE	8. PROETTE
9. SENHORA	9. RAILBUS	9. PUNGLED	9. FLEMISH
10. APLENTY	10. NUCLIDE	10. WOODHEN	10. THEGNLY

Fill-ins

Simply seeing the consonants in their correct position in a word can lead to finding the word. Using only vowels (and no Ys), fill in the blanks to form common words. Answers start on page 163.

Time limit per set: 30 minutes

Average Score: 5 correct   *Good Score:* 7 correct   *Expert Score:* 9 correct

SET A**

1. B__SC__ __T
2. __LM__N__C
3. R__ __DW__Y
4. H__ __RS__Y
5. V__N__LL__
6. __N__T__MY
7. T__BL__ __D
8. C__R__F__L
9. C__H__ __TS
10. M__S__C__L

SET B**

1. CR__N__ __M
2. M__ __LB__X
3. S__ __S__CK
4. PL__G__ __D
5. R__T__ND__
6. __ST__ __ND
7. __NF__D__L
8. P__ __NF__L
9. N__M__R__L
10. F__RT__L__

Time limit per set: 30 minutes

Average Score: 3 correct   *Good Score:* 5 correct   *Expert Score:* 7 correct

SET C***

1. __MN__S__ __
2. C__ __R__G__
3. S__ __W__ __D
4. __RD__ __ __S
5. T__ __T__M__
6. P__R__L__ __
7. B__S__ __G__
8. T__P__ __C__
9. __ __TM__ __L
10. G__N__ __N__

SET D***

1. R__R__ __T__
2. F__ __NC__ __
3. L__M__ __D__
4. T__ __N__ __L
5. __N__W__R__
6. __SC__P__ __
7. M__T__N__ __
8. N__ __V__T__
9. F__T__G__ __
10. B__C__ __S__

Front Extensions

Sometimes you'll have an opportunity to extend from the front of a word already on the game board. This is particularly true when the opening play is a five-letter word starting on Double Letter Score square 8D or H4. You can then extend that opening play to a Triple Word Score square, either at 8A or H1. Below we show you what your rack is and what has already been played. Add three letters of the given rack to the front of the five-letter word to form a common eight-letter word. Answers begin on page 163.

Time limit per set: 30 minutes

Average Score: 4 correct   *Good Score:* 6 correct   *Expert Score:* 8 correct

SET A**

RACK	WORD
1. ACEGMNR	___ ___ ___ ACING
2. EGILOPR	___ ___ ___ AMBLE
3. ACMORUV	___ ___ ___ AMENT
4. EILNTUV	___ ___ ___ AMINS
5. EGHMNOR	___ ___ ___ ANTIC
6. CDEILNW	___ ___ ___ ANGER
7. AEGIORT	___ ___ ___ BORNE
8. CEFILNP	___ ___ ___ CITED
9. ABELMRU	___ ___ ___ DOWNS
10. ACGINPT	___ ___ ___ EATER

SET B**

RACK	WORD
1. ADGLMOU	___ ___ ___ FIGHT
2. ACDILRT	___ ___ ___ FULLY
3. DEGILMR	___ ___ ___ HEADS
4. GIMOPST	___ ___ ___ HOLES
5. ABCDLMP	___ ___ ___ HOUSE
6. AHILOTW	___ ___ ___ LIGHT
7. ACDELMT	___ ___ ___ ORATE
8. CEHNPRV	___ ___ ___ OVATE
9. ABLNORW	___ ___ ___ RAGES
10. CEFIOPR	___ ___ ___ RIDGE

SET C**

RACK	WORD
1. ABEGINU	___ ___ ___ ROWTH
2. EHLMPRY	___ ___ ___ SERVE
3. AEFGLMS	___ ___ ___ TIFFS
4. BENPRTU	___ ___ ___ TONED
5. AELPRUV	___ ___ ___ TICAL
6. CDIMPSU	___ ___ ___ TINCT
7. ABFLMOP	___ ___ ___ TONIC
8. EKLMOPR	___ ___ ___ TALLY
9. AEHLMNR	___ ___ ___ TORIC
10. CEIKLNT	___ ___ ___ WELLS

For the following five sets, there is only one set of three letters that will extend the given word from the front to form a common word.

Time limit per set: 30 minutes

Average Score: 4 correct   *Good Score:* 6 correct   *Expert Score:* 8 correct

SET D***

1. _ _ _ ALATE
2. _ _ _ ALFAS
3. _ _ _ AMIDS
4. _ _ _ AMITY
5. _ _ _ ARGOT
6. _ _ _ AWFUL
7. _ _ _ BARBS
8. _ _ _ BATHE
9. _ _ _ BRUSH
10. _ _ _ CHASE

SET E***

1. _ _ _ CHILD
2. _ _ _ COAST
3. _ _ _ COUGH
4. _ _ _ CUTER
5. _ _ _ DRAIL
6. _ _ _ DUSTS
7. _ _ _ EMBER
8. _ _ _ EVERY
9. _ _ _ GLARY
10. _ _ _ GRATE

SET F***

1. _ _ _ GULAR
2. _ _ _ HANDS
3. _ _ _ HILLS
4. _ _ _ HOMED
5. _ _ _ HOVER
6. _ _ _ IODIC
7. _ _ _ KLONG
8. _ _ _ KNIFE
9. _ _ _ LIFTS
10. _ _ _ LOUGH

SET G***

1. _ _ _ LUTED
2. _ _ _ MOILS
3. _ _ _ NEVER
4. _ _ _ NIVAL
5. _ _ _ OLEUM
6. _ _ _ OVALS
7. _ _ _ PARDY
8. _ _ _ PLASH
9. _ _ _ RATOS
10. _ _ _ REDLY

SET H***

1. _ _ _ NEVER
2. _ _ _ ROILS
3. _ _ _ ROUGH
4. _ _ _ PLUGS
5. _ _ _ SHALL
6. _ _ _ SOLED
7. _ _ _ TEMPT
8. _ _ _ VERBS
9. _ _ _ WHERE
10. _ _ _ TROYS

HOOK WORDS: FIVE-LETTER WORDS

SET A	SET B	SET C	SET D	SET E	SET F
1. THONG	1. SPERM	1. GNOME	1. KEYED	1. CLEFT	1. BRUSK
2. WAGON	2. CHIDE	2. VOMIT	2. AFIRE	2. ALIEN	2. SMIRK
3. TIMID	3. OPALS	3. CHILI	3. AFOOT	3. AGLOW	3. STROP
4. MANTA	4. MAGMA	4. THEIR	4. ICONS	4. ALOFT	4. AVAIL
5. IVIES	5. GHOST	5. SPICE	5. AGAPE	5. GLORY	5. EBONY
6. ABACK	6. VAGUE	6. PLAID	6. GLOBE	6. BLUNT	6. EVERY
7. OVARY	7. KIWIS	7. IDEAL	7. AGREE	7. CHANT	7. LAPSE
8. AFOUL	8. EKING	8. TRIAL	8. IMAGE	8. SMELL	8. AVOWS
9. SPRIG	9. SPLAT	9. GRIMY	9. CHEAP	9. TRUTH	9. TWEAK
10. LEGER	10. FLAKY	10. BROOD	10. THEFT	10. KNAVE	10. DWELT

HOOK WORDS: SIX-LETTER WORDS

SET G	SET H	SET I	SET J	SET K	SET L
1. FACTOR	1. MANTIS	1. ABLEST	1. SELECT	1. CHOSEN	1. FLORAL
2. RADIOS	2. RAPTLY	2. ABORTS	2. MEMBER	2. CHUBBY	2. SUNSET
3. EAGLET	3. HARBOR	3. SCRAWL	3. TENURE	3. SHYING	3. FRIGID
4. WAIVER	4. GARGLE	4. SCURVY	4. TERROR	4. WINDOW	4. COSMIC
5. SALARY	5. JARGON	5. ADRIFT	5. REVERT	5. TIRADE	5. BOVINE
6. BALDER	6. PARSON	6. MEAGER	6. SEXIST	6. SKETCH	6. USABLE
7. MALIGN	7. MASCOT	7. BEAGLE	7. AGREED	7. ELAPSE	7. EQUATE
8. HALOES	8. BATMAN	8. WEBBED	8. SHADED	8. CLINGY	8. ORALLY
9. GAMBIT	9. LAWFUL	9. DEDUCT	9. PHOOEY	9. OLIVES	9. CRAYON
10. LAMENT	10. ABATED	10. REGRET	10. CHORAL	10. SLOGAN	10. TRIFLE

HOOK WORDS: SEVEN-LETTER WORDS

SET M	SET N	SET O	SET P
1. MAGNATE	1. CLEANLY	1. FOXTAIL	1. TRIDENT
2. TANTRUM	2. PLIABLE	2. UPENDED	2. TROUBLE
3. HARMFUL	3. GLISTEN	3. WRECKED	3. CRUDELY
4. WARRANT	4. FLOWERY	4. PREPAID	4. CRUMPLE
5. LAUDING	5. PLUMPEN	5. BRACKET	5. ASCENDS
6. TENFOLD	6. SMARTEN	6. GRATIFY	6. ESPOUSE
7. METHANE	7. AMONGST	7. UPRAISE	7. PLAYOFF
8. AGAINST	8. UNEATEN	8. TREASON	8. ATHEISM
9. ASTOUND	9. SOFTEST	9. PREFACE	9. ZOOLOGY
10. FLATTEN	10. AVENUES	10. UPREACH	10. OVERBID

ANAGRAMS: FOUR-LETTER WORDS

SET A	SET B	SET C	SET D	SET E
1. ACHY	1. ROAD	1. HALT	1. WARY	1. YORE
2. PLOY	2. GALE	2. HAIL	2. BODY	2. FINE
3. IMPS	3. TOOK	3. PAIL	3. BEEN	3. FORE
4. BAWL	4. HEAP	4. MAIM	4. BEER	4. PIKE
5. BATH	5. KNOW	5. VAIN	5. KNOB	5. THEY
6. LACE	6. ZEAL	6. LOAM	6. LICE	6. THEM
7. CHAP	7. FAIR	7. PLAY	7. COOP	7. PILE
8. YACK	8. GAIN	8. MANY	8. DYED	8. WILE
9. CRAM	9. GOAL	9. RAMP	9. FLED	9. NUKE
10. LADY	10. THAN	10. ANON	10. HOED	10. FOIL

ANAGRAMS: FIVE-LETTER WORDS

SET F	SET G	SET H	SET I
1. AHEAD	1. CAMEL	1. MEDAL	1. NAIVE
2. DRAMA	2. CLEAT	2. RAVED	2. ALONE
3. ALARM	3. CAMEO	3. HARDY	3. VALUE
4. BADLY	4. MAGIC	4. DIVAN	4. MEANY
5. BRAID	5. MACHO	5. RADIO	5. AVERT
6. BEAUT	6. CHANT	6. VAPID	6. WATER
7. ALIBI	7. ROACH	7. NOMAD	7. AMIGO
8. GRACE	8. CLAIM	8. GREET	8. TANGO
9. LEACH	9. ACTOR	9. EATEN	9. WAGON
10. REACH	10. SUMAC	10. FLAME	10. WRATH

SET J	SET K	SET L
1. MURAL	1. CHILI	1. GORGE
2. BLEED	2. TONIC	2. GNOME
3. EMBER	3. INCUR	3. HUMOR
4. BONUS	4. TUNIC	4. HOPER
5. LUCID	5. DEMON	5. OTHER
6. DISCO	6. FOUND	6. OLIVE
7. CUPID	7. IDIOM	7. TOWEL
8. CHUTE	8. FIERY	8. YELPS
9. EVICT	9. FORGE	9. FOULS
10. COVES	10. LEFTY	10. GHOUL

ANAGRAMS: SEVEN-LETTER WORDS

SET M	SET N	SET O	SET P
1. ABASING	1. AVOIDER	1. HAILING	1. PURSUER
2. COASTAL	2. SAVORED	2. HAULING	2. AGAINST
3. AVAILED	3. FEATHER	3. NASTILY	3. ASPHALT
4. YARDAGE	4. LEATHER	4. VARIOUS	4. ASCRIBE
5. PEASANT	5. LEAFING	5. OBEYING	5. BRIGADE
6. BONDAGE	6. TEARFUL	6. UNBUILT	6. LIBERAL
7. BEMOANS	7. GRAVIES	7. TERSELY	7. BARONET
8. CHAINED	8. AUGMENT	8. EMOTING	8. CHARIOT
9. CRANIUM	9. TONNAGE	9. WHITEST	9. FIANCEE
10. COOLANT	10. WRAPPER	10. ENVIOUS	10. TRAGEDY

SET Q	SET R	SET S	SET T
1. LEOPARD	1. STATELY	1. CONDUIT	1. KIDNEYS
2. SANDPIT	2. MANURES	2. KITCHEN	2. MEDIUMS
3. SANDLOT	3. RUFFIAN	3. COMPILE	3. DESTINY
4. DOORMAN	4. SHAMPOO	4. COEXIST	4. DIVISOR
5. VINEGAR	5. UTOPIAN	5. CONSOLE	5. REPTILE
6. GALLEON	6. SUSTAIN	6. ECONOMY	6. PENSIVE
7. PASTIME	7. DUSTBIN	7. REDEEMS	7. REQUIRE
8. EARTHLY	8. TRIBUNE	8. DEPRIVE	8. TREETOP
9. HOARSEN	9. BURIALS	9. PLUNGED	9. HIMSELF
10. PENALTY	10. INCLUDE	10. HOEDOWN	10. LENGTHY

FILL-INS

SET A	SET B	SET C	SET D
1. BISCUIT	1. CRANIUM	1. AMNESIA	1. REROUTE
2. ALMANAC	2. MAILBOX	2. COURAGE	2. FIANCEE
3. ROADWAY	3. SEASICK	3. SEAWEED	3. LIMEADE
4. HEARSAY	4. PLAGUED	4. ARDUOUS	4. TOENAIL
5. VANILLA	5. ROTUNDA	5. TEATIME	5. UNAWARE
6. ANATOMY	6. ASTOUND	6. PAROLEE	6. ESCAPEE
7. TABLOID	7. INFIDEL	7. BESIEGE	7. MATINEE
8. CAREFUL	8. PAINFUL	8. TAPIOCA	8. NAIVETE
9. CAHOOTS	9. NUMERAL	9. OATMEAL	9. FATIGUE
10. MUSICAL	10. FERTILE	10. GENUINE	10. BECAUSE

FRONT EXTENSIONS

SET A	SET B	SET C	SET D
1. MENACING	1. DOGFIGHT	1. INGROWTH	1. ESCALATE
2. PREAMBLE	2. ARTFULLY	2. PRESERVE	2. ALFALFAS
3. ARMAMENT	3. REDHEADS	3. MASTIFFS	3. PYRAMIDS
4. VITAMINS	4. POTHOLES	4. BUTTONED	4. CALAMITY
5. ROMANTIC	5. MADHOUSE	5. VERTICAL	5. ESCARGOT
6. ENDANGER	6. TWILIGHT	6. DISTINCT	6. UNLAWFUL
7. AIRBORNE	7. DECORATE	7. PLATONIC	7. RHUBARBS
8. ELICITED	8. RENOVATE	8. MORTALLY	8. SUNBATHE
9. RUBDOWNS	9. BARRAGES	9. RHETORIC	9. AIRBRUSH
10. ANTEATER	10. PORRIDGE	10. INKWELLS	10. PURCHASE

SET E	SET F	SET G	SET H
1. GODCHILD	1. SINGULAR	1. POLLUTED	1. WHENEVER
2. SEACOAST	2. COWHANDS	2. TURMOILS	2. EMBROILS
3. HICCOUGH	3. ANTHILLS	3. WHENEVER	3. THOROUGH
4. EXECUTER	4. FATHOMED	4. CARNIVAL	4. EARPLUGS
5. HANDRAIL	5. PUSHOVER	5. LINOLEUM	5. MARSHALL
6. SAWDUSTS	6. PERIODIC	6. REMOVALS	6. CONSOLED
7. REMEMBER	7. WEEKLONG	7. JEOPARDY	7. CONTEMPT
8. THIEVERY	8. PENKNIFE	8. WHIPLASH	8. PROVERBS
9. BURGLARY	9. AIRLIFTS	9. VIBRATOS	9. ANYWHERE
10. EMIGRATE	10. FURLOUGH	10. SACREDLY	10. DESTROYS

17 DIAGRAMS: FINDING PLAYS OVER-THE-BOARD

PLACE THE WORD

Using the following four diagrams, locate where on the board the given word will score the most points. You may sometimes use tiles already on the board to spell the given word. For example, in Diagram 17-1, LEONE will require all five letters beginning at 14C but only four at L2 through the E at L3; however, LEONE will earn more points at a third spot. As a hint, we show you how many points the word can score. You should refer to the list of two-letter words on pages 23–24 to verify any potential parallel plays.

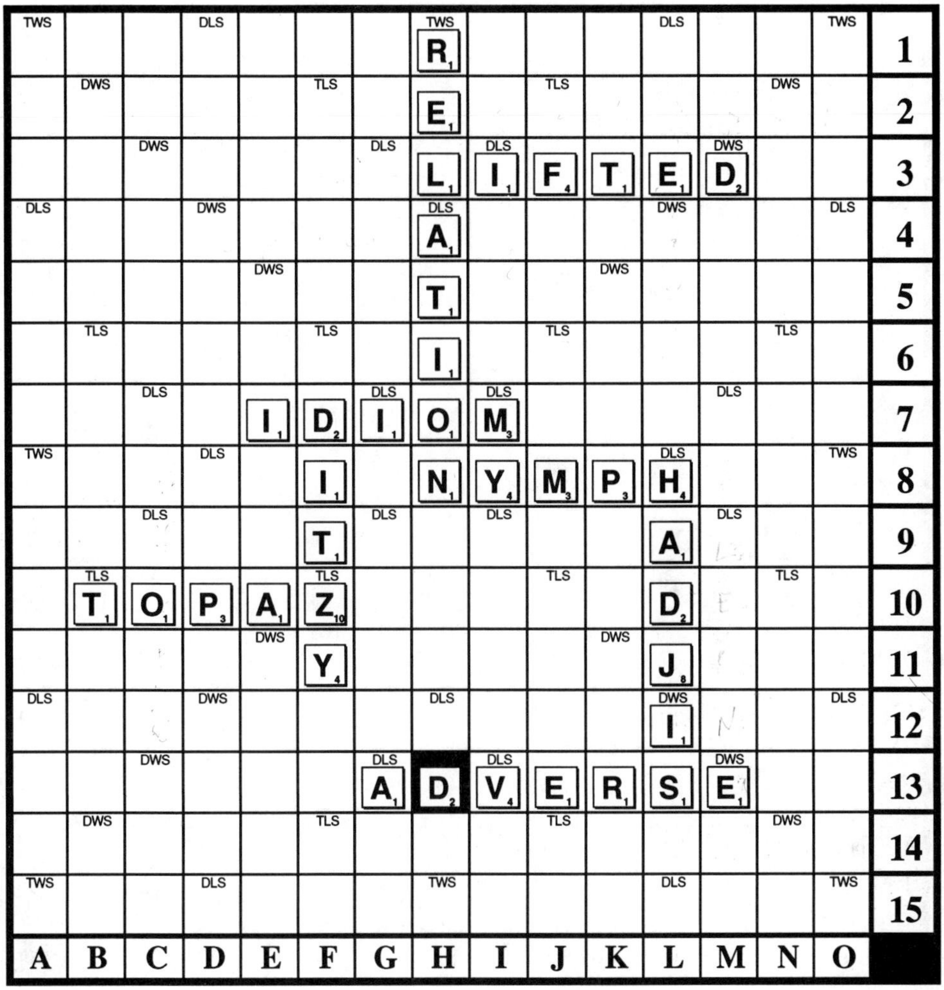

DIAGRAM 17-1

Where on Diagram 17-1 can the following words be played for the most points? Answers on page 185.

Time Limit: 25 minutes

Average Score: 2 correct   Good Score: 3 correct   Expert Score: 4 correct

1. L E O N E   23 _____
2. W A P I T I   38 _____
3. O I D I A   31 _____
4. V O D K A   36 _____

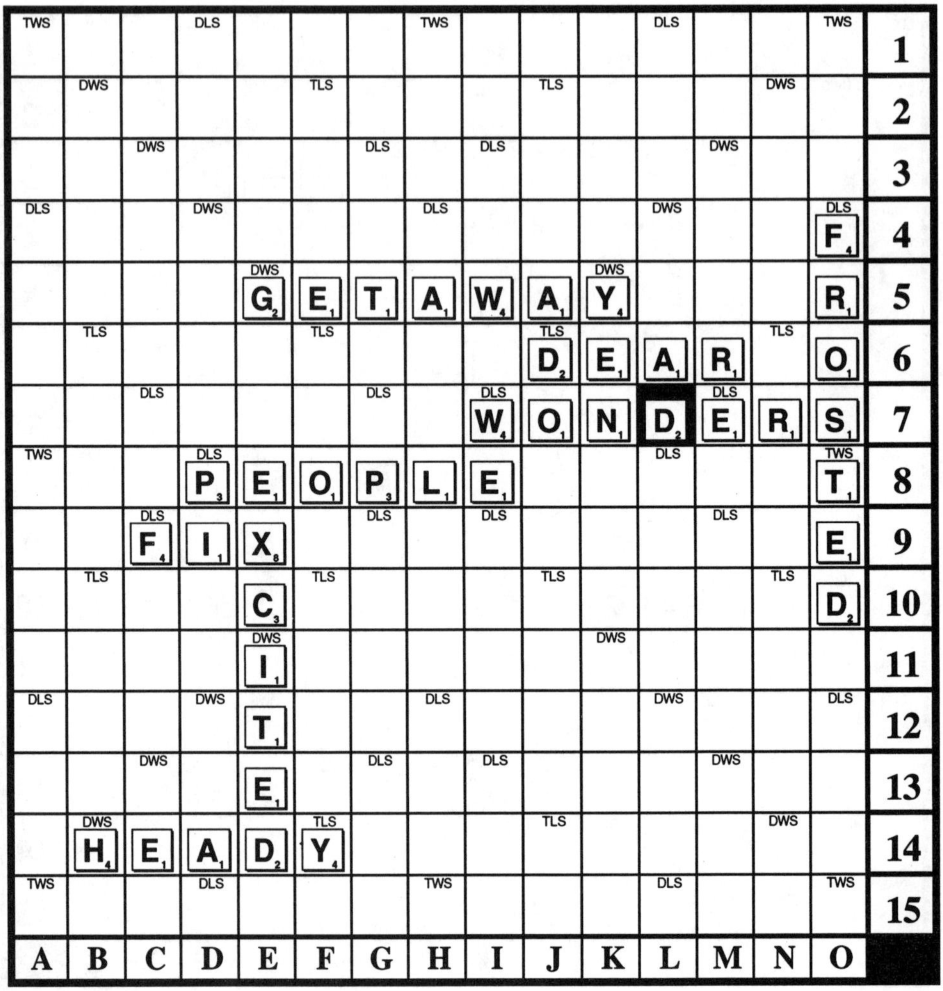

DIAGRAM 17-2

Where on Diagram 17-2 can the following words be played for the most points? Answers on page 185.
Time Limit: 25 minutes
Average Score: 2 correct   Good Score: 3 correct   Expert Score: 4 correct

1. TAMED 34 ____________
2. ASIDE 23 ____________
3. HERD 42 ____________
4. BLOOM 34 ____________

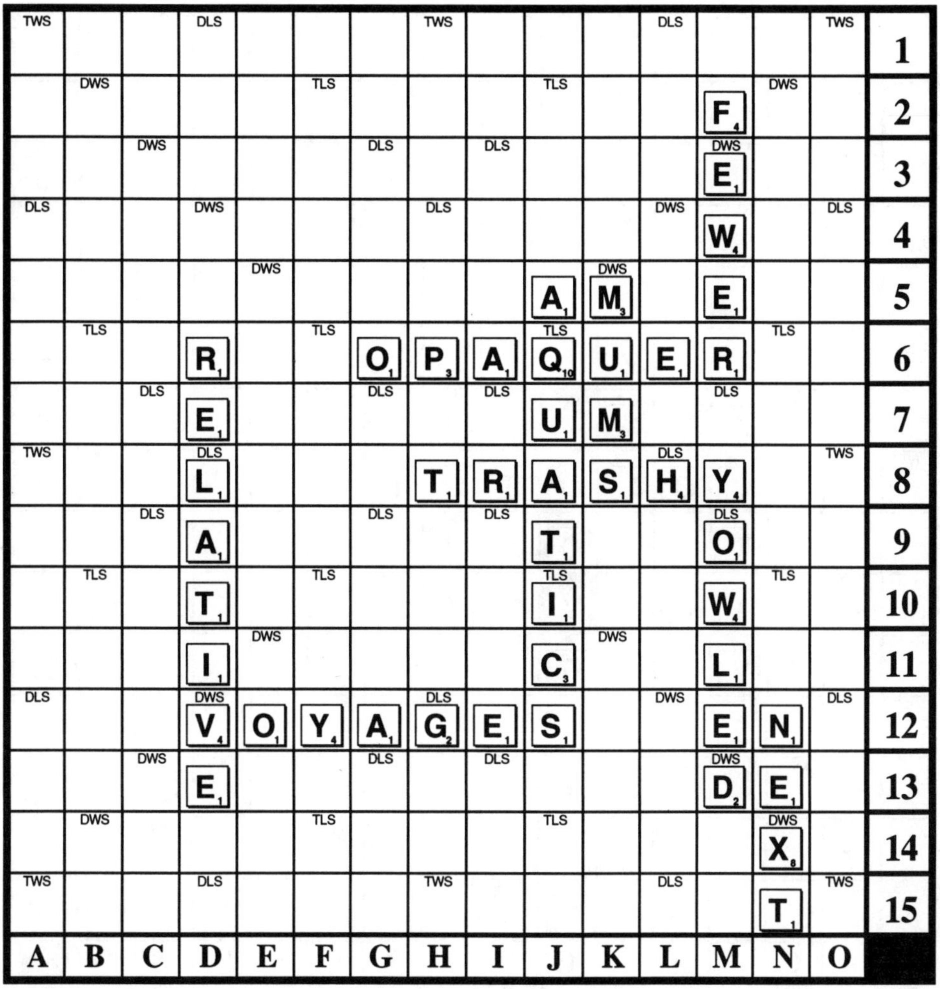

DIAGRAM 17-3

Where on Diagram 17-3 can the following words be played for the most points? Answers on page 185.

Time Limit: 30 minutes

Average Score: 2 correct   Good Score: 3 correct   Expert Score: 4 correct

1. B I O   36 _____
2. D O D O   34 _____
3. F O L D   36 _____
4. C A R O M 39 _____

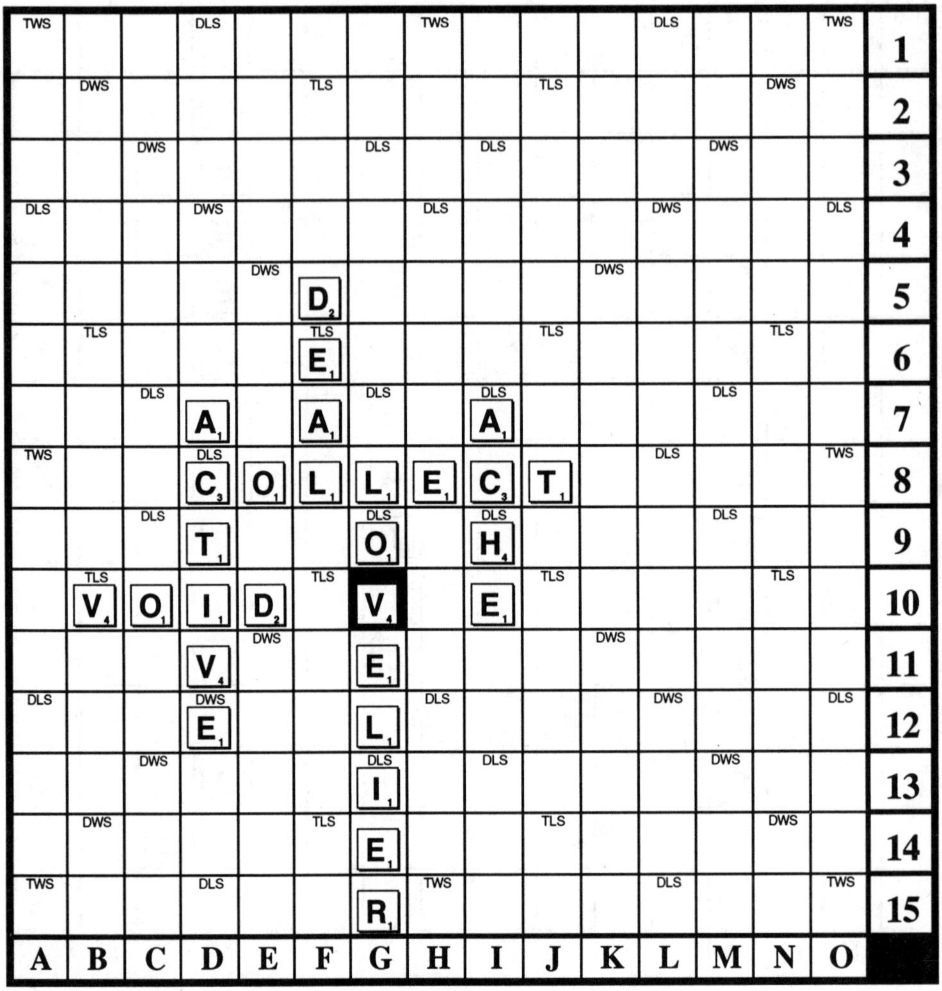

DIAGRAM 17-4

Where on Diagram 17-4 can the following words be played for the most points? Answers on page 185.

Time Limit: 30 minutes

Average Score: 2 correct   Good Score: 3 correct   Expert Score: 4 correct

1. L I T R E   33 _____
2. F R A M E   42 _____
3. H E L P   34 _____
4. U N T I L   20 _____

BONUS SQUARES

In each of the following four diagrams you have different racks and are asked to find the highest-scoring common-word play that covers two specified types of bonus squares. As a hint, we show you the score you're looking for.

#	A	B	C	D	E	F	G	H	I	J	K	L	M	N	O
1	TWS			DLS				TWS				DLS			TWS
2		DWS				TLS		TLS			A			DWS	
3			DWS			DLS	I	N	D	O	W	S	DWS		
4	DLS			DWS				DLS			F	DWS			DLS
5					DWS					B	U	N			
6		TLS				TLS	M	O	R	A	L			TLS	
7			DLS				DLS	DLS	DLS			L	DLS		
8	TWS			DLS				R	A	N	K	L	Y		TWS
9			DLS				DLS	E	DLS				DLS		
10		TLS				TLS		U		TLS				TLS	R
11					DWS			S			DWS				A
12	DLS			DWS				I	T			DWS			Z
13			DWS				DLS	N	O				DWS		E
14		DWS				TLS		G	O	A	T	H	E	R	D
15	TWS			DLS				T				DLS			TWS

DIAGRAM 17-5

Time Limit: 30 minutes
Average Score: 2 correct   Good Score: 3 correct   Expert Score: 4 correct

1. A D E E F M U 53   Find the high-scoring TLS-TLS   _____
2. B F L N P R T 36   Find the high-scoring TWS-DLS   _____
3. B E F H L O S 39   Find the high-scoring DWS-DLS   _____
4. A B C C G I O 23   Find the high-scoring TLS-TLS   _____

Answers on page 185.

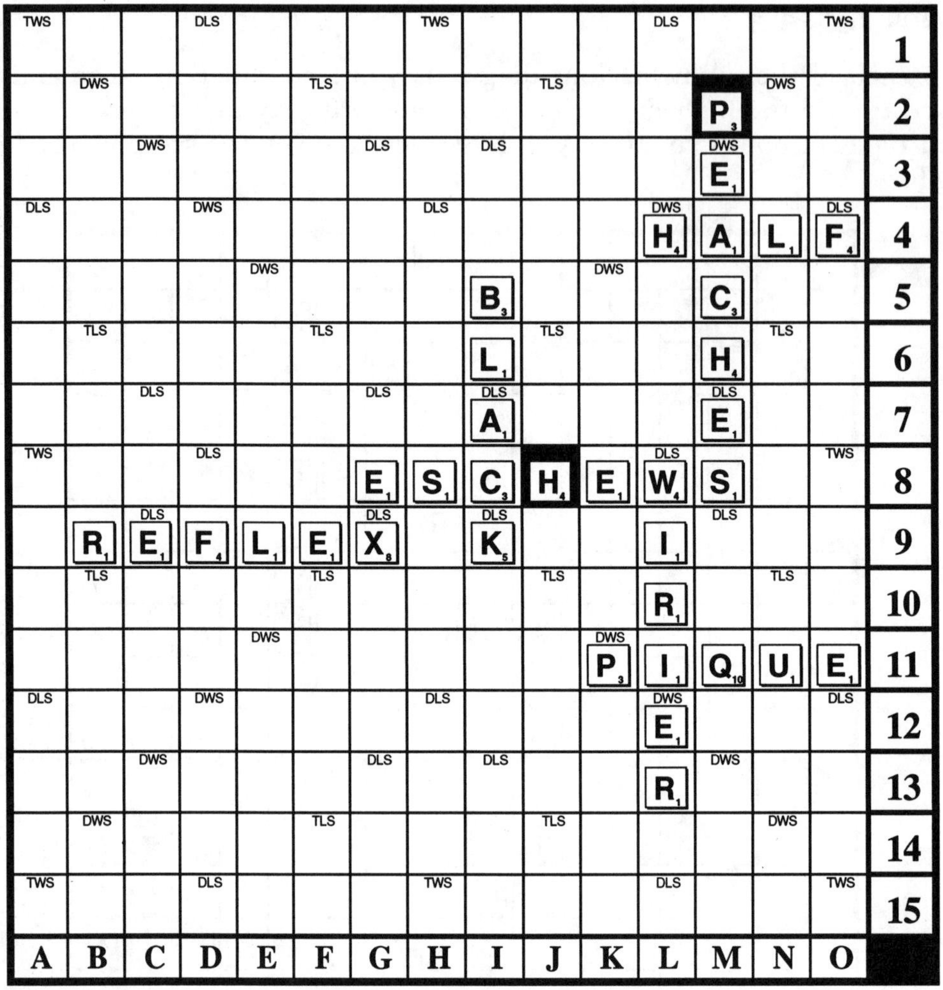

DIAGRAM 17-6

Time Limit: 30 minutes
Average Score: 2 correct   Good Score: 3 correct   Expert Score: 4 correct

1. A J L N O P U 32   Find the high-scoring TLS-TLS _____
2. E L N O P U Z 52   Find the high-scoring TWS-DLS _____
3. A G L M P R V 36   Find the high scoring TLS-DWS _____
4. E G L M R T U 48   Find the high-scoring DWS-DWS _____

Answers on page 185.

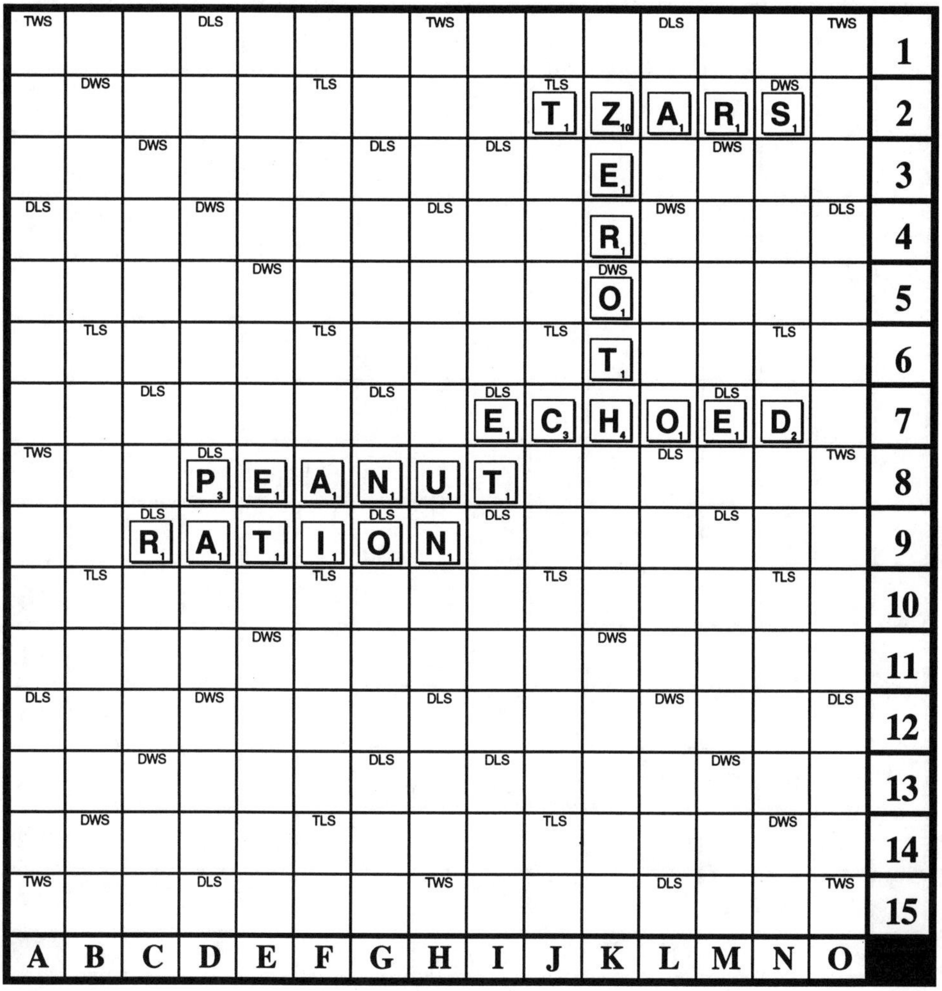

DIAGRAM 17-7

Time Limit: 30 minutes
Average Score: 2 correct Good Score: 3 correct Expert Score: 4 correct

1. A C H L O T V 34 Find the high-scoring TLS-TLS ____________
2. B C E F G I M 33 Find the high-scoring DLS-DWS ____________
3. A D K L P W Y 48 Find the high-scoring DLS-TWS ____________
4. B E F G I L N 48 Find the high-scoring DWS-DWS ____________

Answers on page 185.

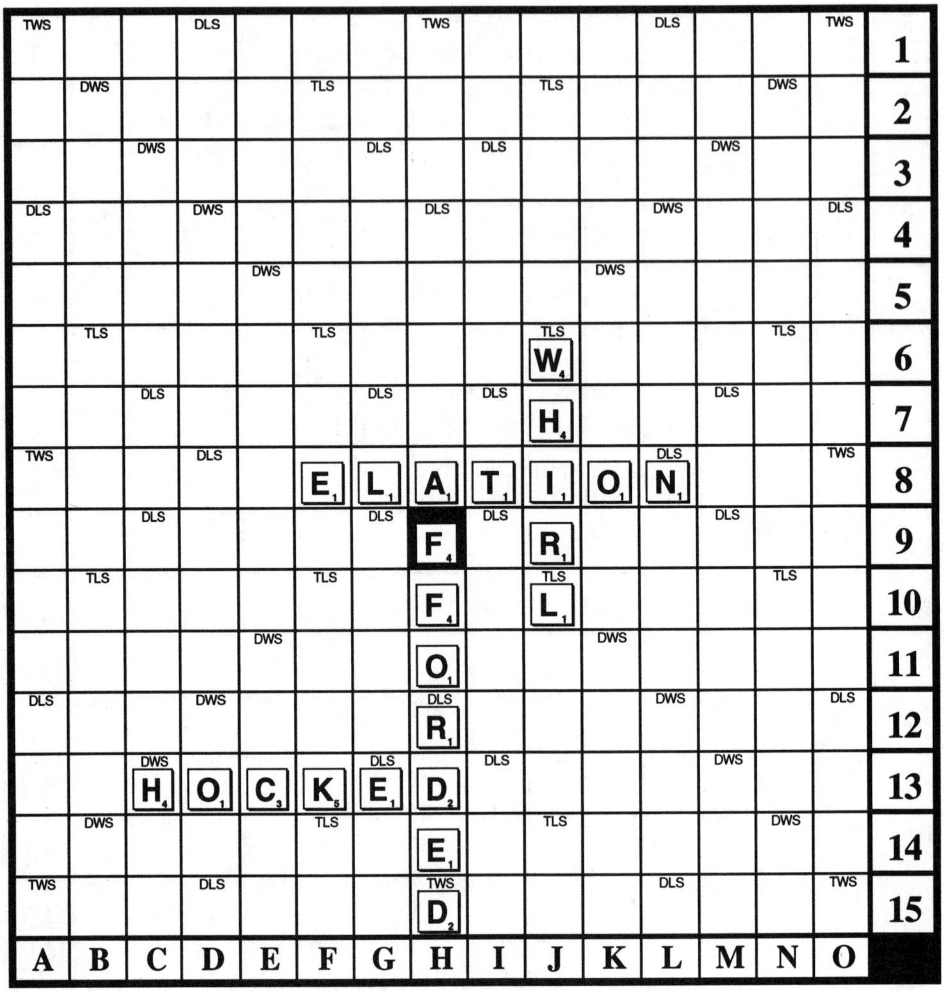

DIAGRAM 17-8

Time Limit: 30 minutes
Average Score: 2 correct Good Score: 3 correct Expert Score: 4 correct

1. A A D F H I U 28 Find the high-scoring TLS-TLS ____________
2. E G H M O R W 45 Find the high-scoring DWS-DLS ____________
3. A B C E G H S 49 Find the high-scoring TLS-DWS ____________
4. E E F M R R S 48 Find the high-scoring DWS-DWS ____________

Answers on page 185.

In an actual game situation, you probably won't be given any clues as to what your best play is. With that in mind, the remaining diagrams present typical game situations and ask you to find the best common-word play.

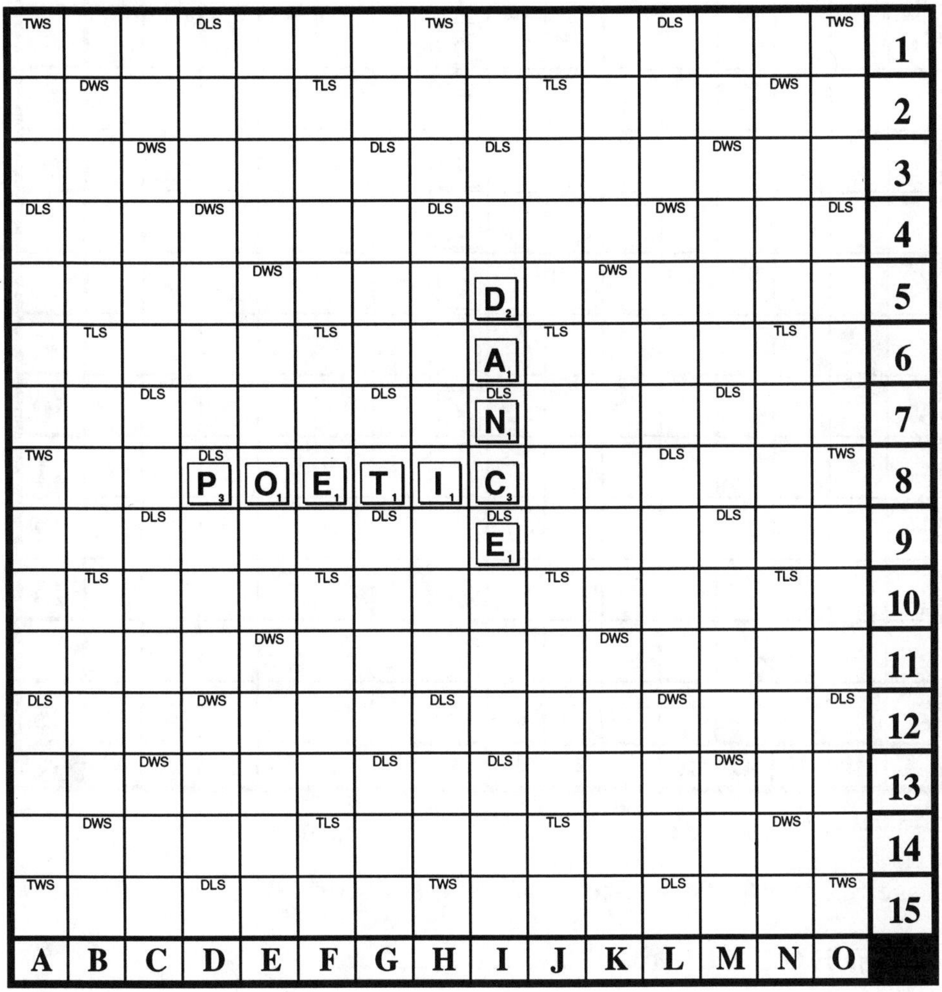

	A	B	C	D	E	F	G	H	I	J	K	L	M	N	O	
1	TWS			DLS				TWS				DLS			TWS	1
2		DWS				TLS				TLS				DWS		2
3			DWS				DLS		DLS				DWS			3
4	DLS			DWS				DLS					DWS		DLS	4
5					DWS			**D₂**			DWS					5
6		TLS				TLS		**A₁**		TLS				TLS		6
7			DLS				DLS	**N₁**					DLS			7
8	TWS			DLS **P₃**	**O₁**	**E₁**	**T₁**	**I₁**	**C₃**			DLS			TWS	8
9			DLS				DLS	**E₁**					DLS			9
10		TLS				TLS				TLS				TLS		10
11				DWS							DWS					11
12	DLS			DWS				DLS				DWS			DLS	12
13			DWS				DLS		DLS				DWS			13
14		DWS				TLS				TLS				DWS		14
15	TWS			DLS				TWS				DLS			TWS	15

DIAGRAM 17-9

Average Score: 22   Good Score: 29   Expert Score: 40

Rack: A D K M N O R   Your Play: _____
Answer on page 185.

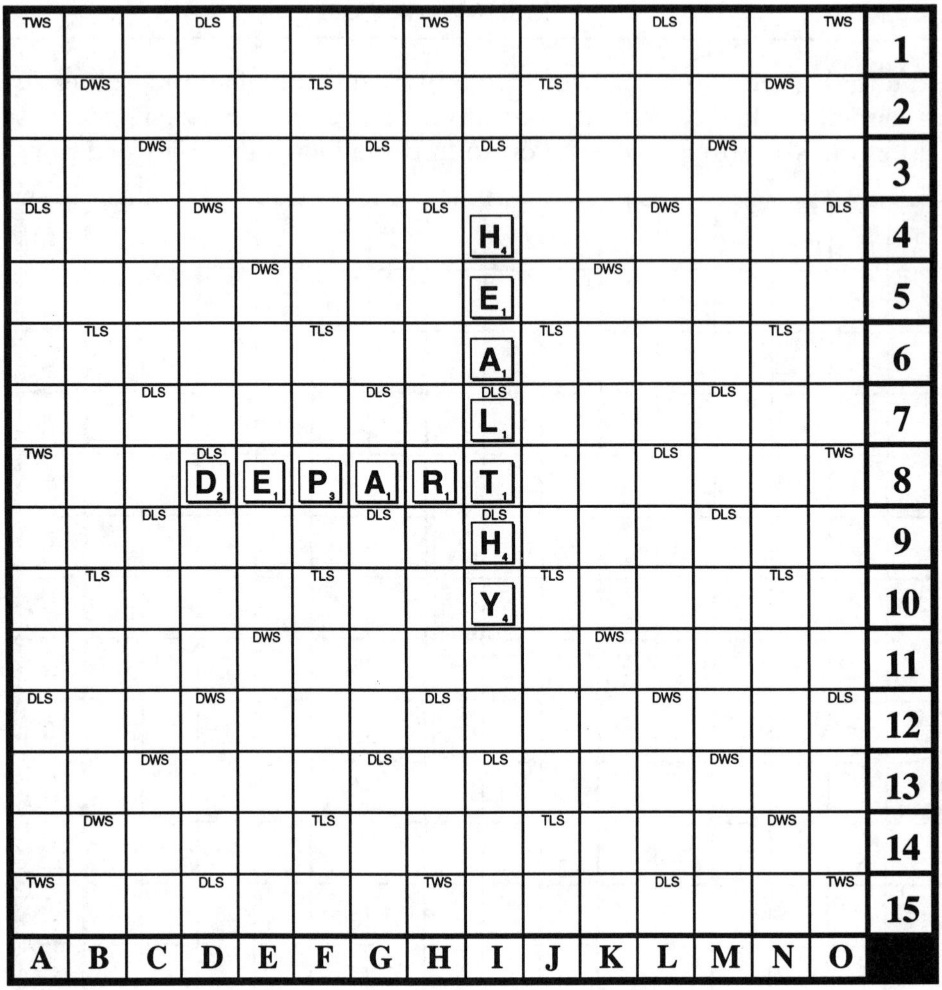

DIAGRAM 17-10

Average Score: 16   Good Score: 33   Expert Score: 43

Rack: B D E G L T U   Your Play: ___________

Answer on page 185.

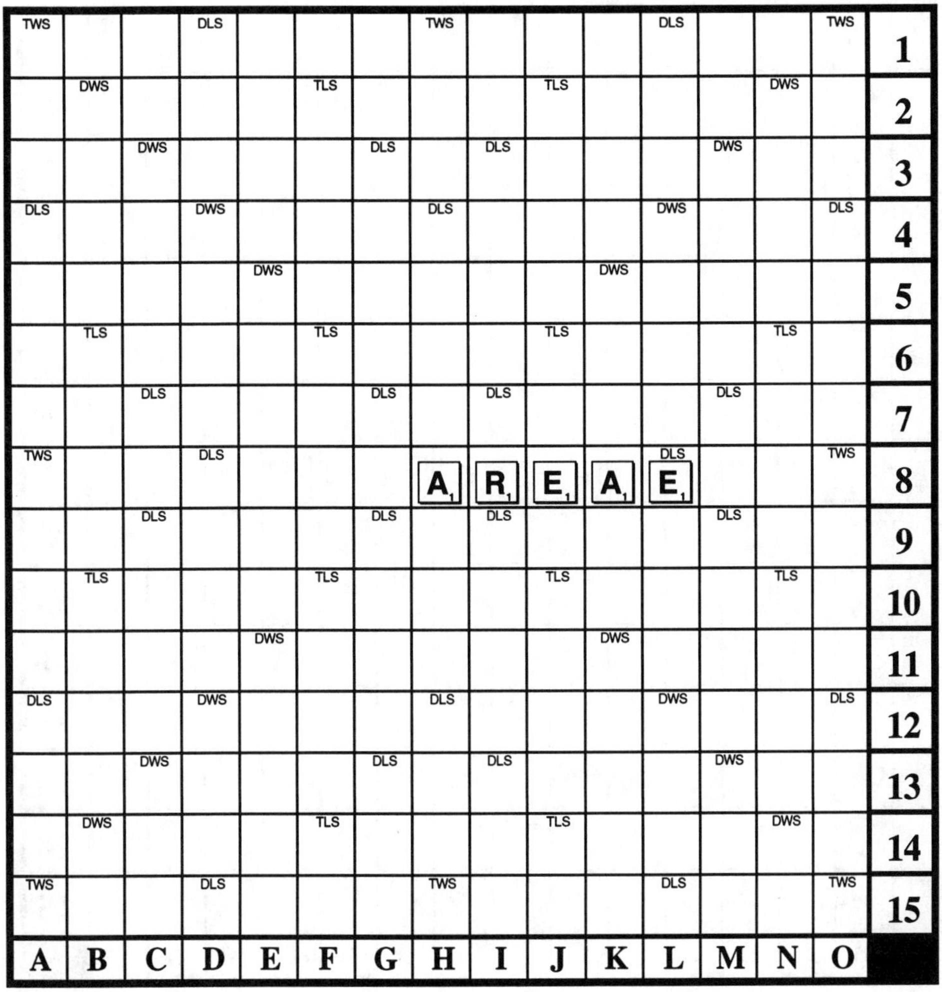

DIAGRAM 17-11

Average Score: 20 Good Score: 24 Expert Score: 29

Rack: A F H L O R T Your Play: ____________

Answer on page 185.

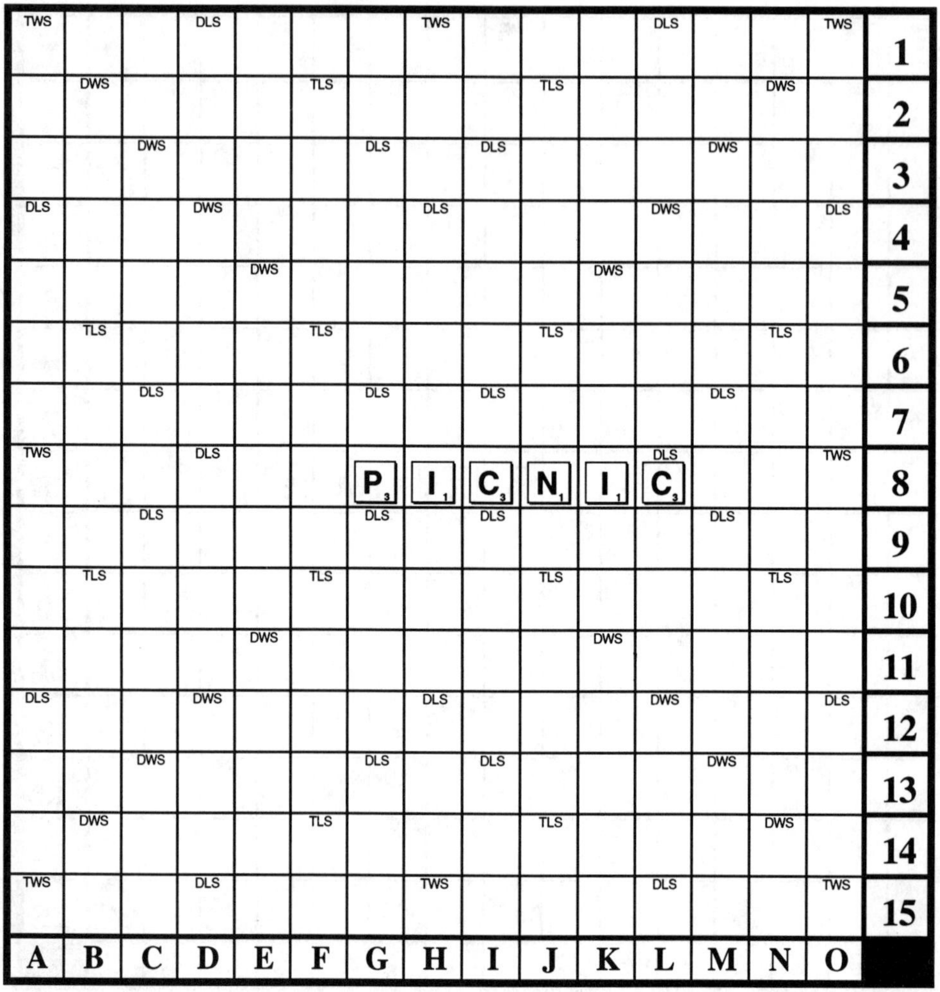

	A	B	C	D	E	F	G	H	I	J	K	L	M	N	O	
	TWS			DLS				TWS				DLS			TWS	**1**
		DWS				TLS				TLS				DWS		**2**
			DWS				DLS		DLS				DWS			**3**
	DLS			DWS				DLS				DWS			DLS	**4**
					DWS						DWS					**5**
		TLS				TLS				TLS				TLS		**6**
			DLS				DLS		DLS				DLS			**7**
	TWS			DLS			P₃	I₁	C₃	N₁	I₁	C₃			TWS	**8**
			DLS				DLS		DLS				DLS			**9**
		TLS				TLS				TLS				TLS		**10**
					DWS						DWS					**11**
	DLS			DWS				DLS				DWS			DLS	**12**
			DWS				DLS		DLS				DWS			**13**
		DWS				TLS				TLS				DWS		**14**
	TWS			DLS				TWS				DLS			TWS	**15**

DIAGRAM 17-12

Average Score: 32   Good Score: 34   Expert Score: 60

Rack: D E I K L Q U   Your Play: _____

Answer on page 185.

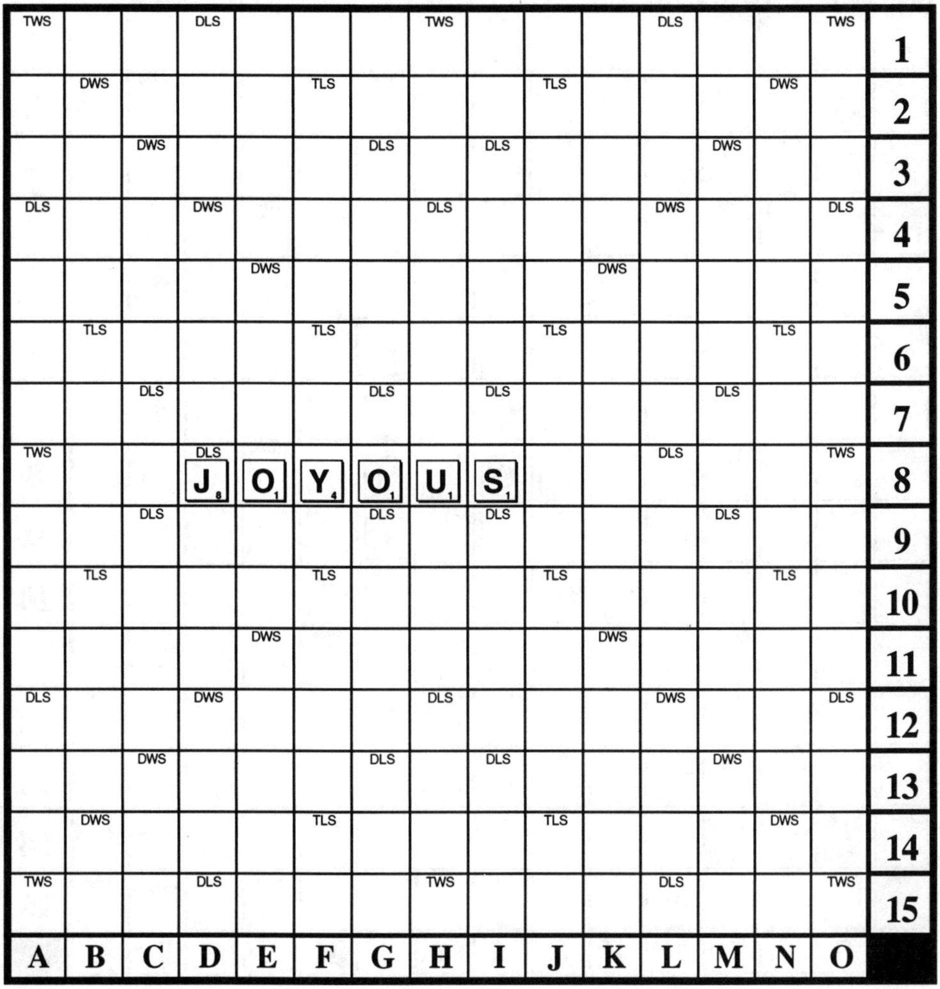

	A	B	C	D	E	F	G	H	I	J	K	L	M	N	O	
1	TWS			DLS				TWS				DLS			TWS	1
2		DWS			TLS				TLS				DWS			2
3			DWS			DLS		DLS				DWS				3
4	DLS			DWS			DLS				DWS				DLS	4
5					DWS					DWS						5
6		TLS				TLS			TLS				TLS			6
7			DLS			DLS		DLS				DLS				7
8	TWS			DLS J	O	Y	O	U	S			DLS			TWS	8
9			DLS			DLS		DLS				DLS				9
10		TLS				TLS			TLS				TLS			10
11					DWS					DWS						11
12	DLS			DWS			DLS				DWS				DLS	12
13			DWS			DLS		DLS				DWS				13
14		DWS			TLS				TLS				DWS			14
15	TWS			DLS			TWS					DLS			TWS	15

DIAGRAM 17-13

Average Score: 30   Good Score: 34   Expert Score: 48

Rack: B D E L M O W   Your Play: _____

Answer on page 185.

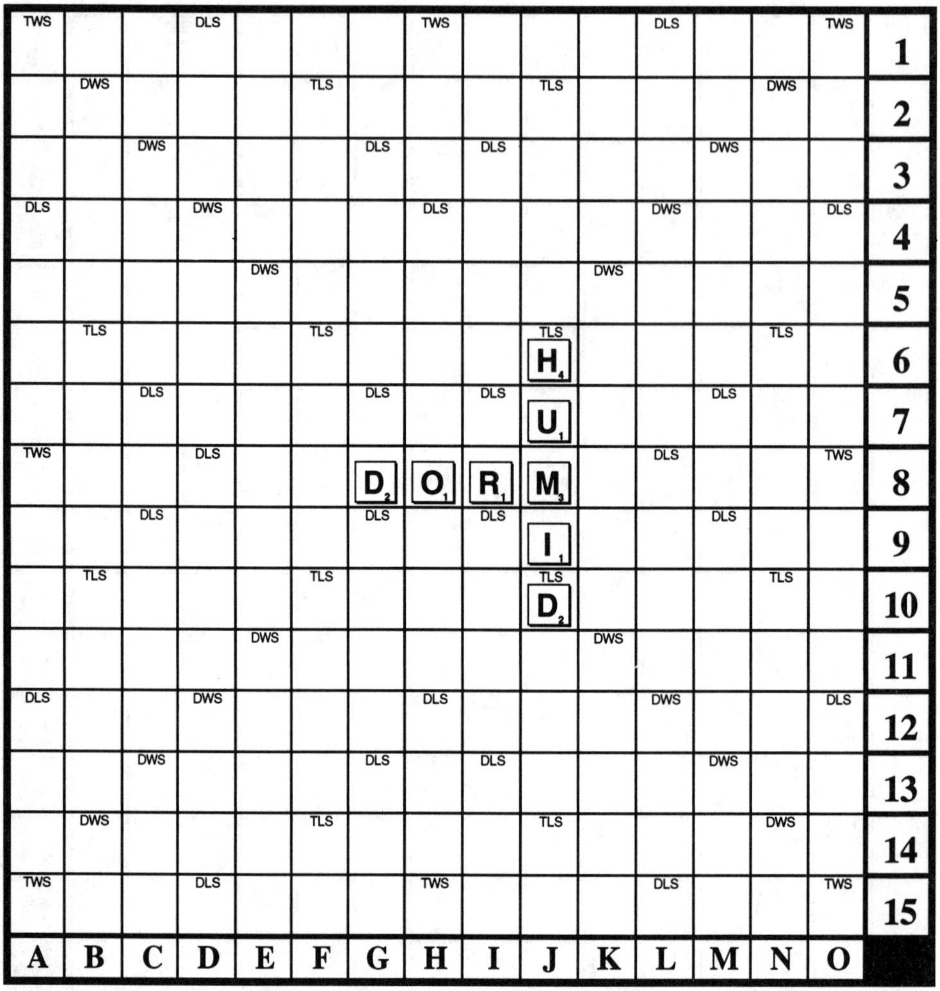

	A	B	C	D	E	F	G	H	I	J	K	L	M	N	O	
1	TWS			DLS				TWS				DLS			TWS	1
2		DWS				TLS				TLS				DWS		2
3			DWS				DLS		DLS				DWS			3
4	DLS			DWS			DLS				DWS			DLS		4
5					DWS						DWS					5
6		TLS				TLS				**H**			TLS			6
7			DLS				DLS		DLS	**U**		DLS				7
8	TWS			DLS			**D**	**O**	**R**	**M**		DLS			TWS	8
9			DLS				DLS		DLS	**I**		DLS				9
10		TLS				TLS				**D**			TLS			10
11				DWS						DWS						11
12	DLS			DWS			DLS		DLS			DWS			DLS	12
13		DWS				DLS		DLS				DWS				13
14		DWS			TLS				TLS				DWS			14
15	TWS			DLS			TWS					DLS			TWS	15

DIAGRAM 17-14

Average Score: 14   Good Score: 19   Expert Score: 48

Rack: C E I O R T Y   Your Play: _____

Answer on page 185.

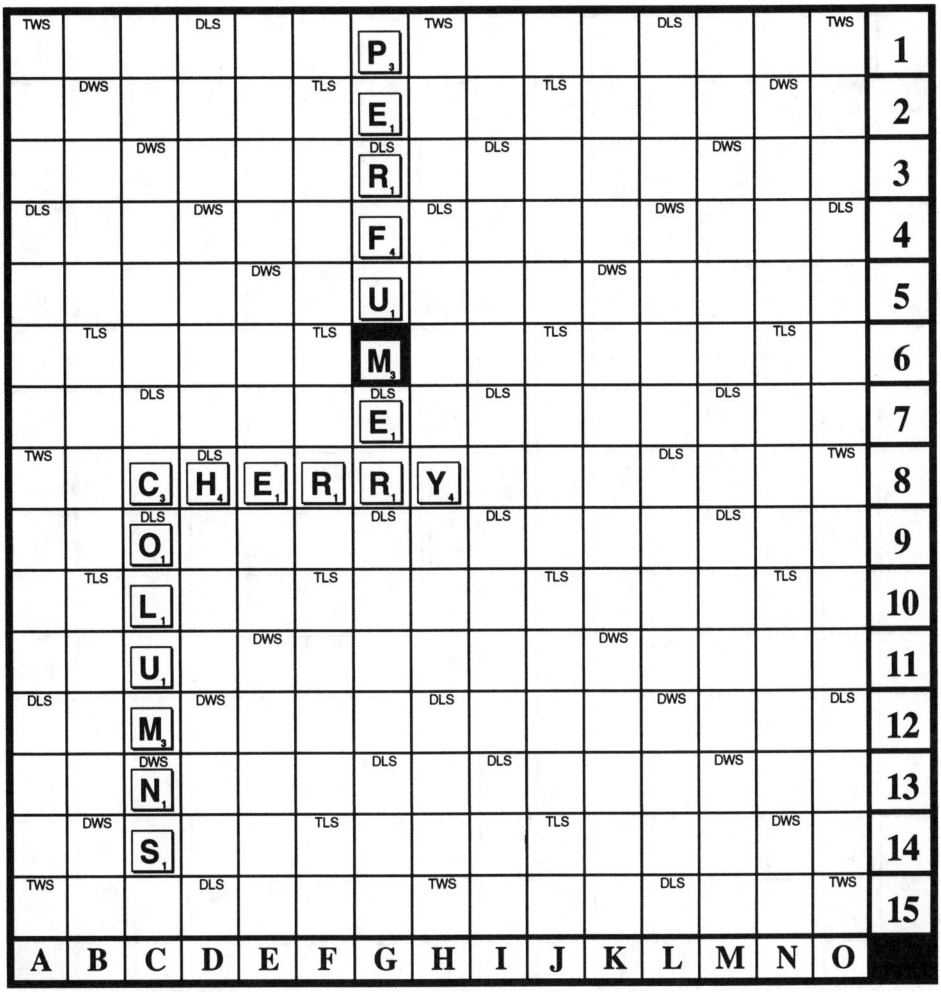

DIAGRAM 17-15

Average Score: 30   Good Score: 54   Expert Score: 60

Rack: E I K M N P U   Your Play: _____

Answer on page 185.

DIAGRAM 17-16

Average Score: 29   Good Score: 40   Expert Score: 38

Rack: A E I M O T V   Your Play: _____

Answer on page 186.

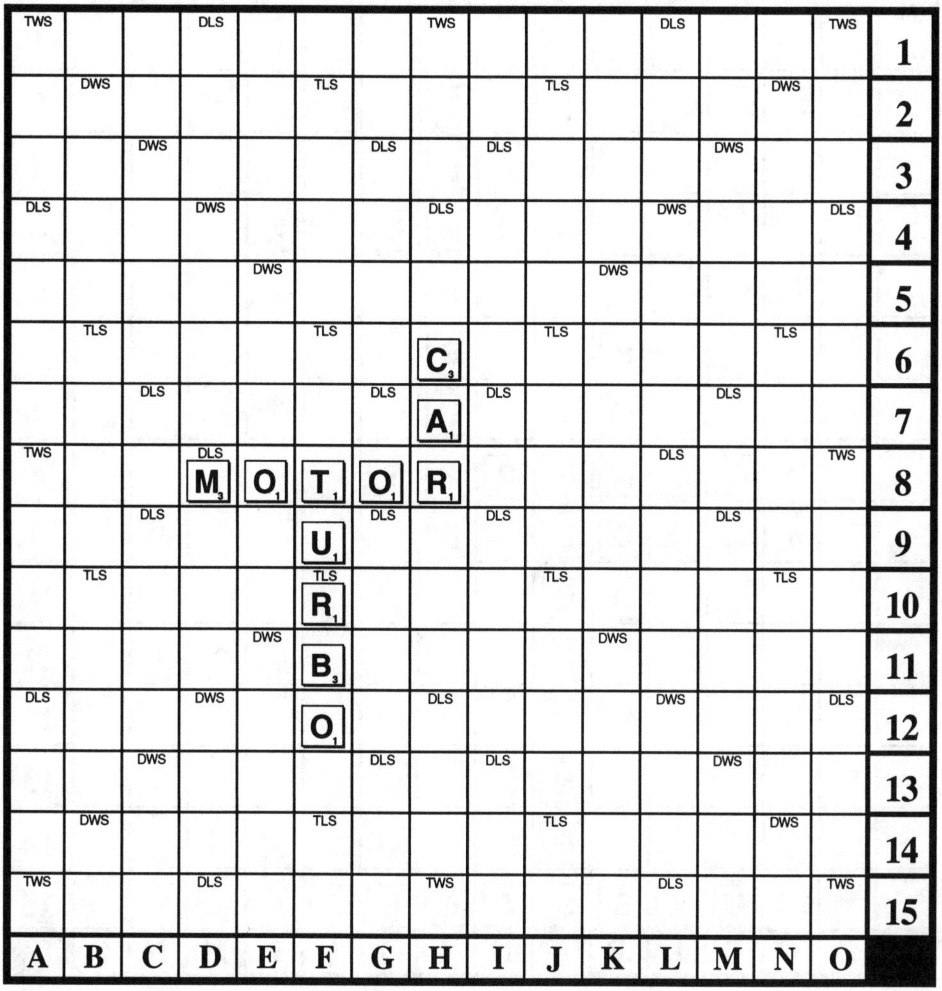

	A	B	C	D	E	F	G	H	I	J	K	L	M	N	O	
	TWS			DLS				TWS				DLS			TWS	1
		DWS				TLS				TLS				DWS		2
			DWS				DLS		DLS				DWS			3
	DLS			DWS				DLS				DWS			DLS	4
					DWS						DWS					5
		TLS				TLS		C₃		TLS				TLS		6
			DLS				DLS	A₁	DLS				DLS			7
	TWS			DLS	M₃	O₁	T₁	O₁	R₁			DLS			TWS	8
			DLS			U₁		DLS		DLS			DLS			9
		TLS				R₁		TLS			TLS			TLS		10
				DWS		B₃					DWS					11
	DLS			DWS		O₁		DLS				DWS			DLS	12
			DWS				DLS		DLS				DWS			13
		DWS				TLS				TLS				DWS		14
	TWS			DLS				TWS				DLS			TWS	15

DIAGRAM 17-17

Average Score: 24   Good Score: 32   Expert Score: 72

Rack: C E J L O S T   Your Play: _____

Answer on page 186.

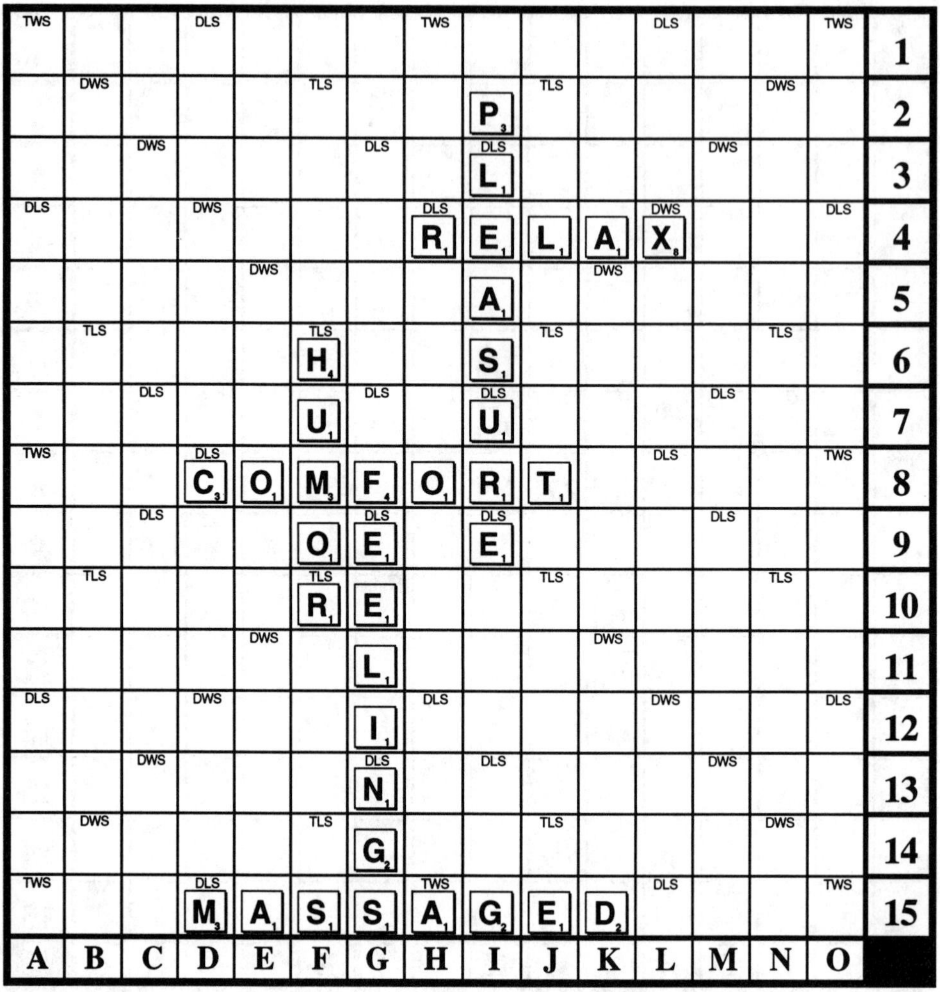

DIAGRAM 17-18

Average Score: 28   Good Score: 40   Expert Score: 57

Rack: D E H L N O R   Your Play: _____

Answer on page 186.

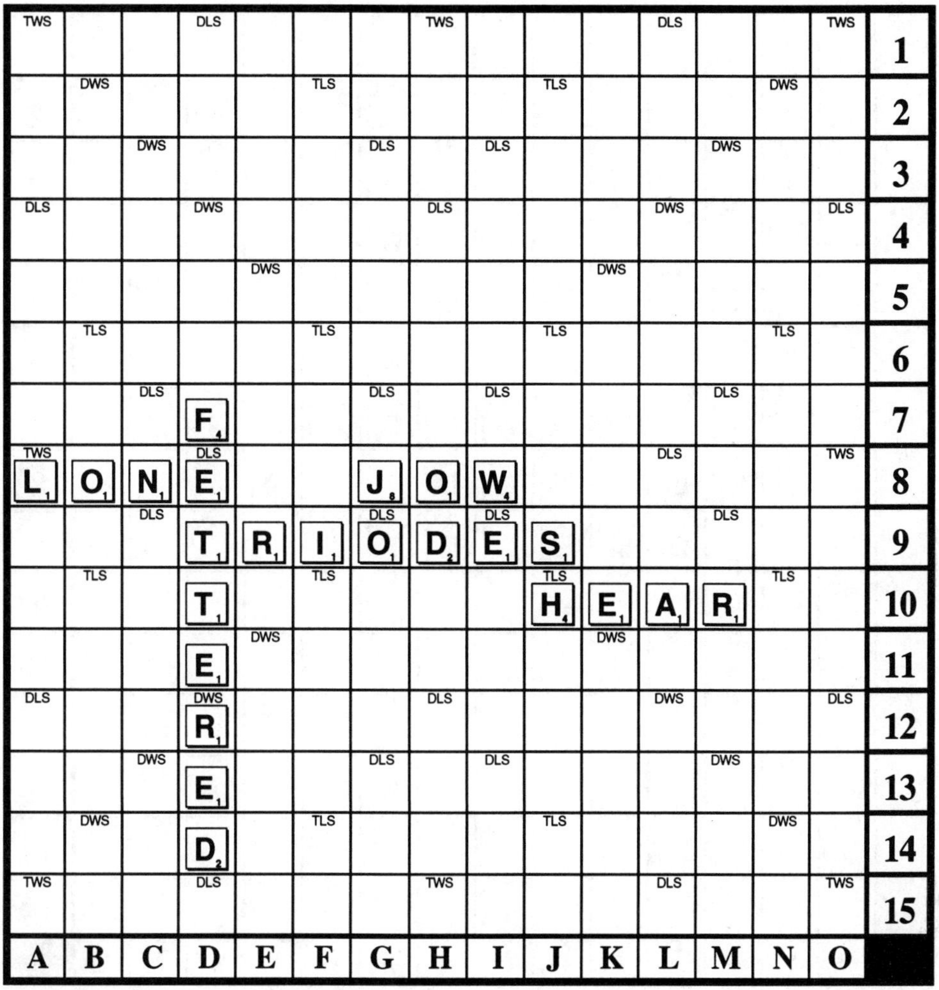

DIAGRAM 17-19

Average Score: 25   Good Score: 33   Expert Score: 39

Rack: A B D I L L S   Your Play: _____

Answer on page 186.

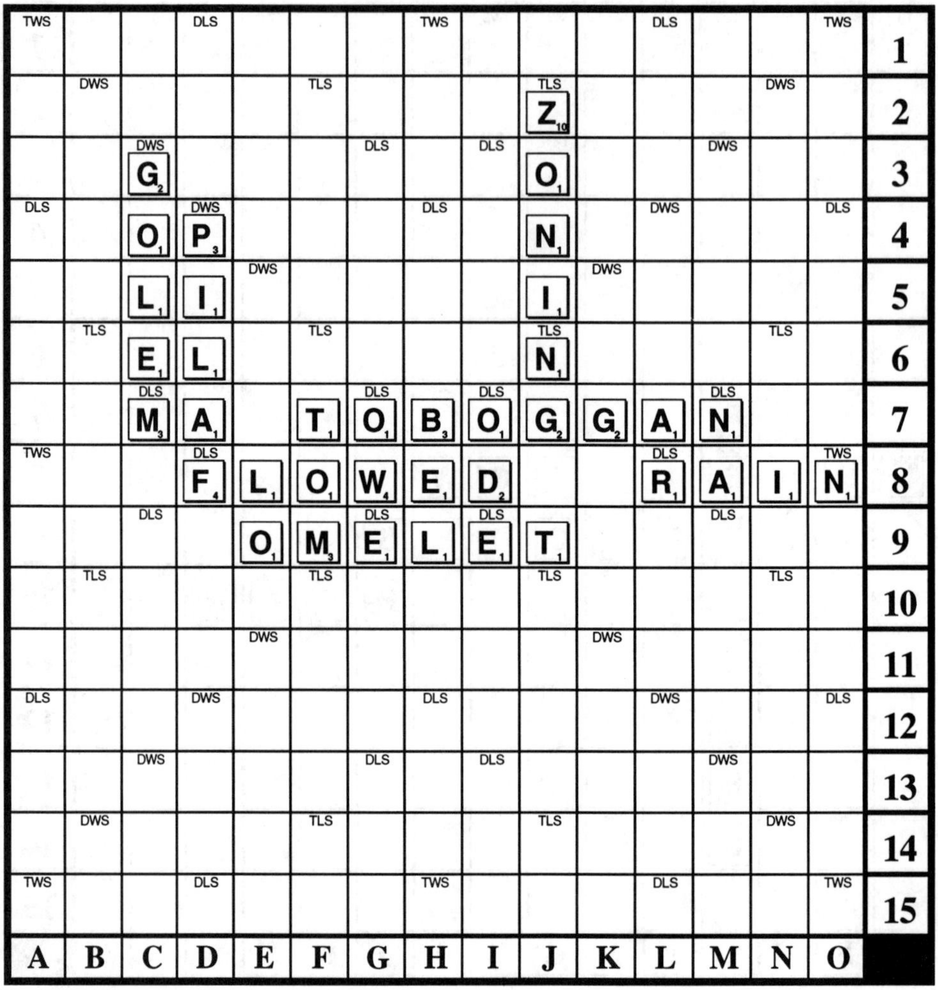

TWS . . DLS . . . TWS . . . DLS . . . TWS **1**

. DWS . . . TLS . . Z₁₀(TLS) . . . DWS . . **2**

. . DWS G₂ . . DLS . DLS O₁ . . DWS . . **3**

DLS . O₁ P₃(DWS) . . . DLS . N₁ . DWS . . DLS **4**

. . L₁ I₁ DWS . . . . I₁ DWS . . . **5**

. TLS E₁ L₁ . TLS . . N₁(TLS) . . TLS . **6**

. . M₃(DLS) A₁ . T₁ O₁ B₃ O₁ G₂ G₂ A₁ N₁(DLS) . **7**

TWS . . F₄(DLS) L₁ O₁ W₄ E₁ D₂ . R₁(DLS) A₁ I₁ N₁(TWS) **8**

. DLS . O₁ M₃ E₁ L₁ E₁ T₁ . DLS . . **9**

. TLS . . TLS . . TLS . . TLS . **10**

. . . DWS . . . DWS . . . **11**

DLS . . DWS . . DLS . . DWS . . DLS **12**

. . DWS . . DLS . DLS . . DWS . . **13**

. DWS . . TLS . . TLS . . DWS . . **14**

TWS . . DLS . . . TWS . . . DLS . . . TWS **15**

A B C D E F G H I J K L M N O

DIAGRAM 17-20

Average Score: 20   Good Score: 30   Expert Score: 40

Rack: G I M N N S U   Your Play: _____

Answer on page 186.

We invite you to try the more demanding puzzles in Chapter Eighteen. Those of you who spend time with them will have the opportunity both to learn new words and to develop a better understanding of what is possible in the world of SCRABBLE® game puzzles. Besides providing the familiar fill-ins, eight- and nine-letter anagrams, and high-scoring plays, we include a contest from the *SCRABBLE® News* that may keep you busy for hours.

ANSWERS: CHAPTER 17

Diagram 17-15
PUMPKIN 1D 60

Diagram 17-14
DORMITORY 8G 48

Diagram 17-13
BLOOMED E5 48

Diagram 17-12
PICNICKED 8G 60

Diagram 17-11
FORTH 7H 29

Diagram 17-10
BUGLED H10 43 or BUDGET H10 43

Diagram 17-9
RANDOM H1 40

Diagram 17-8
1. AHEAD 14F; 2. WHOM 12A; 3. CHASE B10; 4. REMORSE 11E

Diagram 17-7
1. HAVOC B6; 2. CAFE L1; 3. PLAY 8L; 4. FLEETING E5

Diagram 17-6
1. JOURNAL B6; 2. ZONE 8A; 3. VULGAR N10; 4. GRUMBLE 5E

Diagram 17-5
1. DEFAME F6; 2. FLIP H1; 3. SHELF 4D; 4. CUBIC 10F

Diagram 17-4
1. H11; 2. A8; 3. F11; 4. J6

Diagram 17-3
1. O13; 2. L1; 3. L12; 4. N1

Diagram 17-2
1. 4D; 2. 15F; 3. 15A; 4. 6B

Diagram 17-1
1. M9; 2. 8A; 3. 2J; 4. H11

Diagram 17-16
There is a choice of several excellent plays: VIOLATE E5 40 points, MOTIVE H10 40 points, or MOVIE H1 38. We prefer MOVIE because its AT leave is better than the M leave after VIOLATE. Plus, it blocks the TWS square at H1, preventing your opponent from using it. If MOVIE were 3 points less, we would play VIOLATE. Furthermore, MOTIVE keeps the board wide open, allowing many more scoring chances. We prefer MOVIE to reduce opponent's opportunities.

Diagram 17-17
OBJECTS 11E 72

Diagram 17-18
HONORED, E5 57

Diagram 17-19
ODDBALLS H8 39

Diagram 17-20
LINGUINIS 5C 40

TOUGHIES! PUZZLES THAT ARE SERIOUSLY FUN!

Far-Sight***

In each case use only the letters of the given rack to fill in the blanks below to form thirty common words. Answers on page 194.

Time limit per set: 30 minutes

Average Score: 3 correct   Good Score: 5 correct   Expert Score: 8 correct

Rack: A C L N O R W

SET A

1. P __ __ T __ __ I __
2. V __ __ C __ __ I __
3. B __ __ __ A __ __ E
4. __ A __ E __ D __ __
5. __ __ __ __ __ I __ ET
6. __ U __ I __ __ __ Y
7. __ __ U __ __ HE __
8. __ O __ __ TI __ __
9. F __ __ ME __ __ __ __
10. P __ __ __ __ A __ __ E

SET B

1. B __ __ __ __ H __ __ D
2. __ __ __ __ K __ O __ D
3. __ B __ __ __ MA __
4. H __ __ MO __ __ __ __
5. L __ __ D __ __ __ D
6. M __ T __ __ __ __ __ Y
7. M __ __ O __ __ L __
8. N __ __ G __ __ __ E
9. __ __ __ __ D __ M __ Y
10. T __ __ E __ __ __ T

SET C

1. __ __ __ __ __ __ E __ Y
2. __ __ __ __ __ __ D __ Y
3. I __ __ __ __ __ __ __ D
4. F __ __ __ __ __ __ E __
5. __ __ __ __ P __ __ __ __ D
6. __ __ __ __ __ B __ L __
7. __ __ __ __ __ __ DE __
8. __ __ __ __ __ ME __ __
9. __ I __ __ __ T __ __
10. __ __ __ E __ __ __ K

Anagrams

Each of the seventy words below has exactly one very common word as an anagram. How many of them can you find? Answers on page 194.

Time limit per set: 30 minutes

Average Score: 3 correct   Good Score: 5 correct   Expert Score: 8 correct

SET A***	SET B****	SET C****	SET D****
1. ADVANCES	1. ARMONICA	1. URANYLIC	1. IMAGINER
2. TRAPPEAN	2. DRAINAGE	2. DEMERSAL	2. HAPPIEST
3. BIOCIDAL	3. HOGMANAY	3. SULFATED	3. OXHEARTS
4. DECIMATE	4. AMANITIN	4. DISHWARE	4. SARKIEST
5. DECIGRAM	5. FIREBOAT	5. HANDOUTS	5. TALEYSIM
6. DEACONRY	6. AMBIVERT	6. GENERATE	6. ALUNITES
7. CHIVAREE	7. CRATONIC	7. OVERLATE	7. VENATION
8. MINACITY	8. EXCLAIMS	8. EARSTONE	8. SENORITA
9. ADHEREND	9. SAUCIEST	9. MEDALING	9. WORKMATE
10. TARRAGON	10. RUSTICAL	10. UNMARRED	10. PSORALEN

SET E****	SET F****	SET G****
1. TOLUIDES	1. HUNTSMAN	1. CRISPENS
2. INSUREDS	2. ROYALIST	2. ORCHITIS
3. EINSTEIN	3. DEBRIDES	3. REFUNDED
4. GUNFIRES	4. BLOTTIER	4. DISPLODE
5. HEISTING	5. DEMOTICS	5. OVERIDLE
6. KINGLIER	6. CENTROID	6. DESPITES
7. EMPTINGS	7. CLEVEITE	7. FINISHED
8. ORNITHES	8. TECHIEST	8. PIEDFORT
9. POLEMIST	9. ISOCLINE	9. EPHEDRAS
10. ROARINGS	10. COTERIES	10. UNLOADED

Rearrange the letters in each two-word phrase on page 189 to spell a common eight- or nine-letter word. Answers on pages 194–95.

Time limit per set: 30 minutes

Average Score: 3 correct   Good Score: 5 correct   Expert Score: 8 correct

SET H***	SET I***	SET J****
1. LAVA GNAT	1. SLID HOME	1. COSY DRIVE
2. TEA MYTHS	2. OPEN LATE	2. CLAY FAULT
3. TAUT DIET	3. USED CARS	3. EARTH WIND
4. BEST NAME	4. HOLD PINS	4. OLIO STAIN
5. FIND BEER	5. LEG ZONES	5. DAY REPORT
6. ENEMY ORC	6. COME RIDE	6. HEAR SCORE
7. SOUL MICE	7. LARGE HUT	7. DEEP RIDGE
8. LION CAMP	8. LIVE FAST	8. LIMP AURAS
9. BEAN SOUP	9. ACE PILOT	9. TIRE CATCH
10. RING LADY	10. CHIC NAME	10. ART POSTER

Two-Rack Play***

Here are two racks. Start with an empty board and form a play with rack #1. Then use rack #2 to form a second play on the board. What's your two-turn total score?

Average Score: 52   Good Score: 58   Expert Score: 72
Answer on page 195.

Rack #1: A B C D E F G   Rack #2: P Q R S T U V

Six-Rack Play****

Here are six racks. Start with an empty board and form a play with rack #1. Leaving the first play on the board, follow it with a second play using only rack #2. Continue in this fashion until you've made your sixth play with rack #6. Our best solution uses two smaller words (each less than five letters long) that are obscure.

Answers on page 195.

Average Score: 369 Good Score: 458 Expert Score: 602 Our Best Score: 809

Rack #1: D E I I N R W
Rack #2: A I N O P T ?
Rack #3: E F L S T U Z
Rack #4: A E G I N R T
Rack #5: A I I I L N T
Rack #6: C N N O O S U

Highest-Scoring Plays***

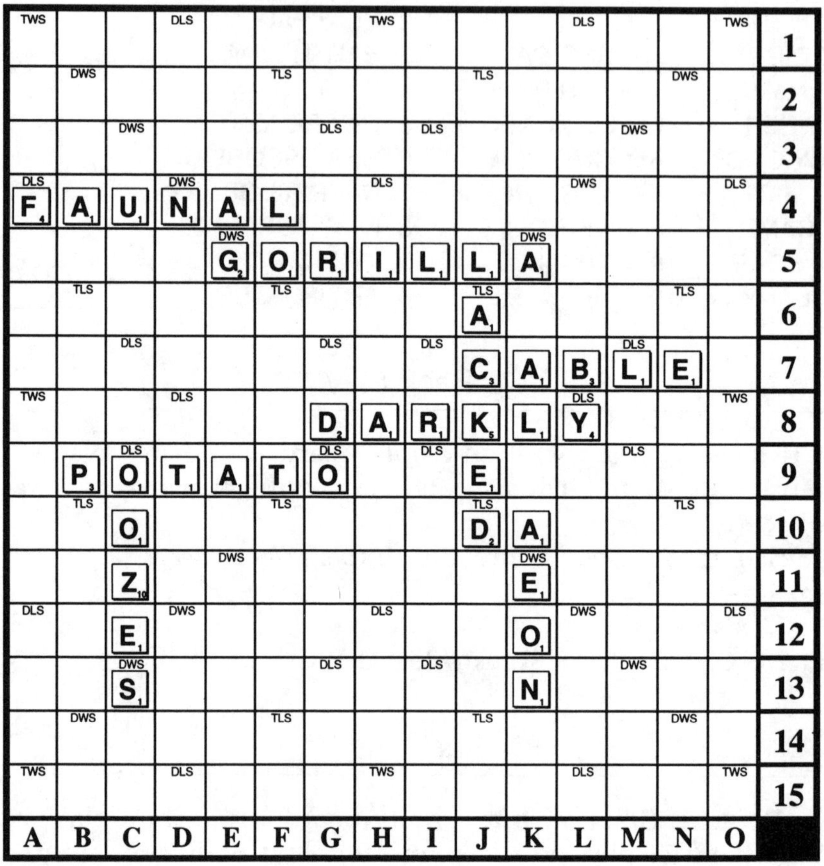

DIAGRAM 18-1

Using any or all of the given letters, find the highest-scoring play on Diagram 18-1 with each rack below. Answers on page 195.

Note: Once you've found a play for Rack #1, don't add it to the board. Always use Diagram 18-1 for each rack.

Average Score: 165 Good Score: 195 Expert Score: 210 Our Best Score: 235

Rack #1: G I L O T T U
Rack #2: B G H M N R Y
Rack #3: I I L N O P U
Rack #4: D E E H L M S
Rack #5: D E F L O R V

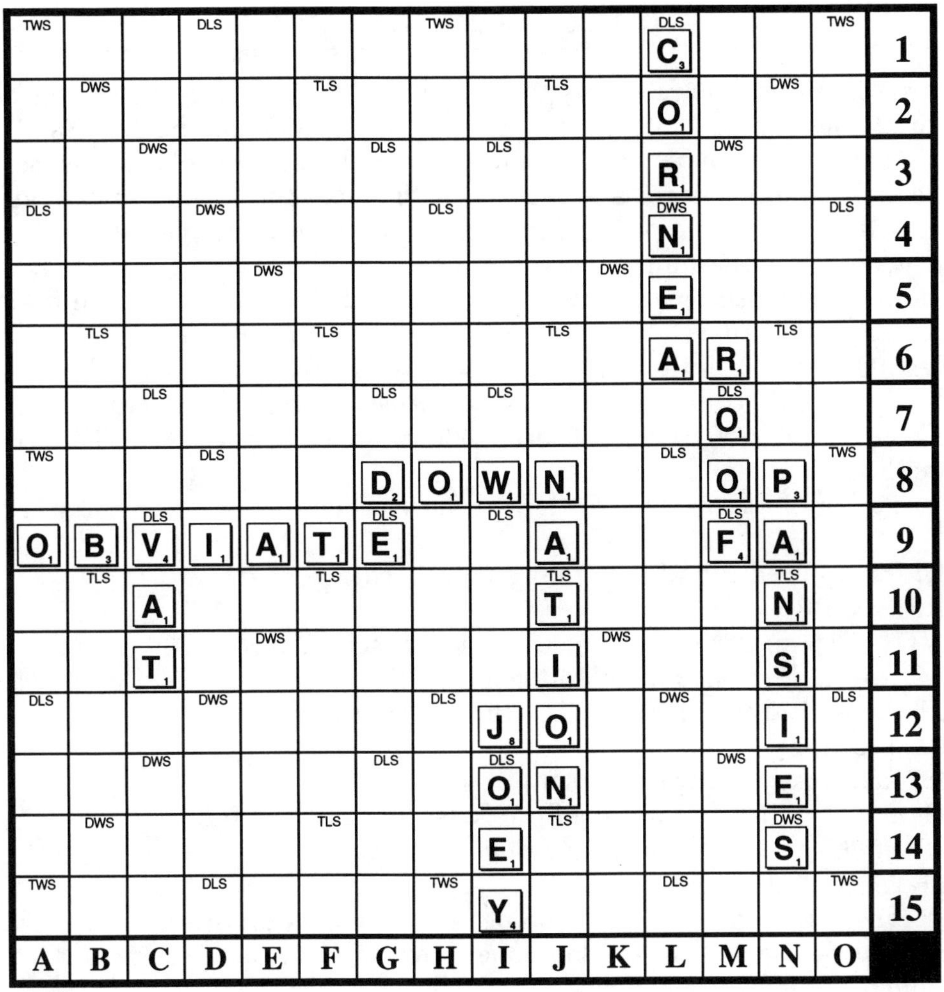

DIAGRAM 18-2

Find the highest-scoring play on Diagram 18-2 with each rack below. Answers on page 195.

Average Score: 220 Good Score: 300 Expert Score: 350 Our Best Score: 409

Rack #1: A C E L M O W
Rack #2: C D E M N O S
Rack #3: E I I N N O V
Rack #4: D D E M O R Y
Rack #5: E E H L N P T

The Consonant Challenge

How well can you score points without vowels? From a standard set of a hundred tiles take out all the As, Es, Is, Os, and Us and the two Ys. That leaves fifty-six tiles to play with, including the blanks. Now choose any seven of these tiles, find a word, and play it on the board, following the standard SCRABBLE® game rules for adding words to the board. Replenish your rack with whatever remaining tiles you choose. Continue adding words to the board and replenishing your rack in a similar fashion until you can find no more acceptable plays. You may use either or both of the two blanks as vowels. Our best solution includes one obscure word not listed below, as well as a few other more familiar words. Answer on pages 195 and 197.

Average Score: 350 Good Score: 400 Expert Score: 450 Our Best Score: 522

Here is a list of acceptable words with no vowels:

BRR: *interj*—used to indicate that one feels cold
BRRR: see BRR
CRWTH: *n* -S an ancient stringed musical instrument
CWM: *n* -S a deep, steep-walled basin
HM: *interj*—used to express thoughtful consideration
HMM: see HM
MM: *interj*—used to express assent or satisfaction
NTH: *adv* pertaining to an indefinitely large ordinal number
PFFT: *interj*—used to express a sudden ending
PHPHT: see PHT
PHT: *interj*—used as an expression of mild anger or annoyance
PSST: *interj*—used to attract someone's attention
SH: *interj*—used to urge silence
SHH: see SH
TSK: *v* -ED, -ING, -S: to utter an expression of annoyance
TSKTSK: *v* -ED, -ING, -S: to tsk

The Alphabet Caper

The *SCRABBLE® News* has a contest each issue. We present here Contest #6. Using each letter of the alphabet and one blank tile (twenty-seven tiles total), score as many points as you can playing a typical SCRABBLE® game. Two readers, Stephen Root, of Massachusetts and Gene Gruhn, of Arizona, tied for first place, having identical solutions of 714 points. Can you find their solution or do better? They play only two unusual words, one four- and one eight-letter word. The eight-letter word uses two of the J, Q, X, and Z. Answer on page 198.

Average Score: 410   Good Score: 550   Expert Score: 650

Below is a sample solution: [See sample Diagram 18-3, page 196.]

1.	JUMPY 8D	54
2.	QURSH E7	34
3.	CHALKING D11	86
4.	FIX I10	13
5.	FIXT I10	15
6.	ADZ F11	13
7.	ADZE F11	16
8.	WOVE 14C	10
9.	BY H7	7
10.	ADZE_S_ F11	14
	Total:	262

This concludes Part III. In Part IV we show what our SCRABBLE® culture is all about. From Alfred Butts, the SCRABBLE game inventor, to SCRABBLE game Clubs and Tournaments to the experts and their skills, it's all there.

Far-Sight
SET A
1. PLATONIC; 2. VOLCANIC; 3. BARNACLE; 4. CALENDAR; 5. CLARINET; 6. CULINARY; 7. LAUNCHER; 8. LOCATION; 9. FLAMENCO; 10. PARLANCE

SET B
1. BLOWHARD; 2. WORKLOAD; 3. ABNORMAL; 4. HORMONAL; 5. LANDLORD; 6. MATRONLY; 7. MONO-RAIL; 8. NONGLARE; 9. RANDOMLY; 10. TOLERANT

SET C
1. CLOWNERY; 2. COWARDLY; 3. IRONCLAD; 4. FALCONER; 5. CROPLAND; 6. CORNBALL; 7. COLANDER; 8. CORNMEAL; 9. CILANTRO; 10. LACEWORK

Anagrams
SET A
1. CANVASED; 2. APPARENT; 3. DIABOLIC; 4. MEDICATE; 5. GRIMACED; 6. CRAYONED; 7. ACHIEVER; 8. INTIMACY; 9. HARDENED; 10. ARROGANT

SET B
1. MACARONI; 2. GARDENIA; 3. MAHOGANY; 4. MAINTAIN; 5. BIFORATE; 6. VERBATIM; 7. NARCOTIC; 8. CLIMAXES; 9. SUITCASE; 10. CURTAILS

SET C
1. CULINARY; 2. EMERALDS; 3. DEFAULTS; 4. RAWHIDES; 5. THOUSAND; 6. TEENAGER; 7. ELEVATOR; 8. RESONATE; 9. MALIGNED; 10. UNDERARM

SET D
1. MIGRAINE; 2. EPITAPHS; 3. THORAXES; 4. ASTERISK; 5. STEAMILY; 6. INSULATE; 7. INNOVATE; 8. NOTARIES; 9. TEAMWORK; 10. PERSONAL

SET E
1. SOLITUDE; 2. SUNDRIES; 3. NINETIES; 4. REFUSING; 5. NIGHTIES; 6. RINGLIKE; 7. PIGMENTS; 8. HORNIEST; 9. MILEPOST; 10. GARRISON

SET F
1. MANHUNTS; 2. SOLITARY; 3. BIRDSEED; 4. LIBRETTO; 5. DOMESTIC; 6. DOCTRINE; 7. ELECTIVE; 8. ESTHETIC; 9. SILICONE; 10. ESOTERIC

SET G
1. PRINCESS; 2. HISTORIC; 3. UNDERFED; 4. LOPSIDED; 5. EVILDOER; 6. SIDESTEP; 7. FIENDISH; 8. PROFITED; 9. RESHAPED; 10. DUODENAL

SET H
1. GALAVANT; 2. AMETHYST; 3. ATTITUDE; 4. BASEMENT; 5. BEFRIEND; 6. CEREMONY; 7. COLISEUM; 8. COMPLAIN; 9. SUBPOENA; 10. DARINGLY

SET I
1. DEMOLISH; 2. ANTELOPE; 3. CRUSADES; 4. DOLPHINS; 5. LOZENGES; 6. MEDIOCRE; 7. LAUGHTER; 8. FESTIVAL; 9. POETICAL; 10. MECHANIC

SET J
1. DISCOVERY; 2. FACTUALLY; 3. HANDWRITE; 4. ISOLATION; 5. PREDATORY or PORTRAYED; 6. RACE-HORSE; 7. PEDIGREED; 8. MARSUPIAL; 9. ARCHITECT; 10. PROSTRATE

Two-Rack Play
1. FACED 8D 30 2. SURFACED 8A 42 TOTAL: 72 points

Six-Rack Play
1. WINDIER 8F 74 2. APPOINT 7I 71 3. ZESTFUL 9I 116 4. GRAT L4 7 5. LATI O9 5 6. CONGRATULATIONS O1 536 TOTAL: 809

Diagram 18-1:
1. OUTFIT A1 27 2. NYMPH B6 38 3. UNZIP 11A 32 4. MESHED 4H 58 5. FLAVORED E7 80 TOTAL: 235

Diagram 18-2
1. CWM H13 61 2. CONDEMNATIONS J2 82 3. INNOVATIVE C5 84 4. DROMEDARY 6F 80 5. ELEPHANT E4 102 TOTAL: 409

The Consonant Challenge
1. SPRIGHT H3 80 2. SPRIGHTS H3 13 3. PFFT 8G 16 4. IN 6H 1 5. JIN 6G 9 6. DJIN 6F 15 7. DJINN 6E 14 8. DJINNS 6E 13 9. CWMS K3 22 10. CRWTH 3K 26 11. SCHMALTZ O1 284 12. TSK 3G 13 13. BRA 5N 4 14. BRR M5 6 15. BRRR M5 6 TOTAL: 522 pt. See Diagram 18-4.

Alphabet Caper
1. LOCKJAW H8 112 2. OX I8 34 3. BY J8 24 4. VOX I7 16 5. FOXY 9G 21 6. AN 13H 3 7. AND 13H 4 8. RAND 13G 6 9. GHI F13 22 10. MEZQUITS 15A 464 11. PE B14 8 TOTAL: 714. See Diagram 18-5.

(Underlined letters represent blanks.)

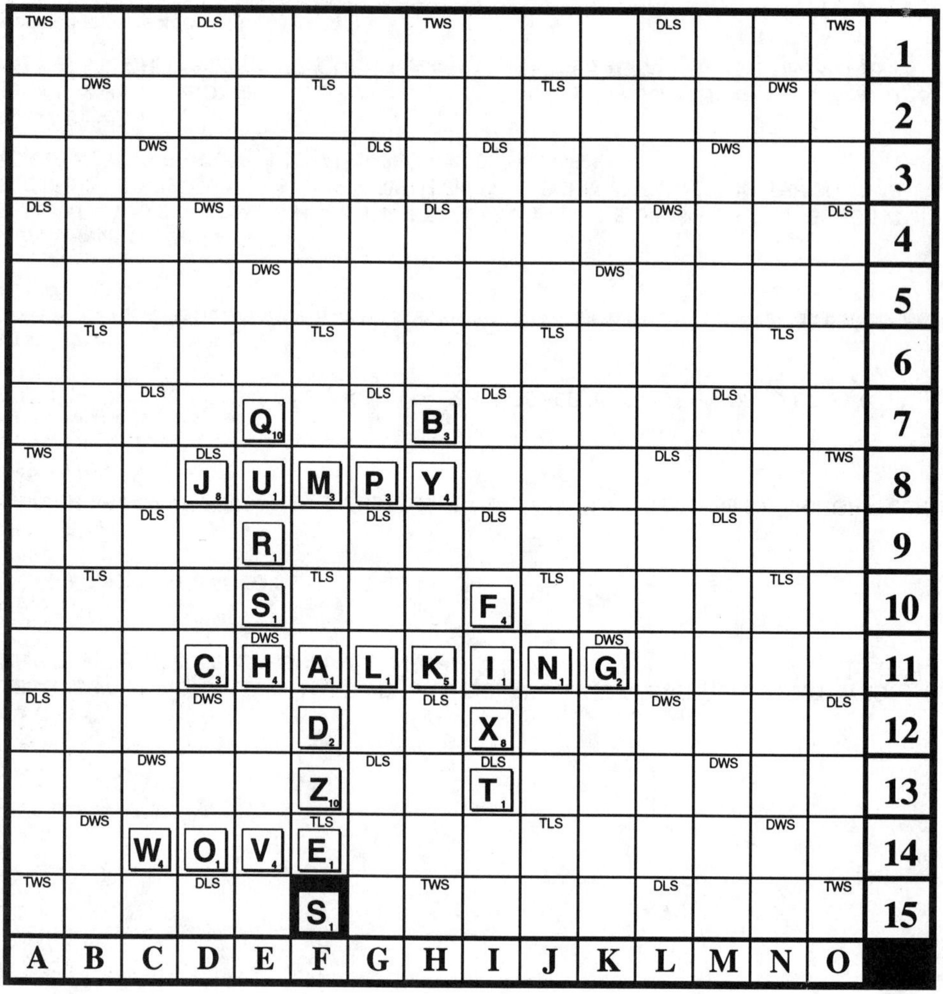

TWS
DLS
DWS
TLS
Q
B
J
U
M
P
Y
R
S
F
C
H
A
L
K
I
N
G
D
X
Z
T
W
O
V
E
S
1
2
3
4
5
6
7
8
9
10
11
12
13
14
15
A
B
C
D
E
F
G
H
I
J
K
L
M
N
O

DIAGRAM 18-3

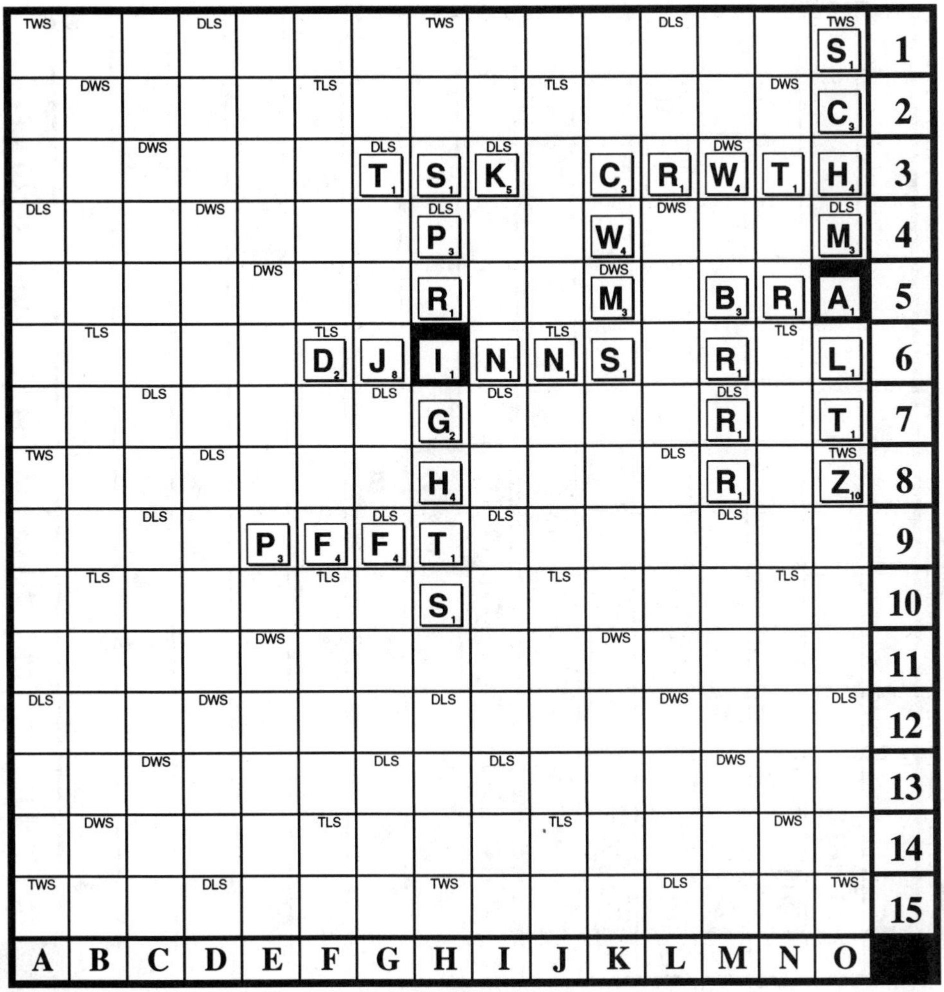

DIAGRAM 18-4

	A	B	C	D	E	F	G	H	I	J	K	L	M	N	O
1															S_1
2															C_3
3							T_1	S_1	K_5		C_3	R_1	W_4	T_1	H_4
4								P_3			W_4				M_3
5								R_1			M_3		B_3	R_1	A_1
6						D_2	J_8	I_1	N_1	N_1	S_1		R_1		L_1
7								G_2					R_1		T_1
8								H_4					R_1		Z_{10}
9					P_3	F_4	F_4	T_1							
10								S_1							
11															
12															
13															
14															
15															

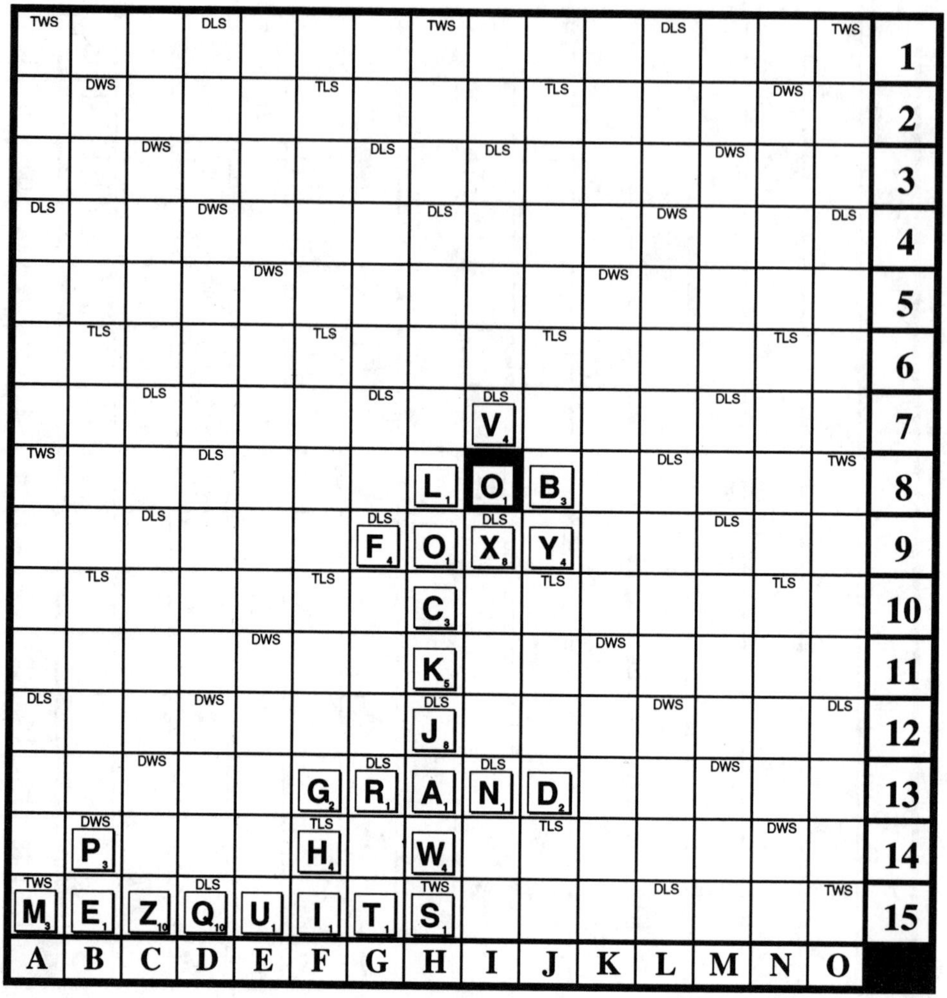
V
L O B
F O X Y
C
K
J
G R A N D
P H W
M E Z Q U I T S
A B C D E F G H I J K L M N O
1 2 3 4 5 6 7 8 9 10 11 12 13 14 15

DIAGRAM 18-5

P A R T · F O U R

EXPLORING THE WORLD OF SCRABBLE®— CLUBS AND TOURNAMENTS

Now that you understand the dynamics of the play of the game, we'd like to show you the larger world of the SCRABBLE® game culture.

Chapter Nineteen introduces you to Alfred Butts, the game's inventor. Chapter Twenty will show you what you'll encounter at SCRABBLE game Clubs and Tournaments. Chapter Twenty-one very explicitly shows you what it takes to become an expert player. Chapter Twenty-two demonstrates just how exciting and beautiful SCRABBLE game play can be, with fifteen examples of outstanding plays by some of the best players. Chapter Twenty-three shows you how best to introduce the variety of SCRABBLE games to your children.

19 JOHN WILLIAMS REMEMBERS ALFRED MOSHER BUTTS

It was the summer of 1983, and I had just become involved as a public relations consultant to what was then called SCRABBLE® Crossword Game Players, Inc. The organization was a subsidiary of the game's manufacturer, Selchow & Righter Company. I had just arrived at Chicago's Drake Hotel for the 1983 North American SCRABBLE® Championship, where thirty-two finalists from all over the continent were going to compete for a $5,000 first prize and a considerable amount of glory in the game and word subcultures.

On the plane from New York I had tried to memorize all the material I had received about both SCRABBLE and the fledgling tournament scene. Among the sheaves of information was a press release describing the upcoming event. One of its highlights was that the championship would be visited by Alfred Mosher Butts, the inventor of SCRABBLE. Interestingly, this would be the first time Butts would see firsthand the kind of worldwide enthusiasm his idea had spawned.

After checking into my room, I headed down to the Tournament Room, where officials, press, executives, and players had already convened. After making the rounds, I noticed a frail man, clearly in his eighties, sitting unassumingly in a corner. He was surrounded by several people, but seemed to be doing more listening than talking. Seconds later, one of my associates informed me that the gentleman was Alfred Butts, and asked if I could keep him company for a while.

When the group around Butts dispersed, I walked over to introduce myself. I had not noticed before, but there was a SCRABBLE game in progress on a small table beside him. We had been talking for a few minutes when Alfred asked if I wanted to finish the game with him.

I was stunned. For openers, I had just started to reacquaint myself with the game as part of my new assignment. Secondly, the prospect of playing SCRABBLE with the game's inventor was more than just a little intimidating. I felt as if I were about to shoot baskets with Dr. James Naismith or change a diaper with Dr. Benjamin Spock.

"I'm really a terrible speller," Alfred told me as we began. I looked around at the crush of reporters across the room. "Maybe you shouldn't advertise that fact." The father of SCRABBLE shrugged. "People find out soon enough."

Adding to my sense of intimidation was a prop that Alfred had casually left on the floor beside him. It appeared to be an everyday plastic shopping bag. It contained, however, the first hand-rendered prototype of the SCRAB-BLE board from decades earlier. "Shouldn't this be in the Smithsonian or something?" I asked him. "You really think so?" he replied.

People still ask me how well Alfred Butts played that first day. Frankly, I can't even remember. I'm not sure it really mattered. The next opportunity I had to spend any significant time with Alfred was at the 1985 National SCRABBLE® Championship in Boston. It was the largest event in organized SCRABBLE game history, with 302 word experts from dozens of states and several foreign countries competing.

Alfred was even more overwhelmed than he had been at the Chicago tournament a few years earlier, but loved the attention and VIP treatment he was afforded. He was also introducing a new product, Alfred's Other Game. It was basically a solitaire version of SCRABBLE, roughly conceived by Alfred and fine-tuned by the people at Selchow & Righter. Each contestant and staff member received a copy of the new game, and Alfred must have signed each one personally during the course of the event.

Happily, there was extensive press coverage of the championship, and Alfred was a focal point of much of it. Although he was an extraordinarily unassuming man, he sat through dozens of interviews and photo sessions, answering the same questions over and over again. It's important to remember that Alfred Butts had no prospect of financial gain from any of this. He had long since stopped receiving royalties on SCRABBLE, and Alfred's Other Game, while certainly playable, never threatened to become a classic. Mostly, he was a man in his mid-eighties who was enjoying an unexpected opportunity for some fun and recognition.

It was during the Boston trip that I really spent a lot of time with this American genius. My chief memory was of our visit to a Sunday morning radio program. We were appearing on a show hosted by a Boston radio legend who called himself "the Culture Vulture." Each Sunday morning he interviewed a featured guest, then opened up the phone lines to his listeners.

It should be noted that WBCN is one of the most famous rock and roll stations in the United States. It's safe to say that many of the listeners were not what you'd characterize as typical SCRABBLE game enthusiasts and that a good portion of them had been awake since the night before.

But Alfred sat there and answered their questions, no matter how outrageous. One caller wanted to know the weirdest word he'd ever played. He couldn't think of any for himself, but repeated a story about his wife playing QUIXOTIC against him years earlier. Later, the family had presented her with a custom made T-shirt with the word emblazoned across the front. Another asked what, if he had to change the SCRABBLE game, he would do. Nothing came immediately to mind, Alfred said. He was sure, however, that his late friend James Brunot would probably have a slew of ideas. An M.I.T. student wanted to know the most points that could conceivably be scored in a SCRABBLE game. Alfred said he had no idea, that it might be too subjective to even figure out. Alfred added that he was happy whenever he scored 300 points.

After the show we received a tour of the radio station, including a peek at what was said to be the largest collection of rock and roll music in the United States. It was a great juxtaposition: eighty-five-year-old Alfred Butts wandering around the bowels of a radio station being introduced to legions of people who looked as if they'd just staggered home from a Grateful Dead concert. People were thrilled to meet the father of SCRABBLE—as in every other setting I'd ever seen him in.

On the way back from WBCN, Alfred asked the driver to pull over when he spotted a huge and impressive example of trompe l'oeil (a photo-realistic mural) on the side of an old brick building. Though a trained architect and accomplished artist, he apparently had not seen that many examples of the form in person; indeed, they are still rare in North America. After we stopped, Alfred got out of the car and walked over to take a closer look. He stood there for a few minutes and admired it, then walked back to the car. "That was really something," he told me. I agreed.

"How long do you think it took to do that?" he wondered. I told him I had no idea.

"Do you suppose they had real artists or just regular sign painters?"

Again, I told him I didn't have a clue. However, there was one thing I *did* realize: a mind like Alfred's is as curious at age 85 as it ever was!

My last memory of Alfred Mosher Butts is from June 1991. I was in a nursing home parking lot a few miles outside of Poughkeepsie, New York. Just before we left the car, my host, Alfred's great-nephew Robert Butts, opened the glove compartment of his car and pulled out a giant bag of M&Ms.

"Alfred is ninety-one years old," he said, "and I think these things keep him going."

"Whatever it takes," I told him, hoping *I'm* eating M&Ms at ninety-one.

How ironic, I thought, that the man who invented the SCRABBLE game,

Alfred Mosher Butts, was "surviving" on a candy named after a letter of the alphabet.

I had not seen Alfred for three years. He had been involved in an automobile accident while driving at the age of eighty-eight and he did not get around as he once had. Still, it would be a mistake to say he was just sitting around a nursing home and eating candy. As Robert Butts explained, "Alfred now listens more than he talks. But there is still a lot going on in that magnificent brain."

I had hoped to actually play Alfred a SCRABBLE game that day. Robert had told me that his uncle still played an occasional lightning-fast game with nurses and other residents. But Alfred was a little tired that day. As a result our visit was limited to a half an hour or so and the conversation, though warm, was mostly me talking and Alfred listening.

While an attendant was checking on Alfred, I experienced a clear and acute sense of privilege just being in the room with him. As he and Robert spoke, I reviewed to myself the remarkable legacy Alfred Butts had created.

A SCRABBLE set was in 30 million American homes, 100 million sets had been sold worldwide. In the U.S. and Canada alone, there were over seventy-five official SCRABBLE game tournaments every year and hundreds of official SCRABBLE game clubs. There was a biennial national championship. A typical American championship has three-hundred-plus word experts from thirty-five states and several countries, all of them battling it out for twenty-seven rounds in just four and a half days. That's about seven hours of play a day. A recent national tournament in Thailand featured nine hundred players.

But this day in 1991 I was delivering a particularly sweet message, a new statistic, to the inventor of the game. I had come to tell Alfred in person that the first-ever World SCRABBLE® Championship was going to be held a few months later in London. After the dramatic events around the rest of the world at that time—the Berlin Wall and Lenin's statue had both been toppled—all factions in the SCRABBLE universe had at last agreed on a way to get together and play.

Propped up in his nursing home bed, Alfred Butts listened as I set the stage. Teams from twenty countries would compete. They would include experts from Sri Lanka, Kenya, Israel, Japan, and Nigeria, as well as the more predictable United States, Canada, England, and Australia. Everyone would, of course, play in English.

However, we would be using both the North American and British dictionaries, which meant all players would try to learn an additional thirty thousand words from the "foreign" lexicon. On the final day of the event, two players would battle it out on national television for a $10,000 first prize.

As I expected, Alfred was stunned at the scope and pageantry of this upcoming international event. That he had started it all six decades earlier—in his living room, in the middle of the Great Depression—was almost impossible for him to absorb. Finally, after processing this information for another minute, he looked at me.

"I wish I could be there," he said.

I waited a beat, too.

"Believe me, Alfred," I told him, "you will be."

When Alfred Butts died in 1993, he had already seen SCRABBLE expand worldwide from local clubs and tournaments to national championships to a world championship that included twenty-two nations. Our next chapter will give you a good introduction to the world of organized SCRABBLE game play.

LEAVING YOUR LIVING ROOM: WHAT YOU CAN EXPECT

Now that you've read much of this book and are anxious to meet new SCRABBLE® partners, the world of SCRABBLE game Clubs and Tournaments is awaiting you! There are over two hundred official SCRABBLE game Clubs throughout North America.

The first thing you should know is that every type of person imaginable plays at our clubs! It doesn't matter who you are or whether you're an expert or novice—if you enjoy the game, you'll be welcome at any of our clubs. We try hard to make sure no one is intimidated, either socially or skill-wise.

PLAYING ONE-ON-ONE

Another thing you should know is that club games are always played one-on-one. One reason is because in two-person games each player has the opportunity to make more plays and has less waiting time between turns. The other chief reason is that in the two-person game it is mostly the players' skills which determine who wins or loses. In three- or four-person games, the luck factor is increased enormously. We estimate that in a two-person game, the outcome is based upon luck 15 percent of the time. In the three- or four-handed game, luck may be an important factor as much as 40 percent of the time.

However, we're not suggesting that you stop playing your four-sided SCRABBLE games if you enjoy them. We just want our readers to know that our clubs provide a venue for players who like the challenge of playing one-on-one.

The only exception to this rule of one-on-one is when two or more players decide to play as a team, pooling their knowledge and competing against another team of players. Often these partnership games are more lively than the regular one-on-one contests. That's because players talk and often joke around with one another about their plays. At the same time, they're trying to avoid telegraphing information to their opponents, which can often produce some clever wordplay, both on and off the game board. This is frequently the way players relax during off-hours at tournaments.

TIMED GAMES

Another important thing you should know about clubs is that most use some sort of device to time the plays. While this isn't universally done, you can expect it at the more established clubs.

There are two types of timers the National SCRABBLE® Association recommends. The older method is to use three-minute sand timers. Each player has three minutes to form his or her play on the board and announce the score. The opponent has to warn the player when the sand has almost all run down; otherwise the player gets a few extra seconds. Games timed this way are ended after an hour, regardless of how many tiles haven't been played.

By ending games after an hour, several can be played during an evening. This allows players a chance to compete against several different opponents. While many of our readers may regularly take two or three hours to complete one game, the timed club play will challenge them to think faster. At first, many new club players have a hard time dealing with the faster pace. But within weeks they are grateful, because they notice a marked increase in their playing speed, which translates into *more playing time!* If you don't believe us, try it at home first.

The newer method for timing SCRABBLE games is to use a chess clock—or, as we like to say, a tournament clock. Clocks are much more popular among tournament players than sand timers, because they typically give each player a total of twenty-five minutes to complete all of his or her turns. (There is a 10-point penalty for each minute or fraction of a minute used over the allotted twenty-five.) A tournament clock comes in a plastic or wooden frame which houses two individual clocks—one for your time, the other for your opponent's. At the top of each clockface is a button that, when pressed, stops one clock and starts the other.

The advantage of the clock is that a fast player can make the easy plays in just a few seconds, thus saving up extra time to work on the difficult racks. An added feature is that an inexperienced player can be given more than twenty-five minutes, while an expert may handicap him or herself by starting with only fifteen or twenty. In addition, using a clock ensures that the game will *always* be played to completion. That doesn't always happen when using sand timers.

Some people initially find the clock intimidating. They're constantly looking to see how much time they have left. And often their opponent has to remind them to press their clock. But after they've played several games and become used to the quicker pace, they settle down and are able to concentrate solely on the game. At first, don't be afraid to ask your club director for more than twenty-five minutes if you're having a difficult time. But don't be surprised when your director urges you, after several weeks of practice, to speed up your pace.

PROTILES

Another thing you should know about club and tournament play is the existence of "Protiles." Robert Schoenman, a businessman who finished eighth in the 1993 World SCRABBLE® Championship, created a plastic set of tiles whose lettering cannot be determined from touch alone. Currently, the regular or deluxe set of SCRABBLE tiles that is included with each Milton Bradley SCRABBLE® Game is engraved. Although most people might not be able to determine which letter they are touching, most people *can* determine whether they have a blank or not. The Protiles are smooth and provide club and tournament players with the security of knowing that their opponents can't feel for blanks as they draw tiles from the bag. Understanding the needs of tournament players, Milton Bradley licensed Mr. Schoenman to create these tiles for the several thousand tournament players. Protiles are made in a variety of colors.

SCRABBLE® GAME CLUB ATMOSPHERE

Although the National SCRABBLE® Association has guidelines for licensed directors, there remains a wide spectrum of experiences for the new club player. Some clubs have a very informal atmosphere. Players at these clubs may play whomever they want, whenever they're available. There may be laughing and talking during play that often helps to develop long-lasting friendships as well as improved word skills.

At the other end of the spectrum, there are other clubs that are more competitive. The players there are very quiet during play—though not between games! New players may be given word lists to help them develop their skills and are often offered instruction. New club players may find themselves losing frequently before they learn enough new words to score between 300 and 400 points a game. Players with patience who can endure losing these early games will reap exhilarating benefits. After some experience, most novices learn the techniques for rack balancing and looking for bingos, and eventually learn how to win their fair share of games.

Somewhere in between are clubs with both competitive tournament players and informal social players. Often these clubs have enough members to allow the social players to play amongst themselves and the tournament players to play a more "serious" SCRABBLE game.

Regardless of the type of club you attend, the feedback reaching the National SCRABBLE® Association is that the players at successful clubs grow into close-knit families. In order to accomplish this, the savvy director will be guided by his or her players' input. That means that as a new member of a SCRABBLE® Game Club, you should let your director hear your suggestions for improving its operation.

Those readers who live in an area where there are no clubs may develop their own by ordering our SCRABBLE® Game Club Director's Kit (see Appendix Three). It has all you'd want to know about organizing and directing a SCRABBLE® Game Club or Tournament.

HOW DO YOU RATE?

We get asked frequently different forms of the same question: "I regularly outscore most of my friends in SCRABBLE. I average 350 to 400 points per game. How good am I? Would I be considered an expert?"

Here's our answer, in two parts: If you've become familiar with most of the two- and three-letter words and your average score is at least 300 points, you'll probably win your share of games at most SCRABBLE® Clubs. Most clubs have players who average anywhere from 250 to 400 points per game.

Those of you who average 350 to 400 against your friends will probably find that initially your average will go down at a SCRABBLE® Club, and will stay down until you become familiar with your new competitors. Regardless of your average score with your friends, a better judge of skill is your average score per turn. Not counting your exchanges, if you average 25 to 30 points per turn, you may be an expert already! The best players average 30 to 35 points per turn against their toughest competitors.

TOURNAMENT PLAY

For competitive players who thrive on testing their skills, the tournament scene can give you everything you'd expect in excitement, drama, camaraderie, and, of course, SCRABBLE games—and plenty of them! While there may be only a few players who win the top prizes, everyone who plays is a winner in so many other ways. Your character, stamina, and skills will be tested and will likely improve. You'll also meet a variety of interesting people, including some who might become regular playing partners.

Those of you who take the plunge will find that most tournaments have several divisions of players. This ensures that you'll be playing against others relatively close to your skill level. After your first tournament, you'll receive a rating which represents your skills in relation to other rated players. After 30 to 40 tournament games, your rating will be fairly accurate to within 200 rating points.

Briefly, your initial rating will be based in part upon the average rating of all your opponents. If you finish with five wins and five losses in your first tournament, and the average rating of all your opponents is 1,200, then your first rating will be about 1,200. If instead you finish with six wins and only four losses against the same opponents, your first rating may be closer to 1,300. The ten highest rated players are rated between 2,000 and 2,100; the lowest ten are below 500.

There are a variety of tournament experiences you may encounter. Some events last only one day and involve playing five to seven games (also called "rounds"). Most last ten to twelve rounds and are played over a Saturday and Sunday. For instance, two of the most popular annual twelve-round tournaments in the country are held in Waltham, Massachusetts, in early April and in Atlantic City near the end of January. These events have three and four divisions of players, respectively, and usually draw over two hundred players. The top divisions of these events regularly draw many of the top twenty players in the nation.

For specific information on the two hundred SCRABBLE® Game Clubs and seventy to eighty tournaments run annually in the United States, contact the National SCRABBLE® Association, Box 700, Greenport, NY 11944; (516) 477-0033.

For a more demanding (some say exhilarating) experience, you might like to try the longer events. The annual Western Championship, held in Reno, Nevada, in July, lasts eighteen rounds, has three divisions, draws two hundred players, and is usually held over a three-day weekend. For a slightly different experience, the eighteen-round championship in Gatlinburg, Tennessee, is held in late March or early April, and has seven or eight divisions of twenty to twenty-six players each. The divisions are formed solely on the basis of rating. That is, Division 1 includes only the highest-rated players, whereas the last division has the lowest-rated players, along with any unrated newcomers. The first prize in *each* division is usually $500. So even an unrated player in the lowest division may win a significant prize.

For the ultimate in tournament play, there is the National SCRABBLE® Championship, held every other summer in even-numbered years. Provided you have earned a rating—*any* rating—in at least one previous NSA-rated tournament, you can participate in this incredible event. The National

SCRABBLE® Championship has three divisions, though the winner of the top division is crowned the new national champion. This event is held in a different American city each time, and extends for twenty-seven rounds over five days, usually from Sunday through Thursday. Each participant plays six rounds each of the first four days, then the final three on Thursday morning.

Our National SCRABBLE® Championship regularly draws between three and four hundred players. It's an unforgettable week of eating, breathing, sleeping, playing, laughing, complaining, and talking SCRABBLE. It's a time to reestablish friendships and make new ones while enjoying one of the best games on the planet. Of course, we're not prejudiced or anything!

Milton Bradley Company, manufacturer and distributor of the game, generously sponsors the National SCRABBLE® Championship. A total of $55,000 in cash and more than 130 individual prizes was awarded in the 1994 championship. First prize was $15,000 in cash. The SCRABBLE game is unique in its ability to provide many different inspiring prize categories. Here is a partial list of the prizes awarded at the 1994 National SCRABBLE® Championship:

Expert Division: 1st place, $15,000; **2nd place,** $7,500.

Division 2 (restricted to those rated below 1700): 1st place, $2,500; **2nd place,** $1,000.

Division 3 (restricted to those rated below 1400): 1st place, $1,000; **2nd place,** $750.

Highest-Scoring Game for each round, in each division: $25.

Highest-Losing Score for each round, in each division: $20.

Highest-Scoring Acceptable Play each day in each division: $25.

Greatest Comeback Award, to the player who was furthest behind during a game, then went on to win that game, in each division: $50.

Tuff Luck Award to the player in each division who lost six games by the smallest total point spread: $50.

Best Win-Loss Record on Day 3 for those in the bottom half of the standings at the beginning of Day 3, in each division: $250.

Best Win-Loss Record on Day 4 for those in the bottom half of the standings at the beginning of Day 4, in each division: $150.

Lowest-Scoring Win, in each division: $25.

Flashiest Bingo, in each division: $50.

Best Strategic Play: $250. Not awarded in 1992 due to lack of entries meeting the requirements: a) must be the best play; b) must be one of several playing options; c) must not be an obvious move, but must be based on clever, thorough, creative, or inspired reasoning. The winner is determined by a panel of experts well after the event.

All the upcoming tournament information can be read in the *SCRABBLE®*

News, which you will receive with your membership in the National SCRAB-BLE® Association.

This is important: Before playing in any tournament, become familiar with the Official National SCRABBLE® Association Tournament Rules. While tournament play is essentially the same as home play, the rules are designed to encompass many unusual situations that may arise in a competitive atmosphere. Club play can be informal, but tournament players are sticklers for following the rules. There are several ways that ignorance of the rules can cost you victories. It's inevitable that some people will learn the hard way, but you can avoid most of the hazards by simply reading the rules a few times. As a new member of the NSA, you will automatically receive a free copy of the Official Tournament Rules.

If you have any questions concerning the National SCRABBLE® Association Tournament Rules, please contact our office at: National SCRABBLE® Association, Box 700, Greenport, NY 11944.

Now that you've read about SCRABBLE game experts, you may be curious as to what it takes to join their ranks. Chapter Twenty-one will show you exactly what the expert knows and how s/he wins.

21

SO YOU THINK YOU WANT TO BE A TOURNAMENT EXPERT?
A Word to the Wise

Based on what you've learned so far, you may now want to join the growing numbers of club and tournament players throughout the world. Some of you may even want to enhance your skills and become a SCRABBLE® expert. If so, we'd like to tell you what to expect. Our reason for telling you these secrets is twofold. First, we want to demystify what many articles in the media have tended to show the public—that SCRABBLE game experts are a strange bunch of people who love to memorize obscure words, and that they have amazing word skills that normal people can't possibly develop without studying for hundreds of hours.

Not true! First of all, we know very few players who like to memorize words. Instead, most players simply play the SCRABBLE game and slowly try to remember all the words played against them. They also look at other players' boards to learn new words. If you drop by a club and watch a few games, you'll quickly pick up many new words. However, we'll repeat what we said earlier: look up all unfamiliar words. You're sure to see some phoneys on many boards.

Do you know anybody who can type sixty to eighty words per minute? Of course. With new computer keyboards, in fact, many experienced typists do better than that. But you don't develop that skill overnight! The same applies to your SCRABBLE skills. First you have to learn the proper techniques. In typing, it's learning the touch-typing method and practicing it that leads to speed-typing. In the SCRABBLE game, it's learning the fundamentals, and then simply practicing by *playing*! While you're at it, toss a few anagrams to your friends and have them likewise test you. It's fun!

We admit that our second reason for this chapter is very selfish. We'd simply like to have more good players to play with! We love to meet new people and have fun playing the SCRABBLE game with them. Since we believe that most anyone can become skilled at the SCRABBLE game—and that with the proper approach it's painless—we want to show as many people as possible how.

A SIMPLE STEP-BY-STEP METHOD

To raise your abilities to the highest level, there are basically four separate skills you'll need to develop. First are the vocabulary and word-finding skills. Second are the over-the-board playing skills, particularly during the end-game. Third are the skills to evaluate your opponent's game strengths and weaknesses and to use that knowledge to your advantage. Fourth, but certainly not least, are the emotional skills, or attitude.

As you read this chapter, please keep in mind that it's our experience that most people, regardless of their initial skills, can eventually earn an expert rating. In the National SCRABBLE® Association, this currently means a rating of 1600 or higher.

STEP ONE: IMPROVE YOUR VOCABULARY SKILLS

In order to make the jump to become an expert, you can't avoid learning new words. While we've mentioned this earlier—suggesting in Chapter Twelve which words to learn first—you'll want to know several categories of words. Here are those you should concentrate on, in the approximate order they should be learned.

All ninety-four two-letter words. You won't find all the great parallel plays unless you know all these words. See Chapter Three for maximizing the usage of the two-letter words.

All the two-to-make-three-letter words. While you won't necessarily need all the three-letter words, you will earn more parallel-play points by learning these gems. For example: On our starter sheet, be prepared to start with each two-letter word and record all its hooks: BA—ABA, BAA, BAD, BAG, BAH, BAL, BAM, BAN, BAR, BAS, BAT, and BAY. When you can create this list accurately and quickly for all the two-letter words, you'll be on a par with the experts.

Most of the three-to-make-four-letter words. The same reasoning as above can be used for these words. Since there are fewer hooks per word, these are actually much easier to learn than the two-to-make-threes.

Most of the four- and five-letter JQXZ non-bingo words. After becoming familiar with this list, you'll be able to take advantage of the many obscure JQXZ words that often form high-scoring plays. Any expert you meet will be able to do this.

The SATIRE, SATINE, and RETINA six-to-make-seven-letter words. Imagine that after several turns you've been able to save your good letters and finally have the rack AEEIRST. What do you play? Any expert will be able to instantly rattle off the two bingos on this rack: AERIEST and SERIATE. Once you learn these words, look at some of the other high-frequency six-letter stem lists (pages 265–67). You'll eventually want to become familiar with most of the words on the top hundred stems—if only to be able to recognize your opponents' phoneys or good words! "High-frequency" stems or bingos are those that show up on racks more often than most others.

Learning these words is actually not as hard as it might appear at first glance. Most of the words have familiar letter arrangements. Once you learn how the various letters combine, remembering or finding these words becomes easier and easier.

RE and UN word lists. By far the most phoneys played are those that begin with RE or UN. You will need to be familiar with the acceptable words in order to know whether you're about to play a phoney, or whether your opponent just has.

Five-letter words with one or more 3- or 4-point tiles (BCMPFHVWY), such as HAKIM or FAKIR. These words are the workhorses that give you 25-to-35-point plays. The more you know, the better you'll be able to score, and to rid your rack of awkward tiles.

The words with multiple vowels. Occasionally, all players draw too many vowels. While the novice is apt to exchange them, the expert will be able to find a play that uses several vowels. Become familiar with the words on pages 268–69; they will show up on your rack repeatedly. As you learn the high-frequency bingos, review the seven- and eight-letter words that have five vowels. You'll be surprised how often they can turn a horrible rack into a 70-point play. The top players typically know most of them.

STEP TWO: IMPROVE YOUR PLAYING SKILLS AND ENDGAME PLAY

There is no substitute for being able to find the high-scoring plays and correctly choosing which one balances your rack the best. But what other strategies are there? We discussed learning how to open and close the board at appropriate times. Is that enough? Can one learn to be an expert without further playing skills? Unless you have the wherewithal to memorize the whole dictionary, the answer is *no*! A further skill the expert develops is how to maximize winning chances when there are very few tiles left to draw.

To illustrate, let's look at the current computer programs and see how their playing abilities compare with those of the best players. From several years of play, we've determined that the computer programs that always make the highest-scoring plays are about as good as the 100th top-rated player. These programs have little concern for rack balance, the endgame, or the openness of a board. That means that if you simply learn all the words in the OSPD2 and are able to find them over the board, you won't need much strategy to beat most anyone.

Moving up a notch, there are at least two outstanding computer programs that consider rack balancing in their decision-making. These programs play about as well as the 50th top-rated player. There is one program that includes rack balance and plays a nearly perfect endgame. At its highest level, the program plays as well as any human being in the world. It is clear that endgame skills are of vital importance to the very best players.

Given the above, we thought we would provide our readers with some tips on how to improve endgame play.

Incidentally, the endgame is the most difficult, yet often the most aesthetically beautiful, part of SCRABBLE. Many games between experts are won or lost in the last two or three plays. And you don't have to know all the words to enjoy playing a good endgame position.

Tracking Tiles

The first thing to know is that you can't play an endgame well unless you know which tiles are left to play. The expert tracks the tiles played during the game so that s/he always knows what's left to draw. In fact, many players include a list of the 100 tiles (9 As, 2 Bs, etc.) printed on their score sheets. This is called either a "frequency list" or a (preprinted) "Tracking Sheet." As the letters are played on the board, they are crossed off the list. Many players create their own special tracking sheets, though some directors provide them free at tournaments.

How does tracking help you win games? As most experts can tell you, SCRABBLE is a game of probabilities. You can make more effective decisions regarding your rack leave and your opponent's next play if you know what tiles are left to play. For instance:

A. It might help you to know the precise number of vowels or consonants left to play. Example: Your rack is AAEKNPT with three tiles in the bag, and your tracking shows that all the vowels but your three have been played on the board. You should be able to take advantage of the fact that your opponent has no vowels! Look to form setup plays that your opponent can't block because s/he has no vowels. (See Chapter Twenty-two, Diagram 22-11, for a good example of a setup play.)

B. Knowing whether you can get stuck with the Q should affect your thinking about the last few plays. Example: There is one tile in the bag. Three of the four Us are on the board and you don't know where the Q is. You're 60 points ahead. The eight unseen tiles are ADELNQUW. You realize there is no way you can lose the game unless you get stuck with the Q. Solution: Pass your turn! Let your opponent either play his Q or draw it. While you may win by fewer points (since most of the time your opponent will get a free turn and 25 to 30 free points), you guarantee the win! If your opponent doesn't have the Q, realizes your strategy, and passes, just remember that after six passes the game will be over, and you'll win!

Instead, if you make a play on the board, you're likely to win only 87 percent to 95 percent of the time, losing when you get stuck with the Q. That's not nearly as good as 100 percent of the time, as many unlucky players will testify. They'll tell you about the games in which they were 100 points ahead with one tile in the bag, then lost because they drew the Q and couldn't play it. In many of these cases, they simply didn't take the proper precautions.

Questions we often hear from those attempting to learn tracking are:

Q: What's the use of tracking? I've tried it and all that happens is that I get confused.

A: That's not uncommon. We find that everyone gets a little rattled when s/he first learns how to track. Although we're not brain scientists, from our own experience it seems that the acts of tracking, scoring, and looking for words utilize different parts of the brain. Doing all three tasks at the same time involves an extra effort—"switching gears," so to speak.

In order to avoid this confusion, track only the ten "power tiles" and the four Us. The power tiles are the two blanks, the four Ss, and the J, Q, X, and Z.

Or if you really want to start slowly, just keep track of the Ss and blanks. Just knowing which of these letters are still available can give you that extra edge in deciding how many tiles to play late in the game. You can learn to track more of the tiles as you gain experience. Many experts will admit it took a year or more before they could track all 100 tiles accurately without negatively affecting their playing skills.

Q: How can I take advantage of tracking?

A: Stop to look at your tracking sheet before you make your final decision to play a word. When at least sixty tiles have been played, use your tracking sheet to answer some of the following questions (or others) which may arise as you look for your best play:

1. "Do I need or want to draw the X or E or any other special tile in order to win?" The answer to this question may tell you whether you should play more or fewer tiles per turn.
2. "Do I need to avoid drawing certain tiles (e.g., Q or Z)?" If yes, you may want to play fewer tiles.
3. "Am I far behind, with no bingo in sight?" In that case look for ways to set up the remaining high-point letters, even if you haven't drawn them yet. Remember that even if your opponent draws them, you'd have lost anyway!
4. "Am I way ahead?" If so, do you need to block your opponent from using certain bonus squares? In that case, be aware of hot spots where the

unplayed X, Z, or J can earn game-winning scores. Then block those hot spots to keep your opponent from catching up.

5. "What's the vowel-consonant situation?" If one player has either no vowels or no consonants, that could give his or her opponent an enormous advantage in the endgame. You'll also want to be alert to whether your next leave should have more consonants or vowels.

6. "Of the vowels left, which am I likely to duplicate on my rack?" Near the end of the game, if there are five Is, two As, and one E left to play, you probably want to rid your rack of Is.

7. "How many Ns, Rs, and Ts are still available? Which am I more likely to draw?" Since you want to avoid duplication of letters, you can use this knowledge to decide which consonant to play when a choice is available.

8. "Can I afford to pass, hoping my opponent will draw the Q, thereby increasing my chances of winning?" See example **B** above. You may not be able to answer these questions confidently at first. If not, then guess. Later, ask an expert what s/he would have done. The more you ask questions and get good answers, the quicker you'll gain the experience to rely on your own answers. See Chapter Twenty-two, Diagrams 22-10 through 22-15, for six examples of excellent endgame play.

STEP THREE: LEARN YOUR OPPONENT'S STRENGTHS AND WEAKNESSES

As you have seen throughout this book, there are several different skills by which you may measure your opponents. As you recognize each of these skills, or lack thereof, you can play accordingly to maximize your chances of winning.

Bingo Vision: Does your opponent have an extensive bingo vocabulary? If so, watch for the telltale one- and two-tile fishing plays. While everyone occasionally fishes for bingos, the true Bingo Master will more often draw for and then actually play the bingo on the next turn. Much of the time you won't be able to do anything about it. But when you have a choice of plays, consider making a blocking play if your opponent has telegraphed his or her intentions.

On the other hand, the would-be Bingo Master may have a weakness: overfishing. There are many who rely too heavily on bingos to win their games. This results in their fishing with a 10-to-15-point play instead of taking a strategically sounder 25-to-30-point play. If you encounter these players, and see that they don't draw their bingos very frequently on their following plays, you can probably rest a little easier about opening the board with a play of 25 to 30 points. In other words: Don't be afraid of opening the board when you have a decent play against those who fish too much!

Defense: There are players who delight in blocking the board. They will often take 10 points instead of 30 just to block the board. If you face one of these people, play as open as you can! They won't take advantage of the opportunities. They'll be too preoccupied trying to block the board. And even if they see their better plays, they'll often be afraid to play them, since they may open the board more!

Turnover: If your opponent plays only two or three tiles per turn, go out of your way to play more tiles whenever you have the choice, even if you score fewer points. That's to ensure that you have a better chance to draw the blanks and Ss ahead of your opponent. The more tiles you play, the better chance you have of drawing the better tiles. However, we caution you to be prudent with this principle, since it's not always optimal. It works best with opponents who generally play too few tiles.

Knowing Your Opponent: What is your opponent thinking? As in poker, there are telltale signs of body language that can help you read your opponent's thoughts. Every player exhibits different signals unconsciously, so you should approach learning about your opponents individually. Furthermore, some may want to mislead you with a variety of silent mannerisms. The more you play with a variety of opponents, the more experience and skill in this area you'll develop.

How do you take advantage of reading your opponent? Here's one way: If you truly believe your opponent has a bad rack, you should consider making the play that opens the board but gives you the best leave. This puts pressure on your opponent. S/he may think: "Do I exchange tiles and leave the opening for my opponent, or make a 12-point blocking play and keep a horrible leave?" By presenting your opponents with such difficult decisions, not only do you take advantage of their poor rack, but you give them a chance to make a mistake.

In conjunction with the above, ask yourself: Do you telegraph your thinking to your opponent? If you do, then you will probably find yourself losing to players with lesser vocabularies and weaker anagramming skills. Try to keep your body movements and facial expressions as neutral as possible. For example, suppose you feel a strong emotional response every time you draw a playable bingo. Many times this won't matter. However, if you show any sign of this emotion when there is only one bingo opening on the board, don't be surprised if the opening is blocked!

Hooks: Some players are known for setting up hook plays. For instance, early in a game at a national championship, one expert played the unusual word OORALIS horizontally. He began this word at 8B, one square to the right of the middle Triple Word Score on 8A. What he was hoping was that his opponent wouldn't know the word WOORALIS, which is a variant spelling of OORALIS. Later, with a W and just a few other letters, he scored 60-

plus points with that hook word. This is good strategy if you think your opponent doesn't know a particular word. And even if s/he does, you may be the first one to draw the hook letter.

Knowing when it's advantageous to leave such dangerous hooks means knowing your opponent's temperament and vocabulary. (Is s/he defensive? Does s/he know the word?) As we said above, any play that pressures the opponent may lead to a strategic blunder that gives you better odds of winning.

STEP FOUR: DEVELOP THE RIGHT ATTITUDES

You now have the necessary vocabulary and playing skills, but you still don't win as often as you think you should. You are ready for the last piece from the SCRABBLE game expert's bag of tricks—the right mental approach.

The first thing you need to know—and always remember—is that everybody loses! You may play as well as the best player in the world and still not win. It's just as important to recognize that as it is to realize that most losses are accompanied by playing errors. To help you keep a perspective, you might want to do what some veteran tournament players do. They count how many of the ten power tiles they drew during a loss. If they drew three or fewer, it's likely that luck was definitely against them.

Luck aside, you need to know how you can guard against making mistakes. Your goal, as a good player, is to:

1. **Always strive to find the best play available to you.**
2. **Once you've found a good play, look for a better one.**
3. **Ask yourself: "How do I know I've found the best play?"**

Let's discuss these elements individually in order to understand them better.

1. Always strive to find the best play available to you.

That may seem like a really silly thing to suggest. We can almost hear the response: "Of course I'm always looking for the best play! You don't need to waste time writing that!"

Our answer is that in the reality of competing against another human being, this simple motto is often forgotten. Here is a collection of thoughts that can interfere with your good thinking:

"Is this a collection of garbage tiles, or what?"

"I'll never win this game! It looks hopeless!"

"If I draw one more U, I'm quitting!"

If you've had these thoughts, or something like them, you're not alone. To compound your task, they're often accompanied by a substantial negative emotional response.

Your ability to find your best play will be affected by how much energy you give to feeling bad about your rack. The more victimized you feel, the more likely your next play will be a poor one.

Watch for these negative thoughts. When they intrude, just notice them dispassionately, then refocus your attention on your rack and the board. **Stay alert about finding your best play among all the poor options.** Our experience is that you're likely to gather tremendous positive energy from a pure, childlike state of curiosity about what plays are possible in a given situation. Remember, you may lose anyway, but if you find a spectacular play you can emotionally accept the loss.

Here are a couple of more attitude traps:

"I've never beaten this guy! He knows far more words than I do. Why even bother?"

"Look who my opponent is. This should be a piece of cake!"

There's probably not a player alive who hasn't had one of these thoughts when facing a particular opponent. When you have such thoughts, *beware*! That's because there is an element of luck in SCRABBLE, and almost anybody can beat anyone else on any particular occasion. We've seen players in tournaments repeatedly lose to opponents whom they beat consistently when there is nothing at stake. Thoughts that either overestimate or underestimate your playing skills definitely keep you from the task at hand. So, when you have such thoughts, just smile to yourself and appreciate the fact that you were alert enough to notice them. Then return to looking for the best play.

Here is another:

"Look what I missed! What an idiotic play that was!"

Everyone makes mistakes over the SCRABBLE game board. If you should catch one of yours before the game ends, especially one that cost you the game, you'll undoubtedly feel a bit frustrated. We've seen many players lose their cool after an ill-timed challenge or missed bingo. When this happens they're practically guaranteed to make a poor next play. In fact, these negative emotional states can sometimes last for several games. We've seen top players go from 6 wins and 0 losses to 6 wins and 4 losses, often due to an accumulation of negative energy. A well-known champion has twice ended important tournaments losing the last three games. In one he still managed to finish in first place. In the other, he finished second by a total of only 30 points. On each occasion, he admitted, it wasn't just luck; there was an element of negativity in his thinking.

Somehow, you need to recognize that mistakes are a part of the game. All the top players make them occasionally. Sometimes, when they're made in a championship tournament, these errors can cost thousands of dollars. It's our experience that you'll feel better, and your opponents will respect you more, if you just hang tough. This is particularly important when you are playing a series of games, either at home or in a tournament. Most experts simply forget their mistakes and losses and move on to the next game, fully energetic and eager to play!

2. Once you've found a good play, look for a better one.

The expert will continue to look for better plays. Keep in mind that only when you know all the options will you be able to make the best choice. Since you don't have an unlimited amount of time to make each play, our suggestion is that you always look for a play that you consider "adequate." Then continue looking for a better one until you've used up whatever time you've allotted for that play.

We know a top player who, early in his SCRABBLE game career, held the tiles OVERDOS against a strong expert. There was an E on the board between two Double Word Scores. He was preparing to play OVERDOES for 98 points if his opponent didn't block him. His opponent kindly played the bingo CLEARING on another part of the board, placing the C in the third position between two Triple-Triples. This expert was so anxious to play OVERDOES that it wasn't until after he had started his opponent's timer and looked at the C that he suddenly realized what he had done. He asked his opponent sheepishly: "Could I take my play back?" What he had missed was VOCODERS for 185 points! Of course, his opponent wouldn't let him change his play.

3. Ask yourself "How do I know I've found the best play?"

You will probably never really know for sure if you've found the best play, given the fallibility of the human mind. But we suggest you'll be confident that you did your best if, before you play, you make a systematic search of the board. Experts routinely spend extra time doing exhaustive board searches to find their best plays, especially if they have a blank tile.

Even after a game is over, experts will often review all the significant or questionable plays of the game. By spending five or ten minutes discussing the merits of alternate plays, you'll learn new strategies and develop friendships with your opponents.

Now that we've given you all the tools, we'd like to show you how the best players put it all together. Chapter Twenty-two shows you some outstanding plays from actual tournament play. Enjoy!

22 | EXAMPLES OF OUTSTANDING SCRABBLE® GAME PLAY

Though most players don't record the words from their games, many like to recall their favorite plays. The following is a collection of fifteen examples of excellent expert play. All but one are taken either from club or tournament play. We offer these positions in order to share with you our appreciation of the possibilities, nuances, and beauty of SCRABBLE® play. Enjoy! Unless otherwise specified, the answers are common words.

Example 1

1990 National Championship, New York: Charlie Carroll, Minnesota (1991 Cincinnati, Ohio, Master's Champion)

	A	B	C	D	E	F	G	H	I	J	K	L	M	N	O	
	TWS			DLS				V					DLS	O	F	1
		DWS			TLS			I		TLS				Y	A	2
			DWS			DLS		R	DLS				DWS		D	3
	DLS			DWS				T				DWS		R	E	4
	C			H	DWS		O	U	T	R	A	N	G	E		5
	A	U	D	I	T	O	R			TLS				E		6
	J		DLS	T		DLS			DLS				DLS	Q		7
	O	F		DLS		K	N	O	B			E	T	U	I	8
	L	A	DLS			DLS	M	O	D	E	L			I		9
	E	X			TLS								TLS	P		10
				DWS			W	H	I	N				S	O	11
	DLS	S	A	R	D	I	N	E			D	U	B		P	12
			DWS			DLS			DLS			Y	A	G	I	13
		DWS			TLS					TLS				DWS	N	14
	TWS			DLS				G	A	S	O	L	I	N	E	15

DIAGRAM 22-1

Carroll's score: 371   Opponent's score: 380
Carroll's rack: A E I L M R T

Carroll can't bingo, but he does find the second-best play. His play would probably be unanimously voted the "flashiest" of most tournaments. You should have a good working knowledge of the two-letter words in order to find the play. Answer on page 241.

Example 2

Joe Edley, New York, vs. Rita Norr, Connecticut (1987 National Champion)

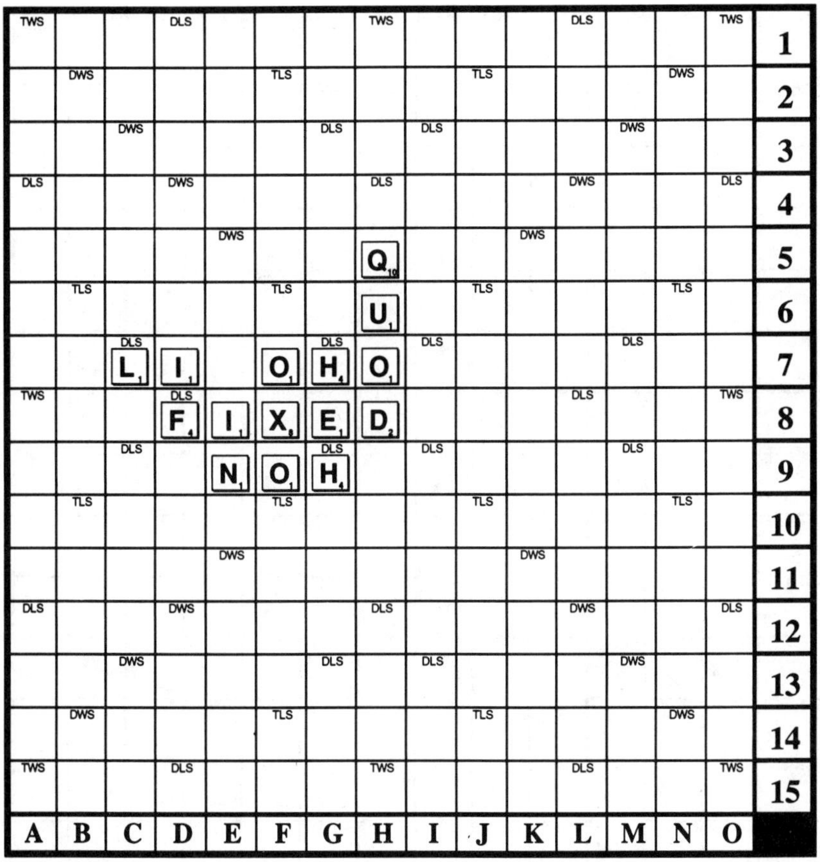

DIAGRAM 22-2

Edley's score: 79   Norr's score: 53
Edley's rack: D E E L P R S

Though PEDLERS is an acceptable bingo, it doesn't play. Answer on page 241.

This game was played during a friendly match prior to an upcoming tournament. Not all of our readers will be familiar with one of the three- or four-letter words considered as a play. We include this example because it shows how a knowledge of hook words can help you score more.

Example 3

1988 National SCRABBLE® Championship, Reno, Nevada: Brian Cappelletto, Arizona (runner-up, 1991 World Championship, England)

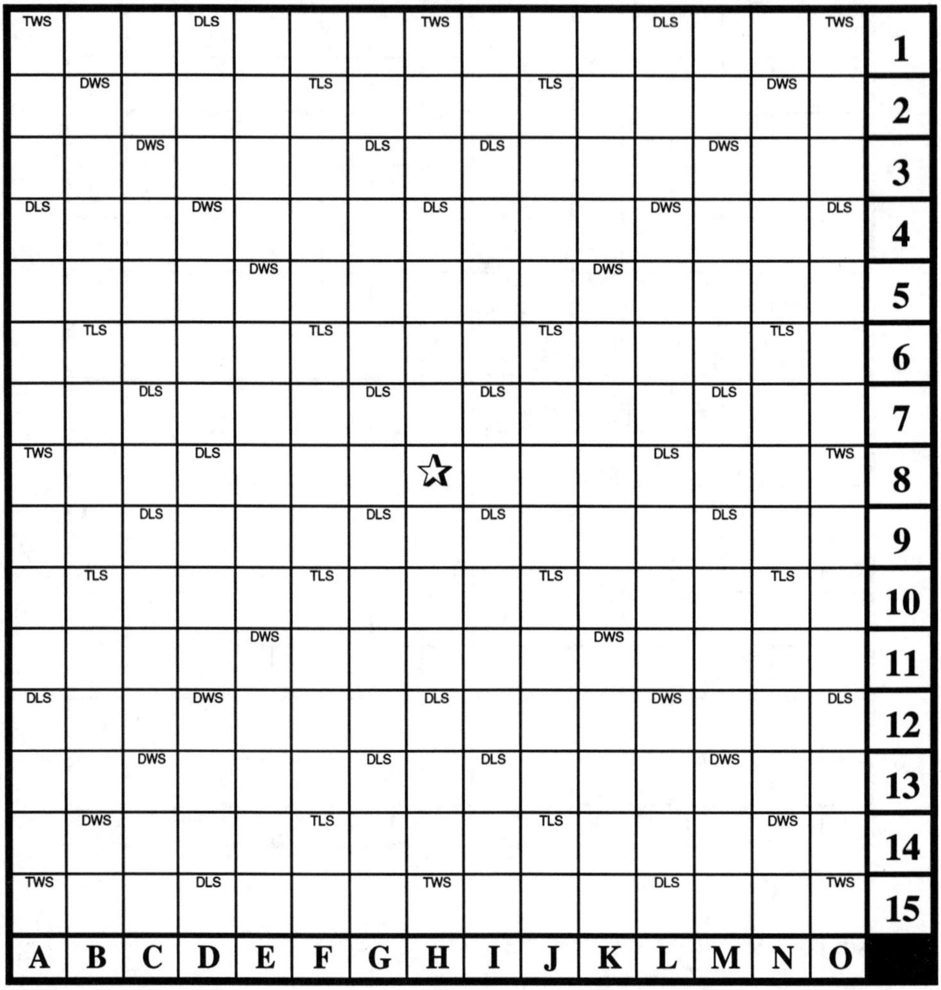

	A	B	C	D	E	F	G	H	I	J	K	L	M	N	O	
	TWS			DLS				TWS				DLS			TWS	**1**
		DWS				TLS				TLS				DWS		**2**
			DWS			DLS			DLS				DWS			**3**
	DLS			DWS			DLS					DWS			DLS	**4**
					DWS						DWS					**5**
		TLS				TLS				TLS				TLS		**6**
			DLS				DLS		DLS				DLS			**7**
	TWS			DLS				☆				DLS			TWS	**8**
			DLS			DLS		DLS					DLS			**9**
		TLS				TLS				TLS				TLS		**10**
					DWS						DWS					**11**
	DLS			DWS				DLS				DWS			DLS	**12**
			DWS			DLS			DLS				DWS			**13**
		DWS			TLS				TLS					DWS		**14**
	TWS			DLS				TWS				DLS			TWS	**15**

DIAGRAM 22-3

Score: 0–0   Cappelleto's rack: A E J M N R T

Though there is no bingo, Cappelletto looks further than the first few plays he sees (JAM, JET, TAJ, RAJ, etc.). Can you find a better play? Answer on page 241.

Example 4

1989 National SCRABBLE® Championship, New York City: Elaine Glowniak, Michigan

	A	B	C	D	E	F	G	H	I	J	K	L	M	N	O	
	TWS			DLS				TWS				DLS			TWS	**1**
		DWS				TLS				TLS				DWS		**2**
			DWS				DLS		DLS				DWS			**3**
	DLS			DWS				R(1)				DWS			DLS	**4**
					Q(10)	U(1)	O(1)	D(2)			DWS					**5**
		TLS				TLS	C(3)	O(1)	Z(10)	TLS				TLS		**6**
			DLS				DLS	R(1)	E(1)	D(2)	O(1)	X(8)	DLS	A(1)		**7**
	TWS			G(2)	R(1)	O(1)	V(4)	E(1)		E(1)		F(4)	I(1)	L(1)	M(3)	**8**
			DLS	A(1)			DLS	H(4)	I(1)	S(1)			DLS		I(1)	**9**
		TLS		N(1)		TLS				TLS				TLS		**10**
	R(1)	A(1)	W(4)	E(1)	R(1)						DWS					**11**
	U(1)		I(1)	F(4)				DLS				DWS			DLS	**12**
	T(1)	O(1)	N(1)				DLS		DLS				DWS			**13**
		A(1)	Y(4)			TLS				TLS				DWS		**14**
	TWS	K(5)		DLS				TWS				DLS			TWS	**15**

DIAGRAM 22-4

Glowniak's score: 177   Opponent's score: 124
Glowniak's rack: D E H N T U V

Though there is no bingo, Glowniak finds a very nice way to both balance her rack and score well. Answer on page 241.

Example 5

1992 Atlantic City Championship, New Jersey: Robert Felt, California (1990 National SCRABBLE® Champion)

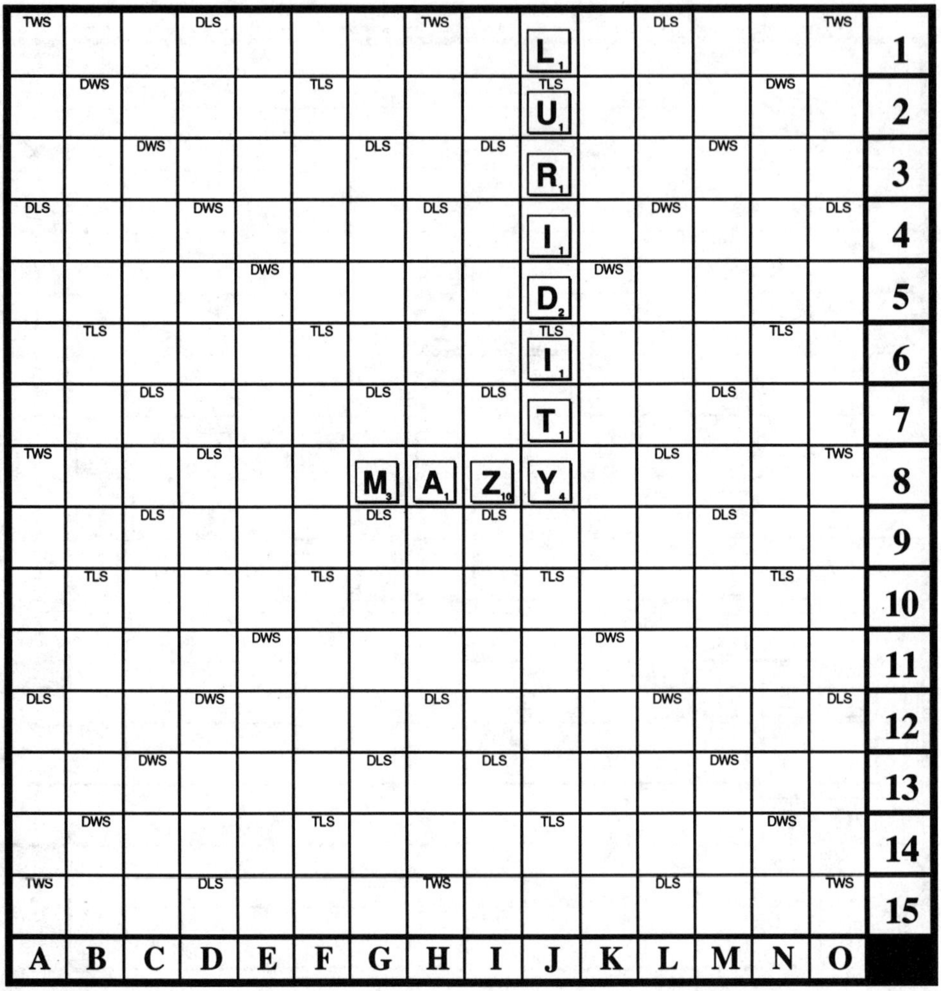

DIAGRAM 22-5

Felt's score: 36   Opponent's score: 0 or 66
Felt's rack: E P P R S T U

Opponent has just played LURIDITY. Felt called "Hold!" and is certain it is unacceptable. Should he challenge it off the board? He could instead play PURPLEST through the L for 89 points. What did he do? Answer on page 242.

Example 6

Michigan SCRABBLE Game Club, January 1993: Chuck Armstrong, Michigan (winner of more than 65 tournaments)

	A	B	C	D	E	F	G	H	I	J	K	L	M	N	O	
1	TWS			DLS				L	TWS			DLS			O	1
2	DWS				TLS			A	P	I	K	I	N	DWS G		2
3		DWS				DLS		N	DLS			DWS F		R		3
4	DLS M	U	DWS C	I	L	A	DLS G	E			DWS F		DLS E		4
5		DWS			DWS		S				DWS	Y		I		5
6	TLS				TLS V		Y		TLS			TLS		S		6
7			DLS		A	DLS	N	DLS	A	D	O	DLS	M		7
8	TWS		DLS B	A	N	N	E	R	S		A	X	I	TWS S		8
9			DLS			DLS		DLS O	U	D		DLS				9
10	TLS				TLS			TLS				TLS				10
11				DWS						DWS						11
12	DLS			DWS			DLS				DWS		DLS			12
13			DWS			DLS		DLS				DWS				13
14		DWS			TLS				TLS			DWS				14
15	TWS			DLS			TWS				DLS		TWS			15

DIAGRAM 22-6

Armstrong's rack: A E H O P R T

Armstrong found a very nice common-word bingo. He eventually wound up playing seven bingos this game. Besides the four already on the board and this one, he later played AWAITER and REOBJECT to finish with 710 points, a new non-phoney high-scoring record at the time. See Appendix Three for the current record. Answer on page 242.

Example 7

1987 National SCRABBLE® Championship, Las Vegas, Nevada: Howard Cohen, Florida

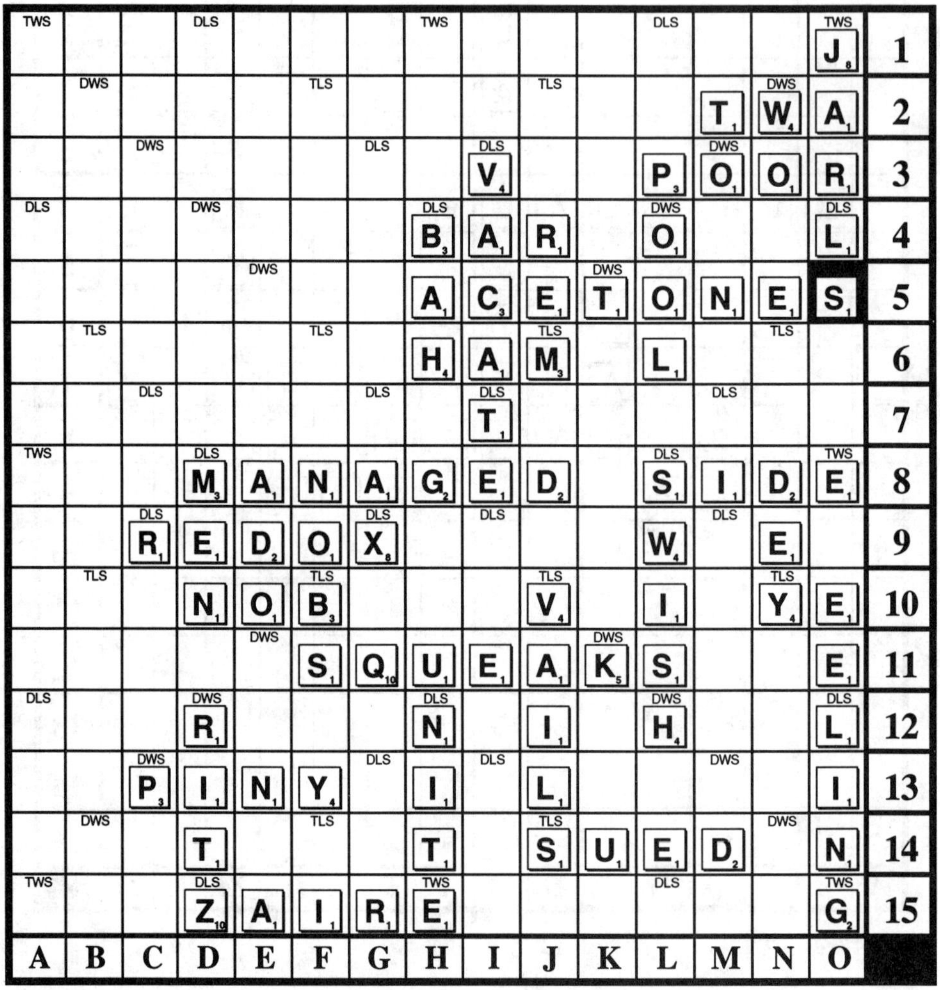

DIAGRAM 22-7

Cohen's rack: C E O R T U ?

Cohen is behind by 150 points and knows he can't win; nevertheless, he's able to find a beautiful play that we're sure he'll never forget. Answer on page 242.

Example 8

1989 Grand Canyon Tournament, Arizona: Alice Van Leunen, Oregon

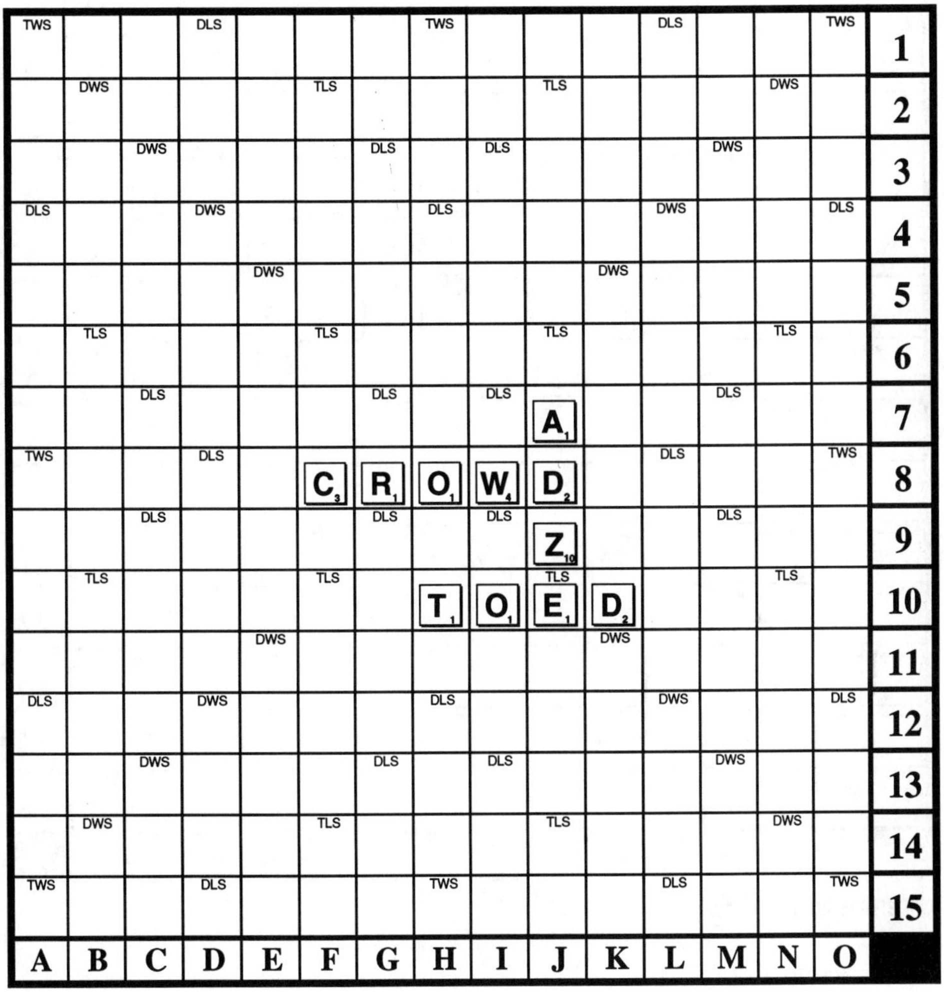

DIAGRAM 22-8

Van Leunen's rack: A C L N R T ?

There is an excellent bingo that can be played from H1 down to the O on H8. But Van Leunen finds an even better play! Answer on page 242.

Example 9

1988 Pigeon Forge Tournament, Tennessee: Dee Jackson, New York

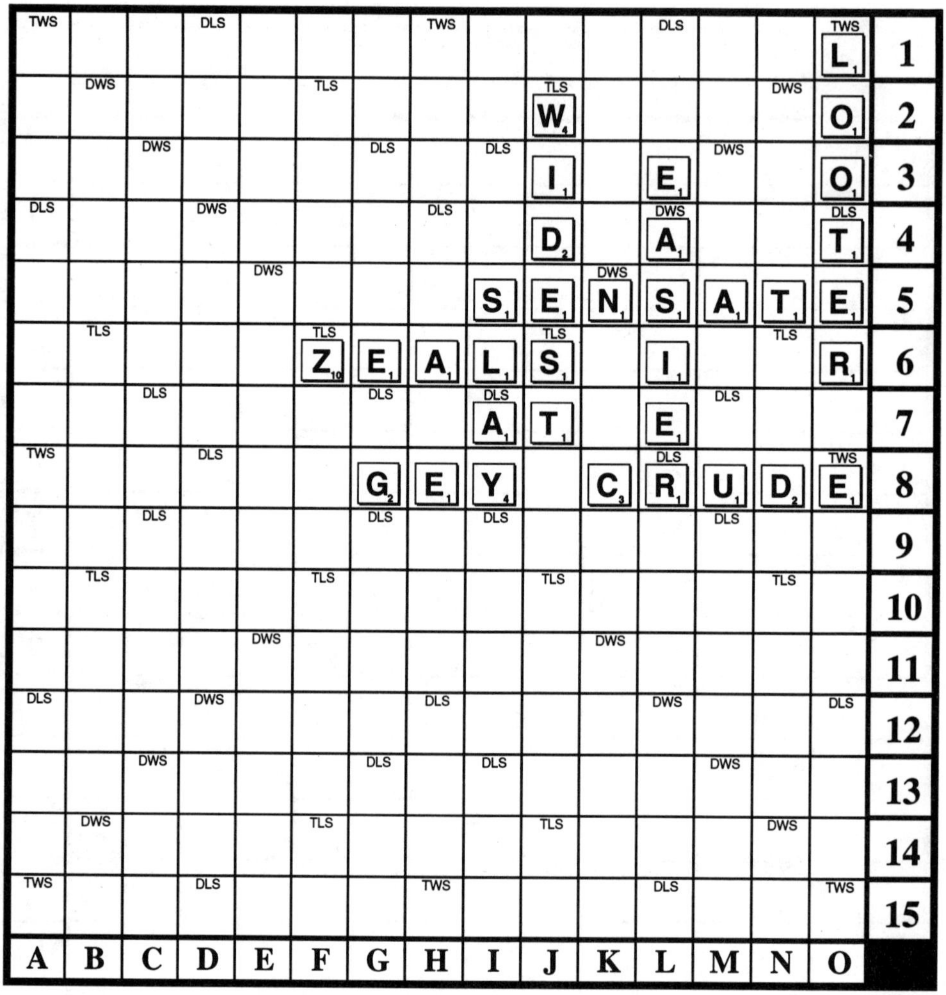

DIAGRAM 22-9

Jackson's rack: E L N O R V ?

We believe she found the only bingo! Answer on page 242.

Diagrams 22-10 through 22-15 show endgame situations. As you're looking at them, keep in mind that the players had no more than five to ten minutes to find the best play.

Example 10

1991 New York City Tournament: Joe Edley, New York

	A	B	C	D	E	F	G	H	I	J	K	L	M	N	O	
1		S	N	O	R	T	E	D			E	Y	R	I	E	1
2		T				M	A	V	I	N						2
3	W	A	F	F	S					D	R	I	L	Y		3
4		R		T												4
5		D		E												5
6		U		R				Z								6
7	O	S		N		I	L	I	A	C						7
8	A	T		B	E	A	N	O		I						8
9	K			S		N	O	I	R							9
10	E	M		A	T			E								10
11	N	O		V		A		I	S	O	L	E	A	D		11
12		O	H	O		G										12
13		A	W	E	E											13
14		R		C												14
15	J	U	T		U											15

DIAGRAM 22-10

Edley's score: 329   Opponent's score: 401
Edley's rack: E E H L P U X   Opponent's rack: G I P Q

The actual score of the game was different from what's shown above. In actuality, Edley was ahead and had no fear of losing. We adjusted the score for dramatic effect to show you how many points Edley will earn. Given the above score, Edley would still have won. You might encounter an unfamiliar three-letter word while you analyze the position. And note that NOIR, which was acceptable in early 1991, is now considered to be only a foreign word and is no longer acceptable. Answer on page 242.

Example 11

Rita Norr, Connecticut, against another expert at the New York City SCRABBLE® Game Club in 1991

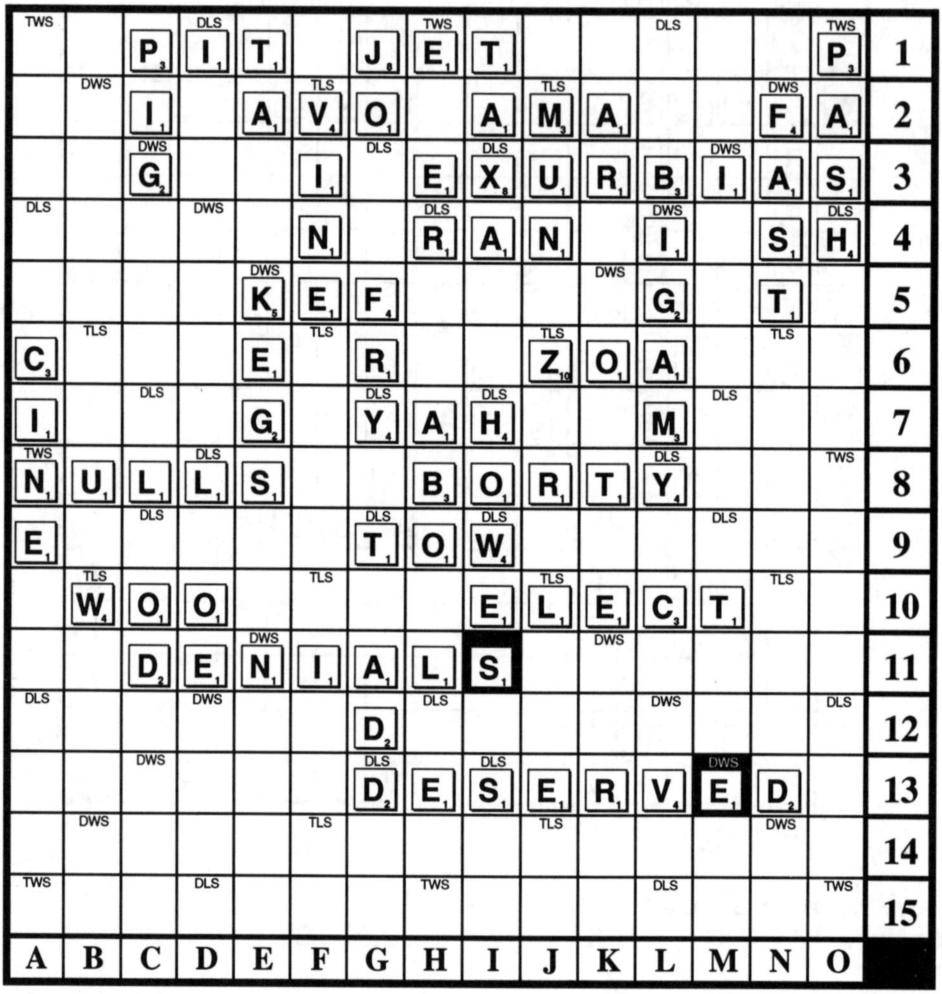

DIAGRAM 22-11

Norr's score: 360   Opponent's score: 420
Norr's rack: E E N O Q R U   Opponent's rack: I I N O U

Though technically she has a lost game, Norr gives herself a chance to win by setting a clever trap for her opponent. Answer on page 242.

Example 12

1985 National SCRABBLE® Championship, Boston: Joe Edley, New York, against Ron Tiekert, New York, who won the event with 20 wins and only 2 losses

	A	B	C	D	E	F	G	H	I	J	K	L	M	N	O	
1				C	M	E	A	T	Y							1
2		I	N	A	N	E	R									2
3			A	B	A	T	E	R								3
4				I											G	4
5				N	U		V								R	5
6				N			I								E	6
7	I		G	O	T		V								E	7
8	D	I	O	X	I	D	E	S							N	8
9	Y				L			H	E	R	O	I	Z	E	S	9
10	L							A								10
11	L					F	O	R	K	M	A	N				11
12	I							P			A	D	O			12
13	S						J	E	T			W	O	P		13
14	T						H	O	R	A	H					14
15					B	O	W	S	E							15
	A	B	C	D	E	F	G	H	I	J	K	L	M	N	O	

DIAGRAM 22-12

Edley's score: 326   Tiekert's score: 350
Edley's rack: A D E E L U?

There is one tile in the bag, and the unseen tiles are C, F, G, I, Q, T, U, and U. With two minutes left to play, Edley wants to find a sure way to win. Simply playing SAD at 15A for 45 points won't necessarily win if his opponent has a good Q play. Answer on page 242.

Example 13

1993 Western Championship, Reno, Nevada: Brian Cappelletto, Arizona

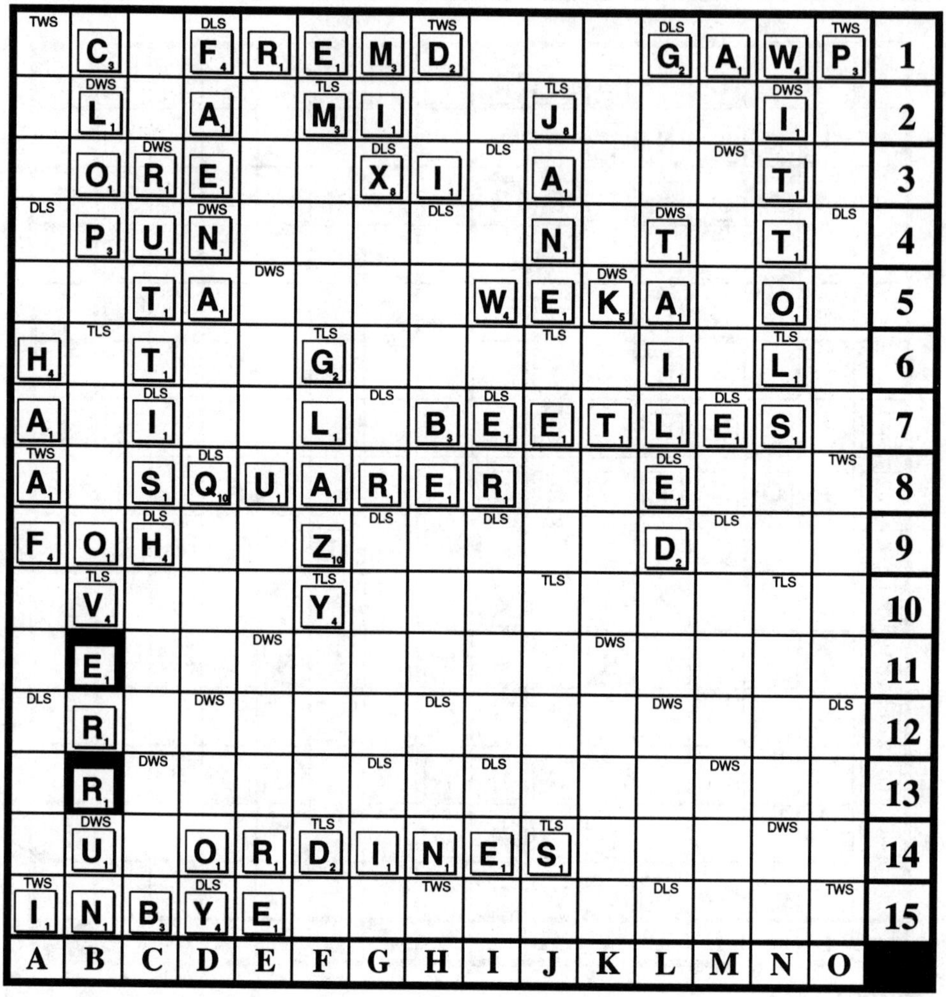

	A	B	C	D	E	F	G	H	I	J	K	L	M	N	O	
		C		F	R	E	M	D				G	A	W	P	1
		L		A			M			J				I		2
		O	R	E		X	I			A				T		3
		P	U	N						N		T		T		4
			T	A				W	E	K	A		O			5
	H		T			G						I		L		6
	A		I			L		B	E	E	T	L	E	S		7
	A		S	Q	U	A	R	E	R			E				8
	F	O	H		Z							D				9
		V			Y											10
		E														11
		R														12
		R														13
		U		O	R	D	I	N	E	S						14
	I	N	B	Y	E											15
	A	B	C	D	E	F	G	H	I	J	K	L	M	N	O	

DIAGRAM 22-13

Cappelletto's score: 305   Opponent's score: 345
Cappelletto's rack: A I N O O O S

There is one tile in the bag. The eight unseen tiles are C, D, G, I, N, O, U, and V. How can Cappelletto play to give himself the best chance of winning? Given the score and his rack, it may seem impossible for him to win, but it's not! Of course, he does need a little help from the "tile gods" and his opponent! Answer on page 243.

Warning: Our average reader won't find the answer to this one unless s/he knows some very unusual, obscure words. We include this position because it so brilliantly shows how you can use both a knowledge of obscure words and a never-say-lose attitude to give yourself the best chance to win. Our answer includes a revealing quote from the opponent, an expert player who finished in the top twenty at the 1993 World SCRABBLE® Championship.

Example 14

1990 National SCRABBLE® Championship, Washington, D.C.: Joel Wapnick, Montreal (1983 National SCRABBLE® Champion)

	A	B	C	D	E	F	G	H	I	J	K	L	M	N	O	
1	TWS			DLS F₄			TWS M₃	A₁	U₁	V₄	E₁	DLS			TWS	1
2		DWS		R₁		TLS	D₂	I₁	N₁	T₁			DWS			2
3	N₁	A₁	T₁	A₁	T₁	I₁	O₁	N₁	DLS			DWS P₃				3
4	DLS			G₂			DLS C₃	H₄	I₁	L₁	L₁	DWS I₁		DLS		4
5					DWS		O₁	E₁			DWS	R₁				5
6		TLS				TLS J₈	O₁			TLS		N₁		TLS Y₄		6
7			DLS L₁		G₂	O₁	R₁		DLS			DLS		U₁		7
8	TWS O₁	P₃	A₁	C₃	I₁	T₁	I₁	E₁	S₁				DLS F₄	TWS A₁		8
9		DLS M₃		B₃		DLS E₁		H₄	O₁	Y₄		DLS	A₁	N₁		9
10	TLS	I₁		B₃		TLS	Q₁₀		TLS				TLS Z₁₀			10
11		S₁		DWS E₁			A₁			DWS	D₂	O₁	G₂	E₁		11
12	DLS	T₁	DWS	D₂	E₁	T₁	I₁	N₁	U₁	E₁	S₁			DLS		12
13		W₄	DWS E₁				D₂		DLS			DWS				13
14		DWS O₁	R₁			TLS				TLS			DWS			14
15	TWS	K₅		DLS			TWS					DLS		TWS		15

DIAGRAM 22-14

Wapnick's score: 327   Opponent's score: 316
Wapnick's rack: E E E L S T W

There are two tiles in the bag. The nine unseen tiles are: A, A, I, N, R, R, U, V, and X. Analysis will involve some uncommon, obscure words. Answer on page 243.

Wapnick's play won the prize for the Most Strategic Play of the tournament. Watch out! Though it's a common word, it's not an obvious play. None of the expert judges initially thought that Wapnick's play was the best, but after a careful analysis they concluded it was.

Example 15

Played during a friendly match; Mike Baron, New Mexico, vs. Jeff Reeves, Louisiana, 1989 (both players are experts and both have won many tournaments)

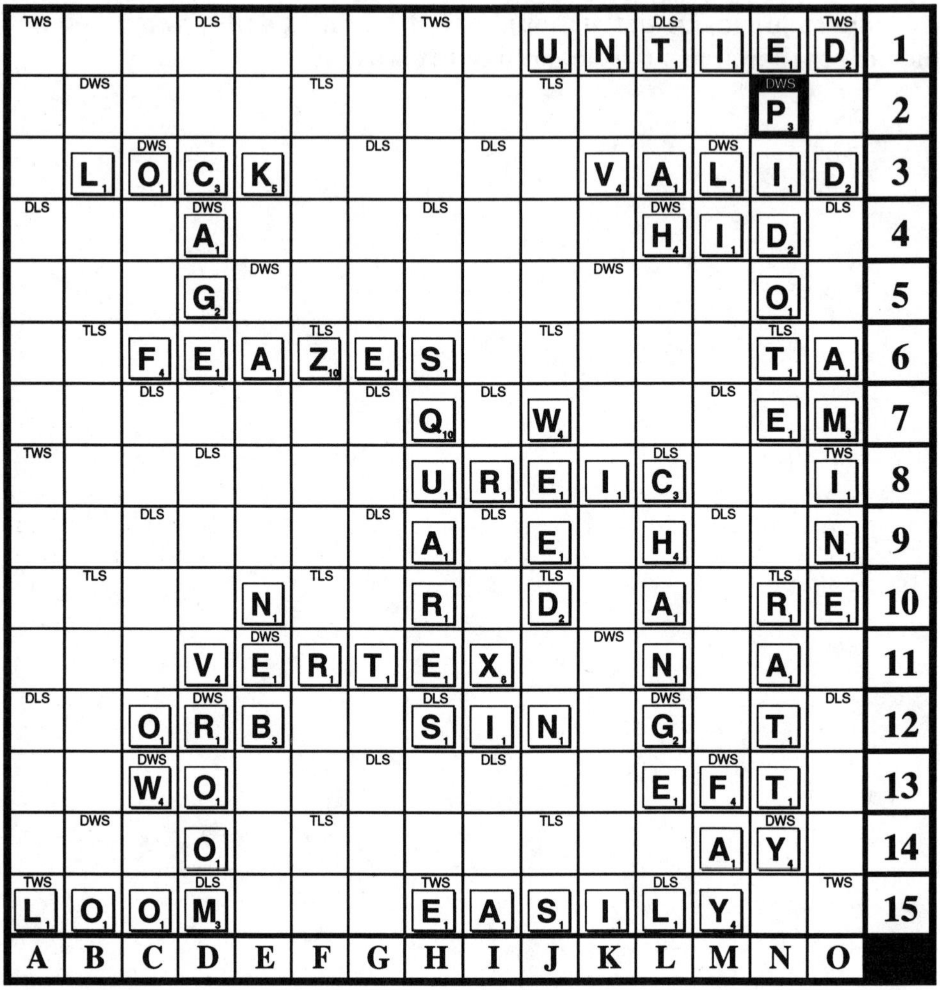

	A	B	C	D	E	F	G	H	I	J	K	L	M	N	O	
	TWS			DLS			TWS	U	N	T	I	E	D		TWS	1
		DWS			TLS			TLS					P			2
		L	O	C	K	DLS		DLS			V	A	L	I	D	3
	DLS			A				DLS			H	I	D		DLS	4
				G				DWS					O			5
	TLS	F	E	A	Z	E	S	TLS				TLS	T	A		6
		DLS				DLS	Q		W			DLS	E	M		7
	TWS			DLS			U	R	E	I	C			I	TWS	8
		DLS				DLS	A		E		H			N		9
	TLS			N	TLS		R		D		A		R	E		10
			V	E	R	T	E	X		DWS	N		A			11
	DLS	O	R	B			S	I	N		G		T		DLS	12
		DWS	W	O		DLS		DLS			E	F	T			13
		DWS		O	TLS			TLS				A	Y	DWS		14
	TWS	L	O	M			E	A	S	I	L	Y	DLS		TWS	15

DIAGRAM 22-15

Baron's score: 267   Reeves's score: 321
Baron's rack: E I N P R S U

There is one tile in the bag. The eight unseen tiles are: A, E, G, J, O, P, T, and the blank. Reeves's last play was LOCK 3B 20 pts. Baron finds a very clever way to give himself a chance to win! If Reeves is less than fully alert to Baron's plan, he will lose. Since the game was not played in a tournament, there was no exceptional motivation for winning or losing. We believe *that* played an important part in what transpired—had the game been more important to Reeves, he might have been more careful.

Note that Baron's rack spells PURINES and UPRISEN, but neither will play, nor will any other bingo. What did Baron do? Answer on page 243.

Solutions to Excellent Plays

Example 1, Diagram 22-1: Carroll played RETAIL 11A 51 points, simultaneously forming CAJOLER, FAXES, TA, AR, ID, and LI. This was a winning play, though REMAIL in the same position would have been slightly better.

Example 2, Diagram 22-2: Even with the board so devoid of scoring opportunities, Edley found a way to set himself up for a huge score on his next play. In order to solve this, you need to know that DEL and DELE are words. Edley played DEL C5 4 points. It would have been very hard for Norr to have blocked his immediate threat of PREFIXED/DELE 8A 68 points. In fact, even if she could have blocked, it wouldn't have been worth it. That's because from her point of view, he might not even have the play (or SUFFIXED, since DELF is also acceptable) and because blocking (for less than 10 points, by playing either DELI, HILI, PILI, SOLI, or TALI, etc. at 7A) would have left Edley with a huge scoring opportunity along column A. Thus, Edley was able to play PREFIXED.

Example 3, Diagram 22-3: Cappelletto found RAMJET 8D 32 points. Some players might have considered exchanging JM and keeping AENRT, since the next rack would likely have allowed a bingo. However, by taking 32 points now, Cappelletto ensured that after his next turn he'd probably have a total score of about 60 points, nearly the score of a bingo. If he didn't draw a bingo after exchanging the JM, he would have ended up with fewer total points and fewer winning chances.

Example 4, Diagram 22-4: Glowniak found UNTRUTH A8 39 points. The DEV leave is excellent considering the collection of awkward tiles on her original rack and the lack of scoring opportunity in the position.

Example 5, Diagram 22-5: Felt challenged LURIDITY off the board and played PUMP G6 14 points, keeping ERST and taking a 50-point lead. If he doesn't challenge and instead plays PURPLEST IF 89 points, he will then have a 59-point lead, but both he and his opponent will have just drawn seven new tiles. In that situation, there is no way to predict who will draw better tiles. However, by forcing his opponent to keep his poor rack of DIILRTU and keeping the bingo-prone tiles ERST with a 50-point lead, he gives himself a better chance to play a bingo first and take a game-winning lead in the next few turns.

Example 6, Diagram 22-6: Armstrong found METAPHOR B4 69 points.

Example 7, Diagram 22-7: Cohen played COUNTERMEN D1 82 points.

Example 8, Diagram 22-8: Although CILANTRO H1 80 points would have been a very nice play, CONTRALTO H7 83 is worth more, and is certainly much prettier!

Example 9, Diagram 22-9: Jackson played the wonderful word WOLVERINE 3D 66 points.

Example 10, Diagram 22-10: There are many good possibilities to consider; HEXED O7 48 points and HELPED O6 36 are the first two we saw. However, both of these fall short of a win, since they give the opponent a good place for his P at N10. The only play that wins is UPHELD O6 36, which sets up EX N5 50. The opponent has to block with LIP N3 or PIU 6M, and then Edley plays LEX L11 to win by 3 points or 1, since the opponent gets stuck with the Q and G and Edley plays out.

Example 11, Diagram 22-11: Norr played OD N12 3 points, because next turn she wanted to play either QUEER or QUEEN O8 48. The truth is that if her opponent ignored the threat and simply played UNDESERVED 13E 14, he would have won by a few points. Not realizing his danger, he blocked with ION 9M 7 thinking that he would now win by a larger margin. That sprung Norr's trap, as she played ER H13 2. Now, with IU left, her opponent can neither end the game nor stop QUEEN 15D 81, which won for Norr. Note that if Norr had played ER H13 first, her opponent would have played ION 15F 15, and would have won.

Example 12, Diagram 22-12: With the possibility of a Q play at either 6K or 7K (QUITE), M6 (QUIZ), or N9 (EQUIP), Edley noticed that DEE N7 9 points would block all of his opponent's Q plays, thereby earning him an extra 20 points and the win. He also saw that if the Q is in the bag, then after DEE his opponent wouldn't be able to stop him from playing the game-winning EQUALS at either 2J or 4H. In the actual game, the Q was the last tile in the bag and Edley went out and won with EQUALS.

Example 13, Diagram 22-13: Cappelletto knew that the only way he could win was by playing a bingo. That looked hopeless unless the G was the last tile in the bag. With that slim hope, he simply dropped his best tile, the S, on the board to form SQUARERS/ES 8C for 19 points. The G *was* the last tile, which gave him OOGONIA, at either M9 or 13I. However, both places could have been blocked with the play ODIC K9 17.

Instead of blocking, the opponent made her best scoring play and was astonished when Cappelletto emptied his rack with his bingo and won! She told us: "As I was tracking tiles I realized that he had three Os. Even though I knew his whole rack, I simply remember thinking: 'Three Os! There's no way he could have a bingo!' So I didn't bother looking closely at all of his possibilities. I know the word! I was just overconfident. It was a good lesson!"

Example 14, Diagram 22-14: Wapnick played STOLE A6 5 points. This blocks the huge X hot spots at B2-6 and B8-10. The opponent very likely had either VARIX B2 62 or PAX B8 57. The result is that STOLE wins 91 percent of the time. SWEET O11 43 only wins 86 percent of the time. The complete analysis of this position took several pages of text to prove. As it turned out, the two tiles in the bag would have lost the game for Wapnick after SWEET, but kept the win after STOLE.

Briefly, the reason STOLE wins so often is that Wapnick now has a 16-point lead with only 5 tiles to play. The opponent has no really good X plays. Wapnick will play out first almost all the time, winning by a hair.

Example 15, Diagram 22-15: Baron's thinking was this: 1. Reeves has the blank or he never would have opened up the A column with the word LOCK, allowing BLOCK, CLOCK, or FLOCK and a vertical play to a TWS. 2. He's probably planning the play JAB or JOB A1 for 37 points if he doesn't draw a bingo. 3. The only chance to win is if Reeves plays the J on A1. With that, Baron simply looked up at his opponent and started Reeves's timer! In effect, Baron had passed his turn. Reeves was surprised, but assumed that Baron was simply frustrated. He shrugged his shoulders as if to say, "Sorry, Mike!" and proceeded to play his highest-scoring play JABOT A1 46 points, emptying the bag and taking a 100-point lead. Whereby Baron plopped down JUNI-PERS 1A 104, winning the game by just a few points!

Where do we go from here? The next generation of SCRABBLE game players is waiting to be taught. If you'd like to join us, Chapter Twenty-three will show you how to introduce SCRABBLE games to your children. Let us know how you do! We're always looking for better techniques. Good luck!

23 SCRABBLE® FOR CHILDREN

Most people agree that one of the greatest gifts one can bestow on a child is a lifelong curiosity about words. This curiosity has a way of leading to other things, such as a love of reading, better communication skills, and much more. Playing SCRABBLE® games with children has proven to be one of the easiest and most effective ways to ensure this love of words.

This has been shown time and again by parents who encourage their children to play the game, and by teachers who have used the SCRABBLE games extensively in the classroom. Few letters bring more satisfaction to the staff of the National SCRABBLE® Association than those that begin:

"My mother and I have been playing SCRABBLE together for thirty-five years . . ." or "My sixth-grade class improved their vocabulary skills remarkably after we played SCRABBLE this semester."

By the time your children are four or five, you can introduce them to SCRABBLE® for Juniors. At eight they should be ready to try the regular SCRABBLE game.

Remember, SCRABBLE games will provide your children with a number of educational benefits. And the best part is that they'll be having so much fun, they won't even notice. Among the things kids learn from SCRABBLE games are:

Vocabulary—This one's pretty obvious.
Spelling—This one's even more obvious!
Math—Remember, SCRABBLE scoring requires ongoing addition, multiplication, counting, recounting, and calculation.

Spatial Relationships—Since words have different values in different places on the board, kids learn to assess and evaluate how many and which tiles to use in their words with the available space on the board.

Thinking—The competition and options provided by the SCRABBLE game force kids to plan ahead and to assess and evaluate options.

Social/Personal—As with any good game, it also helps children experience the value of team play, competition, and need to follow rules. A good score or unusual word builds self-esteem, and a word challenge teaches positive confrontation.

Despite all the obvious fun and educational benefits, however, playing SCRABBLE with children does require a little thought beforehand. As open as they are to new experiences, many children can still be intimidated by a game that involves spelling or a contest that pits them against an adult. With that in mind, you should always consider measures that will give the child both an advantage and a sense of ease.

The most obvious of these is to allow the child to use a dictionary when making any SCRABBLE game move. It's a terrific safety net and one that the child can be weaned from over time. Early on you may also try playing with two children at once, so the child does not have the threat of a one-on-one confrontation. Play a three-handed SCRABBLE game or let the two kids act as a team against you. Both methods work well.

For the most part, you should approach teaching SCRABBLE games the way you teach a child to ride a bike: Jump right in. There is little to be gained by abstract discussion of the process; both of you are far better off getting out the board and going at it!

If the child has never even observed a game before, a good place to start is to have him or her find the tiles for his name—or a favorite word—and place them in the center of the board. Then have him or her calculate the score. Next have the child move the name or word to another place where s/he might encounter a word or letter bonus. A couple of tries should convey the idea of relative scores and the concept of "looking for the hot spots" whenever possible.

Another early exercise might be to place the word ATE on the board. Then have the child find all the letters which can be hooked in front (D, F, R, etc.). Find another word, like BAN, and show what can be placed at the end of a word (D, G, K, etc.). Each time you build a word down with either the front or end-hook letters illustrates that s/he can make two complete new words! This is especially true with the S. For the most part, kids should learn not to use the S unless they are going to make two words.

Take out a rack and have your children draw seven letters from the tile bag. Have them move the tiles around on the rack and wait for words to magically appear. This is a good time to remind them to look for familiar letter combinations: ING, PRE, EST, RE, ATE, ER, etc. Try this several times so that they learn that some letters produce more words than others.

A Couple of Trouble Spots to Look For

There are a couple of areas we've found that tend to confuse kids when they first play SCRABBLE. So you'll probably need to reemphasize the following points:

- Plays may be made only in a straight line, horizontally or vertically. Diagonal plays are never acceptable.
- Bonus squares (Double Word Score, etc.) only count the *first time* they are used. Explain to your child that after a bonus square is covered up, it will provide no more bonus points in that game.
- The blank is always scored as zero points, but it can be used to cover a double or triple word bonus square to take advantage of the extra points.
- They are free to exchange all or some of their tiles whenever they wish as long as there are seven tiles remaining in the pool. But to do so they must skip a turn. Explain why exchanging is sometimes good strategy.
- A child can challenge your word whenever s/he wishes to, but should be aware that an unsuccessful challenge means that s/he misses his or her turn. However, we recommend a "free challenge" rule when an adult plays with a child—at least early on—as it is less intimidating and helps kids to learn words.
- Learn to differentiate between proper and common nouns. This can be confusing. After all, Bill, Rose, Mike, and May are all proper names and generic words as well. Explain this to your child.

The overriding goal is to teach your child that words can be fun. Here are a couple of other ways to do this:

- Have your child see how many words s/he can make out of his or her name. For example, the name Thomas has seventy-nine legal words in it. Use your last name if the first isn't workable.
- Teach anagrams. Show how the letters in the word TEA can also spell EAT and ETA or how CAROB can become COBRA. Find or make up a name and anagram it. For example, Ruth Ardeen can be transformed into: HEAD TURNER, TUNA HERDER, UNDER EARTH, THUNDER EAR.

Probably the single biggest mistake people make in teaching SCRABBLE games to children is pushing them too fast. In this regard, it is no different from baseball, gymnastics, or any other endeavor that requires one to "crawl before you walk." Remember, it is thrilling for a seven-year-old to find a four-letter word on his or her rack and place it *anywhere* on a SCRABBLE game board.

Only after your child is comfortable and confident should you start to introduce other options s/he might have played. Techniques include asking where else s/he might have played the same word, or what other word(s) might have been made with the same letters. If the game is really tutorial in nature, you can ask to see what his or her original rack was and then, together with the child, consider plays from that. Try always to "lead" a child, so that s/he discovers the alternate plays rather than you spelling it out.

Remember, when playing SCRABBLE games with children, the operative word is *fun*. The rest will take care of itself.

The NSA is often asked which SCRABBLE game should be purchased and used in playing with children. Currently, Milton Bradley Company offers four options. They are:

SCRABBLE® FOR JUNIORS

Geared to children aged five and up, this game has a two-sided board. One side helps kids form words through pictures of familiar objects such as a horse or barn. The opposite side is more like a traditional SCRABBLE board.

SCRABBLE® BRAND CROSSWORD GAME

This, of course, is the standard SCRABBLE game. It also comes in Deluxe, Deluxe Travel, and Spanish editions. Most children are ready to graduate to this board by eight years of age.

GAME BOY SCRABBLE®

Slaying dragons and shooting starships isn't the only way to have fun with Game Boy! SCRABBLE® Game Boy allows kids to play solitaire or against an opponent and adds a fast-paced dimension to the classic board game. It also features three levels of play, so that as your child improves there is always a new challenge around the corner. Children can also improve their skills with two other options. One is the computer software version of the game, which features challenging play.

SCHOOL SCRABBLE® KIT

Another option is the National School SCRABBLE® Program, which provides a "School SCRABBLE® Kit" for a classrooms. It includes a video, a teaching guide, six modified Deluxe SCRABBLE® game boards, a SCRABBLE tip sheet, and more.

School SCRABBLE Kits are available to schools for only a modest charge. (Milton Bradley Company makes no profit on them.) Interested teachers should write to the National SCRABBLE® Association on school letterhead. While you're at it, please refer to our appendices for answers to some of your questions. They include a great deal of useful reference materials.

APPENDICES:
Facts, Trivia, and Word Lists

In Part V we've included the following appendices to serve as handy references about the world of SCRABBLE® games.

Appendix One clarifies some often-misunderstood rules pertaining to the SCRABBLE® game.

Appendix Two lists a variety of facts and trivia that have been accumulated over decades.

Appendix Three tells you all about our National SCRABBLE® Association.

Appendix Four has some word lists that you may find invaluable.

COMMON QUESTIONS ABOUT RULES AND CLARIFICATIONS

The National SCRABBLE® Association receives many letters and calls concerning rules. Because of that, we thought we should devote a chapter to clarifying the rules. As a reminder, we want to assure you that it's perfectly okay to play with any variation of the rules you prefer, as long as all the participants know which rules are in effect at the onset of the game.

OVERDRAWING TILES

Many people want to know what happens if a player discovers eight tiles on his or her rack instead of seven?

There is no discussion in the boxed rules about what to do in this situation. The NSA has devised a rule that seems to work very well for our clubs and tournaments: The opponent randomly draws two tiles from the offending player's rack, looks at them both, and then chooses which one to return to the pool of letters. The remaining tile goes back to the player's rack. If a player overdraws two tiles, then the opponent randomly draws three tiles from the player's rack, chooses which two to replace in the pool, and returns the other tile to the player. And so on. In each case, the offending player may see all the tiles seen by the opponent.

This overdrawing penalty influences most players to draw their tiles more carefully. One further note about overdrawing: If the overdrawing player realizes s/he has overdrawn before mixing any of the new tiles with the old ones, then the opponent should randomly choose tiles *only* from the group of newly drawn tiles, while following the instructions given above.

PLAYING WORDS ON THE BOARD

In Chapter Five we discussed what was acceptable play-making. We'll briefly repeat in a slightly different form what we've previously said:

Given that PART is the only play on the board, the following are acceptable plays:

1. PARTY; DEPART; DEPARTING

   It's acceptable to simply add one or more letters to a word, to either the front or back or to *both* the front and back.

2. PARTS: If you want, you can add just an S to a word already on the board.

3. PARTY   G   You may play at right angles to a word.
      O   PART
      U   E
            W

4. FOIL
   PART

   You may play parallel to a word as long as adjacent letters form words horizontally and vertically. In this case, since FA, OR, and IT are all acceptable, playing FOIL as shown is acceptable.

What is *not* acceptable is playing tiles diagonally across the board.

One further point: **All** the letters played in one turn must be contained in **the same horizontal or vertical word.** Example: If PART is on the board and your rack is ADEELMV, it is *not acceptable* to play *in one turn:* the five letters AELMV, forming the words LAME and REV. That's because the five letters are not all contained in one word or played in a straight line.

PART
LAME
 V

PLAYING A BLANK

The official rules do not allow a player, later in the game, to change the letter that the blank represents. Likewise, a player may not replace the blank with the letter it represents and use the blank in another word. At the NSA's clubs and tournaments, this rule is strictly enforced. The NSA also advises that to avoid later confusion, both players record on his or her scoresheet what letter the blank represents at the time it's played.

Those of you who'd like a game with more scoring chances may play the variation that *allows* players to replace a blank on the board with the letter (from your rack) it represents. The drawback (or advantage) to this game is the increased luck factor.

EXCHANGING TILES

A player may exchange tiles (from one to seven) as long as there are at least seven tiles still in the bag. Decide which tiles you want to exchange first. Then remove them from your rack and place them facedown on the table. Only then may you draw your new tiles, place them on your rack, and replace the exchanged tiles back into the pool.

CHOOSING A DICTIONARY

We have discussed *The Official SCRABBLE® Players Dictionary*, 2nd Edition. We recommend it, but whether you use it or not, make sure that all players know exactly which word reference you are using. All words labeled as a part of speech (including those listed of foreign origin, and as archaic, obsolete, colloquial, slang, etc.) are permitted, with the exception of the following: words always capitalized, abbreviations, prefixes and suffixes standing alone, words requiring a hyphen or an apostrophe, and words only formed as part of a two-word phrase. But please remember that some abbreviations and prefixes are acceptable words since they also have separate meanings. For example, RE, which is considered a prefix, is also an acceptable word representing the second note on the musical scale (do, re, mi, etc.).

CHALLENGING

When may a player challenge? And how many words may be challenged at one time?

The rules state that a player can challenge until the next turn. The National SCRABBLE® Association has developed a more precise definition for when a player may challenge:

A) Using sand timers or no timers: Once a player has announced his or her score, the opponent may "Hold!" or challenge. After the player has drawn at least one tile from the pool, the opponent may *not* challenge or hold anymore. To avoid what we'll call "speedy-draw syndrome," the player must take a few seconds to record the total score before drawing replacement tiles.

B) Using tournament clocks: After the player has started his or her opponent's timer, the opponent may "Hold!" or challenge. As above, once the player has drawn at least one tile from the pool, the opponent may not challenge or hold anymore.

Using clocks: Once an opponent has called "Hold!" at the proper time, s/he has as long as s/he wants to think about challenging, as long as s/he hasn't yet made the next play. The player can insist on drawing tiles after one minute, as long as s/he keeps the replacement tiles separate from the old tiles. This is called the "Courtesy Rule." If there is a successful challenge, the opponent may see the replacement tiles before the player returns them to the pool.

Using sand timers: After calling "Hold!" the opponent has only the length of his or her turn—three minutes—to decide whether to challenge or not. The Courtesy Rule is in effect here as well.

SCORING

In Chapter Two, we have already shown how to score the bonus squares. However, there is one scoring question we are asked about so often that we thought it would be helpful to mention it again.

Let's look at two examples:

A	B	C	D	E	F	G	H	I	J	K	L	M	N	O	
TWS			DLS				TWS				DLS			TWS	1
	DWS				TLS				TLS				DWS		2
		DWS				DLS		DLS				DWS			3
DLS			DWS				DLS				DWS			DLS	4
				DWS						DWS					5
	TLS				TLS				TLS				TLS		6
		DLS				DLS		DLS	A₁			DLS			7
TWS			DLS	P₃	A₁	R₁	T₁	S₁			DLS			TWS	8
		DLS				DLS		DLS				DLS			9
	TLS				TLS				TLS				TLS		10
			DWS							DWS					11
DLS			DWS				DLS				DWS			DLS	12
		DWS				DLS		DLS				DWS			13
	DWS				TLS				TLS				DWS		14
TWS			DLS				TWS				DLS			TWS	15

DIAGRAM A-1

You have the above position with the rack: A C E L R T W

Play CRAWL 6G: How much is this play worth?

The play CRAWL 6G forms WAS simultaneously. The W will cover the TLS. Since you form two words at once, and the bonus square is used for both words, and you are *covering* the bonus square *this* turn, the W is scored as a Triple Letter Score square for both CRAWL and WAS. The score for playing CRAWL (spelling both CRAWL and WAS) is: C (3) + R (1) + A (1) + W (12) + L (1) + W (12) + A (1) + S (1) = 32 pts.

A	B	C	D	E	F	G	H	I	J	K	L	M	N	O	
TWS			DLS				TWS				DLS			TWS	**1**
	DWS			TLS					TLS				DWS		**2**
		DWS				DLS		DLS				DWS			**3**
DLS			DWS				DLS				DWS			DLS	**4**
				DWS						DWS					**5**
	TLS				TLS	C₃	R₁	A₁	W₄	L₁			TLS		**6**
		DLS				DLS		A₁				DLS			**7**
TWS			DLS		P₃	A₁	R₁	T₁	S₁		DLS			TWS	**8**
		DLS				DLS	H₄	A₁	T₁			DLS			**9**
	TLS				TLS				TLS				TLS		**10**
				DWS						DWS					**11**
DLS			DWS				DLS				DWS			DLS	**12**
		DWS				DLS		DLS				DWS			**13**
	DWS			TLS					TLS				DWS		**14**
TWS			DLS				TWS				DLS			TWS	**15**

DIAGRAM A-2

Next turn your opponent forms the words HAT/WASH. What does this play score? Answer: H (4) + A (1) + T (1) + W (4) + A (1) + S (1) + H (4) = 16 pts. Notice that the W is not counted as a Triple Letter Score because bonus squares can only be scored as such on the turn they are covered.

ENDING THE GAME

The boxed rules mention that the game is over when a player uses all of his or her tiles and there are no more tiles to draw. That player then earns the points still remaining in all the other players' racks, while the others subtract from their point total the sum of the points still on their rack.

In NSA Club and Tournament play, we use a slightly different rule. The player who ends the game earns **double** the sum of the letters on the other players' racks, and the other players subtract nothing from their total. Example: Player #1, with 323 points, ends the game while Player #2, with 320, still has EMP on his rack. Player #1 should receive 2 × (1 + 3 + 3) = 14 points extra. The final total would be Player #1 337, Player #2 320.

Appendix Two

FACTS AND FIGURES OF THE WORLD'S
FAVORITE CROSSWORD GAME

There are an estimated 35 million leisure SCRABBLE® game players in the U.S. and Canada alone. Among those are over ten thousand enthusiasts who belong to the nearly two hundred sanctioned clubs. Their organization, the National SCRABBLE® Association, is headquartered in Greenport, New York.

❑

Each year over eighty sanctioned North American SCRABBLE® tournaments are held. These attract players of all levels, from curious novices to experts, and usually encompass ten to twelve rounds of play over a two-day weekend. Contestants are allowed up to three minutes per turn, with games limited to a total of sixty minutes. A normal game will have thirteen to nineteen turns per side. Most players use chess clocks to time their moves at tournaments with each player receiving twenty-five minutes to make all his or her plays.

❑

All levels of players are rated by the National SCRABBLE® Association in relation to their tournament results. Players rated over 1600 are considered experts. There are over eight thousand rated players in the United States and Canada, of whom more than five hundred are experts.

❑

The ten best players in the last National SCRABBLE® Championship averaged 405 points per game.

❑

The most points scored in an official game using American-style competitive rules was 770 by Mark Landsberg at a tournament in his hometown of Los Angeles in June 1993. Landsberg's plays included the following words: SHAMEFUL, GRIDIRON, INTRADAY, UNCINATE, and WOBBLIER, of which the last *two* were Triple-Triples.

Mark's opponent was Alan Stern, an expert from Los Angeles who scored 308 that game, making the combined total of 1,108 points a new North American record.

❑

The highest score in one turn in sanctioned U.S. club play was made by Jeff Clark of Flint, Michigan, using the word METHODIZE for 302 points. The highest Canadian score was by Ron Manson of Toronto, who played the word REEQUIPS for 302 points.

❑

The 1993 World SCRABBLE® Championship was held from August 26 to 30, 1993, in New York City at the Plaza Hotel. There were sixty-four competitors from twenty different nations. The official word sources for this tournament were both the American *Merriam-Webster Official SCRABBLE® Players Dictionary,* 2nd Edition, and the British Chambers *Official SCRABBLE® Words.* First prize was $10,000.

❑

This 1993 World Championship event consisted of a preliminary fifteen-round modified Swiss-paired tournament. That means that all contestants play all fifteen rounds, but the players who have the same number of wins are paired off each round. This ensures that the best players play each other near the end of the tournament.

After the initial preliminary event, the player in first place was paired against the player in fourth and the second- and third-place players were likewise paired off to compete in a match of five games. The two winners played in front of closed-circuit TV for the finals. Whoever was the first to win three games would win the Championship. Mark Nyman, a television producer from Leeds, England, won, and is the new world SCRABBLE® champion.

❑

The first world SCRABBLE® Champion was Peter Morris of Michigan, who prevailed over forty-seven other competitors in London in September 1991.

❑

The national SCRABBLE® champions have been: David Prinz (California), 1978; Joe Edley (New York), 1980; Joel Wapnick (Canada), 1983; Ron Tiekert (New York), 1985; Rita Norr (Connecticut), 1987; Bob Watson (Minnesota), 1988; Peter Morris (Michigan), 1989; Robert Felt (California), 1990; and Joe Edley (New York), 1992.

❑

The highest-scoring opening play made in a sanctioned National SCRABBLE® Association Club or Tournament is CAZIQUE for 124 points, by Sam Kantimathi (California).

□

The youngest North American SCRABBLE prodigy was Brian Cappelletto of Arizona, who, at seventeen, finished fifth in the 1987 National Championship. At twenty-one, he was runner-up at the first World SCRABBLE® Championship in London. The current youngest prodigy is Allan Saldanha of England, who, at fifteen, won the 1993 British SCRABBLE® Championship and finished fifth at the 1993 World SCRABBLE® Championship. The oldest active SCRABBLE expert is Horace Davis of California, who is still winning games at clubs and tournaments at ninety-six years old.

Appendix Three

THE NATIONAL SCRABBLE® ASSOCIATION

The National SCRABBLE® Association does the following:

❏ Publishes the *SCRABBLE® News* eight times a year, which includes:
   Lists of upcoming tournaments
   News of tournaments and their results
   Word puzzles of all kinds
   SCRABBLE game strategy for new and/or experienced players
   Annotated tournament games
   News items about what's happening in the world of SCRABBLE games
   Word lists for learning new words
   Contests
   Lists of newly formed clubs and club changes

❏ Licenses Official National SCRABBLE® Association Clubs and Directors

❏ Sanctions tournaments and advertises them to nearby clubs and media

❏ Oversees a rating system that assigns tournament players Official National SCRABBLE® Association Ratings.

❏ Awards Expert Points to club players.

❏ Formulates rules and regularly updates guidelines for ensuring fair standards and practices at official SCRABBLE® game Clubs and Tournaments.

❏ Maintains membership records for over ten thousand SCRABBLE game players.

❏ Sends Starter Kits to each new member, including: word lists (the twos, the two-to-make-threes, and the three-to-make-fours among others), membership cards, glossary of SCRABBLE game terms, Official Tournament Rules, and club roster and the *SCRABBLE® News*.

❏ Organizes and promotes a biennial National SCRABBLE® Championship tournament that is open to all rated players.

❑ Publishes a Director's Bulletin geared to keeping directors aware of the latest developments in the SCRABBLE world.

❑ Answers hundreds of letters and phone calls received each year concerning rules on unusual over-the-board situations and a variety of other questions and concerns that the general public has about SCRABBLE games.

❑ Maintains constant liaison with the Milton Bradley Company, the game's manufacturer, to consider new mutual promotional ventures.

Do you have an interest in:

Starting your own licensed SCRABBLE® Game Club?
Computer programs that can enhance your word-game skills?
Specialized lists of useful words?
SCRABBLE T-shirts or other memorabilia?
Tournament clocks?
Books devoted to word puzzles?
Other SCRABBLE-related resources?

If you have any questions about any aspect of SCRABBLE® games or would like to find out more about some of the resources mentioned above, please contact:

THE NATIONAL SCRABBLE® ASSOCIATION
BOX 700
GREENPORT, NY 11944
(516) 477-0033

As a member of the National SCRABBLE® Association, you'll receive a membership card; a roster of SCRABBLE® Players Clubs in the U.S. and Canada; 3 special word lists to help improve your play; and 1-year subscription to the SCRABBLE® News. That's 8 exciting issues with . . .
• News about clubs and tournaments in your area
• Official National SCRABBLE® Association Tournament Rules
• Special word lists and helpful playing hints
• The latest in strategy
• Challenging quizzes & puzzles
Fill out the form below (print clearly) and send to:
NATIONAL SCRABBLE® ASSOCIATION,
P.O. Box 700, Greenport, NY 11944

YES! I'd like to join the National SCRABBLE® Association. I enclose a check or money order for $15.00 ($20.00 for Canadian membership; $25.00 outside the 50 states and Canada). **Only U.S. funds will be accepted.**

☐ *I am interested in starting a club in my area.*

NAME _____

STREET _____

CITY _____

STATE _____ ZIP _____

Appendix Four

IMPORTANT WORD LISTS

The following lists represent the most useful SCRABBLE game words to learn. They will appear on your rack repeatedly as you learn to balance your rack.

THE TOP TEN 6-LETTER STEMS

SATINE

A:	ENTASIA		EATINGS		SALTINE	R:	ANESTRI		TISANES
	TAENIAS		INGATES		SLAINTE		ANTSIER	T:	INSTATE
B:	BASINET		INGESTA		TENAILS		NASTIER		SATINET
	BANTIES		SEATING	M:	ETAMINS		RATINES	U:	AUNTIES
C:	CINEAST		TEASING		INMATES		RETAINS		SINUATE
	ACETINS	H:	SHEITAN		TAMEINS		RETINAS	V:	NAIVEST
D:	DESTAIN		STHENIA	N:	INANEST		RETSINA		NATIVES
	DETAINS	I:	ISATINE		STANINE		STAINER		VAINEST
	INSTEAD	K:	INTAKES	O:	ATONIES		STEARIN	W:	TAWNIES
	SAINTED	L:	ELASTIN	P:	PANTIES	S:	ENTASIS		WANIEST
	STAINED		ENTAILS		PATINES		NASTIES	X:	ANTISEX
E:	ETESIAN		NAILSET		SAPIENT		SESTINA		SEXTAIN
F:	FAINEST		SALIENT		SPINATE		TANSIES	Z:	ZANIEST
G:	EASTING								ZEATINS

SATIRE

A:	ARISTAE		STAIDER		RETAILS		RETINAS	T:	ARTIEST
	ASTERIA		TARDIES		SALTIER		RETSINA		ARTISTE
	ATRESIA		TIRADES		SALTIRE		STAINER		ATTIRES
B:	BAITERS	E:	AERIEST		SLATIER		STEARIN		IRATEST
	BARITES		SERIATE		TAILERS	P:	PARTIES		RATITES
	REBAITS	F:	FAIREST	M:	IMARETS		PASTIER		STRIATE
	TERBIAS	G:	AIGRETS		MAESTRI		PIASTER		TASTIER
C:	CRISTAE		GAITERS		MISRATE		PIASTRE	V:	VASTIER
	RACIEST		SEAGIRT		SMARTIE		PIRATES		VERITAS
	STEARIC		STAGIER	N:	ANESTRI		TRAIPSE	W:	WAISTER
D:	ARIDEST		TRIAGES		ANTSIER	R:	ARTSIER		WAITERS
	ASTRIDE	H:	HASTIER		NASTIER		TARRIES		WARIEST
	DIASTER	I:	AIRIEST		RATINES	S:	SATIRES		WASTRIE
	DISRATE	L:	REALIST		RETAINS				

RETINA

C:	CERATIN	GRATINE	RETINAL	S: ANESTRI	ITERANT
	CERTAIN	INGRATE	TRENAIL	ANTSIER	NATTIER
	CREATIN	TANGIER	M: MINARET	NASTIER	NITRATE
D:	ANTIRED	TEARING	RAIMENT	RATINES	TERTIAN
	DETRAIN	H: HAIRNET	N: ENTRAIN	RETAINS	U: RUINATE
	TRAINED	INEARTH	P: PAINTER	RETINAS	TAURINE
E:	ARENITE	I: INERTIA	PERTAIN	RETSINA	URANITE
	RETINAE	K: KERATIN	REPAINT	STAINER	URINATE
	TRAINEE	L: LATRINE	R: RETRAIN	STEARIN	W: TAWNIER
F:	FAINTER	RATLINE	TERRAIN	T: INTREAT	TINWARE
G:	GRANITE	RELIANT	TRAINER		

ARSINE

C:	ARCSINE	G: EARINGS	SERINGA	M: MARINES	P: PANIERS
	ARSENIC	ERASING	H: HERNIAS	REMAINS	RAPINES
	CARNIES	GAINERS	I: SENARII	SEMINAR	S: ARSINES
D:	RANDIES	REAGINS	L: ALINERS	N: INSANER	T: *See*
	SANDIER	REGAINS	NAILERS	INSNARE	SATINE *list*
	SARDINE	REGINAS	RENAILS	O: ERASION	V: RAVINES
F:	INFARES	SEARING			

IRONES

A:	ERASION	ORDINES	H: HEROINS	M: MERINOS	OESTRIN
C:	COINERS	ROSINED	INSHORE	O: EROSION	ORIENTS
	CRONIES	SORDINE	I: IRONIES	P: ORPINES	STONIER
	ORCEINS	G: ERINGOS	NOISIER	R: IRONERS	U: URINOSE
	RECOINS	IGNORES	J: JOINERS	S: SENIORS	V: RENVOIS
D:	DINEROS	REGIONS	REJOINS	SONSIER	VERSION
	INDORSE	SIGNORE	L: NEROLIS	T: NORITES	

ITONES

A:	ATONIES	HISTONE	SENTIMO	POINTES	S: NOSIEST
B:	BONIEST	I: INOSITE	N: INTONES	R: NORITES	T: TONIEST
C:	NOTICES	L: ENTOILS	TENSION	OESTRIN	W: TOWNIES
	SECTION	M: MESTINO	O: ISOTONE	ORIENTS	X: TOXINES
H:	ETHIONS	MOISTEN	P: PINTOES	STONIER	

ANTRES

B:	BANTERS	EASTERN	TANKERS	O: ATONERS	RANTERS
C:	CANTERS	NEAREST	L: ANTLERS	SENATOR	T: NATTERS
	CARNETS	G: ARGENTS	RENTALS	TREASON	RATTENS
	NECTARS	GARNETS	SALTERN	P: ARPENTS	U: NATURES
	RECANTS	STRANGE	STERNAL	ENTRAPS	SAUNTER
	SCANTER	H: ANTHERS	M: MARTENS	PARENTS	V: SERVANT
	TANRECS	THENARS	SARMENT	PASTERN	TAVERNS
	TRANCES	I: *See*	SMARTEN	TREPANS	VERSANT
D:	STANDER	SATINE *list*	N: TANNERS	R: ERRANTS	W: WANTERS
E:	EARNEST	K: *RANKEST*			

EINRST

A: *See*	**F:** SNIFTER	**M:** MINSTER	STONIER	**U:** NUTSIER
SATINE *list*	**G:** RESTING	MINTERS	**P:** PTERINS	TRIUNES
C: CISTERN	STINGER	REMINTS	**S:** ESTRINS	UNITERS
CRETINS	**H:** HINTERS	**N:** INTERNS	INSERTS	**V:** INVERTS
D: TINDERS	**K:** REKNITS	TINNERS	SINTERS	STRIVEN
E: ENTIRES	STINKER	**O:** NORITES	**T:** RETINTS	**W:** TWINERS
ENTRIES	TINKERS	OESTRIN	STINTER	WINTERS
RETINES	**L:** LINTERS	ORIENTS	TINTERS	

ENORST

A: ATONERS	SNORTED	THRONES	MONSTER	STONERS
SENATOR	**E:** ESTRONE	**I:** NORITES	**N:** TONNERS	TENSORS
TREASON	**F:** FRONTES	OESTRIN	**O:** ENROOTS	**T:** STENTOR
B: SORBENT	**G:** TONGERS	ORIENTS	**P:** POSTERN	**U:** TENOURS
C: CORNETS	**H:** HORNETS	STONIER	**R:** SNORTER	TONSURE
D: RODENTS	SHORTEN	**M:** MENTORS	**S:** NESTORS	

AEERST

A: AERATES	**F:** AFREETS	**L:** ELATERS	NEAREST	SEATERS
B: BEATERS	FEASTER	REALEST	**O:** ROSEATE	TEASERS
BERATES	**G:** ERGATES	RELATES	**P:** REPEATS	TESSERA
REBATES	RESTAGE	RESLATE	RETAPES	**T:** ESTREAT
C: CERATES	**H:** AETHERS	STEALER	**R:** RETEARS	RESTATE
CREATES	HEATERS	**M:** REMATES	SERRATE	RETASTE
ECARTES	REHEATS	RETEAMS	TEARERS	**U:** AUSTERE
D: DEAREST	**I:** AERIEST	STEAMER	**S:** EASTERS	**W:** SWEATER
REDATES	SERIATE	**N:** EARNEST	RESEATS	**X:** RETAXES
SEDATER	**K:** RETAKES	EASTERN	SEAREST	

WORDS THAT INCLUDE AT LEAST 66% VOWELS

AA	NAOI	ACULEI	AUCUBA	EASIES	IODINE
AE	OBIA	ADAGIO	AUDILE	EELIER	IODISE
AI	OBOE	ADIEUS	AUDIOS	EERIER	IODIZE
OE	ODEA	ADIEUX	AUGITE	EIDOLA	IODOUS
	OGEE	AECIAL	AUNTIE	EKUELE	IOLITE
EAU	OHIA	AECIUM	AURATE	ELODEA	IONIUM
	OLEA	AEDILE	AUREUS	ELUATE	IONIZE
AEON	OLEO	AEDINE	AURORA	ELUVIA	IONONE
AERO	OLIO	AENEUS	AUROUS	EMEUTE	KOODOO
AGEE	OOZE	AEONIC	AUSUBO	EOLIAN	KOOKIE
AGIO	OUZO	AERATE	AUTEUR	EONIAN	LAMIAE
AGUE	QUAI	AERIAL	AUTOED	EOSINE	LAURAE
AIDE	RAIA	AERIED	AVENUE	EPIZOA	LEAGUE
AJEE	ROUE	AERIER	AVIATE	EPOPEE	LIAISE
AKEE	TOEA	AERIES	BAILEE	EQUATE	LOOIES
ALAE	UNAI	AEROBE	BAILIE	EQUINE	LOUIES
ALEE	UNAU	AERUGO	BATEAU	ETOILE	MEALIE
ALOE	UREA	AGAPAE	BAUBEE	EUPNEA	MEANIE
AMIA	UVEA	AGAPAI	BEANIE	EUREKA	MEDIAE
AMIE	ZOEA	AGORAE	BEEBEE	EURIPI	MEINIE
ANOA		AGOUTI	BOOBOO	EXODOI	MEOUED
AQUA	AALII	AIKIDO	BOOGIE	EXUVIA	MIAOUS
AREA	ADIEU	AIOLIS	BOOHOO	FAERIE	MILIEU
ARIA	AECIA	AIRIER	BOOKIE	FAUNAE	MOIRAI
ASEA	AERIE	ALEXIA	BOOTEE	FEIRIE	MUUMUU
AURA	AIOLI	ALODIA	BOOTIE	FERIAE	NAUSEA
AUTO	AQUAE	ALULAE	BOUBOU	FLOOIE	OBELIA
AWEE	AREAE	AMADOU	BOUGIE	FOODIE	OCREAE
BEAU	AUDIO	AMEBAE	BUREAU	FOOTIE	ODIOUS
CIAO	AURAE	AMOEBA	CAEOMA	FOVEAE	OEDEMA
EASE	AUREI	AMUSIA	CAIQUE	GALEAE	OEUVRE
EAUX	COOEE	ANEMIA	COATEE	GATEAU	OIDIUM
EAVE	EERIE	ANOMIE	CODEIA	GIAOUR	OILIER
EIDE	LOOIE	ANOPIA	COOCOO	GOALIE	OLEATE
EMEU	LOUIE	ANOXIA	COOEED	GOATEE	OLEINE
EPEE	MIAOU	ANURIA	COOEES	GOODIE	OOLITE
ETUI	OIDIA	AORTAE	COOKIE	GOOIER	OOMIAC
EURO	OORIE	AOUDAD	COOLIE	GOONIE	OOMIAK
IDEA	OURIE	APIECE	COOTIE	GUAIAC	OORALI
ILEA	QUEUE	APNOEA	COTEAU	GUINEA	OOZIER
ILIA	URAEI	APOGEE	COULEE	HEAUME	OPAQUE
INIA	ZOEAE	AREOLA	CURIAE	HOAGIE	OPIATE
IOTA		AREOLE	DAIMIO	HOODIE	OPIOID
IXIA	AALIIS	ARIOSE	DAUTIE	HOOLIE	OREIDE
JIAO	ABASIA	ARIOSI	DEARIE	HOOPOE	ORIOLE
LIEU	ABULIA	ARIOSO	DOOLEE	HOOPOO	OROIDE
LUAU	ACACIA	AROUSE	DOOLIE	IGUANA	OTIOSE
MEOU	ACAJOU	ATAXIA	DOOZIE	IODATE	OURARI
MOUE	ACEDIA	AUBADE	EASIER	IODIDE	OUREBI

OUTAGE	RESEAU	URANIA	YAUTIA	AREOLAE	OOGONIA
OUTATE	ROADEO	UREASE	ZAIKAI	AUREATE	OUABAIN
OUTEAT	ROADIE	UREDIA	ZOUAVE	AUREOLA	OUGUIYA
OUTLIE	ROOKIE	UREIDE		AUREOLE	ROULEAU
OUTSEE	ROOMIE	UREMIA	ABOULIA	AURORAE	SEQUOIA
OUTVIE	SOIREE	UTOPIA	ACEQUIA	COUTEAU	TAENIAE
PEERIE	SOUARI	UVEOUS	AECIDIA	EPINAOI	URAEMIA
PEEWEE	TEEPEE	UVULAE	AENEOUS	EUCAINE	
PEREIA	TENIAE	VEEPEE	AEOLIAN	EUGENIA	ABOIDEAU
QUAERE	TIBIAE	VOODOO	AEONIAN	EULOGIA	ABOITEAU
QUALIA	TOUPEE	WEENIE	AEROBIA	EUPNOEA	AUREOLAE
QUEUED	UBIQUE	WEEPIE	ALIENEE	EVACUEE	EPOPOEIA
QUEUER	UNCIAE	WEEWEE	AMOEBAE	EXUVIAE	EULOGIAE
QUEUES	UNEASE	WIENIE	ANAEMIA	IPOMOEA	
QUINOA	UNIQUE	WOODIE	AQUARIA	MIAOUED	
REDIAE	URAEUS	WOOLIE	AQUEOUS	NOUVEAU	

THE TWO-TO-MAKE-THREE WORD LIST

Listed below are all the two-letter words. Before and after each two-letter word are listed each of the letters that can be added to the word to form a three-letter word. For example: NU takes a G front hook to form GNU, as well as any of the back hooks B, N, S, and T to form NUB, NUN, NUS, and NUT.

b	AA	hls		LI	bdenpst
bcdfghlmprstw	AD	dosz		LO	bgoptwx
ghkmnstw	AE		a	MA	cdegnprstwy
bdfghjlmnrstwz	AG	aeo	e	ME	dlmntw
abdhnpry	AH	a	a	MI	bdglmrsx
	AI	dlmnrst	hu	MM	
abdgps	AL	abelpst		MO	abdglmnoprstw
bcdghjlnprty	AM	aipu	ae	MU	dgmnst
bcfgmprtvw	AN	adeity		MY	
bcefgjlmoptvwy	AR	bcefkmst	a	NA	beghmpwy
abfghklmprtvw	AS	hkps	ao	NE	betw
bcefghklmopqrstvw	AT	e		NO	bdghmorstw
cdhjlmnprstvwy	AW	aeln	g	NU	bnst
flprstwz	AX	e	bcghmnprsty	OD	des
bcdfghjklmnprswy	AY	es	dfhjrtvw	OE	s
a	BA	adghlmnrsty		OF	ft
o	BE	deglnty	fnop	OH	mos
o	BI	bdgnostz	dmnrty	OM	s
a	BO	abdgopstwxy	cdefhimstvwy	ON	es
a	BY	es	bcfhklmpst	OP	est
	DA	bdghklmpwy	cdfgkmnt	OR	abcest
o	DE	beilnsvwxy	bcdkmnsw	OS	e
au	DO	ceglmnrstw	bcdhjlmnprstvwy	OW	eln
kr	EF	fst	bcfglpsv	OX	oy
fhpy	EH		bcfghjst	OY	
bdegmst	EL	dfklms	s	PA	cdhlmnprstwxy
fghmr	EM	esu	ao	PE	adeghnprst
bdfhkmpstwy	EN	dgs		PI	acegnpstux
fhps	ER	aegnrs	aeio	RE	bcdefgimpstvx
dhopry	ES	a	a	SH	aehy
bfghjlmnprstvwy	ET	ah	p	SI	bcmnprstx
dhklrsv	EX			SO	bdlnpstuwxy
	FA	dgnrstxy	eu	TA	bdegjmnoprstuvwx
ae	GO	abdortxy		TI	celnpst
asw	HA	deghjmopstwy		TO	degmnoprtwy
st	HE	hmnprstwxy	h	UH	
cgkp	HI	cdemnpst	bcghlmrsy	UM	mp
o	HM	m	bdfghjmnprst	UN	s
mortw	HO	bdegnptwy	cdhpsty	UP	os
abdfghklmr	ID	s	bjmnp	US	e
kr	IF	s	bcghjmnoprt	UT	as
abdfghjklprstvwy	IN	kns	aeo	WE	bdent
abchlmpstvwx	IS	m	t	WO	eknostw
abdfghklnpstwz	IT	s		XI	s
	JO	begtwy		XU	
os	KA	befsty	pr	YA	hkmprwy
a	LA	bcdgmprstvwx	abdelprtw	YE	ahnpstw

THREE-LETTER WORDS

AAH	ANI	BAT	BYE	DAD	DUD	ERS	FOE	GIN	HEW	INK
AAL	ANT	BAY	BYS	DAG	DUE	ESS	FOG	GIP	HEX	INN
AAS	ANY	BED	CAB	DAH	DUG	ETA	FOH	GIT	HEY	INS
ABA	APE	BEE	CAD	DAK	DUI	ETH	FON	GNU	HIC	ION
ABO	APT	BEG	CAM	DAL	DUN	EVE	FOP	GOA	HID	IRE
ABY	ARB	BEL	CAN	DAM	DUO	EWE	FOR	GOB	HIE	IRK
ACE	ARC	BEN	CAP	DAP	DUP	EYE	FOU	GOD	HIM	ISM
ACT	ARE	BET	CAR	DAW	DYE	FAD	FOX	GOO	HIN	ITS
ADD	ARF	BEY	CAT	DAY	EAR	FAG	FOY	GOR	HIP	IVY
ADO	ARK	BIB	CAW	DEB	EAT	FAN	FRO	GOT	HIS	JAB
ADS	ARM	BID	CAY	DEE	EAU	FAR	FRY	GOX	HIT	JAG
ADZ	ARS	BIG	CEE	DEI	EBB	FAS	FUB	GOY	HMM	JAM
AFF	ART	BIN	CEP	DEL	ECU	FAT	FUD	GUL	HOB	JAR
AFT	ASH	BIO	CHI	DEN	EDH	FAX	FUG	GUM	HOD	JAW
AGA	ASK	BIS	CIS	DES	EEL	FAY	FUN	GUN	HOE	JAY
AGE	ASP	BIT	COB	DEV	EFF	FED	FUR	GUT	HOG	JEE
AGO	ASS	BIZ	COD	DEW	EFS	FEE	GAB	GUV	HON	JET
AHA	ATE	BOA	COG	DEX	EFT	FEH	GAD	GUY	HOP	JEU
AID	AUK	BOB	COL	DEY	EGG	FEM	GAE	GYM	HOT	JIB
AIL	AVA	BOD	CON	DIB	EGO	FEN	GAG	GYP	HOW	JIG
AIM	AVE	BOG	COO	DID	EKE	FER	GAL	HAD	HOY	JIN
AIN	AVO	BOO	COP	DIE	ELD	FET	GAM	HAE	HUB	JOB
AIR	AWA	BOP	COR	DIG	ELF	FEU	GAN	HAG	HUE	JOE
AIS	AWE	BOS	COS	DIM	ELK	FEW	GAP	HAH	HUG	JOG
AIT	AWL	BOT	COT	DIN	ELL	FEY	GAR	HAJ	HUH	JOT
ALA	AWN	BOW	COW	DIP	ELM	FEZ	GAS	HAM	HUM	JOW
ALB	AXE	BOX	COX	DIT	ELS	FIB	GAT	HAO	HUN	JOY
ALE	AYE	BOY	COY	DOC	EME	FID	GAY	HAP	HUP	JUG
ALL	AYS	BRA	COZ	DOE	EMS	FIE	GED	HAS	HUT	JUN
ALP	AZO	BRR	CRY	DOG	EMU	FIG	GEE	HAT	HYP	JUS
ALS	BAA	BUB	CUB	DOL	END	FIL	GEL	HAW	ICE	JUT
ALT	BAD	BUD	CUD	DOM	ENG	FIN	GEM	HAY	ICH	KAB
AMA	BAG	BUG	CUE	DON	ENS	FIR	GET	HEH	ICK	KAE
AMI	BAH	BUM	CUM	DOR	EON	FIT	GEY	HEM	ICY	KAF
AMP	BAL	BUN	CUP	DOS	ERA	FIX	GHI	HEN	IDS	KAS
AMU	BAM	BUR	CUR	DOT	ERE	FIZ	GIB	HEP	IFS	KAT
ANA	BAN	BUS	CUT	DOW	ERG	FLU	GID	HER	ILK	KAY
AND	BAR	BUT	CWM	DRY	ERN	FLY	GIE	HES	ILL	KEA
ANE	BAS	BUY	DAB	DUB	ERR	FOB	GIG	HET	IMP	KEF

KEG	LEX	MIG	NIT	OOH	PER	QUA	ROW	SIR	TAU	TUX
KEN	LEY	MIL	NIX	OOT	PES	RAD	RUB	SIS	TAV	TWA
KEP	LIB	MIM	NOB	OPE	PET	RAG	RUE	SIT	TAW	TWO
KEV	LID	MIR	NOD	OPS	PEW	RAH	RUG	SIX	TAX	TYE
KEX	LIE	MIS	NOG	OPT	PHI	RAJ	RUM	SKA	TEA	UDO
KEY	LIN	MIX	NOH	ORA	PHT	RAM	RUN	SKI	TED	UGH
KHI	LIP	MOA	NOM	ORB	PIA	RAN	RUT	SKY	TEE	UKE
KID	LIS	MOB	NOO	ORC	PIC	RAP	RYA	SLY	TEG	ULU
KIF	LIT	MOD	NOR	ORE	PIE	RAS	RYE	SOB	TEL	UMM
KIN	LOB	MOG	NOS	ORS	PIG	RAT	SAB	SOD	TEN	UMP
KIP	LOG	MOL	NOT	ORT	PIN	RAW	SAC	SOL	TET	UNS
KIR	LOO	MOM	NOW	OSE	PIP	RAX	SAD	SON	TEW	UPO
KIT	LOP	MON	NTH	OUD	PIS	RAY	SAE	SOP	THE	UPS
KOA	LOT	MOO	NUB	OUR	PIT	REB	SAG	SOS	THO	URB
KOB	LOW	MOP	NUN	OUT	PIU	REC	SAL	SOT	THY	URD
KOP	LOX	MOR	NUS	OVA	PIX	RED	SAP	SOU	TIC	URN
KOR	LUG	MOS	NUT	OWE	PLY	REE	SAT	SOW	TIE	USE
KOS	LUM	MOT	OAF	OWL	POD	REF	SAU	SOX	TIL	UTA
KUE	LUV	MOW	OAK	OWN	POH	REG	SAW	SOY	TIN	UTS
LAB	LUX	MUD	OAR	OXO	POI	REI	SAX	SPA	TIP	VAC
LAC	LYE	MUG	OAT	OXY	POL	REM	SAY	SPY	TIS	VAN
LAD	MAC	MUM	OBE	PAC	POP	REP	SEA	SRI	TIT	VAR
LAG	MAD	MUN	OBI	PAD	POT	RES	SEC	STY	TOD	VAS
LAM	MAE	MUS	OCA	PAH	POW	RET	SEE	SUB	TOE	VAT
LAP	MAG	MUT	ODD	PAL	POX	REV	SEG	SUE	TOG	VAU
LAR	MAN	NAB	ODE	PAM	PRO	REX	SEI	SUM	TOM	VAV
LAS	MAP	NAE	ODS	PAN	PRY	RHO	SEL	SUN	TON	VAW
LAT	MAR	NAG	OES	PAP	PSI	RIA	SEN	SUP	TOO	VEE
LAV	MAS	NAH	OFF	PAR	PUB	RIB	SER	SYN	TOP	VEG
LAW	MAT	NAM	OFT	PAS	PUD	RID	SET	TAB	TOR	VET
LAX	MAW	NAP	OHM	PAT	PUG	RIF	SEW	TAD	TOT	VEX
LAY	MAY	NAW	OHO	PAW	PUL	RIG	SEX	TAE	TOW	VIA
LEA	MED	NAY	OHS	PAX	PUN	RIM	SHA	TAG	TOY	VIE
LED	MEL	NEB	OIL	PAY	PUP	RIN	SHE	TAJ	TRY	VIG
LEE	MEM	NEE	OKA	PEA	PUR	RIP	SHH	TAM	TSK	VIM
LEG	MEN	NET	OKE	PED	PUS	ROB	SHY	TAN	TUB	VIN
LEI	MET	NEW	OLD	PEE	PUT	ROC	SIB	TAO	TUG	VIS
LEK	MEW	NIB	OLE	PEG	PYA	ROD	SIC	TAP	TUI	VOE
LET	MHO	NIL	OMS	PEH	PYE	ROE	SIM	TAR	TUN	VON
LEU	MIB	NIM	ONE	PEN	PYX	ROM	SIN	TAS	TUP	VOW
LEV	MID	NIP	ONS	PEP	QAT	ROT	SIP	TAT	TUT	VOX

THREE-LETTER WORDS *(cont.)*

VUG	WAR	WED	WIG	WON	WYE	YAR	YES	YOK	YUP	ZIG
WAB	WAS	WEE	WIN	WOO	WYN	YAW	YET	YOM	ZAG	ZIP
WAD	WAT	WEN	WIS	WOS	XIS	YAY	YEW	YON	ZAP	ZIT
WAE	WAW	WET	WIT	WOT	YAH	YEA	YIN	YOU	ZAX	ZOA
WAG	WAX	WHA	WIZ	WOW	YAK	YEH	YIP	YOW	ZED	ZOO
WAN	WAY	WHO	WOE	WRY	YAM	YEN	YOB	YUK	ZEE	
WAP	WEB	WHY	WOK	WUD	YAP	YEP	YOD	YUM	ZEK	

GLOSSARY

Abbreviations: DLS: Double Letter Score; **DWS:** Double Word Score; **TLS:** Triple Letter Score; **TWS:** Triple Word Score; **?:** Blank; **PTS.:** Points.

Alphagram: The alphabetic arrangement of a group of letters. Example: BEGNU is the alphagram of the word BEGUN.

Anagram: A word that is spelled with the exact same letters as another word. Example: KITCHEN is an anagram of THICKEN, and vice versa. GAPE is an anagram of PAGE.

Back Extension: See "Extension Play."

Back Hook: See "Hook."

Balancing Your Rack: Making a play that leaves the letters on your rack which will most likely help you to score well next turn. This often means leaving a favorable ratio of vowels and consonants. Also known as Rack Balance.

Bingo: Any word played that uses all seven letters of the rack, earning a bonus of 50 points. British players use the term "bonus" instead of bingo.

Bingo-Prone Tiles: A group of tiles that are likely to produce a bingo. Often used to describe a player's set of three to six tiles just before drawing his or her replacement tiles. Example: ERS?, AL?, or AERST.

Blank: One of the two tiles that have no letter printed on them. The blank is worth zero points, but is widely regarded as the most valuable tile due to its chameleonlike ability of being able to represent any letter. Having one increases the odds of playing a bingo.

Blank Bingo: A bingo that includes a blank tile.

Blocking: The act of playing a word on the board that stops the opponent from making a potentially large score.

Braille: To feel the surface of a tile while your hand is in the bag in order to draw a blank or other specific letter. This is strictly forbidden.

"Challenge!": An opponent calls "Challenge!" when s/he thinks a word is not acceptable (i.e., not in the OSPD2). The opponent records the challenged words on a "challenge slip" and a word judge is called to verify the acceptability of all the words formed on a play. If any of the words challenged are unacceptable, the whole play is unacceptable. The player must then remove his or her play from the board and lose that turn. If all the words are acceptable, then the challenger loses his or her turn. Only one turn is lost on any challenge.

Challenge Slip: The slip of paper upon which the words being challenged are printed by one of the players (and double-checked by the opponent). These slips are generally preferred to a player's simply pointing to the challenged word on the board. That's because mistakes are much more likely to be made unless the words are recorded.

Chess Clock: see "Tournament Clock."

Closed Board: The opposite of an open board: when there are few or no places on the board to put down either bingos or other high-scoring plays.

Coffeehousing: To make small talk, crack knuckles, or do any of a number of things meant to distract or mislead your opponent. This is unethical and strictly forbidden in clubs and tournaments. It is generally considered impolite to talk during a tournament game unless it is pertinent to the score or the play.

Contestant Score Card: On this card each player keeps a record of each game's results: opponent's name and signature, who plays first, final score, total number of wins, and his or her own total point spread.

Courtesy Rule: If an opponent takes more than a minute to "Hold!" a play, the player may draw new tiles but must keep them separate from the others until the hold is resolved. Often, a third rack is used to hold these new tiles.

Credits: A seldom-used but effective method of deciding tournament results. One "credit" system has each player beginning each game with 30 credits. The winner automatically earns 10 credits, plus 1 credit for each 10 points of point spread (rounded off). The loser subtracts 1 credit from his or her original 30 for each 10 points of spread. Arbitrarily, no more than 60 credits nor fewer than 10 credits can be earned. For example, if Player #1 beats Player #2 400–350, Player #1 earns 30 + 10 (for winning) + 5 (for winning by 5 × 10 points) = 45 credits. Player #2 earns 30 − 5 (for losing by 5 × 10 points) = 25 credits. For ties, both players receive 35 credits.

Double-Double (DWS-DWS): When a player makes a play with letters that cover two Double Word Score squares, it is known as playing a "Double-Double." The bonus for covering two DWSs on one play is four times the sum of the value of the letters of the Double-Double word. The sum should include the extra values earned from any DLS covered that turn.

Dumping: Making a play that scores few points but rids the rack of a poor combination of letters.

Endgame: That portion of a SCRABBLE game when there are fewer than seven tiles left to draw from the bag.

Exchanging Tiles (or Trading Tiles): Instead of playing a word on the board, the player may use his or her turn to exchange from one to seven tiles for new tiles drawn from the bag. There must be at least seven tiles in the bag in order to exchange. To exchange, place the unwanted tiles facedown in front of you, announce the number of tiles you are exchanging, draw an equal number of tiles from the bag and place them on your rack. Finally, return the unwanted tiles to the bag.

Extension Play: The extension of one word by adding two or more letters. Example: With QUEST on the board, adding CON to the front creates the extension CONQUEST. Also called Front Extension or Back Extension.

Fishing: To play for only a few points or exchange only one or two tiles, keeping five or six really good tiles, with the hope of making a high-scoring play next turn.

Frequency List: See "Preprinted Tracking Sheet."

Front Extension: See "Extension Play."

Front Hook: See "Hook."

"Hold!": An opponent calls "Hold!" when a player plays a word that the opponent considers challenging. Calling "Hold!" signals to the player not to draw new tiles until either the challenge is officially resolved or the hold is canceled. To cancel a "Hold!" the opponent simply tells the player "I accept the play." Using chess clocks, an opponent may hold as long as s/he desires; with sand timers, a hold may last as long as three minutes. After one minute of holding, the player may draw tiles, but must keep them separate from the others. See "Courtesy Rule."

Hook Letter (or Hook): A letter that will spell a new word when it is played either at the front or end of a word already on the board. Example: With HARD on the board, the Y is a hook letter, since HARDY is acceptable. "Hook" is also used as a verb. Example: The letter C can "hook" on to HARD, since CHARD is acceptable. Also called Front Hook or Back Hook.

Hot Spots: These are either specific squares or areas on the board that have excellent bonus-scoring opportunities. Players will do well to look for these areas before looking for words on their rack. Examples: Triple Letter Score squares or Double Word Score squares adjacent to vowels; a single letter placed between two open Triple Word Score squares; words that take a variety of hook letters (ARE, ON, CARE).

Leave: The group of tiles on a player's rack after s/he makes a play and before s/he draws new tiles.

Natural: A bingo that does not use a blank tile. Also called a Natural Bingo.

Nongo: A bingo that won't play on the board.

Neutralizing the Timer: Stopping the game clock. Neither player's time continues during challenges, rule disputes, or score verifications.

Official SCRABBLE Players Dictionary, 2nd Edition: The Bible for all National SCRAB-BLE® Association Clubs and Tournaments. The official source for all of the two- to eight-letter words. For words over eight letters, the NSA uses Merriam-Webster's Collegiate Dictionary, 10th Edition.

Open Board: During play, the board is considered "open" when there are many places to play either bingos or other high-scoring words.

Overdrawing Tiles: When one player draws more tiles from the bag than is appropriate.

Parallel Play: A word played parallel to another word. Example:

MAR
LATE

With MAR on the board, LATE is a parallel play that simultaneously forms MA, AT, and RE, all of which earn points for the player.

Passing: A player may pass his or her turn by not exchanging tiles and not making a play on the board. The player says "Pass!," scores zero, and starts the opponent's timer. It is now the opponent's turn. In club or tournament play, when there are six consecutive scores of zero in a game, the game is over. A player scores zero when s/he either exchanges, passes, or loses a challenge.

Phoney: Any unacceptable word. An unacceptable word is one that is not found in *The Official SCRABBLE® Players Dictionary*, or, if the root word has more than eight letters, it is not found in the *Merriam-Webster Collegiate Dictionary*, 10th Edition. However, if a phoney is not challenged, it will stay on the board for the remainder of the game.

Point Spread: The algebraic difference between the winner's and loser's score of a game. Example: If Player #1 wins over Player #2 by 400 to 300, Player #1's point spread is +100; Player #2's is −100. See "Total Spread."

Power Tiles: There are ten power tiles. They are the two blanks, the four Ss, and the J, Q, X, and Z.

Preprinted Tracking Sheet: Also called Frequency List or simply Tracking Sheet. This sheet of paper has printed on it either the alphabet or a partial or complete list of the one hundred lettered tiles used in a SCRABBLE® game.

Rack Balance: See "Balancing Your Rack."

Rack Management: How a player develops his series of racks toward the goal of putting down a bingo and other high-scoring plays.

Rating: For each sanctioned National SCRABBLE® Association tournament, a new rating is computed for each of the contestants. The rating represents how well a player is doing in relation to other rated players. The higher the rating, the more skillful the player. Ratings currently range from 200 to 2,100.

Rounds: In club or tournament play, one game is one round. Typically, there are five or six rounds (games) per day at most tournaments.

Sand Timer: In some tournaments and clubs, where chess clocks are not available, three-minute sand timers are used to time each player's turns.

Second Opinion: If a player believes the word judge has made a mistake, s/he may ask for a second person to research the challenge. That second judgment is known as the second opinion. If the second opinion contradicts the original one, a third opinion may be called for.

Stems: Certain five- and six-letter combinations of letters are so useful for forming bingos that lists of bingos have been printed that include these stems. Some of the more useful ones are: STARE, STANE, RETINA, SATINE, and SATIRE. By learning these lists and saving these letters, players will learn to play bingos more often.

Team (or Partnership) Game: Two or more players may pool their knowledge and play as one team against another.

Total (Cumulative) Spread: Over the course of many games the + (plus) or − (minus) spread for each game is added together. At the end of a tournament each player has a total spread for the event.

Tournament Clock: Often called a Chess Clock, it is actually two clocks housed in one plastic or wooden case. Sanctioned tournament games are timed using these clocks. Each player has twenty-five minutes to play the entire game. After making a move, the player presses the button on his or her side of the clock, which starts the opponent's time. The clock is used in this fashion until the game is over. Players are penalized 10 points per minute for every minute or fraction thereof used over the allotted twenty-five.

Tracking (or Tile Tracking): The process of keeping track of the letters played on the board. This can give the astute player an advantage as the game progresses. Careful trackers can deduce an opponent's rack after there are no letters left to draw. By knowing the opponent's rack, the player can often make moves to block the opponent's best plays or set up high-scoring plays that the opponent can't block. Players are allowed to play with their own Preprinted Tracking Sheet alongside their score sheet.

Tracking Sheet: See "Preprinted Tracking Sheet."

Triple-Triple: When a player makes a play with letters that cover two Triple Word Score squares, it is known as playing a "Triple-Triple." The bonus for covering two TWSs on one play is nine times the sum of the value of the letters of the Triple-Triple word. The sum should include the extra values earned from any DLS covered that turn.

Turnover: Players are playing for "turnover" when they play as many tiles as they can in order to draw as many new tiles as possible. By playing for turnover, a player maximizes his or her chances for drawing the better tiles.

Two-to-Make-Threes: Two-letter words that will take a third letter placed either in front or back to form a three-letter word. Example: AN is a two-to-make-three because BAN, CAN, etc., as well as AND, ANT, and ANY, are words. The three-letter words BAN, CAN, and ANT, and ANY, are also known as two-to-make threes. This description may seem confusing. When in doubt, consider any word on our Two-to-make-Three List on page 270 to be a two-to-make-three. Also note "three-to-make-fours," etc.